REVOLUTION TODAY: U.S.A.

Revolution Today: U.S.A.

A Look at the Progressive Labor Movement and the Progressive Labor Party

PROGRESSIVE LABOR PARTY

An Exposition-Banner Book

Exposition Press *New York*

Clothbound edition distributed by

EXPOSITION PRESS INC.

50 Jericho Turnpike Jericho, New York 11753

FIRST EDITION

LIBRARY OF CONGRESS CATALOG CARD NUMBER: 71-136979

0-682-47181-X

Contents

The articles reprinted in this book are given as they originally appeared. Therefore, if the reader rejects—or warmly welcomes—particular ideas in the earlier articles, he or she should realize that some of them failed to stand the test of experience. The book should be taken as a whole, as a record of the party's development.

union movement's history and the role played by left-wing, class-conscious workers.

THE FUTURE IS BRIGHT, *June 1970* 346

The Progressive Labor Party believes a historic trend is taking place. With the class struggle in the United States reaching a new intensity, the advanced, class-conscious workers are making their presence felt. We believe that the 1960's were the years in which Marxism-Leninism re-appeared in the United States and that the 1970's will see the working class seizing the world outlook that will guide them to socialism. Our party has the opportunity to take the initiative and become the leader of that revolutionary movement.

Introduction

During the last decade militant action and revolutionary ideas have become an important trend in our country. Millions of Americans have been inspired by revolutionary action around the world. And, certainly, heroic action by millions of black people in our country against ruthless racist and ruling class oppression, was admired by countless Americans.

At the root of revolutionary ferment in our country is the fact that the Capitalist system is in contradiction to every vital aspect of the lives of students, intellectuals, and workers. At this writing, millions of Americans know the imperialist bosses must be swept away. Thousands know Capitalism must be replaced by the Dictatorship of the Proletariat.

But it is not sufficient to simply know this. It is decisive to organize to make revolution and socialism a reality. For this reason the Progressive Labor Movement was organized eight years ago, and the Progressive Labor Party was organized five years ago. Contained in this book are some of our important ideas. Articles are reprinted as they first appeared.

By reading these articles one can trace our development. At least two serious errors stand out. First, in the earlier period we had many illusions about Nationalism. Our line went something like this: There are two kinds of Nationalism. There is the reactionary kind which openly aligns itself with U.S. imperialism and Soviet revisionism. The current rulers of Indonesia fit this description. The other kind of Nationalism is "revolutionary." The political rationale was that these Nationalists were essentially at odds with imperialism and revisionism. One example of this is the leadership in Hanoi, or Algeria. This mistaken idea is developed at some length in the article "Road To Revolution—I." And, it is set straight in other pieces.

The other error which persisted in our party was not clearly understanding how to rely on the working class. We always advanced the idea that to make a revolution in our country required winning the majority of workers. But in practice we relied on students. Our strategy was good; our practice was in contradiction to our strategy. Within the past year we have begun to solve this contradiction. Now we can safely say the working class is becoming the key force in our party.

Workers are responding to our party. The current circulation of our paper *Challenge-Desafio* is 100,000 each issue, and growing. Most of our newer circulation is among industrial workers. We see in this development the ascendancy of Marxism-Leninism in our country. Communism is not a dead letter in the U.S. It is becoming the most important idea to thousands of workers and students.

The articles in this book will, partially, show the basis upon which we in the Progressive Labor Party are organized, and how we act. Guided by Marxism-Leninism, we think the main thrust of our work is positive, revolutionary. Armed with theory and practice we will be able to correct our many errors. One of the most important aspects of Marxism-Leninism is the ability for self-correction. The imperialists cannot do this. Imperialism, and its partner revisionism, stand opposed to the revolutionary sweep which is the reality in the world. Because of this basic contradiction it is impossible for them to find a correct strategy. They can only change tactically. We, on the other hand, are in step with the revolutionary march of the people. Our interests are one and the same as workers and oppressed people of the world. We can grow and change, because in the growth of revolution we have everything to gain and nothing to lose. Thus, we can serve only the workers. Our loyalties are only to our class—the working class.

The only way the working class can emancipate itself is through revolution. Workers' power over their own lives is not a gift of God, and it is not going to be handed over by the ruling class. To end capitalist oppression, requires Marxism-Leninism. It stands as the beacon for the working class to utilize and act on. All of our experiences and world experience show workers will seize the banners of Marxism-Leninism and carry them forward. Capitalism is the dead letter of reaction, retrogression and decadence. Revolution is the only way forward. And revolution it will be.

REVOLUTION TODAY: U.S.A.

Build a Base in the Working Class

JUNE 1969

Be a Party of the Working Class Among the People

Report Opening the PLP Pre-Convention Discussion March 1968

This report deals primarily with a few big obstacles within the party and among the people that impede class consciousness. The most significant of these is our limited basebuilding. Despite some progress, this vital work is weak. If we are to be prepared for a long, hard battle against the enemy, we must have confidence in the masses—and especially in workers. Because our party members are generally young, they are enthusiastic. This is excellent. However, this will soon turn into its opposite if they aren't fortified by ties and experiences with the people. Obviously young people are limited in experiences. Even the fact that our line seems to be generally correct, will turn into the opposite if the party has no real base. We must drive this home continuously!

I would like to make some comments about myself. I believe that all the weaknesses displayed by party members are also exhibited by myself. The differences between myself and others is one of degree. I do not believe that any party escapes the imprint of its leaders—especially its chairman. This includes weaknesses as well as strengths. Even after 22 years of trying to help build a revolutionary movement, I believe that one of my main motives still is self-serving. That is, I do my work more to satisfy something within me than to serve the people. Nonetheless, I would say that the biggest reason that I have been able to do the little I still do over these 22 years is that some part of my devotion stems from the fact that I really believe the working people will, eventually, defeat imperialism. I have never been a world-beater making ties among people. But, all my life, I have had some few close ties, as a boy in the neighborhood and school, in the army, at work, where I live, in the C.P. and in the PLP. Most of my "communist" relations evaporated over the years. All of my

C.P. friends went completely to the other side. While I have been greatly encouraged by the growth of PLP, it still doesn't sustain me, yet, as much as other experiences in my life. These can be summarized in the following way: I have seen all sorts of people "come through" for me and for others under all sorts of difficult circumstances. This is in addition to the general revolutionary sweep in the world, which–to me–is still more of an objective phenomenon. I really believe, in my bones, that the workers and students will eventually "come through." I believe in this based on the most limited experiences. Today, our party members have a far greater chance than I did to do more and go much further—both ideologically and politically (ties with the people). They are receiving better training all around. But advance, granted it will happen, must not be self-serving, but in the interests of the people. Fulfillment should come through serving the people. No one in our party has achieved this yet. Nor do many of us grasp this point completely. It is very easy to maintain the values of the ruling class, only obscured by a thin veneer of militancy or self-sacrifice. Some members may view their working in a big factory in the same way that someone puts money in the bank. Working in industry becomes a status symbol within the party rather than another good act in the process of serving the people. Some middle class person may view his living in a slum like the rich view their Park Avenue address. Years ago, if you asked most white or Black C.P. members who lived within two miles of Bedford-Stuyvesant where they lived, they didn't mention the street; they just said "Bed-Stuy." Status–that's what they're after. It was the "in thing" in the C.P. to live there. This is a hard thing to defeat–self-serving. I feel that I have a long way to go. I try, with ups and downs, to curb this. I don't feel sure that I'll ever win completely. Now I feel I can still be useful to the party. I believe I will remain so. But this is tied very closely to what everyone else does as well as my own individual effort to improve. In other words, the stronger our base, the more confidence will develop among us all.

This is a very limited attempt at a few self-critical remarks. I could go on. I just didn't want anyone in the party to feel that the "leader" was spouting orders to others. I am part of the process. And I want to underline the entire matter of relations with the people.

Begin a Real Transformation—Work and Study

Since our founding convention a number of serious changes have occurred in the world, in our country and in our party. It will be useful to examine some of these developments to see where we are and to help us decide how to improve our work.

The transformation of our Progressive Labor Movement to the Progressive Labor Party was, objectively, a very serious step. Whether we understood it or not, we were telling the ruling class that we were organizing under the banners of Marxism-Leninism in order to crush them. (Certainly the ruling class understands this act.) At the time, our members, in the main, were a group of middle-class students. We had all the characteristics of such a group: rootless and baseless; isolated for the lack of previous political strategy, and sectarian to the core because we had no real working class outlook. Moreover, individualism was rampant, and it expressed itself most sharply in the pathetic way in which many of us lived. We didn't work, we didn't build political bases, and we were generally lazy. Joining the movement or party was still a step toward personal fulfillment, and not a step to defeat the enemy, let alone serve the people.

Our principal strategy, up until the time we became a party, was to rely on open mass agitation for socialism coupled with various activities which were often militant and spectacular, but not always helpful in base-building. Much of this work was useful, because it brought our ideas boldly to the people. Our boldness encouraged others to various levels of defiance against the ruling class. But over-reliance on it helped maintain our isolation from the working class.

The key ideological breakthrough of the convention was posing the question of having a serious party, or having more of the same. What differentiated the two was whether the new party was to be a party of the working class, or whether it would preserve all the same middle-class aspects of other new formations among Black and white student types. We chose to become a party of the working class. For PLP this was a profound decision. Because, to accomplish this meant not a partial transformation of the party, and the individual member of the party, but a total transformation of both. Therefore, when we evaluate our progress during the last few years it must be viewed from this vantage point. What have we done, or what are we doing, to become a real Marxist-Leninist party?

One of the first steps in this arduous protracted process was simply to go to work. Work at least would give us a greater sense of discipline and put us in touch with people. Work would give us the contact and experiences among the working class which could nourish and expand our political consciousness. Working could be the first real step toward becoming a real party, and not a collection of political playboys. In the beginning we were very timid about pressing this process. Indeed, working was a revolutionary step. As in all processes, distortions developed. Many felt that working for the party was going to work. If you worked for the party this allowed you to work full time among the masses. For a while we had almost as many working for the party as working in factories. By and large, working for the party meant keeping busy to accomplish little or nothing.

After allowing this to go too far, the leadership, laggardly, intervened, and stopped this distortion. Today, most of our members who can or should work are doing so. And, here and there, we have begun initial work toward industrial concentration. That is getting people to work in areas which over the long-run are vital to our perspective. All this has shown that our members are willing to start the long process of transformation to become real communists.

Being Marxist-Leninists we know that merely working is not the final solution to problems. With our program of bringing the party closer to the working class we initiated a more comprehensive educational program within the party. All of our people study a little. And most of our clubs have involved non-members in Marxist study groups. Our study reflects our over-all limitations. It is often not concrete nor related to our work. And it usually requires very little from teacher and student. This encourages superficiality and learning by mimicking rather than struggle.

The process of work and study has helped us develop the long-range strategy that political power can be seized in our country only when a significant section of the working class becomes politically conscious. Consequently our immediate strategy is governed by this outlook. Our attempt to develop a worker-student alliance is a manifestation of this. In the Black Liberation Movement we recognize that the present level of the struggle is national in form and class in content. We say that national struggle must eventually give way to class struggle, and that in the long run we will try to unite the entire working class.

This class outlook is still the main contradiction between us and many good forces within the "New Left" and in the Black Liberation Movement, inasmuch as their ideology is still based on bourgeois ideas. And, of course, it is the principal contradiction between us and the enemy. The ruling class is well aware of the danger of a revolutionary working class outlook, because their political survival depends on passivity at least among the working class.

So since our founding convention we could say that we have moved closer to the working class. We have raised our ideological level, developed more of a long-range class outlook, and we have improved ourselves organizationally. However, this improvement can only be viewed as partial and fragmentary. We have only scratched the surface of becoming a party of the working class. A total transformation is a process. We have made the initial toddling steps.

The International Revolutionary Movement Helps Us Grow

At our founding convention we made certain political estimates. Based on our estimate of the national and international situation we said the class struggle is sharpening, and that our party could grow if it overcame its weaknesses. At the time we pointed out that the U.S. war of aggression in Vietnam was part of a world-wide counter-revolutionary strategy of the U.S. We felt that the war was against the interests of most Americans and that opposition would surely mount as the consequences of the war were felt in the country. The war has turned out to be the primary contradiction in our country today, sharpening all aspects of the class struggle.

The rapid growth of opposition to the war is today a fact. More people than ever are actively opposed to the war, and millions of others have been moved to other actions partially because of the war. Since the founding convention, the Black Liberation Movement has mushroomed all over the country. Strikes against the "national interest" have been the largest since 1953.

Internationally the past period has been characterized by the sharpness of the class struggle. Several things stand out as vital. The Great Proletarian Cultural Revolution (GPCR) in China is the most significant feature. Here the struggle by the working class to hold state power goes on sharply even after the seizure of state power. The lessons of this revolution are basic, for what is the use of winning power if the old ruling class can always take it back? In the course of this revolution, certain old questions have been posed in a new light. These are questions that are very germane to our work, even though we are in our infancy. The question of how to serve the people, the relationship of the party to the people has everything to do with some of our problems. We have a vital stake in the outcome of this Proletarian Cultural Revolution. If it is lost revisionism will gain a vast, vise-like hold over the revolutionary movement. The revisionist defeat of China would be a terrible set-back to us and to all revolutionaries. Of course we are partisan in this historic event. Naturally we wish the revolution well and hope for its victory. The GPCR is a significant expression of class struggle, not only in China but in the world. It shows that the international capitalist class will never give up. The complete defeat of imperialism can occur only after Marxist-Leninist ideology triumphs among the people. So the GPCR is a mass movement acting to correct errors. Errors are not corrected administratively but by mobilizing the masses under the leadership of the Marxist-Leninists in the party. To insure victory, the working class and its vanguard must be firmly in the saddle, resolutely defeating bourgeois ideas and forces at each stage. Any let-up will be exploited by the defeated class and its international allies. No party can be immune from revisionism as long as the class struggle exists.

The GPCR based on the Thought of Mao Tse-tung, has made an invaluable contribution to all revolutionaries by bringing this question home so sharply. By waging the war against revisionism in their country the Chinese are serving all workers and oppressed people. To merely attack revisionism in the Soviet Union would have only a limited value. To vigorously oppose revisionism in China is the essential struggle against international imperialism and modern revisionism.

People's War in Vietnam has proven its invincibility. The Vietnamese people are giving a profound demonstration in revolutionary action. We cannot say too many times how this revolution has inspired and encouraged anti-imperialist and revolutionary developments the world over. We have been in the forefront of compelling the U.S. to get out of Vietnam now, despite all obstacles, and this has shown our class consciousness. Internationalism, the support of the revolutionary process everywhere, the subordination of the local struggle to the over-all class struggle, is a sign of growing maturity. In the final analysis internationalism, the knowledge of the fact that the working class and the oppressed people are united in a common cause and against a common international enemy, gives the working class a great deal of leverage. It enables the revolutionary forces on a world scale to concentrate their strength against a common enemy as well as to vigorously develop the revolutionary process at home. Obviously our complete support of the people in Vietnam has helped our struggle at home. This struggle has not only raised our own consciousness but also raised the understanding of millions of our people.

We would be foolish to overlook setbacks in the international movement that took place in this period and not try to summarize what they mean. Counter-revolution has scored several significant temporary victories: Indonesia, Algeria, Cuba and the complete transformation of class power in the Soviet Union and in all the eastern European countries except Albania. Additionally, U.S. imperialism has launched attacks in the Mid-East, Latin America and Africa.

Generally speaking, we should view the international revolutionary movement in this way. Because of the importance of the Cultural Revolution in China, and the overwhelming significance of Vietnam the international movement is strategically stronger. Marxism-Leninism is stronger because it is more thoroughly developed than ever before. The concept of the dictatorship of the proletariat has been clarified and strengthened. People's War has been proven to be a vital contribution to the arsenal of Marxism-Leninism. The understanding of how to fight revisionism in a revolutionary party by clarifying the relationship of the party to the people is invaluable. Three little words—"Serve the people"—if properly understood and applied are a weapon for the working class of incalculable force. So, in fact, if the international movement is smaller in numbers than before, its development is higher than ever. Newly emerging revolutionary forces all over the world can benefit enormously from the Thought of Mao Tse-tung. They can avoid the mistakes of Indonesia, the Algerians, and the Arab world, to mention a few.

Today the interrelationship between armed struggle (People's War) and the fight for the winning and holding of the dictatorship of the proletariat is clearer than ever. It can more easily be grasped as an integrated whole instead of in isolated fragments. It is precisely this interrelationship which is being vigorously obscured by the "new" revisionists in Latin America. Castro and Debray have opened a full assault on Marxism-Leninism. Only by understanding the entire question of the dictatorship of the proletariat can Marxist-Leninists be able to guide the revolutionary process through its different stages to a successful conclusion.

The lessons of People's War in Vietnam are so profound that even if the revisionists were able to betray this revolution tomorrow, the international movement would have learned indispensable lessons. One of the key ones would be how the vanguard plays its independent role within a revolutionary united front, how it should transform the national revolution into a class revolution.

Consequently, the international movement is strategically stronger, while in several places it has become tactically weaker.

"Left-Wing" Liberals Oppose Workers' Dictatorship

Finally, at our founding convention we posed liberalism as the main ideological danger to the developing radical movements. But we estimated that liberalism had received a crushing defeat and had lost a great deal of its potency. This was an over-estimation. Liberalism is a more durable duck than we thought. While a good deal of the newly emerging radical and revolutionary forces have recognized the danger of liberalism, their failure to develop revolutionary consciousness–even class consciousness–enables the liberals, à la RFK, to endure politically. So even though many recognize the dangers of liberalism, the ruling class still preserves its class strength through the illusions of liberalism. If you don't develop a really fundamental alternative to capitalism, you inevitably retrogress. RFK (and his ilk) simply waits until your gas runs out, and is there all ready to tow you away. We have estimated that RFK and company pose the main danger to the anti-war movement, and for that matter to all movements in this country. The carrot and the stick still works. The ideological struggle against liberalism must go on sharply, even though we have won limited victories.

In our country the class struggle is sharpening. However,

liberalism inside and outside of the movement poses the main danger to the revolutionary process. It impedes a further development of the class struggle. Liberalism inside the movement has many guises. Sometimes it takes the "independent" radical form of *Studies on the Left, Monthly Review, National Guardian* and various New Left publications. The essential quality of liberalism as it appears within the movement is that it opposes a working class outlook–hence opposes the dictatorship of the proletariat. So this really leaves the people the "choice" between the good and bad imperialists. Without a revolutionary outlook, the "lesser of two evils" theory must endure, no matter how people may speak against it. There is only one alternative to the dictatorship of the bourgeoisie–the dictatorship of the proletariat. This is why the struggle against those who consciously oppose revolutionary ideology must be waged vigorously and sharply, preventing them from misleading tens of thousands of good people who can be won through mutual experiences against the class enemy.

Build a Revolutionary Political Base

If our party is to continue to make slow but steady progress there are several things we must curb and eventually defeat. Sectarianism, the main way revisionism appears in our party, is the main weakness in our party today. This is reflected in the low level of base building in all of our work, in each area. We must say self-critically that we could have done much better these past few years than we have done. We could not have become a mass party, nor could we have become decisive in any area of work. We could be bigger and with more influence than we now have. A careful examination of almost every member of the party will show that he has a limited political base and is not doing a hell of a lot to change this situation. How can you serve the people if you have no relationship, or extremely limited relationships, with them? Under these circumstances, membership in the party is primarily a selfish act, and while that may be a valid point of departure it isn't good enough if we are talking about defeating U.S. imperialism. Selfishness, or a "what's in it for me" attitude, is the essence of revisionism. Lack of base can sometimes be dismissed as mere ineptness. More often, it manifests an ideological deviation. Unwarranted isolation is diametrically opposed to class consciousness. Class consciousness has nothing to do with how well you can vocalize Marxist-Leninist propositions. It has everything to do with your relations to people, and how they can eventually be moved into battle against the class enemy.

Whom Do We Serve?

At each step of the way we must evaluate our commitment to building the party and serving the people. Our fulfillment as individuals can best be accomplished to the degree we make the party the central thing in our life. Sectarianism can best be described as fear of the people, or lack of confidence in the people. Since we aspire to be a working class party, lack of ties, no matter in which area you work, means a lack of confidence in the working class. And, while you may verbally oppose all the middle-class notions in other groups or periodicals you essentially share their outlook. Moreover, we do not want our members to view their participation in the party as a "sacrifice." Being in the party is a great opportunity to do something useful with your life. It can give you an unprecedented opportunity to serve the people. If you view your activities as an infringement on your personal prerogatives–hence a sacrifice–you are still completely under the influence of the enemy. You are not making very much progress. Your progress can best be measured in terms of your relationships with other people, especially non-party people. To overcome individualism and to achieve collectivity means defeating narrow selfish motives. For most of us developing relations with the people is an effort. Bourgeois ideology trains us to be loners, cynical of everyone else, particularly with people who do not fall over to agree with us.

If we want to overcome narrow "craft" interests in the various areas in which we work, if we want to win people to think in terms of how their actions should be designed in order to aid the entire class, then obviously we must train ourselves to view all of our actions from the point of view: "Is it helping the party to build and grow?" If we cannot do that, then we will be unable to win the masses to our line. When we go among the people and tell them we are communists they usually take us at our word. They evaluate us far differently than they evaluate other people. After all, we give them new yardsticks for judgment. If you claim you are for all the good things, but in your actions are not, the people will see this. This will compound their cynicism and reduce their desire for change. To the people you will simply be another guy who talks big and acts small. Workers have plenty of experience with this phenomenon in the unions. Many students and intellectuals are already using this yardstick to evaluate various bourgeois institutions.

We have a great responsibility to overcome our shortcomings and win a commitment to long, protracted revolution. In the past we tended to leave the matter of evaluation of one another to ourselves in the party. We have partially developed self-criticism and criticism. But even if we developed it fully within the party this would still give us an insular view of one another. In the coming period we should encourage people whom we know personally or work with politically and know personally to give their impressions of us as communists. We should train ourselves that being in the party means loyalty to the people. We should train ourselves to encourage the people's participation in our development. This would also tend to prevent the party from becoming a club. The party would be better oriented to improve its work and the work of its members if we had more insight into what non-party forces thought of us. We should encourage this no matter what the "risks"!

Personal Relationships Key to Basebuilding

In our quest to build bases we should take a closer look at one another. We should start from the ground up. Like, "who do you know?" "What is the nature of the relationship?" In doing this we should take a broader view of what constitutes a political base. Many of us come from campus activity, where the action is usually hot and heavy, and personal living is less than stable. We think in terms of knowing people solely on an action basis. However, if you live in a community or work in a shop you build your relations based on a long range commitment to the shop or neighborhood. The pace of struggle now may not have the intensity of campus struggle. While we should certainly try to know and work with those who are active, it is important to have many relations in the shop or community with people who may not be active at all now. It is impossible to predict who will rise to the fore in the long run. It is valuable to have relations with people of a "purely" personal character. The fact that people like you on a personal basis, knowing you are a communist, is important to you and them. Even if they do not agree with you politically, their relationship with you will often lead them to defending your right to function. This can often lead to enhancing your ability to function in any area.

At a later date, under different circumstances, experience with you and confidence in you could lead to a transformation in someone you thought to be passive. Having a wide circle of relations gives the party more maneuverability. Your relations with people should lead to enlightenment for them. As a communist you should impart confidence in the eventual overcoming of this society, which destroys the fabric of life. You can help people change, just as they help you change. Don't forget, we are not building a narrow minority movement. We are opposed to an elitist concept of historical change. Eventually we hope to involve tens of millions in sharp struggle. Where are they to come from? They are not about to fall from the sky. They are going to be those who at the moment don't often seem interested in changing society. But we say that sooner or later objective processes will sharpen the contradictions between most working people and the system. Then whom will the people work with and trust? Those whom they know and have confidence in.

What are we doing today to make trust in us a reality tomorrow? Are we becoming "tribunes of the people"? In other words, do we participate in all the seemingly endless struggles the people go through until their consciousness is more fully developed? Do people see us as totally interested in the affairs of the people? Are we respected, if not necessarily agreed with? Can anyone in our shop, school, or community come over to us in complete confidence on any matter, knowing that he will be listened to and helped? Do workers say about us, "I don't agree with that guy, but you got to respect him because he always tries to help. Maybe I better pay attention to his ideas."

Integrating the Fight for Reforms With Revolutionary Basebuilding

To avoid becoming merely "do-gooders," to become real revolutionaries requires class hatred. We have to fight the system not because "these poor need help" but because we are actually part of the working class and are oppressed by the system.

Are we learning how to align the fight for reforms with our revolutionary framework? Or do we abstain from struggles on reforms because it will "confuse the people"? because "the ruling class can co-opt success"? Perhaps some of us use this notion, that reforms should not be fought for, as a crutch to avoid struggle and ties. We ought to ask ourselves what issue is being fought over today that isn't a reform. Communists introduce revolutionary consciousness into the struggle for reforms, and use any victory as an example that the strength of the people is limitless. If this or that issue is won, we can go further, constantly sharpening the class struggle. This is an important preparation for revolution. The alternative to this is "the worse the better" notion. In other words, generally our work must start at the level people are at, with the issues that concern them. For an example, in a shop would you start with wages and conditions or the war and socialism? On a block would it be housing, sanitation, schools and racism or the war and socialism? Would you ignore questions regarding academic freedom and student-faculty problems when fighting the war on campuses? However, we would introduce revolutionary and anti-imperialist ideas into immediate struggles, and show the interrelationship. But we must use many issues to bring people into battle against the ruling class, and through these battles we learn together.

Several examples from our work in the shops make this clear. We have followed a line of working on, and helping to initiate struggles on, the issues closest to the workers: on-the-job grievances, safety, overtime, company hearings, wages, etc. These certainly are not revolutionary issues. Yet through activity around these issues, and our members participating fully in this activity, we have been able to start raising the larger, more long-range issues. This reveals us as left-wingers and communists to the workers in a way that means they won't reject us, even if most of them (at this point) don't agree with our long-range solutions.

In one area, where a comrade has been working for six years, he has consistently fought on the shop issues, the sellouts of the union mis-leaders, the contract struggles, etc. He has won a reputation as a fighter (and been elected steward) and was able, in the course of moving with the workers in struggle, to point out the relation to the war, to the capitalist parties, and even (among some workers) that socialism is the only answer. Thus, this comrade is able to take the floor at large union meetings and point out the phony Kennedy line advanced by the leadership on the war, is able to attack them sharply over their support for imperialism in the Arab-Israeli war, and is able to call for support for our party in a political campaign. All this does not cause him to be isolated from the workers precisely because they know him as one who produces against the boss in the immediate class struggle. Without the latter he would be "dead" as far as a base among the workers is concerned; but this way he is someone to be listened to and is able to influence a few workers over to his position. At the very least the workers in his local and his shop recognize the value of having a communist leading their fight and make it difficult for the boss or the union mis-leaders to red-bait him out of his job. Of course, the next step is to recruit to the party, which becomes a test of how much influence is being exerted on more advanced issues.

In another more recent example, a club in one industry has been able to initiate struggle in their shops over purely economic questions—wages, overtime, enforcement of the union contract. While they constantly talked to workers about more political issues in the course of making friends with them, it was not until the actual on-the-job class struggle against the boss was launched (and partially won) that the workers saw our comrades as necessary to their success on economic questions. And in preparation for, and during, these reform-type struggles, our comrades were able to make the workers aware that they were communists, in PLP, and attempted to relate long-range solutions to the current struggles with some workers. They are now able to sell CHALLENGE to their fellow workers, and while many may disagree with the advanced line, they respect our comrades as fighters who produce and stand up to who they all agree is the enemy—the boss. And gradually a few of the workers will be won over and recruited to the party. But again, without the fight on reform issues, there would have been no basis to relate the longer-range, revolutionary ideas or sell our revolutionary newspaper.

Still another example exists in a basic industry where one comrade helped launch a small-scale struggle that has won some victories (saved one worker's job, for instance), propelled him into a shop steward's position, created the real necessity in the workers' minds for a permanent caucus to fight all the time, and given a good basis for our comrade to fight racism as a divisive weapon of the bosses. All this has enabled him to raise our line on the war, and established a left-wing or "red" reputation for him without isolating him from the workers. On the contrary, they have drawn closer to him (electing him steward) and he has been able to give our literature to some workers in the course of these struggles (and brought one worker into a PL study group). None of this would have been possible without actual struggle for economic reforms, because it is only through such struggles that lessons can be taught (both on the weaknesses after defeats and the counter-attack to be prepared for after "victory"). This enables the struggle to be raised to a higher level. In the course of these low-level reform struggles, more advanced points are won beyond just the reforms themselves: in the latter two of the above-mentioned areas the workers realized that drinking and stealing put them in jeopardy with the boss–and therefore puts the whole struggle against the boss in jeopardy–and some stopped (which puts them in a better position to conduct more advanced struggles). Workers also realize the destructive nature of racism in real terms, not based on intellectual theorizing (although the latter plays its part). And they begin to realize that "reds" are not the ogres they're painted to be but, in fact, are very necessary (or at least useful) to their own struggles. This is a great leap forward.

In any event, the conclusion from these and other experiences is clear: we participate in (and help launch) reform-type struggles in order to raise the struggle to the next highest level. This IS the job of a revolutionary. Not raising the level is opportunist. Not participating in most reform struggles is sectarian. Both help the enemy.

See who you can win to your side by going up and down the block hollering "Socialism–let's seize state power neighbors." But if you do the necessary spadework, and when objective conditions change, this seemingly ridiculous act could take on real meaning. Never write off the masses and their ability or capacity for struggle. Either we learn to love, honor, respect, and rely on the masses, or we close shop.

What makes us think that we can postulate to the workers about selfishness—like don't take that poverty money, because you weaken the struggle; or telling skilled workers that they have to fight for the rights of the unskilled in the shop or weaken their own battle; or tell white workers the paltry, temporary crumbs that may come from white chauvinism should be cast aside for class unity; or tell Black workers the road to freedom can be achieved, eventually, by establishing class unity–that setting up a Black bourgeoisie hating whitey solves nothing; or tell the working class that their allegiance must be to oppressed workers in Vietnam, and not the oppressive U.S. bosses? We want workers to subordinate what appears to be their immediate interests for the good of the entire class at home, or even the international working class, but are we willing to subordinate what seems to be our immediate interests?

If we are going to defeat U.S. imperialism we all have to enter into the struggle wholeheartedly. We must use all our initiative, thoughtfulness, and discipline. While the general work of the entire party can help the individual member to build a base, in the final analysis each member has to produce. No one can do it for you. Party directives, articles, and agitation are helpful, but these devices cannot do the job. Without real base-building the party will shrivel up and die. If the individual member doesn't build a base the same fate awaits him politically. Oh, there are always rationales, always issues to "struggle" on, but finally you run out of dodges.

Build People's Organizations

Naturally a broader view of base-building must include more than just individual ties. It should include some examination of forms. At the moment there are a couple of objective problems to deal with. In recent years there has been little success for anyone who tried to build organizations in working class communities. For the most part there is strong resistance by workers to community organization. This resistance, in part, is based on cynicism and the lack of political development to overcome cynicism. Also, many people still have strong illusions about the state. They still rely on the state to solve their problems.

So very often you see the contradiction between powerful mass action, and lack of organization. This is most apparent in the ghettos. Hundreds of thousands act against the system spontaneously, in an extremely sharp way. But two weeks after the action only the tiniest segment considers organization. Most often it is the government and their nationalist stooges who move in to mis-organize the community. Too few good forces act organizationally. This failure to organize against the state in a serious way indicates more faith in the system than meets the eye, real faith. This is becoming more obvious with the spate of Black candidacies across the country, including the South. Illusions about the parliamentary process still run deep in the country. Deeper than we realize.

In the past we put a lot of emphasis on open agitation. Our ability to grow from this has been very limited. People in the community are not generally ready to organize directly against the war, or under revolutionary banners, although huge numbers are opposed to the war, and some forces are deadly opposed to the system. Therefore, we must continually probe for the level around which people are ready to organize. Any consistent struggle against the system is useful. Within these efforts all sorts of political lessons can be drawn by us and the people. This is why we should consider building organizations that are geared to the everyday problems people face, and relate the larger political questions to them. Education, housing, sanitation, women's problems, prices, etc. are all questions which bear organizational investigation. In the past we have been too quick to pass up existing groups which might have some potential, like PTA's or Tenants Councils.

Of course this proposal will provoke the cry of opportunism. However the essential question is how do you play a vanguard role in a mass organization? How do you "work with and struggle against"? In student work we are seeking out forms of struggle and organization which do not necessarily start out from the point of opposition to the war.

We are working under the assumption that the majority of students can eventually be mobilized against the system. At this point, the majority are not ready to organize against the war. Many are ready to fight for various aspects of academic freedom, (more student-faculty control of the schools), and will generally support working class battles. So within these issues we should find the forms to work with more people. And in the course of this work we develop the ways and means to raise the consciousness of more people.

Develop New People's Leaders

In the course of expanding our ties in an all around way—personally, politically, organizationally—we will be beginning to solve a very pressing problem. This is the scarcity of new people's leaders who are ready to fight the system, at least in a limited way. Within the working class especially, this is a burning question. Where are the new leaders in the Black Liberation Movement? Not many. You might count them on your two hands. Where are the new leaders in the labor movement? Few and far between. Where are the new leaders in the various communities? Let's face it. The old has-beens or the newer never-wases are still around. They still control most of the existing organization. While this helps to explain the cynicism mentioned before, it doesn't excuse us from trying to solve the problem. People's leaders will not descend from Mars. We must have a conscious policy of bringing new leaders forward. And, when new decent forces do spring up we must try and prevent their corruption by the old-line leaders and the government. If we don't intercede more skillfully we will always be able to say with some certainty that virtually any new leader is a "phony." This "truth" will be a pyrrhic victory for us. Until the people have real leaders their struggle will be throttled by the state. Smugness will not overcome this problem. Only close political-personal relations based on struggle can begin to change this situation.

Given this objective reality–little organization and leadership –within the working class, we must take a closer look at the development of the united front.

The United Front

First, let's review a few things about the united front. Our revolutionary efforts can't succeed without the development of the united front. Each stage of the revolutionary process requires a united front. This is true because at any stage large numbers of people will not necessarily be under our direct leadership, or agree with the long-range strategy of the party. But many forces will be willing to work with the party on short-range goals, or even on intermediate goals. Within these struggles we must try and win the confidence of these people and win more and more to the idea of the dictatorship of the proletariat. So the united front is a contradiction. It is the unity of opposites.

What are some of the characteristics of this situation? Unity with some is transitory and unstable. At some stage of the game, as the struggle against the enemy grows sharper, those who haven't advanced their consciousness will split. This is good because those who are left are at a higher level. And this development must grow and grow. Each new stage of the struggle should see more forces, more politically developed, and able to break with those who would retard the struggle.

At each stage of the struggle we must determine what is the correct slogan to organize the united front around, and with whom to unite. Also, while there may be one overriding question, there may be other questions in various areas to organize the united front around. The slogan to organize around must be principled, and must sharpen the struggle against the enemy. We should avoid the two classic errors by realizing (1) The united front is not a popularity contest. (2) The united front cannot be a replica of the party program.

In the anti-war movement "U.S. get out of Vietnam now" is the slogan around which we are trying to build the united front. We believe this slogan fits the conditions mentioned above. We try and work with forces who either believe this correct or at least can be won to this premise. It is important that they have either a base among the people or influence. Naturally there will be some forces who do not believe this slogan correct, but, because they have no base, try and co-opt the united front by claiming allegiance to the slogan. We should try and prevent these forces from penetrating the united front and mis-leading it.

In the labor movement today, especially at the shop level, the conditions of the united front are different. Here we would start out at the level of sharper union efforts against the boss. Within these struggles we would relate the question of the war, either publicly or individually, or both, depending on the tactics required.

In the Black Liberation Movement the war has emerged more centrally as a key aspect of the united front. But, even here, the essential question of the united front for the Black Liberation Movement is super-exploitation.

Flexibility Within the United Front

Very often a united front on one question can lead to a broader united front on other questions. This can lead to involving more people in struggle and winning more people to the more fundamental point. The recent Brooklyn College experience is very germane. At the school the united front—PL and SDS—were acting against some aspect of the war. The school attacked. The students defended the right of the united front to carry on its actions without harassment. The school called the cops. The focus of the united front shifted momentarily away from the war to "cops on campus and student-faculty control."

The anti-war forces acted flexibly within this new front to help make these two issues central, while relating them to the war. They were also able to show very clearly the role of the police and school authorities in regard to the state. Ten thousand students supported the strike and the anti-war united front. Many of these students previously supported the war or were passive. Because of this broader involvement some changed their minds and some were won over from passiveness to opposition. The SDS grew, we will grow, opposition to the war will grow, and opposition to the administration will grow. Naturally, there will be attacks and complications. But the action proved our basic premise that the majority of students can be won to struggle against the system. At some point the contradiction will sharpen, provoking action even at this middle class bastion. Here we saw a good example of how the united front, flexibly applied, raised the consciousness of thousands. Consolidation and consistency becomes the next stage.

In united front work the idea of "struggle with–struggle against" must be skillfully applied. We must be very sharp against those who consciously betray the struggle, like Socialist Workers Party, Communist Party, *Guardian, Monthly Review,* etc. At the same time we must use wisdom in winning those who are influenced by the wrong line, but who are essentially honest. Distinguishing between friends and enemies, it is called. Perhaps two ways could be used to evaluate the united front. Did we grow in influence and numbers? Did the center grow likewise, including more vigorous leadership?

United Front is Built From the Base Up

There must be two strategic premises guiding our united front work today. The united front, in the main, must be built from below. Therefore we are helping to build left-center coalitions in every area of work. We say build from below because our estimate is there are few real people's organizations championing the needs of the people–and damn few leaders who take this path. Here is where our united front policies are interrelated with our base-building. Base-building is bound to help develop people's leaders and organizations. Building people's formations to fight the enemy in different places, at different levels, means building the center. We unite with this center to defeat the ruling class and its stooges among the people, advancing the struggle to new levels. In this fight we raise our consciousness and that of the forces with whom we are fighting. In doing this we build our party, and with more of the direct leadership of the workers. As this process grows our leadership spreads to wider and wider sections.

Even after the seizure of state power, the united front is a strategic weapon to defeat revisionism and imperialism. Under different conditions it is still necessary for the Left to unite with the Center to defeat the Right.

In trying to judge the long-range tendency of attempts by communists at united front work in this country one would have to conclude that the long-range weakness was right opportunism. This is not to say that Left-sectarianism was not (and won't be) a problem. But to get the best appraisal of what is most likely to happen requires a long-range view of historical weakness. We didn't invent this concept of taking a long-range view–Lenin did.

So even in our initial steps we are making both mistakes at once. If you agree with the idea of "struggle with–struggle against," and that the long-range tendency has always been right opportunism, then you must conclude that "struggle against" was, and probably will be, weak. Within the anti-war movement, for example, we have waged a struggle against the C.P.-SWP forces; while they have footing and influence, still it is easier to hit them because the militants whom we want to influence can more easily see their deviation. Hence they are an easier target. And even if the C.P.-SWP axis adopts a more militant line–like "get out"– this can still be seen through more easily.

It is also not too difficult, at this point, to attack liberalism in the anti-war movement. If we attack RFK & Co., people won't get up tight about it even if they don't agree with us. In any event, the more radical forces, for the moment, agree that RFK is rotten.

Where we get the most static from militants, forces whom we are trying to win, is where we have differences with them, and where we fight for our own line. When we advance a class line, it will not be immediately accepted by radicals. When we reject tactics like "resistance" because these tactics will not only isolate radicals from workers, but from other students and intellectuals that could be won, our line will also be momentarily rejected by many.

By advancing a class line and tactics that will strengthen and broaden the base we are, in fact, advocating the only genuine militancy. This is so because these are ideas necessary to win. In the face of opportunism many of us will retreat. Some of us will panic, and suddenly nothing we say or do will seem right. Why? Because at the moment many do not agree. "Struggle against" becomes a sometime thing. It is easier to be popular.

Our fight for a class line within the anti-war movement is in no way contradictory to the aspirations of those who want to defeat the U.S. policies. In fact, it helps them from being drawn into various traps by the enemy to crush the movement. However, when you oppose something which appears to be militant, or forces who genuinely desire militancy but who are being side-tracked, the cry of "arrogance" or something like it will arise.

For example no matter how we hailed the struggle of the Vietnamese, the moment we questioned and criticized their taking Soviet "aid" we were attacked as "arrogant." Why? Because most people with whom we work do not understand, as yet, the dangers of a united front with the Soviets. Even though some people in the party were willing to go along with the line, although they disagreed, they finally couldn't go along with it because of the character of their base. Lydegraf and Coe for example had for their base mainly ex-C.P. people or similar types. They couldn't take the gaff from friends and both ended up attacking the party.

So it is true that in fighting deviations there are temporary losses. But these losses are more than offset through strengthening the party and the people's movements in practice and ideologically. This is not an instant process. When we conducted an ideological struggle against *Studies on the Left* many condemned our articles criticizing them. Some did it politically, some raised "style" questions. Today these articles are used in our study in many places in the party because events seem to prove our line. Our party was strengthened and many forces in the New Left were aided, and rejected the *Studies*' line of parliamentarianism.

A clear polemic against what appears to be popular ideas is like swimming up-stream, going against the tide. And that's what is going to be in store for us for a long time. If we present ourselves and our ideas carefully and develop our work well, slowly but surely we will gain more and more footing and win the initiative. Struggles against deviations—particularly seemingly non-class ideas, which are really ruling class ideas covered up by militancy–are going to be with us for a long time. And it is necessary to always distinguish between the misleaders and those who are misled. If attacking those who mislead implies that those who are misled are in error by accepting misleaders, this is a real act of friendship–because without trying to point out that which is correct we would be of little value to the people.

One of the aberrations developing in our efforts to broaden out community work or industrial work is the tendency to become popular at all costs. Make ties one way or another, good or bad. So if we adopt a line in the community around the war which is the same as the C.P. or someone like them, it's O.K. because we are "good guys." We know what we are doing. Or if in a shop, we go along with all kinds of racism and anti-communism when we might be able to fight it, that's O.K. because we are "good guys" and we do not want to be isolated. But "glorious isolation" is far better than advancing opportunism.

Once again, remember that we can be corrupted not only directly, but through our base. We are developing ties not merely to have them, but to slowly but surely try to raise revolutionary working class ideas with those with whom we work. In correcting sectarianism let's not swing over to opportunism. This will be a constant danger in the period ahead.

The most important point in any of these polemics is our political ties, our relations with the people whom we are trying to win. Here the "struggle with" becomes dominant. Without these ties any polemic will just turn people off. There will be no force to clarify matters for those who have no crystallized opinion.

This is the essence of our sectarianism: our relations are still too limited and fragile to win people to our line in many cases. In the face of disagreement we flounder. We are more at home dealing with obvious opportunist errors, but we are thrown off by Right errors covered by a militant veneer.

The united front is the most difficult strategy to apply. You need a base. You must be able to work with people who not only don't agree with you, but may even be vigorously anti-communist. And there is a thin line between opportunism and sectarianism. The correct line is very hard to achieve. Errors are bound to occur. The work must be evaluated continuously to achieve the right mix. To use an unscientific term, you need common sense.

Strengthen the Party: Defeat Servility

Inner-party struggle is vital to the life of our party. Inner-struggle is made necessary by the weaknesses that we bring into the party and by the weaknesses that exist in the people with whom we are working. The influences on us are not just the open efforts of the ruling class. We are also influenced by the ruling class through the people we are trying to win.

At this point we want to try and deal with two important contradictions which we have not mastered yet. One is servility and discipline. The other is individualism and collectivity. Servility is really an essential aspect of bourgeois society. When the ruling class prattles about individuality and initiative they are really only referring to themselves. They train the working class and the students and intellectuals to be servile. (There is a trifle more latitude for students and intellectuals. But actually this is skin deep. Latitude is only allowed in trifles, so long as it is harmless and shows up on profit charts.) We are taught to be used to having other people think for us and direct us. We are trained to be mentally lazy. Problems and decisions are usually solved or made by someone else. Even individual problems are settled in a bad way. If you have a little money you go to the great wizard, tell him your troubles while he strokes his chin. Supposedly he illuminates the contradiction for you and steers you to the "solution." While the myth is created that "you solved your own problem," the reality is that you were driven to the couch. If you don't have money to throw away on Dr. Cronkite you drink or take dope. And in some cases you do it all. The essence of this is servility, because you do not relate your contradictions to the system, and you capitulate to some form of non-struggle.

When you join the party you are faced with the idea of democratic centralism. While some may complain about the centralism the truth is that many like it. The antagonism to centralism is only skin deep. Centralism is really what we are accustomed to and what we have been trained to accept. The party leaders often like this, deep down, because it makes the task of "leading" so much "easier." So, in the party, you can easily arrive at a boss-worker relationship. Bureaucratic-centralism can easily develop from democratic centralism if we are not alert. Keeping quiet will replace inner-party struggle if we are not alert.

But servility goes even further in robbing the party of vigor and creativity. People are often loath to act unless told what to do and guided at each step. Even very simple work, like selling literature, requires an order from the boss. Obviously this is debilitating. Under these circumstances direction and leadership, which are necessary, really become orders from the boss. The collective aspect is gone because collectivity really belongs only to the party leaders in the same way democracy really belongs just to the ruling class.

More membership participation must be encouraged and welcomed. The responsibility for correction is the leaders!

Because our party stems from a large middle-class group we bring another deviation into the party–individualism-anarchy. In rebelling against the boss-like domination in life we come to believe our mothers and fathers who told us that we are geniuses and wonderful. Some never really meant their accolades. They were trying to establish their status through their children in their middle class world. "Murray, you are the smartest boy alive. You'll be a lawyer, at least." So now when we participate in party discussion we will never relinquish our point of view. We will never shut up. Secondary differences are elevated into primary differences. "The party must be defeated because they don't agree with us. If we can't defeat the party from within we must do it from without." So beating the party becomes some immature people's battle.

There is a common denominator between servility and individualism-anarchy. Usually it is manifested by not carrying out the party line among the people. By staying isolated the individualism is hard to curb and defeat. Or, if a base is being built, it is not really for the party. It is a personal base, to be used not in the interest of the party, but in the interest of the individual. Kingdoms and fiefdoms are being built. Eventually, these are taken over or handed over to the enemy. After all, it is the enemy's ideas that are predominant.

In all this there is a thin line between what is good and what is bad. Liberalism in the party is wrong and so is autocracy. Perhaps we could summarize this question in the following way. Everyone should be active and developing ties based on a collective determination of perspective and line. We each should fight all proposals we don't agree with. We should question all that is not understood. We should accept all the decisions of the party for a time but insist on reevaluations based on experience. None of us should accept anything that challenges basic Marxist-Leninist concepts, as for example, the need for revolution, the dictatorship of the proletariat, proletarian internationalism, U.S. imperialism is the main enemy of the people of the world, PLP is a party of the working class and class struggle is the driving force of history.

Many times in the past we have raised the idea of being constructive in inner-party struggle. It is imperative to have a friendly, non-sarcastic attitude. If there isn't an open, friendly atmosphere this will distort the fight over differences. We still have many instances of nastiness and organizing others against "them" and for "our" position. When things like this happen, people should intercede. Don't wait for the leadership. Put down rudeness and attempts to organize for one's position outside of regular discussions.

Remember that every difference can't be resolved immediately or just through reasoning. This means that comrades have to decide what they think is right and what wrong. This means that someone has to accept the decision, subordinate his position to others, maintain an open mind and see what experience teaches. This means that the minority cannot conduct a nasty, wise-guy, on-going struggle against the line when others are trying to apply it. Time and experience must be allowed to really get a good idea of the validity of a particular effort.

Proper relations between members is essential to party growth. Take nothing, and no one, for granted. Consider all your actions from the viewpoint of how they affect others. The idea is to help one another, not to destroy one another. The latter is the road to success in the bourgeois world. In our world helping the people, helping each other, is our success.

More people must come forward to be responsible for building the party. More have to view all their actions from the point of view of what is good for the party. Obviously, no deviation from Marxism-Leninism helps this. Fighting deviations within ourselves and within others mean helping to lead the party. A thorough-going collective outlook will enhance our inner struggle. Inner struggle is, after all, aimed at strengthening all of us.

In the coming period we have to improve our recruitment procedures. First our recruitment should stem more from contacts we are making in activity. We must put the question of joining the party as the most important step in that person's life. Joining the party means a qualitative change between the individual and the ruling class. As stated earlier, you are challenging the ruling class to a life and death struggle. At least, the enemy understands it this way. Therefore he hates you. Of course his tactics vary, from period to period. So we shouldn't let this momentary period of limited bourgeois democracy for some to fool us.

Perspective–Performance–Perseverance

When people join the party a perspective should be worked out with them based on the needs of the party. The perspective should also be determined by the skills, abilities and desires of the member. This perspective should go beyond just tomorrow! This means that the party group into which the person is recruited should have a perspective. The candidacy period can really become meaningful only if there is some way to gauge the person. In trying to carry out something in particular, and by discussing the perspectives of the club and individuals, the new member can make a better judgment as to whether he wants to stay in the party. It is in the pre-recruitment period that we should get to know as much as possible about the person, so the club can better evaluate membership, not the candidacy period.

In recruiting we should not have the ridiculous idea that we are looking for a perfect communist. Where do we have perfection now? Becoming a good communist is a long-term process. The fight for commitment is constant. Who in our party doesn't have to fight for his commitment? Don't create standards for new members that we have not yet achieved in old members. Some yardsticks to be used: Know your person well. Is he active? Is he stable? Does he agree with the basic ideas our party is founded on? Personal and political shortcomings, if they are not crucial, have to be overcome in time–in the party, in struggle among the masses.

In the past we have made both possible errors: sometimes too liberal and sometimes too demanding. As in every question raised here too our skill, thoughtfulness and maturity must be developed.

Chauvinism—Who Needs It?

Another deviation which exists in our party is white chauvinism. This doesn't have the overt crass forms that one finds in American life. Nonetheless chauvinism exists! If it is not fought it will grow, because the ruling class is sharpening up its racist axe in the face of sharp struggle by Black people in the U.S., and oppressed people all over.

There are three main forms in which it develops in the party. (1) The failure to advance the needs and aspirations of Black people if this seems to fly in the face of temporary needs of white workers. (Of course there is a tactical question involved concerning length of time in a place and progress in base-building. But let us assume this tactical question is settled.) We are not in a popularity contest. Our ideas have to be publicly advanced if we are to eventually see them become dominant. In fighting any deviation among the masses our position in the beginning will not be popular. Naturally, the ability for our ideas to get a decent hearing depends on our relations with white workers. If such relations don't exist you have fallen down on the key aspect of the battle. Many, perhaps most, white workers believe that Black workers' advancement, in any form, takes bread out of their mouths. This idea has been consciously planted by the bourgeoisie and in the narrowest sense seemingly confirmed by life.

But racism is one of the bulwarks of the white workers' own enslavement. So by persisting in the fight against racism we will win white workers in the long run. Because if they want to achieve their aspirations they must eventually develop unity with Black workers.

Recent events in the schools in New York have posed this particular question sharply. There is a sharp contradiction between teachers and the state over working conditions. There is a sharp contradiction between the parents and the state and the parents and the teachers. (Contradictions within contradictions.) At the time of the (1967) strike the secondary contradiction between parents and teachers was sharpened. The state and its various stooges have done this. But the union and the workers have done this also by venting their racism. So the key contradictions between the parents and the state and the teachers and the state get somewhat derailed. Winner—the state.

In the course of the teachers' struggle against the state our people and friends can't see how to reverse this trend of parents and teachers fighting each other. To some extent they play down the racism of the teachers and the union, and don't hit it nearly hard enough. A feeling is generated that if you attack racism among the teachers you may be hurting the class struggle aspect, as well as endangering your own relations with teachers. People often see only the nationalist deviation. But the nationalist deviation, which must be combatted, thrives primarily because of chauvinism. Which is the main danger to the working class, chauvinism or nationalism? We say chauvinism! If you are going to make a one-sided error, for crying out loud, make it combatting chauvinism.

At our past convention there was a strong Black nationalist tendency. This was encouraged by chauvinism. Black people were brought into the party and to the convention for "composition." They were not ready for the party. "White people shouldn't work in the ghetto." However, in our work this has gone too far. Under the guise of following the party line, and by bowing to nationalism many white members in the party have little or no contact with Black people. In reality many people feel relieved that they don't have to have relations with Black people. "After all if white people scrutinize us closely because we are communists, Black people will do it more so. We really have to be on our toes. Who needs it?" There is great truth that Black people will judge us carefully. Why shouldn't they? And that's how we are forced to think and learn and change. Do we want it handed to us on a silver platter? Do you think it will be handed to you on a silver platter?

We believe white communists can influence Black workers, especially in industry where the oppressor is more obviously a common one. While white communists must mainly develop ties with white workers, and not fawn over Black workers, they must eventually become the unifying force between the two.

In brief, chauvinism is displayed in our party by not fighting as sharply among workers where we can; by not developing ties with Black workers and trying to recruit them; and by pandering to nationalism. Marxism-Leninism is the science of the working class, Black and white. While the nationalist current places obstacles in the fight for Marxism-Leninism among Black people, it can be overcome by a resolute fight against chauvinism in and out of the party.

Understanding the Dictatorship of the Proletariat

Within the radical movement and within the Black Liberation Movement the key concept to fight for and win is the dictatorship of the proletariat. This is the concept which draws the greatest fire from various forces. But if we are to win this fight for a working class outlook we have to be clear on this question ourselves. There are only two classes in the world today that are capable of holding state power and who actually hold state power: the bourgeoisie or the working class. There are no in-betweens. Any political development is judged by evaluating its class-power implications. And where there have been revolutions we can determine their nature by seeing which class really holds state power. Ask yourself this question: "Who holds state power in Algeria, Ghana, Guinea, Soviet Union, Cuba, Albania?" Only in China and Albania do the workers hold state power. What other class holds it in the others if you agree that it isn't the working class?

Some people think that revolution can be successfully carried out without Marxism-Leninism, that is, without a party, and without the strategy of the dictatorship of the proletariat. There are revolutions and revolutions. There are working class revolutions, and bourgeois democratic revolutions. There are National Democratic revolutions which may or may not be transformed into Socialist revolutions. If they are not, power may simply be transferred from one section of the bourgeoisie to another. Such is the case of Algeria. The reason why so many people in and out of the movement can be taken in by Debray is precisely because they do not understand this question. Many people in our party don't recognize the counter-revolutionary role of Debray. They can't understand that Castro and company have launched an all-out assault on Marxism-Leninism in this hemisphere. It is hard for people to understand revisionism, if it isn't stamped "made in Moscow or Yugoslavia." But clearly if revisionism is to succeed it must fool the people. Therefore, in each period, in each country, it takes on that coloring most helpful to conceal itself. It trades on the hopes of the people, it builds itself on these hopes, but actually revisionism works against them. Does anyone believe that revisionism openly opposes Mao in China? The red flag is used to obscure the red flag. Mao is "drowned in a sea of Mao."

So today the newer variety of revisionism drowns revolution in a sea of "revolution."

How is it done? Can anyone who claims to be a revolutionary come before the Latin masses and oppose armed struggle? The Soviets are completely discredited because of this. So modern revisionism advocates "armed struggle." But the armed struggle is separated from the concept of People's War. In this way Marxism-Leninism and the dictatorship of the proletariat are opposed. All you need are a few good guys and a gun. Where has armed struggle in and of itself won state power? If that were all that was necessary Al Capone would have been President. Armed struggle is an important aspect of the revolutionary struggle. But it must be based on People's War, the mass line leading to the dictatorship of the proletariat. Revolutionary violence is not limited to terrorism. Revolutionary violence must be a matter the people embrace.

We believe the strategy we are pursuing to be generally correct. It can be improved, and is being improved by experience. More significant adjustments are needed in our trade union program. It was here that we had the least experience, and it was here that the revisionist influence was strongest.

Our main changes have to take place in ourselves, in the way we try to carry out our line. That is why this report deals with those aspects more directly related to base-building.

The principal manifestation of revisionism in our party really comes from a limited ability to transform ourselves and become real forces of the working class. In the final analysis our line can best be demonstrated in life by how many workers we can move into battle against the enemy. If we can't do it today what are we doing now to make it possible tomorrow? This is what will really distinguish us from those petty bourgeois forces within the Left whom we are carrying out an ideological struggle against. Are we really different than they are? Do we mean what we say? Base building is the only way for us to carry the day and in the long run make the revolution. The battle won't be won on the pages of the magazine. That can help. But action in life is the basic answer.

If there has been repetition or you have heard this song before, ask yourself why? It is because we are not doing well enough in becoming a party of the working class. The concept is not yet clear enough in anyone's mind. Without a base everything turns out to be a hollow joke, an exercise in romanticism. We know, even where we have tiny toe-holds, the influence we can exert. From our most limited experiences in the schools, communities, factories we can see the power of Marxism-Leninism even if applied in the minutest doses. We have been a positive influence on almost all the new political developments in the country. But this is scratching the surface. We can be wiped out one way or another unless we do better. We have progressed. But we have not made indestructable ties to the workers. We are not serving the ruling class but we are not as yet thoroughly committed to the working class. We are moving in the right direction, but we must do better . . . better . . . better.

Unlimited opportunities await us. Hundreds of millions are fighting U.S. imperialism everywhere. Millions in our country are beginning the long march.

Wipe out obstacles in the party!
Build a base for the party!
Bc a party of thc working class among the people!
Serve the people, not ourselves!

Fight Individualism

Speech Opening, Second PLP Convention, May 1968

Three years ago, at our initial convention, we made the point that we had to become a serious party, a party of the working class. We had to begin to transform ourselves into genuine revolutionaries, people completely devoted to Marxism-Leninism, to the party and to the concept that the party serves the people.

As I am sure many of you who were at that first convention understood, or many of you who were members of the PLP at that time understood, there were a lot of shortcomings in our party, and there were certainly a lot of shortcomings in us as individual members of the party. And, at that time, I think, if we would have gone around the room (and that time we had a convention, I don't recall exactly how many people were there, perhaps 200), if we would have gone around that room, and asked those people who had some tangible relationship to the working class to raise their hands, I don't know if you could have gotten a baker's dozen to put up their hands. If you asked people at that convention, "Who among you works for a living and goes to work every day?" you might have gotten less. I don't know. You would not have gotten too many. [Walter Linder says: "Four."] Four you would have gotten. Well, Wally's a stickler, precise; so it's probably true. Let's rely on his preciseness.

And I think one of the main things that came out of our first convention, one of the most important things, was this idea that we would become a party of the working class, a revolutionary party. We would develop close ties with the working class. And, of course, one of the first steps was to go to work.

I think that in the last three years, in taking the first toddling steps along this path, we've made progress. Just looking around the room today, I see a lot of people here who work in industry. There are a lot of people here who are carrying on much more serious activity where they live or in school than was the case at our first convention. I think that's an accomplishment. And I think that's something we should take a very positive view about. This was a serious step forward for our party.

We Must Go Further in Integrating With and Stimulating the Working Class

We have brought into the American scene way beyond our ranks the idea that if you want to make a revolution in this country, then you had better win the working class politically. And we know that during the last few years, we have carried on a political battle to win people to this idea, because this idea was generally alien, certainly in our student and intellectual movement. And the working class itself, because it had little or no political consciousness, doesn't necessarily conceive of itself as that class which will be the key, the instrumental class, in bringing about revolutionary socialism in our country. This is one of our biggest contributions in our country, and this is something we have to pursue with a lot more vigor and skill than we have. That is to say, to make the PLP a party of the working class and win other sectors of the population to understand that it is on the shoulders of the working class that socialism will triumph in the United States. We made a little start in this direction but we have to go much further.

Certainly anybody reading about the political situation in France can see this proposition a lot more clearly. That is to say, a lot of people can start the revolutionary process. But it is only the workers, in the modern industrial countries, that are going to finish it. When we were kids we used to say "Before you start something, you better see who's going to finish it." If we want to start a revolutionary movement we'd better have a clear idea how it is going to get finished, upon whose shoulders it is going to be finished.

France certainly refutes the notion, which has been spread around by all sorts of forces (sincerely or otherwise) that the working class in capitalist countries is so hopelessly corrupt that it is not going to make the revolution, and revolution can only come in the more oppressed sections of the world, and therefore, our task is simply to somehow or other assist these colonial revolutionary movements. They say we should write off our own working class. This is, of course, one of the biggest victories the international bourgeoisie can accomplish. Nothing would make them happier. Well, I wouldn't say nothing; it would make them very happy if the workers in all the capitalist countries would just stay put, so they would only have to fight colonial workers. Then they wouldn't have to fight on both fronts.

But if France were repeated in our own country, we might ask ourselves what we'd be doing; which is an interesting question. Certainly you can see the enormous value such an event would have for the revolutionary forces in Asia, Africa, and Latin America. If the American bourgeoisie was so hemmed in by its own working class here that it could not deal effectively with the oppressed outside its boundaries, and would be forced to weaken the struggle against them, or perhaps even let go, this for all intents and purposes would be the beginning of the end, or the end for imperialism. So when we talk about being a party of the working class and introducing Marxism-Leninism, the ideology of the dictatorship of the proletariat, into the ranks of the working class and into the people's movements generally, we are talking about big stakes. And it is not just an abstraction.

You know, some say "Would you believe that the Progressive Labor Party is going to lead the revolution? Would you believe that?" Everybody would say to himself, "That's pretty funny." Well, it's all right to have a sense of humor about things and to take things in stride but we better understand that that's what we are trying to do! We are trying to destroy the system and we are trying to bring revolutionary ideology into the working class and our outlook is that we can succeed. We can do this because the system that we are fighting cannot satisfy the working class and the people generally, and Marxism-Leninism can help workers achieve a new system. They come into sharp contradiction with the system. And we have to have the will, the guts, or whatever you want to call it, to bring our revolutionary ideas into all of these struggles. We should take this perspective very seriously, and we should think from the point of view that "We can do it; it can be done." Not from the point of view of pompousness, but from a point of view of being serious about what we are doing, of seeing that the opportunities are there, and that whether or not we succeed rests on us, not on the enemy, but on us. And it's no use in crying over spilled milk, like others have done: "We failed because they beat us." "We failed because they were too strong." "We failed because of whatever the enemy did." No! The enemy can do his thing. He does it all the time, to all revolutionaries. He tries to crush and defeat them.

But revolutionaries fail and revolutionaries don't succeed in carrying forward the revolutionary process mainly because of their own shortcomings, primarily because of their own limitations. If this weren't true there would be no point in starting. There would be no point in organizing to smash the system. Because superficially the system appears much stronger than the revolutionary forces; so, if you are taken in by appearances, you will give up the ghost. And, unfortunately, too many of us are still taken in by appearances, although going through the motions of playing revolutionary. After all, it's interesting. It keeps us off the streets. It gives us something to do. It gives some purpose to our lives, it makes us feel noble and that sort of thing. But in our guts all of us question whether it can be done, or whether we can do it. As I said, we'd better take the approach that it can be done, that we are going to do it, and that the only one who can defeat us is ourselves. Nobody is to blame but ourselves.

Develop Revolutionary Leadership

Now one of our main tasks since our inception has been to bring about this transformation in the party and in ourselves, to become serious revolutionaries, and not through an abstraction, but actively to play a certain kind of role. Of course, one of our main perspectives, one of our key tasks, has been to develop a core of people who would be considered professional revolutionaries in the traditional sense. That is, to serve the revolution and the party and the people comes first, that is the primary thing in their life. Because no serious revolutionary party can exist, and be successful, without serious revolutionaries, without a cadre, without a leadership. And, during the last three years, I think small steps have been taken along this road. That is to say, there is a number of such people in a growing core in our party, represented broadly by the people at this convention. By and large, this growing core of cadres slowly but surely (with ups and downs, still trying to equivocate a little bit) is making this revolutionary outlook the primary thing in their lives, is trying to defeat the "I" mentality and develop the "We" mentality. This convention is a reflection of this process.

Now are we developing cadre as an abstraction so as to be able to say we have 60 or 100 or 120 or whatever the number is of people who are dedicated? That's nice of course. But what is the purpose? The essential purpose is to bring leadership into the party, to develop revolutionary leadership among the people. There is the tendency in America, and probably in all countries to some degree, to say, "What do you have to be a leader for?" Somehow or another, movements can succeed without leaders. Now, of course, the ability of movements to succeed is based on two things. It is based on the objective circumstances, but also on the subjective circumstances. And it's the interrelationship of these two that determines the outcome of the movement. For example, to refer back to France, there perhaps we could say a revolutionary situation existed objectively. But was there revolutionary leadership? There may be revolutionaries, but is there a leadership in the sense that it has that political relationship with the masses that they can take advantage of this objective situation, and consummate that revolution? I doubt it. I hope I'm wrong, but I doubt it.

What is the role of leadership in the Soviet Union? In Indonesia? What is the role of leadership in every area where the revolutionary movement is moving ahead or retrogressing? Very important. Decisive. Just as the objective situation is decisive. We could all go into the street and cry "Rise up, fellow citizens. Let's seize City Hall." And unless that has some objective basis in reality, people will throw ash cans at us, or laugh at us. So I'm not putting forward a superman view of history. I'm simply putting forward what I believe is one of the most important elements of revolutionary ideology, of Marxism-Leninism: the need of the people to have a revolutionary leadership. And, therefore, if we think in terms of playing a role among the people and within the party, and in terms of leading the people in struggle, then we better now view it seriously. View it from the point of view that we are undertaking a tremendous responsibility.

We are involved with other people in fighting the system, and we better not view that arrogantly, or conceitedly or pompously, but as a struggle of life and death. We are at war with the system: the class struggle is not some abstract concept. It is a struggle of life and death. It is a struggle of one class to defeat and to destroy the other one. That is what it is. And that is the struggle we're in. You get into a life and death struggle with your enemy, you better understand that. And you better think accordingly. And you better try to get everyone else to think accordingly because the class forces who are involved besides ourselves are being constantly victimized by the other side and in the long run have to destroy the other side's ability to oppress and repress them. And this is a life and death fight. This is an all-out fight. It's not a partial fight. Because if it's a partial fight, then we're reformists. We can say revolution, we can say a lot of nice things, but sooner or later, we'll stop saying that. Sooner or later the part of us which is reformist will become primary because we really don't think we are in a life and death struggle. We really don't think we are in an all-out struggle with the enemy. We really just think we are doing some good things, and hoping it all works out for the best. We are really thinking that history has its ups and downs but history is on our side, so if we don't do it, some others will come along and they will do it.

Well, that's true. You might draw some comfort out of that, but that's what's known as opportunism. That's what's known as not taking into full account one's responsibilities to the revolutionary process, abdicating responsibility and working piecemeal. And when you do something piecemeal, sooner or later you retard, you hurt the revolutionary movement. In the long run, and maybe it doesn't take so long, the little good that might be done turns into its opposite and becomes counter-revolutionary. So our efforts have to be transformed and made complete.

What we are trying to do is to develop revolutionary leadership among the masses and win the majority of the working class and other sections of the population to political consciousness, to

Marxism-Leninism. And this requires, of course, many attributes but it requires, above all, serious devotion, dedication and confidence in the working people. It requires the ability–politically, ideologically and tactically–the ability to develop ties with the working class and with the people which are tight, which cannot be broken by the enemy, so that the revolutionary process develops, and as the people become more conscious, we are able to guide this revolution to its consummation, which is the dictatorship of the proletariat. Therefore, these years of patient, slow winning and training people and developing ties among the masses, no matter how protracted they may seem, no matter how slow they may seem, are vital. They are vital to developing a revolutionary party and a revolutionary leadership among the people.

Obstacles Within the Party

Now within the party there are many obstacles to developing revolutionary leadership, within the party and outside the party, and we see this all the time. What we are dealing with to a great extent is a petty bourgeois ideology, the ideology of the enemy within our own ranks. And it manifests itself in many ways. And we know that if we are going to move ahead that we have to fight this ideology even more vigorously than we have till now. And some people say with a certain amount of justification, "Well, if we do that we'll lose people." That is to say, if you really make Joe work in that shop, and he wants to do something else, and you insist, he'll quit. He might. We see that in every stage of the game, as we develop.

Whenever the party felt it was ready for the next big step, there was always a certain amount of dropping away from the party. This happened even when we formed the party out of the Progressive Labor Movement which we felt was a serious step, because we felt there was enough unity of ideas to form the Progressive Labor Party. This was a serious step because now you are telling the enemy in a sharper way, and you're telling one another in a sharper way, "Look, we are intensifying the struggle." So, at our first conference, I don't recall exactly when it was, a number of people got up, and challenged this idea of a party, raised a lot of ideas to show why it was wrong. And when we went ahead and formed the party, they dropped away. On the face of it, there was no particular reason for them to drop away over our forming the party or not forming the party. They all said they agreed with us on all the main points like dictatorship of the proletariat. They all said they were not defending imperialism, or most of them did. They all said a lot of the right things. But when the party was formed, these people recognized that that was a step forward, a sharpening of the struggle and they fell away.

Now, sure, we don't say "That's wonderful, we're losing all our members!" We are trying to win these people. We try and make a fight for these people. But, nonetheless, this process does go on. When we came out with *Road to Revolution* there was a struggle in the movement. Because what was *Road to Revolution?* That was the opening, the public declaration of struggle against revisionism. A lot of people said, "You can't do that." When the arguments were raised none of these guys said they were against the dictatorship of the proletariat, none of those guys said they were for the war in Vietnam; they didn't say anything on the surface so terrible. They recognized that *Road to Revolution* was a sharpening of the struggle against revisionism and imperialism. Some of them dropped away.

When we came out with *Road to Revolution II* and we tackled revisionism even more sharply, other people dropped away. None of them were raising what appeared to be primary differences. Nobody said that the party was founded on the wrong premise, that we weren't based on the working class. Nobody argued that. They were all for that. But they dropped away. When we start the process within the party of "Look, we have to have more discipline based on collectivity, based on understanding, people have to become more accountable to the party, people have to work, people have to go to school, people have to accomplish something in the community," certain people fall away because the screw is getting turned a little more tightly.

It's not simply a subjective thing, it's not that we decided, "Let's turn the screw and see who we can get rid of this week." It's that our political estimate is that the class struggle is growing sharper, and that in order to just keep abreast of the class struggle we have to do better. And I don't believe we are even keeping abreast of the class struggle. I think, to some extent, we're lagging behind. I don't think we can do everything we'd like to do or we ought to do. But nonetheless, there is this tightening of the screw.

Now, we make our estimate based on our understanding of the international situation of imperialism, based on its growing limitations, based on the growing sweep of revolutionary struggle. The class struggle in our country will grow sharper. We said that several years ago. People laughed in our face. "Oh, those workers won't even go on strike." "They won't do this, they won't do that." "The students are all rotten." "Black people are all lumpen proletariat." So on and so forth. We didn't come to our estimate out of the blue. We came to it based on a somewhat scientific estimate of the objective situation of imperialism. And our estimate has been proven, by and large, correct. The class struggle has grown sharper, outside the country and within the country, and our estimate still holds. One of the recent articles in PL on imperialism tries to give a careful economic evaluation of the falling rate of profit as a barometer of the maneuverability of imperialism. If you say the rate of profit is falling, then you are also saying the imperialists' ability to maneuver is growing less and less, and this forces them more and more to attack and tighten up on their own workers, and oppress workers all over the world. And we think this is the situation we're in, and we think that the coming period will continue to see the sharpening of the class struggle, continue to see the sharpening of struggles in our own country.

That is the sweep of it. We don't have a precise blueprint, but we see that pattern. And it will be protracted, the revolution will take time, and it will not succeed unless there's a serious revolutionary party in the field, a party that has a fundamental relationship with the key sections of the masses. No gimmick, no sleight of hand, no cute trick is going to pull it off, although in America the gimmick and the sleight of hand is part of the culture. But we are not working with this culture. We are working with a Marxist-Leninist outlook. The revolutionary process is protracted. It's always been protracted, it always will be protracted, and it continues even after the seizure of power.

Individualism

Lack of confidence in the working class, lack of confidence in the party, lack of confidence in Marxism-Leninism, is manifested often in a very individualistic attitude toward what one does. A lot of people say (in one way or another) "I'm going to do what I want to do, when I want to do it, and how I want to do it, and I really don't give a damn what the rest of you people think." And that comes out in a million and one ways. If all of you who are here think about yourselves a little bit, and think about most of the people in the party a little bit, I think you will agree that that attitude is still fairly prevalent.

We had a fellow here in New York just recently who was committed to working in industry, committed to developing industrial concentration, who said he was at the disposal of the party. In other words, you wouldn't think it would matter to this guy whether he worked in shop A or shop B. His club said "Go to work in shop A, we think you should work there, not here." Naturally he got a job in shop B. They said he should work in shop A. You wouldn't think that's a primary question, inasmuch as this fellow is saying "I want to work." But he got into an all-out struggle. The club said, "Well, look, you're not raising any principled objections to working in A or B, so we want you to work in A. You're not saying 'I don't want to work any more,' or 'I don't believe the line.' "

We got guys who went to work in industry a few years ago based on the line that grew out of the last convention. We tried to place people in industry with discrimination. We tried to take into account background, personality, so on and so forth. Perhaps some people would be better off teaching, or as welfare workers, or succeeding in the academic world. After all, in every area in American life we have an important role to play. And some guys said, "Oh, never mind, I want to be on the front line. I'm going to be on the front line." Where's the front line? Steel! Auto! Coal mines! Sewers! Front line. So I'd say to these guys, "It's not so easy on the front line. We should evaluate ourselves, maybe you should not be on the front line. Maybe you should be a half step behind the front line." There's a qualitative difference being in the front line and being 300 or 400 yards away from the front line. There's a big difference between living in Harlem or living on the West Side. Big difference. Front line is here, and you're a little bit away, you can still play a good role.

"No, no, front line." All right. "Look, if you change your mind, if you find it's too hard, let's talk it over; you can always change your perspective." After all, it's not a closed corporation here. We have not captured the market every place. Let's evaluate a guy's work. It gets hard on the front line. It gets hard. Working in one of these automobile plants is hard. You work 10 hours a day, six days a week during the busy season. It's hard. In Buffalo, Murray worked many years in an automobile plant. They used to have a saying in Buffalo among the workers. The guys used to say, "If you work for Ford for three years, Chevy won't hire you." The other guys said, "If you work for Chevy for three years, Ford won't hire you." Because workers used to get burnt out; nervous breakdowns and all that kind of thing were very common, particularly in the highly automated, rapid assembly line places.

So now you work there six months or a year. Front line. Hard. Now, instead of coming to the club or collective and saying, "Look, this is very hard for me. Maybe I made a mistake. Maybe we made a mistake. Maybe I should be doing something else; look, I'm still devoted to Marxism-Leninism. I certainly can make a contribution." No, instead of that honesty we've got our "front line theory." We've got to justify it. We can't be honest because that's not romantic any more. That's not the "flowering of the individual." "I work in auto!" But actually you think this whole business of working in the factory is a load of shit. "Workers are no good. I agree with Marxism-Leninism. I agree with the Progressive Labor Party. But these workers ain't going to do nothing. And we're not going to do nothing."

A person has the right to change his mind. We certainly can't prevent people from changing their minds. We're a voluntary organization. But you see, it's very individualistic. It's not completely honest. It's basking in status symbols, preening for your friends. Instead of coming out and saying what it is, you try and cover it up with a theory.

People do this work for a year or two, young guys or even older people. It doesn't matter that much actually. I don't think age is any indication of patience, stability or understanding. It's hard. Things don't move the way you want. The revolution isn't around the corner. And you could be doing this for a long time. You don't think of it just that way, but somehow in the back of your mind is the idea "I can be a lawyer, I could be a doctor, or something; maybe my mother was right. I'll give this thing a whirl for another year, and I'll get a theory. I'll come up with some big theory, that will speed the whole thing up, and get it all over within a year or two. And I'll get a theory to go with it. I'll get some guru or somebody who'll come up with some new 'Marxist-Leninist' theory and a big plan." We've all heard this. It's just another way of creeping out. That is to say, when ideological differences arise within the party (which is not a bad thing, which is a good thing) we have to be very objective and determine what is the reason for the difference. Is it a serious attempt to influence the movement, or is it merely giving vent to a great deal of individualism?

Take the National Committee as an example. I think I mentioned once before that out of the original 20 National Committee members elected at the previous convention about a third dropped away from the party. Now sure, there were differences, but yet in none of these differences was there a basic challenge to the party's line, a challenge to the dictatorship of the proletariat and all the basic bedrock principles. I don't think there was open challenge to that. In each case secondary differences were elevated to primary differences and these people left the party. When you delved into it a little more carefully you saw two or three things. When you examined the outlook, the attitudes, there was a complete difference on base-building, on how to build a base, and whom to build a base among. There was a lot of individualism and arrogance. "You don't agree with me, screw you, that's all. It's my way or no way." And, unfortunately, to a great extent, this is still a very prevalent attitude in the party.

Now, you want to give leadership to the party, and you want to give leadership to the masses (that's what we're talking about). How are you going to do it, when a good deal of your ideological thinking is based on individualism? "Me, me! My mother told me I was the smartest guy alive, and she was right! I am! Nobody could tell me I'm wrong, because I know everything. And no one else in the party knows anything. They don't understand." Now it may be that the party is wrong, and individuals are right. That has happened before. It's happened in this party. It's going to happen again. That is to say, the party will make mistakes, an individual or a couple of individuals in the party will say, "Look, the party's making an error" and you know, it won't be understood, it won't be accepted. You have to take a serious attitude to that kind of struggle. You have to take a protracted attitude to that kind of struggle unless you feel that the party renounced the fundamental ideas for which you joined it. If that's the case, then I would say, "Why wait, split, that's right." But if it's a tactical or even a strategic difference, you have to take a protracted attitude in dealing with that. There's always a possibility, God bless you, you may be wrong, and maybe the collective was right. And even if you are right, if you have any confidence in the collective, well, somehow or other they'll get enough wisdom to understand how smart you were, to see maybe you were right. People change.

We have made many changes in the party, and have had many changes in our line and in many of our strategies and tactics. And unfortunately, that's right, in many cases it's taken us too long to make changes. But, nonetheless, there have been changes. And we have to take a protracted attitude, to fight in a sharp, but principled way, from the point of view of really building the party. And if you really want to build the party when you have a difference with it, you have to think about that because it's not so simple. That's a very difficult contradiction. That's right, I don't say it's simple. But the way to solve it is not to break up the party, to try to make the party become the main enemy, and beat the party. Because that's a very bourgeois attitude.

Well, we have a lot of that in the party. That's bourgeois arrogance, individualism, thinking of yourself over the needs of the party and the people. Sooner or later this brings you into contradiction with the people. If you're working, as all of us are trying to, among the people, you can't be Dr. Jekyll and Mr. Hyde. Your attitudes will appear in your work among the people. You can't be the bad guy in the party and the good guy among the masses. Maybe for a little while you will be on your best behavior among the masses; you will put on a little better show. And you will cover it up a little bit because you have a certain kind of political consciousness (political in the Democratic Party sense) and you can keep a poker face and cover it up a little bit. "Oh, he's a nice guy. But we won't work collectively with the masses, because after all, we know everything. What do these dumb people know? All we have to do is tell them. And if they don't do what I want, they're stupid."

And that's how seemingly good people become enemies of the working class. They don't sit down and will it, they don't sit down and say "I'm going to screw the workers, I'm going to screw the party, now I'm going to do it." They are usually seemingly good guys who want to do a good thing, who do what they think is right. But really they are not working collectively, they don't give a damn about anybody but themselves. They have an axe to grind, and they are going to grind it.

People come to the convention but they don't necessarily view this convention as a way of solidifying the party. How many of us sat down and thought, "Now what am I going to do at this convention to make the party a stronger party; what am I going to do at this convention to unify and build the party, to strengthen the party?" And how many people really view the convention as a forum to win people to their ideas? "I came here to win somebody to my idea. I wrote a leaflet and really, I wrote this paper to win people to my idea." Well, I think most of us are like this. Many of us view the convention as a forum to get our point across, rather than a process in which the party can emerge stronger than ever, renewed in its dedication to going out and building the party among the people in their own areas. So, therefore, I think that on this question of individualism, we have a long way to go, we have not licked it by a long shot.

We can't take a superficial view of the development of the party. It would be a big mistake. We must dig deeper. We can take nobody for granted. We must take everybody into consideration, and work with one another very closely and collectively to help one another overcome individualism, and to progress in the work.

Criticism and Self-Criticism

Now, I think that one of the biggest weaknesses in the development of the international movement, and it certainly manifests itself in our own movement, is the failure to develop criticism and self-criticism. Because without the process of criticism and self-criticism there is no scientific way that the party can correct itself, no way at all. That's the only way. Without it we are robbed of the real ability to correct ourselves. And so, inevitably if self-criticism isn't elevated we will sink into the wrong ideology. We'll develop the wrong ideas, because there will be nothing in operation to fight the wrong ideas.

I think that we have to think about this a little more. For example, in almost all the papers written for the convention discussion, (and there weren't that many, 30, 40, however many there were) how many were self-critical? Who wrote any that said, "I have been trying this work, and I screwed up. And I am not doing what I could have." That at least would be an attempt, weak as it is, to set a self-critical tone. One comrade wrote a list of criticisms of the party. And this comrade, before he got into the criticism, wrote two sentences of self-criticism, but he crossed it out. Crossed it out! Could not bear that everybody in the party should read something of a self-critical character! And yet the whole paper was a critique of the party's line! All crossed out.

And at first I thought I'd be nasty and just have it photographed, just like that. But fortunately (or maybe unfortunately) Wally saw it and, I don't know why, he thought I crossed it out, so when he pasted it up, he took it out.

Now, that's a little bit of a phenomenon, that not one member of the party, (I might be wrong, maybe there was one) but most members–almost nobody had anything self-critical to say. There was some criticism, which is good. But that's only one aspect of criticism and self-criticism. Self-criticism is very important, because if we don't evaluate ourselves it's very hard for others to get a handle on some of the real shortcomings that we may have. Of course it's easier to "self-criticize" somebody else than to be self-critical of oneself. And that's another way of showing that we still consider ourselves to be primary and the party and the people to be secondary.

Now many times people say, "Well, I'm for all that. That's all true. What can we do to change? What can be done to change?" Well, there's no panacea. I think in the first place one has to be aware of this problem. Self-criticism is still the primary thing. One has to have some evaluation of oneself and the people one is working with, and deal with shortcomings self-critically and critically. But after having said that, then of course there are certain procedural things that have political content which can help people change. Now one of them is check-up. When someone is asked to do something, and he agrees to do it, there should be careful examination to find out whether it is being done. How well is it being done? Examine it. Evaluate it. What was done? What was the person's perspective? Does he have a perspective? What did this thing have to do with the person's perspective? In this way we have some way of evaluating a person's political role. It isn't a mystically psychological procedure with somebody hating himself saying, "Well, I'm this and I'm that, I'm a bad fellow," and everybody answering, "That's true." No! There is a process by which we help the individual member to make positive changes.

And this has to be a constant thing. So that when we are engaged in activity, even in the heat of a battle so to speak, we have to find the time to examine what it is we are doing. Somebody says, "Ugh, we'll do it later, when it's all over." Yeah–when we're all dead, we'll examine it. When it's all over, then we'll do it. "I have no time. I have a million meetings. I got to meet this one.

I've got to see that one. I'm all tied up." All tied up! Can't stop for a minute to think about what it is we are doing. Can't stop for a minute. Got minutes for everything else, got minutes to write criticism, got minutes for this, got minutes for that, ain't got five minutes to sit down and ask "What are we doing?"

I have seen it happen in strikes; we had it here in New York in a welfare strike, where our club in the Welfare Department (I don't know why I'm picking on them, it's one that comes to mind) was in the middle of a strike. The club hadn't met. The left-wing caucus that they were working with hadn't met. Too busy. I asked why hadn't the club met. "We're too busy." Well what the hell do we need a party for? What do we need a party for? What is the collective process of the party? The left-wing caucus that they were working with hadn't met.

The students at Columbia are tearing up the pea patch. SDS is the organization leading it. The SDS has not met, we haven't gotten it to meet yet. Our people are active members in it. What is the collective? "I went up to Columbia. I went up to the front lines. I showed my face." Yeah, that will help a lot at Columbia! You know, individualism. How does one distinguish himself in struggle? He's a hero. That's America. That's how you distinguish yourself in the struggle. You're a hero. Somebody gives you a medal, and when you come back, "Boy, were you brave. The cops hit you 18 times. Were you brave!" Big bravery. I think we should be brave. I'm not denigrating bravery. But by balls alone you won't do it. You won't do it. You have got to have brains, you've got to think. You've got to work together. You've got to evaluate, and in the middle of a struggle you've got to do it. In the middle of a struggle.

I once read a book about the Chinese Army written by a bourgeois general, and he described how in the middle of a battle they managed to hold meetings. Now they won. So you can't knock that. That's very interesting. How do you hold meetings in the middle of a battle? They figured it out. They worked it out. Guys were having meetings in foxholes. "What should we do now? Let's think it over." Almost ludicrous when I read it. I said to myself, "What a jerk you are Milt. These guys know that this is part of how we overcome this individualism, by working together collectively within the party and with the people we're working with politically outside the party.

Of course, if you've got nobody to work with politically outside the party, you're in trouble. You've got no relationship to the masses, there's no process. The main door is closed. You don't know anybody, that's a problem. And there's still many of us who, by and large, really don't have relationships with the masses that are meaningful. We say hello to somebody, and get up in the morning and say hello to the neighbors, but we don't really know them. And I think to a great extent that is the case with many people yet. Relationships are too superficial. We don't know people well. They don't really tell us too much. You know what I think we should do? We should ask people, "What do you think of me? How do you think I am working? What do you think of the role of my party in this situation now?"

It doesn't mean that everything that somebody says, whether he is in the party or outside the party, is correct. But it's interesting to hear what people have to say. You might learn something. And that process might help toughen one's skin and make one stop and think. We have to think about this question of criticism and self-criticism, and not do it abstractly, but do it in the process of work. Do it in relationship to what it is we're supposed to be doing, what we voluntarily agreed to do, and what everybody else expects us to do. Otherwise, where's the responsibility to one another? None!

So we had a meeting, we agreed, and now everybody goes out and does what he wants anyway. Of course, the masses spot that. They will pick it up. They will see that you guys aren't serious. Guys from the party in various mass struggles, two lines: one guy says one thing, another guy says another thing. People there, some people, know they're in PL. "Say, that's a funny party, that's a funny party. Gee, they're not 'Stalinists.' They're jerks." Try to get away with it in the union. See how long you will last.

Right Opportunism

Now in our party these deviations appear in very specific political ways. One could sum it up by saying there's a lot of right opportunism in the work and in the thinking, and on the other side of the coin, there's a great deal of sectarianism which we have been attacking by paying attention to developing our individual relationships with other people. And in our opinion these are two sides of the same revisionist's coin. This manifests itself in the unions and in Black liberation work, and among students.

We had a fellow working in a good shop in the Baltimore area and he came up with the absurd of the absurdities. You know, everyone reacted: "Would you believe that!" He said the blasphemy that Walter Reuther was better than George Meany. And you'd think, "Well, oh boy, after six years in PL, how could some guy say something so foolish? The year before that guy would have said 'Line them both up.' " That same guy would have said "Put them to the wall." He went to work in a shop, and within six months he "discovered" that Walter Reuther was better than George Meany. How did that happen?

And you know Wally went down to see him. "Oh no, you know that Walter Reuther is just as bad as George Meany," and we give him the line. This guy says, "No, there's a difference, there's a difference." So what's the difference? "He's better." Why's he better? Well, he lists the usual little things, he's against the war, or something, whatever it is, he likes Kennedy better than Johnson. You know those things, whatever people are saying. He's better. So Wally says, "Well, that's not our line."

So why did this change come over this fellow? Why? Six months ago he would say shoot Walter Reuther, and now Reuther became "better." Why? Because among the workers with whom he's working, every day he goes and lives with these guys, and maybe he got among a group of guys who had a little different type of consciousness, who maybe concerned themselves (because in that particular plant and around that area there are guys who are "more sophisticated" in this sort of thing) and they started butchering him with "Walter Reuther is better." And he would have to go in every day, and he would have to argue for our position. So after a while, you see, instead of him winning them, or at least him saying, "Well I can't win them now, but maybe in time I could win them," figuring how that process could be done, (or "maybe these guys are unwinnable, maybe I'm working with the wrong ones," or whatever the situation is) instead they won him. Why? Because it was very hard for him to work this out himself because these guys have logical arguments. There's nothing totally illogical about what these workers were saying. George Meany, what could be worse than George Meany? But we say that Walter Reuther is a reflection of liberal imperialism within the labor movement and it is neither here nor there whether he is a crook or not. The point is he reflects a certain class ideology. And in a certain sense that ideology is more pernicious than

Meany's. But nonetheless in six months our guy was spouting the Communist Party's line.

Now, you can take more sophisticated twists on this. When Martin Luther King was assassinated our party came out with a line, be it as it may, and some guys working in a union among a lot of Black workers came out with a different line about Martin Luther King. Why? Well because it was a very sensitive situation. A lot of Black people were grieved by King's assassination. And to take it on in the way the party took it on publicly was too hard, so they came out with something that was "less hard." Well, maybe tactically they should not have come out with anything. I think, you know, you're better off coming out with nothing than coming out with the wrong line. The ruling class' ideas are prevalent among the masses. If you're working with, or you're talking to, a number of people who are sympathetic to LeRoi Jones (who is another manifestation of reactionary nationalism among the Black people, but somebody whom we worked, or attempted to work with, so we're not talking abstractly, and I don't want to personally vilify him, I won't bother) they would say LeRoi Jones was a wonderful man. "Look, he was arrested. He went to jail. How can you attack or criticize somebody when he is a 'victim' of the ruling class?" Why can't we say that about Martin Luther King? He went to jail plenty of times. Why can't we say that about Walter Reuther? They blew off his arm.

Somebody said recently "Well, look at Dr. Spock. How can PL criticize Dr. Spock? They tried to put him in jail." And so on. We said Dr. Spock may be an honest man, he may help babies, it's very useful, but nonetheless, he's either consciously or unconsciously being used by the ruling class within the antiwar movement to mislead us. "But he's gone to jail, he's on trial." Well somebody picked this out of the paper last night: "Dr. Spock involved in Whitehall Street demonstration, was indicted by the government, charged with engaging in a conspiracy to help young men resist the draft and to disrupt induction centers throughout the country. Today, during opening statements of five defense lawyers, Leonard Boudin, counsel to Dr. Spock, said the 65-year-old pediatrician had testified that his arrest for disorderly conduct was staged with the foreknowledge of the New York City officials. The object of the peaceful tableau, in which the police would let Dr. Spock stage a symbolic disruption of the Selective Service machinery by sitting briefly on the steps of the Induction Center before being arrested, was to encourage youth to avoid violence in their antiwar, antidraft demonstrations, Mr. Boudin said. The demonstration was conceived, he said, by David McReynolds, Executive Secretary of the War Resisters League, who told Mayor Lindsay and Chief Inspector Garelik that the arrest of Dr. Spock and others would have a pacifying effect on young people because it would show them that the adults were going forward and getting arrested. Mr. Boudin said that before the announced demonstration Dr. Spock and Mr. McReynolds met with the Mayor to discuss the episode."

Now you see, here's a guy who's either too stupid, or whatever you want to call it, who's consciously being used by the ruling class to mislead the movement. We should support him! And yet, when we attacked those Resistance demonstrations, and made these very observations, that for the first time in history there were planned encounters, that the two so-called antagonists planned the whole thing out and said, "You hit me here, you arrest me there, I'll be symbolic here," you know, and when we attacked that, a lot of people in our party said "Oh, you guys are rotten to attack Resistance. Resistance is helping the struggle." Yeah, you see how they helped the struggle! Sure! There are a lot of good people in the Resistance. Most of the young people in the Resistance Movement are good. But how are you going to point out to them what is bad unless you say it? We aren't attacking them, we're attacking the leaders of this thing. We're attacking the relationship between these leaders and the ruling class. We're attacking the class character of the demonstrations. Were these demonstrations going to hurt the anti-war movement? Or were they going to help the anti-war movement?

But people said, "Well, when I showed that article to people I'm working with they said, 'That's terrible. PL is criticizing these people! We can't use it. It's a bad thing. Very bad.' " But yet we know that the Resistance Movement has been harmful. We're not opposed to resistance. We're not opposed to what happened at Brooklyn College. We're not opposed to what happened at Columbia. We're for making it bigger and better. But we say those are good because they are related to a base-building effort. That has a great deal of significance. It's not an isolated action off someplace where they can beat your god-damned brains out and use it to cause a lot of mistrust and demoralization in the movement, and isolate us from the sections of the people with whom we're trying to work. But we know that in the party some people backed away from that line. In Boston they wrote something else. "We agree with the line. But we'll put out something different because that's the hard line. I'll tell you why we're putting our thing out. It's the words. The language. It's a very funny language, so we'll put out something different." So when they came out with their own different thing it didn't help them. It didn't help them at all. Even opportunistically it didn't help.

Yes, present it as well as you can, present it and improve it as much as you can, but the basic thing is whether your line is right or wrong. What is the right line?

Fighting For Correct Line is Key to Leadership

We have the responsibiilty to bring forth the right line in every area. That's leadership. You bring forth the right line no matter how difficult it may be in the short run. That's leadership. Whoever said it was easy to fight for the right line? Who said it is easy? Do you think it's easy? No. That work is hard. It's not easy. It's hard. That's what it is all about. The name of the game is "hard." Not easy. And that's right, most people at this point are not going to agree with us. If they would we'd have to have Madison Square Garden to hold the convention. And that was always true with every revolutionary movement. You have to start small and then slowly but surely, with a very sharp uphill struggle, get among the people and fight for your ideas.

But the way to win acceptance for your ideas is not by abandoning them. The way to win for your ideas is not by creating illusions among the masses, and helping the ruling class make phony leaders among the masses. Unfortunately, enough phony leaders are already imposed on the masses. Why do we have to make new ones, Doctor Spock or LeRoi Jones, or Mr. Carmichael? What do we need it for? What's it gonna help? Bad enough we got Walter Reuther and George Meany and a host of others who already have leadership in the labor movement. We don't have to help them make new ones.

So part of our job is to struggle against these things. And very often it's unpopular. Very often it's very hard to struggle against these things. Very often the people we like the most, the very person we want to win, doesn't like us and will attack us, and will say "I don't want anything to do with you because you're attacking Dr. Spock. And you're a son of a bitch for doing it. You got a lot of nerve for saying that." A lot of people got very angry with me because we took a critical position on King when he was assassinated. "How can you say that? He was such a nice man." Well, I'm not saying we should not take into account people's sensibilities or sensitivities but you can't square it by changing the line. You can't square it by retreating from a class position, from a politically conscious position. You can't do it.

And you can't resolve the problem of errors in the work by making a bigger error. That's to say, in our work in industry, of course there's a danger of economism. Of course there's a danger of right opportunism. You work in this atmosphere, under the nose of the company, under the nose of the state, under the nose of the trade union bureaucracy, with the illusions that the workers have, you're more likely than not to make opportunistic errors. How do you cure it? By making a correct political fight. Not by coming out with bigger and better economism. That's not going to solve the problem. Economism is going to be resolved by bringing political consciousness into the labor movement and into the people's movements.

That's right, the question of state power. That's not an abstraction. It only becomes an abstraction to us because it is hard. So it seems that it's not relevant to what we're doing. But in the course of struggle the question of state power always becomes relevant. Do you know of one struggle in the country today where the question of state power and the dictatorship of the proletariat didn't come to be essential? At Columbia, on a strike, in the rebellions in the ghetto? Why? Because in every struggle in this country the state moves with all its force, either round about or directly in every struggle. That is the main lesson. What struggle has there been in this country where this isn't a main lesson? That is the lesson we have to pound home and home and home again.

Let's say, for the sake of argument, that all these demands in France that we read in the *New York Times* today are the true limit of demands. (Because we don't know all the demands. We're not that informed.) Who in France today is raising the question of state power, from what we can scc? Nobody. That's probably true. Some students and anarchists have taken over the factories. So, that's nothing new. That's syndicalism. That's the IWW. Get the factories. The workers, under the revisionists' leadership, want a bigger raise. There's nothing wrong with a bigger raise. They want the taxes reduced. Nothing wrong with the taxes reduced. They want all these things. That's fine. How are you going to get them? How are you going to resolve the problems of the French workers? By seizing state power! Who's going to seize state power? The workers and the students. Who's for seizing it? Probably nobody. Or probably a group, maybe like ourselves, which is so small, and so divorced (because of objective or subjective circumstances) from the class struggle, that even if it raises it, it carries little weight. So even there where it almost appears like "here is state power right under your nose," where it looks like "all you have to do is reach out and take it,"—they are reaching for the wrong thing. They are trying to reach out and take the wrong thing. And yet, there it is.

Without Ties to Workers Line is Irrelevant

Now I hope I'm wrong. I hope that what we read is wrong. Let's hope that there is a group in France, a political sect in France that has state power as its outlook, and can win the workers to snatch it. Fine. That's great. We'd love it. But in my opinion it's not likely, not at all. Here's the struggle in France. And now it comes down to what are your ties. It doesn't just happen, it's a process. Nobody in France has been advocating seizing state power. The revisionist party in France for the last 30 years has been saying popular front, this front, that front, Mitterand, Mendes-France front, every front but the right thing. And they educated the workers away from the idea of state power. So if you said to somebody in France 20 years ago, why don't you raise state power? "Oh, I'm for state power, but what does state power have to do with the price of tea in India? 'State power.' Let's be practical. Let's reduce the taxes, get higher wages, let's get parliamentary representatives elected." Well, you see, this is the background from which the rebellion in France broke out. After 20-30 years there's nobody for state power. And now because ten guys are getting up and saying state power, who's going to listen? What relationship do they have to the masses?

You don't win people just because you make an announcement. If we could then we could close shop now, wait 'til it happens here and when it happens I'll call you all up on the phone and say, "Here it is." It will take 10 years or 15 years or 20 or tomorrow. Whatever. I'll call you up and we will all go out. But of course people will all laugh in your face and say "Who's this nut? Where do you live? Where did they let you loose from?"

Sure, fighting for the right line seems like an abstraction. Yes, it's "irrelevant," because we don't see that our essential political task among workers is, yes, to get involved, to win them, to engage in a day-to-day struggle, and to introduce political ideas. Now, when we talk about political ideas we're mainly talking about winning state power.

How do we move the struggle from one level to another? Very often people can't see how to move. It's hard. People don't see what they can do to move the struggle from one level to another. Sell magazines and our other literature, that may be the best thing you can do. You can't get the Columbia students to go and take over City Hall; the workers won't shut down the factories now. Maybe at Columbia or any place one of the biggest things you could do is to recruit people into the party. Why? Because you will politicize guys and you will have more forces to go among the masses to politicize them, and try to improve them. The revolutionary movement doesn't come out of the air. You have to raise political ideas among a lot of people. That is the most important thing you can do. It gives the revolutionary Left, our party, much more strength and footing, and when there's a bigger change in the objective circumstances, we'll be in a position to do a lot more and really raise the struggle to a higher level, going further and if possible, all the way. The essence of our political role among the working people is to advocate class consciousness, unity of the people in struggle, to clear out misleaders, and bring political consciousness into the movement.

Clear the Enemy's Ideas Out of the People's Movements

Now, a lot of people say, "But we're not hitting the main enemy, we're hitting too many other people." All right, you show me where Lenin polemicized against the Czar!

To look at it from another aspect, in this country people have more illusions in the ruling class than the Russian people had in the Czar. The problem of exposing the ruling class was less necessary for Lenin. In our country, it's true, we have spent a lot of energy, exposing the ruling class, explaining what it is and how it operates, showing all the ins and outs of the Kennedys. That's one of the peculiarities of our situation. We have to do a lot of that.

But we also have to expose and show the class relationships of the forces that exist within the people's movement. If you have not done that, you have not done anything. The old Communist Party sat around and said, "Attack the enemy, the worst one, the main enemy." They always had the "main enemy." The ultra-right, the main enemy. "Don't attack Johnson, only the main enemy. Certainly don't attack Walter Reuther. Don't attack King, don't even attack George Meany. Who's the enemy? The ruling class. Who's the worst of the ruling class? The ultra-right. Let's attack them." See?

How does any movement overcome its obstacles? It has to clear away those within its ranks who have the enemy's ideas. You have to clear away those obstacles in order to move ahead. Now it's true you can make a lot of mistakes. That's right. You can't act indiscriminately. And we have to be careful not to attack our friends, and to know who our friends are. But we are trying to make a differentiation between the people and the false leaders, the misleaders, because the people are our friends and it's often the leadership who are bad. Because just to say that the system is bad is not enough. It's good to say this, it's decisive to say this, but it's not sufficient. It's only the first step. We have to fight the class struggle within the movement and within our party. Not because we're trying to dance on the head of a pin, but because we're trying to make the movement and the party stronger, and defeat those obstacles that prevent us from moving ahead. That's why we try to carry on struggle from within.

Now maybe, here and there, maybe on any specific points the party is wrong. Maybe Dr. Spock is our friend. Maybe Walter Reuther is our friend. Maybe LeRoi Jones is our friend. Maybe we're wrong. How will that be proven, that the party is wrong? How will we prove that the party's wrong and made a wrong estimate of these people? Life, struggle, will show if we're wrong. And if we have a self-critical ability then the party will reverse itself. Then the party will say, "Look, we made a mistake." I'm not saying we must consciously go out and make errors. I'm just saying that there's got to be a delineation, a method of establishing who are friends and who are enemies and some method of resolving problems, some method of moving ahead, and some method of self-correction.

Ideological Struggle in the Party

We have to see that this ideological struggle, within the party, and outside the party, is basic to giving leadership to the party and to the masses. It is an essential aspect of struggle. It means breaking down lazy thinking, getting off our asses and it means taking initiative to do things we don't like. That's right. Very often we don't do the best thing in these struggles. And we have to learn to fight in the best possible way and respond to these struggles in the best possible way. Even if at this particular moment you're not expert at giving and taking criticism the answer is not to avoid doing it. You will learn how to do it by doing it and that's just as hard as any other work. It's just as difficult. As we said many times, we must begin to curb liberalism in the party. We must intensify the class struggle in the party in a way which reduces antagonisms and contradictions among our friends and sharpens them with our enemy.

That's right. This is the class struggle in the party. All these differences of opinion reflect the various trends among the people. These differences don't fall out of the sky. It's got everything to do with working with people. Of course we can't not work with people. That's why you need the collective: to throw all these ideas into the hopper. The collective sorts it out and puts it together, and tries to make a scientific plan based on the various experiences that we all have had.

I think that if we don't develop this collective approach in the party, and if we don't see what the essence of our political role is among the masses then we're going to lose the perspective of state power and we're going to become a reformist party. We're going to become like the others. That's a big responsibility that we have, to try and prevent this from happening, to try and see that our party plays its revolutionary role. Because, as we said before, U.S. imperialism is the oppressor, the main enemy of the peoples of the world and those of us who are communists have the responsibility of helping to destroy this system.

And up until this point I think we have made some progress. But, speaking for myself, I feel that we have been very weak in conducting political and ideological struggles within the party and outside of the party. I feel we have been very lax in allowing a lot of shortcomings to exist, to sort of look the other way. It's hard to struggle within the party. You know, we grow cozy with one another. We're all pals. We all know one another. And when you work with people in the mass movement, that same thing happens sometimes, you know, and it becomes a touchy thing to criticize this one and that one. And I have certainly been one of the main culprits in the party in allowing a lot of things to go by the board, even many times repressing or diverting political struggle and trying to soft-pedal it.

Naturally you try to use common sense. You don't want to turn the party into a football field where you can have anarchism and everybody just vents his spleen. There's a scientific way of developing political struggle so that it helps the party, so it helps the masses and helps our people to become political leaders. We have an understanding, we have some guidelines, democratic centralism, some sense of communist discipline, some hatred of the enemy. Therefore, I hope that one of the uses this convention might serve, besides developing our program in various areas, is to sharpen these political and ideological struggles in the party so that we can get all our party members to work more seriously, more acceptably and consequently, serving the masses.

Because when we are talking about serving the masses, this is what we're talking about. We're not talking about bringing them coffee and cake. We're talking about bringing communist political ideas into their ranks so they can conduct the struggle against the enemy in a better way, so they can achieve their aspirations. A lot of shortcomings that exist in the party can be overcome because most of the people in the party, perhaps almost everyone in the party has the desire to do this work. But that desire won't be fulfilled unless a collective effort is made.

Very often people hang back and don't overcome their problems precisely because they are not fought with. If you take the easy way with them, they will take the easy way with themselves, and nothing changes. If you don't criticize somebody and raise things with him it retards his ability to develop self-criticism. Because we are working under the assumption that most people are trying to do a political job and if things are pointed out to them in a constructive political way it will help them reflect on it and make a self-critical evaluation of this criticism. And I think that very important, and not an academic question.

Become a leader to people, a people's tribune, but not a boss. Become someone whom people will rely on and respect and who will recognize your respect and admiration and loyalty and devotion to them. Become someone whom they recognize as a serious, committed person, not somebody who is frivolous, not someone who is like the trade union bureaucrats or the rest of the fakers that exist in the people's movements, somebody that's in it just for themselves. Because you know how people talk about these types. "Ah, he's in it for himself. He's out to get what he can." That's how they think about most leaders, and unfortunately, there's a lot of truth about that.

People say that's the way it is in our country. "Yeah, everybody is out for himself." So, they accept it. But when you come before somebody and you say, "Look, buddy, I'm a communist, I'm not out for myself. I'm out to serve the people," and list all the good things they'll say, "Ah, it sounds good." But they're going to watch you and see if it's true. And the minute you start acting for yourself, they'll say, "Ah, just like the others. Out for himself."

You see that's what people all over the world are saying about the Soviet revisionists. That's what they are saying. "Just like the other capitalists, out for themselves, get what they can." Of course that may be the simple man's way of summing up history. But I want to tell you, that's a very essential point because that's the way most of the people's leaders in this country act. They are out for themselves. "What's in it for me?" That's what the guys said about Hoffa. "Ah, I know he's out for himself. But at least he's trying to get me something." That's the way people refer to Hoffa. "Well, at least he's not like Meany. Meany doesn't even bother. Hoffa will try to get us a dime or something. So let him have his million dollars, or whatever it is."

But that can't be good enough for us! "Well, Murray is so-so, but at least he's better than I am." That's a pretty crummy way for people to evaluate us. That would be a real criticism. If people think of us like that then we'd better either change or pack it in.

I think we have the goods to transform ourselves, to really serve the people, to really be responsible to one another, and to really go all the way. Our responsibility is to our party, and our loyalty is to the people and to Marxism-Leninism. It is up to us. Do we really believe that, do we really act in that way, and do everything necessary to make that so? And that really means becoming persons of integrity. All of us. I'm talking about myself, because I don't think I am developed to that point. I have a long way to go. And I hope that after this convention we interact with one another and with the masses to bring everyone of us as quickly as possible up to that level. If you do that, if we act in that way, then these three days that we spend together will be of some use.

Improve Our Base Building

Summary of PLP National Committee Meeting, January 1969

At our founding convention in 1965 we made a decisive turn in vowing to become a party of the working class, and we went to work. We said—and still say—that the working class, especially its industrial segment, is the key force for revolution in the U.S. It is that group which, potentially, holds decisive power in a modern capitalist country. And recently we have refined that to demonstrate that currently in the U.S. Black workers are a decisive factor within the industrial working class.

But because our party may have 50% or 60% or even 90% of its members working in trade unions does not necessarily mean that we will have become a proletarianized or working class party. While we have concluded that the objective conditions are certainly ripe and full of class struggle out of which workers can be recruited to our party, whom have we been recruiting? It is mainly teachers, welfare workers and students, independent radicals and professionals. This is good, and should increase. But whom have we NOT been recruiting? Industrial workers (except in rare instances).

Generally we have traced the reason for this imbalance to "objective conditions": young professionals are recently off the campuses, "hot-beds of radicalism," and are more open immediately to radical ideas. Industrial workers are more removed from the radical, anti-war movement and therefore not as prone to listen to our advanced ideology. But if these industrial workers are not being won to that ideology, then the whole thesis of the role of the working class breaks down, assuming objective conditions are favorable to their being won.

There is a gap—a subjective gap—between our party and the industrial workers. We think the thesis of the industrial workers being decisive and our being able to win them to Marxism-Leninism is valid. It is we who have not been equal to that task. While we have been growing quantitatively in the unions, we are not qualitatively changing into a working class party. And, in fact, if the qualitative change does not occur, the quantitative change can easily turn into its opposite and we can either begin to lose members and/or easily become moribund like the revisionist C.P.

Getting people into auto or steel or transportation is important, but it is far from the whole story. It is really just the barest beginning. There are at least two main reasons why we have not really gone beyond that point: (1) based on our predominantly middle class background we tend to more easily relate to middle class problems and set up rigid barriers to dealing with working class problems; and (2) we have not really recognized the POLITICAL nature of establishing close ties with, especially, industrial workers.

(1) One of the reasons that our people have been able to recruit many more teachers and welfare workers is that our members doing the recruiting have backgrounds similar to many of those being recruited and therefore are more ready to deal with the kind of problems–essentially middle class–that these professional workers have. This is not bad, necessarily, especially if the politics of the recruitment is at a high level, and, also, if it grows out of struggle against the boss or the system. But many of our members who are working among industrial workers also come from middle class backgrounds and are not yet ready to come to grips with the kinds of problems these workers have–which take a different form than the ones our members are used to–and therefore set up a far more rigid line on recruiting them to the party than do those working with professional workers.

For example, not only do we spend far more time in dealing with the problems of members with middle class backgrounds; we also tend to bring them into the party with these problems on the grounds that we will continue the struggle there, provided their "political line" is good. So if a prospective member feels the need of a psychiatrist, or has been living with a man or woman for a couple of years without resolving the situation by marriage or splitting up, or tends to live a somewhat bohemian life–all problems relatively foreign to industrial workers–we tend to mount a struggle on these middle class-oriented problems, even as we draw them closer and into the party. But if workers run around with other women (or men) or drink heavily, or "watch TV all the time," or any other aspect of life that ruling class ideology engenders in workers–a wall gets set up between our members and these workers which not only rule them out "for the forseeable future" as party recruits, but tends to prevent us talking (or doing) politics with them because they are somehow beyond our rigid (middle class) specifications of who can join the party. We don't think of these workers as prospective–and actual–recruits with whom we will wage a protracted struggle, to change their bad habits (just the same as we would do with the weaknesses of middle class people or students whom we recruit). And therefore we tend less to bring them our line and win them to it.

There are numerous examples of this, of members with middle class backgrounds having gone to work in industrial situations, and reinforcing the barriers between themselves and their fellow workers rather than trying to remold themselves and break down these barriers. One member worked two years without ever seeing any worker socially off the job (although this has started to change, but a fight is still to be waged to have this member really immerse himself in the working class). Another member criticized a fellow worker for "going out with other guys" while she had a boyfriend. But our member, at that time, was living with a guy (a nice, comfortable arrangement) without having to face the problems of her fellow worker (who was not living with her boyfriend) and could then take a "holier-than-thou" attitude. Yet she wasn't aware of the double standard of male-female relations she was adopting towards her fellow worker, stemming from the class differences in their ways of life.

Still another member who had worked for many years before coming into the party had all the problems of a single worker in his forties. On the one hand we rarely, if ever, struggled with him on these problems. Secondly, we allowed his bad politics to go on unchecked within the club for a long time (since "he had long trade union experience" and "we'd better look after newer people"). Then, when the bad politics became predominant in the club (and union) situation, we tied that to his personal weaknesses, proposed he not be chairman, whereupon he quit. Now there is a thin line between being liberal on politics and engaging in protracted struggle with someone. The point is, here we never engaged in any real political struggle–more or less left this guy alone, based on his previous union experience–and then found ourselves at a point where he felt pushed to the wall and not prepared to wage any kind of struggle. So we lost him.

Now, this brings up another point. Even if we recruit workers who have spent all their lives in a working class situation, what's to say they'll stay in the party once they're recruited? What kind of problems do our clubs deal with now? Supposing one such worker were to come to our next club meeting; how do you think he'd react to what's being talked about? Would the high degree of intellectualizing that goes on in many club discussions scare him or her away? Have we become that close to and really immersed in the problems of workers around us so that we are prepared to deal with them, wage a long-range struggle with them, involve them in joint struggle, bring them our politics, learn from their much longer experience in the class struggle, and bring them into the party?

(2) Our efforts at having all our members fight for a political base for the party's line on the job has started to bear some fruit. Many more members are raising many political questions for discussion with their fellow workers: racism, the war, the state, socialism, the dictatorship of the proletariat, etc. Many more members have begun to give our literature to their fellow workers especially among industrial workers. And more of our members have begun to tell workers that they are in PL and why, what that means. Furthermore, this has been done in a number of instances while going through real class battles together. Yet when the question of establishing unbreakable ties with these workers is brought up, many of our members nod agreement but at the same time feel somehow that this is not really political (just a means to a political end). When it is raised that one important reason why workers don't defend our members–whom they know to be communists and are friendly with–when they get fired is that our members don't have unbreakable ties with their fellow workers (the workers don't really feel our member is part of them)–then our reaction is usually that this is not the reason, that there is something "more political" that is missing. Yet what could be more political than workers defending a communist–knowing him or her to be one–based on the feeling that this person is so much a part of them, so inextricably woven into their lives, that they just can't sit by and do nothing, that they HAVE to fight for his or her job? Of course, that doesn't necessarily mean that the fight will win–but at least it will take place.

Developing close personal-political ties with our fellow workers is one of THE MOST POLITICAL THINGS WE CAN DO, provided, of course, it goes along with the raising of our line, the party's program. But we, paradoxically, seem to be doing more of the latter than the former. And maybe this is because we haven't actually changed our life style, the friends we have, the time we spend with people in PL as against time spent with our fellow workers, and the QUALITY of the time spent with our fellow workers. If we don't reorient, especially toward industrial workers, we'll never recruit them to the party, or if we manage to recruit some, we won't hold them, and, ultimately, as we put forward our political line and draw attacks from the ruling class, the workers won't find the overwhelming need to maintain us among them. Of course, that might sound "non-political" ("they're defending us because we're their best friends") but, in reality, if we don't develop that kind of relationship, we won't get close enough to workers to understand and work with their problems (which in many cases are different than our members have experienced); we won't win them into the party; and those that we do win, we won't hold. In other words, we won't become a working class party, but will continue to recruit only professional workers with middle class problems and outlook, and there won't be any proletarian section of our party to help these members become more identified with the industrial working class, more proletarianized.

We aren't saying that we shouldn't continue to work among non-industrial workers, students, etc. We aren't saying these areas are not important for our political struggle. But we are saying that if a decisive turn isn't made among industrial workers, the recruitment of even those professional unionists will begin to turn into its opposite, draw the party into thinking that is the main area of political work, spend all our time there, get no real proletarian character to the party (the "new working class" stuff), and won't develop a real party of the working class. And how many years do we have in which to do this? How long can we go along in our present condition without recruiting industrial workers without turning into a party dominated by middle class ideas, backgrounds, problems–and solutions?

A lot more concentrated effort must be made by the party leadership among our comrades in this area, giving their own past experiences and raising more pointed, detailed questions about the members' relations with their fellow workers. A plan of work is to be developed in each club and industry, against which each member is to be held accountable. An examination of each comrade as to whether realistic possibilities exist for he or she to remold himself into a person more closely related to the workers around him; and if not, to what kind of other situation should he be shifted in which a better possibility exists (if it exists at all) and whether the comrade should turn to another area of work from which an important political contribution can be gotten. A list of every worker to whom we have a relation should be made; what the level of our base is with them; how we intend to pursue it to a point where they can be recruited. Examine searchingly how we spend our lives and how that relates to the workers around us; what kind of personal-political lives we lead. What do we consider the barriers between us and these workers? Do we have double standards for recruiting?

On the Party

JANUARY 1965

The launching of a revolutionary party in the U.S. is a most serious undertaking. In the first place, it is attempting a difficult, but possible task of defeating U.S. imperialism on its own territory. Secondly, because it is a party unlike other political parties—a party of the U.S. working class built upon the theoretical foundation of Marxism-Leninism—it has the sacred responsibility of whole-heartedly serving the U.S. working class. Finally, because we are revolutionaries we have the duty of supporting fellow workers and oppressed people all over the world who are engaged in sharp battle with the U.S. ruling class.

Obviously, such a party must bring together the most loyal, most courageous, most conscious, best disciplined forces in order to wage irreconcilable struggles against all enemies of the U.S. working class, and against enemies of people fighting for freedom and socialism all over the world. This party must eventually be capable of applying Marxism-Leninism to our own conditions, and be able to defeat or correct, within our own ranks, various errors that will arise.

If our party can do these things it will take deep roots among the working people of our country, as well as other groups necessary to achieve workers' political power in the U.S.

In order to carry forward the political line of the party and to defend ourselves from the state machinery of oppression, it is important that the party's organization be built along revolutionary lines, and that the party's activities be carried out in a militant disciplined manner. The organizational theory of the party is democratic centralism. The scientific method of evaluating and learning from all experiences, good and bad, is criticism and self-criticism.

Our party is being formed in a period in which revolution is the dominant political trend all over the world. It comes into being at a time when Marxism-Leninism is being affirmed and reaffirmed time and time again. This has been demonstrated through the debate in the international movement, a debate concerning two lines: one for revolutionary socialism, the other for surrender and retrogression to capitalism. Revolutionaries all over the world are uniting under the banner of Marxism-Leninism, because they see in life the true unchanged character of imperialism. Most important they see that through militant battle they can defeat U.S. imperialism! In our own country workers, students, black people and intellectuals are in ever-sharpening struggle with the U.S. rulers. They are learning, slowly but surely, that their security and freedom cannot be won under capitalism. We have seen through our own limited experience that some of the best forces in these movements can be and are being brought to see the necessity for applying the science of Marxism-Leninism in our country. They see, too, that the science of the class struggle must be mastered and is entirely applicable to our own conditions.

We can take great pride in the small forward steps of our young movement. In three years we have emerged as a national movement. We have openly carried forward the banners of revolution. We have established some important ties to the key political movements in the country. As a result of our limited work we have incurred the wrath of the ruling class, which is good, and have already received many blows. In the face of these attacks our members and leaders have stood fast, have answered tit for tat, and have grown politically as well as numerically despite the assault. It is in the course of all these various battles that we will achieve the testing that is necessary to call ourselves with full confidence revolutionaries worthy of serving the U.S. workers. In the course of our activities we will learn how to develop and apply revolutionary theory to our country's problems.

The U.S. ruling class has its state apparatus, which not only serves as the instrument of repression against the workers, but also acts as the general staff for the ruling clique. U.S. workers need their own general staff. The party can serve this function if it is capable, and wins the confidence of the broad masses of workers. The party must be in a position to evaluate every facet of the class struggle in every area. It must review all the parts and piece together the whole, in order to develop the strategy and tactics for revolution. It must be able to see the inter-relation of the class struggle in our country to the global class war that rages continuously. It must provide our working class with the strategy of victory, a strategy based upon the scientific evaluation of all the political phenomena.

In order to do this the party must be able to recognize all contradictions in the class struggle, and see how to utilize them or overcome them in the interest of the workers. The fundamental contradiction in our country today is between the workers and the owners of production. It is becoming clearer to many of our people that their problems will never be solved by this system. It is becoming clearer to others that their problems will get worse under this system. And it is becoming clearer to some that the system must be changed. Conditions of most workers in the country are worsening. Intellectuals are being straight-jacketed to the military industrial complex. Students are recognizing the factory environment of the educational system. Many in all categories are beginning to link the subjugation at home to the oppression abroad. So deep is this contradiction, that the U.S. rulers are afraid to commit U.S. workers and students to fight in their armies. These contradictions can be harnessed to step up the class struggle in favor of the workers.

Within the people's movements negative contradictions arise and must be overcome. Antagonisms have been created between workers and student-intellectuals; contradictions between black and white workers; between old and young workers; between organized and unorganized workers; contradictions between farmers and workers; between the petit-bourgeoisie and all workers. These contradictions must be solved so that the class struggle can move along more dynamically. Can anyone, scientifically, deal with these questions other than a revolutionary party? Can anyone advance the strategy and tactics for workers' power? Can these things be accomplished on an individual basis? Can you defeat U.S. imperialism by yourself? Only a well developed, theoretical, disciplined organization with class ties of trust and confidence with the entire working class could accomplish this; an organization which is committed collectively and individually to defeating the U.S. ruling class; an organization that can learn how to withstand not only the attacks of the moment, but the attacks to come over a long period of time.

The struggle in this country will be of a long range character. As was said, we are dealing with the strongest ruling class in history. Only the most careful organizational and ideological preparation, leading to unbreakable ties with the masses will sustain us through many dark nights. Despite this difficult long range outlook, we can have great confidence in the final outcome. The U.S. working class, despite defeatist conceptions by self-professed "Marxists" and "radicals", abounds in revolutionary heritage and potential. We revolutionaries cannot see things statically. We cannot fix on things as they are at the moment. Young lovers can afford this luxury. Not us. Every day shows the growing militancy in all sections of the working class arena. Strikes and turmoil in almost all industries, and other key sectors, are a fearsome thing to the bosses. They recognize the potential of all workers to rebel, and act accordingly. This is not to see things only through rose colored glasses. We must recognize the low level of class-consciousness that exists. But, that is precisely our job—to bring class-consciousness into the workers' movements; to win political leadership of the working people.

If we have no confidence in the working class, let's not even try. Because only the working class, due to its relationship to the means of production, and because of its strength, can be the leading class in the revolutionary development.

We don't have to stand in awe of the profit-princes. Their world is rapidly crumbling under hammer blows from revolutionary forces all over the world. Revolutionary socialism is triumphing everywhere. We can learn from all genuine revolutionaries. Our science is far stronger and more durable than the bourgeois "ideology." We are on the side of the great majority. Our enemy is small in number, has few real friends, and can depend only on what it can buy—sometimes. We will win if we learn how to develop ourselves into bona-fide revolutionaries, and our party into the party of the working class.

WHY THE PARTY?

Most of the members in our movement have never been in the organized left before. This is good! It is good because we do not have to defeat years of incorrect ideology and wrong methods of work of the old movement. Most of our people are young, many do not come from working class backgrounds. These members however, bring to the movement not only their enthusiasm, militancy, and courage—but their ignorance of revolutionary theory and their petit-bourgeois tendencies.

We are all surrounded by bourgeois ideology. The pressure exerted against us, as against all the people, is enormous. There is not a clear cut revolutionary situation in our country, therefore functioning is not so simple. Many of our people are still committed to their own self-advancement. They can still exist within the system. Middle-class forces can still "escape," at some point, from the class struggle. As a result illusions still persist about the capitalist system. Tremendous ideological work must be done among our people to burn out all vestiges of bourgeois thought. This must be a collective process, requiring intensive, systematic criticism and self-criticism, based on study and practice. Because of petit-bourgeois influence, individualism is a dominant tendency among some of our forces. They are not used to solving problems together. In this society you solve your problems on your own—if you can. The strong survive. The collective process is still foreign. Individual evaluations are made about things and people. If one decides someone or something is wrong—that's it. He simply goes around and acts on his own assumption. He has no concern for whom or what he undermines. He knows he is "correct," so why talk it over.

Many of us would rather consult our friends than the collective. If we like someone he must be good, and everything he says must be so. This breeds elitism, and of course, he who has the most friends will have the most "influence."

Many of us still have a short range approach to our lives. Therefore if things do not go as well or as fast as we think they should we get easily discouraged. We do not embark on our work in a scientific manner. We make false estimates of what we think can be accomplished. We are subjective in our set-backs, instead of being analytical. This happens because we are not yet sure of the need for a life-long commitment to socialism—to revolution. Not enough of us are ready to give our very lives if need be. These are attributes that must be pursued, and won't be achieved by saying it's so, or in a short period of time. Naturally, objective conditions could change things drastically, but given the present period these are things we will have to grow into.

Only in a party apparatus, where people are serious and disciplined, can we begin the necessary cadre development—the winning of people at various political levels to a total revolutionary perspective. People may join the party for various reasons, but the party has the responsibility to train its cadre into revolutionary forces. The party and its work becomes the center of our lives, the most important thing in our lives, the thing that we hold closest and value the most in our lives. This is why in other countries revolutionary parties have triumphed over apparently superior forces. This is why the ruling class fears communists. The morality of a real communist is unconquerable because of a class outlook, and total devotion to the ideas to which he is committed. This is what the ruling class cannot buy, cannot destroy. We will develop these cadres in our country. Only a revolutionary party can and will do it.

SELF-CRITICISM AND CRITICISM

The purpose of self-criticism and criticism is to strengthen the individual communist, and of course, the party. We have to learn from our experiences, and be able to appraise positive and negative developments objectively. If we do not strengthen ourselves in this process we will not have practiced this method correctly. The results will be destructive. This is a real danger, because capitalism—the U.S. version is the worst—produces the "dog eat dog" mentality. People who are in error are to be scorned and cast aside. People with whom we disagree must be put down in bitter debate in order to demonstrate our "correctness." And, if you can't win a debate on its merits, scheme a little, get off in the corner with your friends, talk the "adversary" into the ground, finish him off.

We have to understand that in this particular period, due to our general inexperience, low level of political development, no great amount of U.S. revolutionary theory to draw from, tremendous pressures of coercion and repression from the enemy, and no brilliant leaders to emulate, we will make mistakes. This will happen collectively and individually. If we understand some of our weaknesses, and develop a patient scientific attitude in dealing with them, in time we will be able to overcome most of them. If we develop a working class attitude in dealing with errors, then the proper atmosphere will exist for criticism and self-criticism. Our members will welcome this vital aspect of party building as much as other work. We will not get upset and bristle at such exchanges, but have the attitude of thanks that the criticisms came out. For in this process the party will be strengthened, and, after all, this is the thing nearest and dearest to us. However, it would be incorrect if we view this process of strengthening our work in a formalistic way. Criticism cannot be done by appointment or command. It must become an integral part of party life. If we spent as much time evaluating our work and the party's work as we do debating other matters we would be better off. Criticism must be developed in a consistent-systematic way, involving all leaders and members.

We must develop an attitude of mutual respect for one another. The party's members are its most important asset. Why should we trifle with them? Some people feel that because someone is in the movement, he can be taken for granted. They do not understand the need for warm political and personal relations. A member in error is considered an enemy. People who have no consideration for party members, in all probability, have no consideration for anyone. You can't be a "Doctor Jekyl and Mr. Hyde"—tough on the inside, sweet on the outside. Train yourself to be a sincere person in the party, one who can work collectively, and these traits will carry into your mass work.

In the course of practice of criticism and self-criticism problems develop that must be dealt with in a more flexible manner. Some forces get into a bad state because of many blows from the enemy, and tremendous internal pressures from the party. It can lead to the inability to practice criticism and self-criticism in the "normal" way. Such people are in no position to accept formal collective criticism at this moment. They have to be restored by various methods: by extra efforts to be closer on a personal and political basis; by more individual gentle criticism; sometimes rest is needed, as in the case of any battle fatigue. In any event every cadre must be assessed on an individual basis. We are not all the same. We all suffer ups and downs. We must never become hardened to one another. Great care is needed in developing durable comradely relations.

At other times, some of our cadre receive criticism, accept it in words, and don't change one iota. They continue their wrong harmful ways. They in fact act in such a way as to undermine the movement, *unintentionally*. No matter how persuasive, patient, or correct the criticism is, the comrade shows no change; perhaps he gets sicker. This requires a different approach. One must become a little rougher. Actually, the patient is not sick enough to recognize his illness. Make him "sicker". Yell at him, "knock" him in the head. When he is sick enough maybe he will respond to loving care. If not he needs a leave of absence to reflect more on his attitudes, his political development. Remove him from the scene, *temporarily,* before more damage is done.

Many of us come from the middle class. Those of us who do not, suffer enormous middle-class pressure. Only through the development of the party and its scientific processes can we defeat these influences and become real people. Then we can break the ruling class hold over our lives, and make the recruiting of petit-bourgeois forces into the party a most positive development. Through practice these forces can overcome the contradiction between workers and themselves and develop full working class relations with many potential revolutionary workers.

DEMOCRATIC CENTRALISM

As we have noted—we are taking on a powerful adversary. He can be defeated, because he faces a whole series of insoluble contradictions. One of the key contradictions is between the U.S. ruling class and its workers, students, intellectuals, and certain sections of the petit-bourgeoisie. If we learn how to deal with these contradictions we can win. But this implies that we must have real ties to these groupings of people. We must win their confidence, and eventually be the vanguard of the people's movements. Democratic Centralism, then, is not a series of arbitrary organizational rules. Democratic Centralism enables us to gather the ideas from the people, fashion them into programmatic and strategic positions, and then go back to the people with our plans. It is, in fact, the scientific organizational theory that enables us to draw closer to the masses, enabling us to develop our theory, strategy, tactics, while preserving the movement from the blows of the enemy.

Democratic Centralism enables the party to act as a united solid phalanx against the enemy, making the effect of a smaller force far greater than usual. Democratic Centralism unites leaders and members, develops mutual confidence, develops iron discipline based on voluntary association. This discipline is higher than military discipline, because it is based on understanding not command, on voluntary association rather than enforced relations. These kinds of organizational concepts are foreign, and feared by, the ruling class. Essentially, *they* hold *their* cadre through buying them, and by fear.

These are three concepts to be fought for to make Democratic Centralism work. First, the ability to engage in full frank discussions from top to bottom on basic political questions. Second, ties to the people, to prevent the discussions from becoming academic personal exercises in rhetoric. Third, the willingness to subordinate your individual desires and thoughts to the will of the majority.

By utilizing these three concepts we can accomplish the following: arrive democratically at decisions; be able to carry them out among the masses, and at a later date re-evaluate experiences democratically, based on serving and learning from the people; by being able to curb or destroy bourgeois individualism, we can act unitedly in all situations, giving us our maximum strength and strength beyond that.

To fully develop this method it is important to achieve the following. The party needs a core of *tested, devoted, competent* leaders. Leaders who can earn the hatred of the enemy, the respect and devotion of the party's members and the masses. If this is achieved it is more likely that the members will react more quickly to the decisions of the leaders once the general line is hammered out at conventions, plenums, etc.

Of course, we have not as yet achieved this situation in our movement. Some of our leaders have various portions of these qualifications. None comes close to having all. One could say that our leadership is thoroughly committed, but not fully developed. Therefore, our leaders need a lot of help from the members. The democratic aspect must be developed with a capital D. In time, our working class will produce leaders that approach some of the other great revolutionary leaders in other countries. Fortunately, these other great leaders and movements existed and exist, and we can learn from them. Naturally, we are independent and cannot simply ape other experiences, and try to fit them into our situation. But, we can always learn from others. All fundamentals of Marxism-Leninism are applicable in our situation. And some of the particular experiences of others can be utilized in our own country.

Another key aspect to develop is the fullest participation

possible of our members in the work. Naturally, everyone isn't the same. Some members have different situations than others, but all should be encouraged to carry forward the work of the party. In this way greater experience is gathered by leaders and rank-and-filers, making criticisms and decisions more meaningful. Too many of our people still take a casual attitude to party decisions. All too many cannot work in a sustained way. Many of us are simply lazy. This is because many of our people have never had work experience. Many are from school. Others shun work like the plague. Others have the mistaken notion that being a revolutionary means working full time for the organization. Some won't give the organization a lot of their time unless they are paid. All of these faults indicate low political level and poor leadership. Democratic Centralism can become an abstraction (this rule to fight over, or that rule to fight for . . .). Our members and leaders must be vigorous, conscientious, responsible—all adding up to doing real political work on the job or in the community.

Factionalism or "tendencies" or groupings or cliques based on personal relations cannot be tolerated in our movement. No revolutionary movement triumphed over a powerful enemy divided into such formations. Debate, and criticism, when open, constructive are the life blood of the movement. When conducted surreptitiously, outside the body of the party, not in front of the group or individual concerned, they become the death of the party.

Many high sounding notes are put forward to justify factionalism. "Tendencies are the history of movements." This Trotskyite notion is one of the reasons these counter-revolutionaries never led a revolution anywhere, and why they never will. This notion, in fact, expresses bourgeois concepts in the revolutionary movement. It breeds mistrust in one another, and in the masses. If you have criticisms raise them openly, constructively. If you are unsure how to pursue this method discuss it with the leadership. No one need fear the raising of criticism. No one should fear the *collective* disposition of the criticism. Cliques dissipate the energies of the movement. People's time is taken up not with planning or carrying out the line of the party and collectively evaluating its results, but with preparing schemes against one another. Meetings are held to prepare for meetings. Splits within splits. Meetings within meetings—within meetings. This is at best trade-union mentality, at worst the mentality of the enemy. Nothing can dress this nonsense up—nothing can justify it. Our movement, if it is serious, can tolerate almost anything but this.

Of course, one should take into account the intensity applied in pursuing criticism, or differences. Not every matter is a question of life or death. A member should always be prepared to compromise on matters of secondary importance. Not every difference is a matter of principle. On matters of fundamental questions one should pursue things to the end so to speak. For example, if the party or a member was opposed to the principle of the dictatorship of the proletariat, this a fundamental proposition. Fight for it all the way. Whether to have this picket line or that one, would not be a question to go all out on. Don't turn the party into a perpetual battle field over every question. In many cases the other fellow's judgment is as valid as yours. If, in the event, things prove you right, the party will have another chance to do it that way.

We have been a flexible movement till now. This has been good. We still must be flexible, but we must tighten up. We must demand more from one another. We are under attack. People face long jail sentences. Can we continue to accept slovenly political work or attitudes? Can we slide over or shy away from criticisms? Do we not have to be more disciplined; spread our influence among the masses; raise, through consistent study, our ideological level? Can anyone of us be satisfied with ourselves or with one another? This is not the signal for a ruthless purge, etc. But it is a call to put into practice a rational, scientific method of work; to do in a healthy way what most of us already believe.

In our short existence we have had virtually no organizational expulsions or punitive actions. *This is good!* Our people in general have grown, but not enough. We will be ruthless with agents within our ranks. We will save our ruthlessness for them. With one another, we will, in a patient, constructive way, demand higher and higher levels of participation and devotion, until we justify the term "vanguard." We will not become automatons, unable to consider personal problems, etc., but we will try and give every consideration to the party. The party is and must become first and foremost in our lives.

We have picked up the banner of patriotism and revolution. It is we who are acting in accordance with the desires of the U.S. workers. But we have no allegiance to a corrupt dying system, led by a ruthless, vicious class.

Road to Revolution—I

MARCH 1963

U.S. Workers Require Revolutionary Theory

Two paths are open to the workers of any given country. One is the path of resolute class struggle; the other is the path of accommodation, collaboration. The first leads to state power for the workers, which will end exploitation. The other means rule by a small ruling class which continues oppression, wide-scale poverty, cultural and moral decay and war.

The task of Marxist-Leninists is to lead the working class in its conflict with the oppressor class; to destroy capitalism's grip on the people—ideologically, politically, economically; to defeat it. In order for a vanguard to accomplish this, it must be free of the ideology of the ruling class. It must have a strategy, based on the science of Marxism-Leninism, that takes into account the general development of the science and understands the particular circumstances of any given situation.

Marxism-Leninism has always been under sharp attack by the entire international capitalist class. They have always sought to undermine the ability of the science and its practitioners to win the working class and other key sectors of the population. Yet, despite every conceivable obstacle placed in the path of Marxist-Leninists by the ruling class, one billion people are now in the process of creating their socialist societies.

Fear of Revolution Sparks an Imperialist Counteroffensive

The decline of the world capitalist system has been so rapid that imperialism has renewed and invigorated an all-out drive against Marxism-Leninism, hoping to keep the rest of the world from revolution and socialism; and to subvert, roll back, crush and destroy countries that have moved to socialism or that have won independence from colonial rule.

The imperialists of the United States have for the past twenty years assumed the leadership of this drive. They hope to accomplish what Hitler and company failed to do: establish their political and economic hegemony over the capitalist world, then use this powerful base to dominate the entire world.

When applying intense pressure, intimidation, confusion or plain corruption in the past, imperialism has been able to win adherents from the Marxist movement to its side. Now the situation is more desperate than ever for imperialism. There is a powerful socialist and anti-colonial system in the world which has the potential power to crush imperialism.

In order to reverse the historical trend to national revolution and socialism, U.S. imperialism has mounted a significant counter-offensive. This counter-offensive has many components, including: a mighty military build-up of nuclear and conventional armaments in the United States; a determined effort to subvert, take over and contain colonial and national freedom movements around the world; an active policy of counter-revolution in regard to the socialist countries; support for fascist forces all over the world (most notably the rearming of West Germany with nuclear weapons); a consistent attempt to compel "allies" to follow blindly U.S. imperialism's policies; and finally, a massive ideological campaign directed against the people of the world in general and the socialist camp in particular. The content of this campaign is that: U.S. imperialism is a force for peace, a force for freedom, a force for people's welfare; if imperialism has shortcomings, they can and will be overcome; that U.S. imperalism is itself the most progressive social system in the world. But the key force of the argument imperialism uses to "convince" the world of its new "beautiful" nature is the force of its nuclear weapons and its threat to use them.

Fear of Imperialism Sparks Revisionism

Confronted by this offensive many important elements in the international Marxist movement have resurrected revisionist political positions that were buried many times in the past. Some of the main premises of the classic revisionism of Bernstein and the Second International are presently reappearing in transparent disguises, namely: that the state in a bourgeois society is above classes and mediates the class struggle, and that revolution is no longer desirable or necessary, especially in the advanced countries where parliamentary democracy provides the vehicle for an evolutionary and gradual transfer of power to the working class.

The defeat of these false concepts in the past removed an important stumbling block and made possible the triumph of the Russian Revolution.

Four other revisionist ideas that must be dealt with today by Marxist-Leninists are:

(1) that U.S. imperialism will not wage war because of the catastrophic effects of nuclear weapons; that the "sober circles" dominating bourgeois society are "rational"–meaning they are not guided by class interests and not subject to the objective economic laws of society as outlined by Marx and Lenin;

(2) that all wars, no matter what their size or character are bad, since any one may escalate into a nuclear war;

(3) that in time the USSR will have such material wealth that underdeveloped countries will be irresistibly attracted by its example, and this will be the primary reason for their moving into the socialist camp; that the USSR, by extending large-scale aid to bourgeois nationalists, can use this aid to win them to a socialist outlook; that the tremendous success of socialism will capture the imagination of the workers in advanced capitalist countries to such a degree as to guarantee a socialist transformation there;

(4) that since U.S. imperialism can prevent economic crises it has no need to expand and can disarm of its own free will; that armaments are not a necessary part of imperialism but hurt its profit position and therefore that a welfare state can be established in the U.S., mitigating the class struggle at home.

Such revisionist fallacies have the effect of sapping the revolutionary will of the people to struggle in the face of imperialism's mounting aggression.

Which Path—Revolution or Revisionism?

A great debate has broken out in the international movement. The outcome of this decisive debate will determine to a great degree the character of the class struggle in every country in the world.

The nature of the class struggle in our country is a very important factor for the workers of our country and also for the workers of the entire world. If the workers in our country can defeat or weaken their own ruling class then the path to freedom and peace will be easier for all other workers. The more workers that defeat imperialism in their own countries the easier it will be to defeat the U.S. ruling class at home. Therefore the line that prevails internationally will affect the class struggle in every country, including our own.

Obviously, if the international working class takes the line of collaboration with U.S. imperialism the U.S. ruling class will be greatly strengthened. It will be better able to conduct class war against its workers. U.S. workers are more and more paying a stiff penalty for the class collaborationist policies that have been carried out at home by their union leaders and by the leaders of the Communist Party for the last twenty years.

Consequently, the dispute in the international movement is not merely a political debate but a matter of life and death for millions of people. The fundamental question is whether a revolutionary line is to be adhered to and strengthened or weakened and abandoned. Revisionism, which always describes itself as a "creative development of Marx and Lenin based on new circumstances," has always been the first step in the abandonment of revolution itself.

Origins and Results of Class Collaboration in the United States

To build a serious Leninist movement in our country it is necessary to understand what has been the dominant weakness of the U.S. communist movement.

From the earliest days of the communist movement in the United States to the present, revisionism and its political manifestation, class collaboration, has been the chronic weakness.

Revisionism has usually been identified with individual leaders: Lovestone, Browder, Gates. But revisionism, which permeated the entire fabric of the Party, could not be uprooted by the mere removal of its chief spokesman. The C.P., still led today by many who led that party together with Lovestone, Browder and Gates, stands as a fitting memorial to their ideas.

Revisionism always came forward in this country based on the theory of "American exceptionalism," that the development of capitalism in the U.S. was different than in other countries; that a revolutionary outlook was not necessary: for the U.S. imperialists, it was claimed, were different from other imperialists, as they did not follow an expansionist policy. Enlightened capitalists, they could make automatic concessions to their own workers. Therefore, there could be an evolutionary path to socialism rather than a revolutionary one.

These illusions were fostered by the rapid development of American imperialism after World War I–from 1920 to 1929 it exported the then unheard of amount of $20 billion capital. This unprecedented expansion gave the U.S. ruling class the maneuverability to buy off sections of its working class. And this, despite some resort to violence, was the policy followed even in the most severe times of depression.

After the expulsion of Lovestone, the Party developed a militant pragmatic approach which appealed to workers during the Depression and produced a mass base for the C.P. But even at that time there was no long range revolutionary strategy developed which could sustain the Party when the objective conditions of the Depression changed.

Nonetheless, by utilizing its militant pragmatic approach the C.P. was able to recruit tens of thousands because of its hard-hitting fight for reforms. The C.P. fought for social security, industrial unionism, unemployment insurance, wage and hour laws, public welfare and all the other gains credited to the New Deal. And, of course, the Party, standing on the side of bourgeois democracy, was in the forefront of the anti-fascist struggle.

The CPUSA played a heroic role in this period among American workers, defending the Russian Revolution and its gains. As such, it was the sole group in this country that opposed the attempts of U.S. imperialism to "strangle the baby in its cradle."

Of special significance, in its defense of Negro victims of white ruling class oppression and its writings on this matter, the C.P. heightened the social consciousness of the country as a whole to a level unknown since the Civil War era.

On balance, despite thousands of devoted revolutionary-minded members, the C.P. was a party of reform not revolution. Earl Browder, who led the C.P. in its most influential period, later aptly characterized the Party's revisionism:

> . . . the C.P. rose to become a national political influence far beyond its numbers (at its height it never exceeded 100,000 members), on a scale never before reached by a socialist movement claiming the Marxist tradition. It became a practical power in organized labor, its influence became strong in some state organizations of the Democratic Party (even dominant in a few for some years), and even some Republicans solicited its support. It guided the anti-Hitler movement of the American League for Peace and Democracy that united a cross-section of some five million Americans (a list of its sponsors and speakers would include almost a majority of Roosevelt's Cabinet, the most prominent intellectuals, judges of all grades up to State Supreme Courts, church leaders, labour leaders, etc.). Right-wing intellectuals complained that it exercised an effective veto in almost all publishing houses against their books, and it is at least certain that those right-wingers had extreme difficulty getting published. It displaced the old Socialist Party of Norman Thomas as the dominant influence on the left, and that party split up during the 1930's . . . it gradually merged with the organized labour movement and the New Deal in all practical activities, while retaining the facade of orthodox Marxism for ceremonial occasions. It became the most successful reformist party in the Marxist tradition that America had seen, while remaining unchallenged as spokesman of revolutionary Marxism in its ideological aspects. While championing the Soviet Union in international affairs, it turned to the Jeffersonian American tradition as equally authoritative as that of Marx.[1]

The development of a significant Left in the country and a powerful trade union movement which organized mass-production U.S. workers posed a big problem for the ruling class. Heretofore the ruling class had the majority of the organized workers pretty much under control. For the most part these organized workers were in the skilled craft categories under reactionary leadership in the AFL. The ruling class had not been able to solve its many contradictions. Mass unemployment was widespread and unchecked. A section of the ruling class supported Roosevelt's candidacy and program of limited, minor reforms in order to head off revolutionary action. However, unemployment, poverty and racism continued. In the course of winning concessions, and with the advent of World War II, the C.P. developed an uncritical, non-class attitude to the Roosevelt administration. Once again

[1] Browder, Earl, *Socialism in America,* reprinted from "St. Anthony's Papers," Cahier on International Communism, St. Anthony's College, Oxford, Chatto & Windus, London, 1960, pp. 101-102.

illusions about "progressive capitalists," capitalism's ability to solve its fundamental contradictions, the neutrality of the state and about U.S. imperialism were spread.

United States imperialism emerged from World War II stronger than ever. Its capitalist competitors–"enemies" and friends–were on their knees, ravaged by the war. European economic recovery was underwritten by further export of U.S. capital. The Soviet Union, which had borne the brunt of the war against the Nazis, was devastated. Unlike the war-torn capitalist powers, it could rely only on its own resources for economic recovery. Indeed it seemed it was to be the "American Century." U.S. monopolists were to pick up the pieces and assemble them as they saw fit. They would rule the world in any manner necessary for maintaining their control.

To make matters easier, U.S. workers had gone through a period of full employment because of the war. After the war a four-year unfulfilled domestic demand for consumer goods and large scale export throughout the world produced nearly full employment. This further enhanced the notion that capitalism could solve its internal contradictions, could overcome cyclical crises. Capitalist ideologists crowed about "people's capitalism," the "welfare state," unlimited production and full employment forever.

By this time, despite sincere but inadequate attempts by William Z. Foster and others to change the situation, and subsequent paper reversals of the line, the Communist Party USA was unable to recover from the body-blow of revisionism. Even so, because some struggle did continue within the organization, militant positions sometimes prevailed. This was true up through the end of the Korean War.

In order to understand the inability of the Party to overcome revisionism, one has to know the depths to which the Party leadership and some of the membership had sunk. Browder's famous Bridgeport speech on the agreements reached at Teheran put the CPUSA in complete unity with the U.S. ruling class. He said:

> Every class, every group, every individual, every political party in America will have to re-adjust itself to this great issue embodied in the policy given to us by Roosevelt, Stalin and Churchill. The country is only beginning to face it so far. Everyone must begin to draw the conclusion from it and adjust himself to the new world that is created by it. Old formulas and old prejudices are

going to be of no use whatsoever to us as guides to find our way in this new world. We are going to have to draw together all men and all groups with the intelligence enough to see the overwhelming importance of this issue, to understand that upon its correct solution depends the fate of our country and the fate of civilization throughout the world.

We shall have to be prepared to break with anyone that refuses to support and fight for the realization of the Teheran Agreement and the Anglo-Soviet-American coalition. We must be prepared to give the hand of cooperation and fellowship to everyone who fights for the realization of this coalition. If J. P. Morgan supports this coalition and goes down the line for it, I as a Communist am prepared to clasp his hand on that and join with him to realize it. Class divisions or political groupings have no significance now except as they reflect one side or the other of this issue. . . .

Marxists will not help the reactionaries, by opposing the slogan of "free enterprise" with any form of counter-slogan. If anyone wished to describe the existing system of capitalism in the United States as "free enterprise," that is all right with us, and we frankly declare that we are ready to cooperate in making this capitalism work effectively in the post-war period with the least possible burdens upon the people.[2]

The entire leadership of the CPUSA except William Z. Foster and possibly a few others endorsed Browder's line. The ensuing "self-criticism" failed to get at the roots of revisionism. Not only weren't there significant changes in leadership, but those few who had fought Browderism before and after the exposure were expelled from the Party as "factionalists." Jacques Duclos, a leader of the French C.P., who now hails Khrushchev's views on co-existence, and who seeks to unify the French C.P. with the "socialists," the same "socialists" who only a short time ago wanted to fight the war in Algeria to the finish, attacked Browder in 1946 for this very same line he himself holds today. He then said:

Earl Browder made himself the protagonist of a false concept of the ways of social evolution in general, and in the first place, the social evolution of the United States. Earl Browder declared, in effect, that at Teheran capitalism and socialism had begun to find the means of peaceful co-existence and collaboration . . . with a view to reducing to a minimum or completely suppressing methods of struggle and opposition of force to force in the solution of internal problems of each country.[3]

---

[2] Browder, Earl, *The Communist*, Speech at Bridgeport, Conn., January, 1946, p. 8.

[3] Duclos, Jacques, *Cahiers du Communisme*, Paris, France, April, 1945.

Browder's expulsion after World War II had little effect, because, except for the Chairman, the leadership remained the same. The essence of the Party's line became united front behind Wallace (the New Roosevelt), with the liberal imperialists, not the working class, as the leading element. Therefore, the C.P. failed to fight for an independent position for the working class, failed to present socialist aims and a socialist perspective and failed to expose the nature and the aims of U.S. imperialism.

This failure to play an independent role had deep roots. William Z. Foster, writing in 1945, said that central to Browder's role

> was the constant playing-down of the independent role of the party . . . (It) expressed itself in various forms of tail-ending after the bourgeoisie. . . . For at least ten years it had the effect of facilitating the demagogy of the Trotskyites, and Dubinsky Social Democrats . . . Browder refused to criticize more sharply the reactionary policies of the A. F. L. Executive Council, except in the most flagrant cases. . . . But the worst . . . (was) shameless tail-ending after American finance capital . . . as progressive bodies and as qualified to lead the nation. . . .[4]

These tailist policies carried into the good work done in organizing the CIO. The C.P. gave many of its best forces as organizers, who instead of being known as communists, playing an independent role, lost their identity in a false conception of the united front. Instead, they became CIO bureaucrats and not communists, and eventually together with other pie-cards voted to kick communists out of the leadership of the trade unions.

In an attempt to make it appear that they were moving in a new direction the Party leadership proposed a line explained by Eugene Dennis, the general secretary:

> For a people's government that will advance the cause of peace, security and democracy! For an anti-imperialist, anti-monopoly government! What is projected in this slogan, it should be made clear, is a political objective that reflects the united front program which is bringing into a broad coalition all the democratic and anti-imperialist forces including the third party movement.[5]

Actually this line was opportunistic in that it substituted this

---

[4] Foster, William Z., *The Struggle Against Revisionism,* New York, 1945.

[5] Dennis, Eugene, *Political Affairs,* March, 1948.

false and unrealistic strategy in place of developing a revolutionary strategy to socialism.

> . . . the Communist Party holds that the workers and their allies could elect such a people's front government under the Constitution by vigorous action. Beyond this point, in practical policy, the Communist Party has not planned. But it is clear that such a people's government would be elected, probably, when the great masses of the people, facing conditions of a serious political crisis, would feel the urgent need of it.[6]

The tactics flowing from this ridiculous strategy were necessarily sectarian because it was patently impossible to elect such a government in 1948.

Years of revisionism came home to roost with a vengeance as the government mounted a powerful anti-labor, anti-communist offensive which neither the trade unions nor the C.P. could effectively deal with.

McCarthyism, and the steps leading up to it, were a necessity for the ruling class, which needed a "treasonous conspiracy" to win the people for a cold war crusade against the USSR. (The second world war had left behind anti-fascist, pro-Soviet feelings among the people which were dangerous to America's rulers.)

Illusions prevailed that the government would always act impartially, that the government wouldn't allow the bosses to trample on workers' rights, and that the government wouldn't allow unemployment to return in force. The workers felt that in the final analysis the government wouldn't let the workers down. For a while class collaboration looked as though it could satisfy the needs of the workers, at least a section of the organized workers in the crafts and in the heavy basic industries. But millions of Negro workers never shared in the "mutual trusteeship." Millions of unorganized workers never received any part of the big "payoff." Millions of workers in the lighter industries never shared in the gravy train.

Events internationally began to contradict the "incontradictable" economy. A great deal of the world was breaking away from imperialism, thus limiting the areas of foreign exploitation. To offset this, and the increasing competition from other capitalists,

---

[6] Foster, William Z., *History of the Communist Party of the United States,* International Publishers, New York, 1952, p. 554.

U.S. imperialism was forced to turn the screw on its own workers in an effort to sustain maximum profits.

To consolidate the grip of reaction over the labor movement, the AFL and the CIO were merged in 1955. This "unity," hailed at the time by the CPUSA, enabled Meany and Co. to completely dominate labor and prevent the re-emergence of militant tendencies. Instead of using the enormous potential of 16 million organized workers for their own interest, the AFL-CIO leaders abandoned any fight in the workers' interests–proceeded to intensify red-baiting and called on the workers to support the cold war.

With the working-class leaders hog-tied by class collaboration the ruling class was able to stifle dissent. The cold war, with its military buildup which was to provide full employment forever, became a noose around the workers' necks. Arms production was a source of maximum profits for the bosses. Since the arms had no social function and cost fantastic sums, the workers' tax money became a prime source of profit. This was the post-war version of Keynesianism. Schools, hospitals, housing, roads were all in a state of decay in the areas where the workers lived. Overproduction reasserted itself in almost every consumer industry in the country. Plant capacity, expanded with the workers' tax money, was unable to be fully utilized. Unemployment began to mount and remain at high levels due to a stagnating economy and the development and wide-scale introduction of automation.

The labor aristocracy was beginning to feel the pinch. It was getting more and more difficult to get concessions. Real wages began to decline. Working conditions deteriorated as the men were forced to keep up with, or outproduce, the new machines. A worker's "patriotism" was measured by how well he adjusted to his worsening conditions. In the preceding period the ruling class had succeeded in denuding the labor movement of communists, helped in great part by the C.P.'s opportunist policies. To prevent any possibility of struggle, the ruling class passed a series of repressive measures. More and more the government, intent on stripping the workers of their main weapon, shed its "impartial" air and moved to outlaw strikes. Anti-communist legislation was passed and utilized as a further measure to control the workers.

Obviously, if the workers were to reverse the situation a counter-offensive would have to be launched. Such an offensive would bring them into direct conflict with the cold war line of the ruling class. This would, of necessity, bring them into collision with their own leaders, who in the main supported the policies of the ruling class. For the most part the labor leaders are prime practitioners of class collaboration and reflect the ideology of the bosses in the labor movement. Such "leaders" came on to the scene riding the wave of the ruling class' anti-communist crusade.

One of the factors making it possible for them to consolidate their power was the C.P.'s failure to lead a militant fight against the monopolies' onslaught.

The bitter fruits of the labor leaders' collaboration were loaded onto the backs of the workers. These "leaders" hailed the system, urged reliance on the government and made no answer to the bosses' assault. Instead of carrying on a militant struggle for jobs and conditions most unions were converted into centers of ruling class propaganda.

They ignored their own official program for a shorter work-day, for organizing the South, and for independent political action. Reuther's and Meany's claim that capitalism was "people's capitalism" became a hollow joke.

The trade union leadership tried to cover up its sell-out by adopting the bosses' slogan: "national interest." The C.P. tried to obscure its betrayal by attempting to shift the workers away from struggle. This was done either through perpetuating illusions about the Democratic Party as the "lesser of two evils," or by generally diverting the workers from recognizing the ruling class and its state apparatus as the main danger.

More recently it has continued to pursue this line by advancing the notion that the ultra-right is the main danger. In doing this it separates the ultra-right from its class base—the ruling class. The C.P. thus tries to divert the workers from fighting the main sources of monopoly power which control the state apparatus and manipulate it in their interests. It attempts to mislead the workers into believing that the Pentagon and/or other "hot-heads" are separate and apart, and not dominated by the state (acting for the ruling class) or its "reasonable" Commander-in-Chief, the President.

Thus, according to this logic, the threat of war, or the onslaught against workers' conditions and hard-won gains comes not from the ruling class but from various and sundry irresponsible individuals and "mad-men." The C.P. views the late President and the present administration as a vehicle for progress. After the assassination the *Worker* described the administration as one of

> reason and reasonableness in groping toward universal disarmament; the attitude of concern for the economic and social welfare of the working people; the policy of urgent and definitive elimination of segregation, for securing to the Negro people their full and equal rights.[7]

As a matter of fact, the Kennedy-Johnson administration is the most cunning and dangerous to date. On the one hand it practices aggression abroad and oppression at home; on the other hand it poses as the champion of world peace, Negro rights, and workers' conditions. The records show unemployment increased; more virulent anti-labor legislation was passed; the infamous McCarran Act was enforced; the war of genocide in south Vietnam was stepped up; Cuba was invaded; the world was brought to the brink of nuclear war by Kennedy's Cuba policy; the arms budget was increased by billions; preventive war concepts were adopted.

These policies nourished the development of the open fascists; the growth of a significant openly fascist trend points up the growing contradictions of U.S. imperialism. It indicates a class in trouble, unable to fully operate through bourgeois democracy. The people had to be kept in line—had to accept deteriorating conditions. The ruling class adopted the double tactic of using the ultra-right as a diversion to protect its moderate image and to mask its aggressive policies. At the same time it used the ultra-right to crush the people's will to resist.

Thus the ruling class creates a system of blackmail: if you don't support "us good guys" the extremists will take over. In fact, the ruling class uses the ultra-right to prepare fascist reserves as its deterioration continues. Therefore, the people's main blows must be aimed at the heart of repression—the ruling class—while at the same time striking at all manifestations of open fascism.

An Alternative to Class Collaboration Is Needed

The heart of any alternative program to be fought for by communists, is based on the fact that the problems of the workers will never be solved under capitalism. Only socialism can organize

[7] *The Worker*, Editorial, November 23, 1963.

automation (presently wiping out 40,000 jobs per week) to suit the needs of U.S. workers.

What is required is an alternative path of struggle which would open up an all-out fight for the shorter work day, along with a drive to unionize the South. The emergence of a labor movement organized around an independent class program, and the complete eradication of segregation and discrimination in the labor movement–which in classic "divide and conquer" style prevents unity –are goals to be fought for.

A genuine vanguard would help the workers fight for a new leadership in the labor movement. It would try to organize sections of the more conscious workers in the trade unions into formations that could make their leverage felt. It would unmask, not conceal, the actual character of the state. It would expose the role of imperialism in relation to oppressed people. It would make clear to workers the relationship between their own battles and the battles of oppressed people everywhere. It would point out how every and any revolutionary victory assists them in their struggle at home. It would continuously and openly advocate socialism as the only fundamental solution to the problems they face. It would consistently show the need for state power in the hands of the workers. It would strive to build a revolutionary party based on Lenin's concept of workers' rule.

As the screw is turned on the U.S. worker he is slowly but surely beginning to understand that collaboration is no answer. Despite intense pressures he is beginning to grasp the relationship of the state to the ruling class. Armed Kentucky miners, printers on long strikes, longshoremen tying up the country, rail workers compelling their union to make a pretense of struggle, rank and file activity bypassing the union leaders, workers refusing to accept government-controlled settlements, government arbitration boards being characterized as phony, almost two million workers in the Teamsters union and the expelled unions from the old CIO still following paths somewhat different from the one laid out by the ruling class—all show in a small way that battle lines are beginning to be drawn and that millions of workers will not sacrifice themselves on the altar of the money men.

The direct corollary to the squeeze on U.S. workers is the intensification of the drive for U.S. monopoly domination throughout the world. U.S. arms have bolstered reaction and fascism all over the earth. They have been the decisive factor wherever counter-revolution has developed. The policy of nuclear intimidation and blackmail was foreshadowed in the closing days of World War II, when the U.S. unilaterally dropped the atomic bomb on a defeated Japan. This act was a warning to the people of the world–a warning which John Foster Dulles developed into the doctrine of "massive retaliation."

After the Second World War the Soviet Union was ringed by a network of military bases. In quick succession there unfolded a series of counter-revolutionary efforts in Greece, Iran, the Philippines, Guatemala and Hungary. With its invasion of Korea, and the ultimate goal of reversing the victory of socialism in China, the U.S. initiated a policy of open aggression to roll back and defeat revolution in Asia. Coinciding with counter-revolution was the systematic restoration of Nazis and militarism in West Germany, preparing that country to once again take her "rightful" place as the chief tormentor of the peoples of Europe. West Germany's payoff for following U.S. policy dictates was unlimited financial aid and her promotion to "U.S. ally number 1" in the "European Community." The ultimate reward: a new Wehrmacht with nuclear arms, preparing the way for an atomic version of the traditional "drive to the East."

Here at home the new trend slowly but surely developing in the ranks of the workers because of sharpening contradictions is paralleled by a new trend emerging in the radical movement. This trend among radicals is, to a degree, a development and extension of the efforts of those forces who, over the years, tried unsuccessfully to defeat revisionism in the C.P. Many genuine communists tried to transform the C.P. into a revolutionary party. Today the C.P. leadership is a hopeless apologist for imperialism. By its consistent collaborationist line the C.P. has compromised itself irrevocably with advanced workers. The process of political corruption of the C.P. leaders has been intensified and given a new mantle of "respectability" by the revisionist line propounded in the international movement.

A genuine Marxist-Leninist party could have made a tremendous difference in the struggles of the working class of our country. Had the C.P. followed a truly Marxist-Leninist course it could have retained, even under the severe blows of the class enemy and even in periods of necessary tactical retreat, a secure base among the people. The total penetration of the C.P. leadership by the ideology of the ruling class was an important ruling class victory.

However, this is not a defeat from which the workers cannot recover. So long as there is a class struggle in this country there will be a revolutionary force. Because of the developing contradictions of U.S. imperialism a new revolutionary party will arise in this country stronger than ever.

Black Liberation: The Key to Revolutionary Development

The ability of U.S. imperialism to amass maximum profits, an absolute necessity for modern-day monopoly, rests to a great extent on the super-exploitation of the Negro people. Hundreds of billions of dollars in profits have been accumulated over the years from the labor of the Negro people. The direct exploitation of Negro workers has, moreover, enabled the ruling class to increase its oppression of white workers to a degree not generally recognized.

The ruling class has been able to maintain the South as a low wage sanctuary, holding the cheap labor market of the South as a club over the heads of northern whites. At the same time, the existence of millions of low paid Negro workers in the north also tends to depress the wages of all other workers. Maximum profits achieved through discrimination enable the ruling class to amass enormous capital to develop neo-colonialism, automation and extend capitalist productive capacity—all of which produce still more profits. Racism is a bulwark of U.S. imperialism. A powerful fight against racism is an important blow against the very foundation of imperialism. Its eradication is tantamount to the smashing of imperialism.

Under these circumstances recognition that the Negro liberation movement is the key to the development of a successful revolutionary movement in this country is mandatory.

Although the liberation movement is in its early stages it is clearly the most revolutionary development in the country today.

A common resistance to a common racial oppression; racial solidarity; a common historical tradition and cultural identity; a common desire for dignity and equality are the motor forces of the freedom movement.

At the same time the class aspects of the movement have come increasingly to the forefront because Negroes have become an important component of the industrial and non-industrial working class and a small Negro bourgeoisie has emerged.

But since, in fact, the reason for the racial oppression is economic exploitation, Negro workers, because of their interlocking interests as colored people and colored workers are objectively being placed as the leading element of both the freedom movement and the class struggle generally.

The post-war surge of the anti-colonial liberation movements, along with the victory of socialism (particularly in China and Cuba) have had tremendous impact on, and accelerated the pace of the Negro freedom movement. Events in Africa also have special significance for the Negro people. However, increased militancy was not easily come by. It was accomplished practically without allies. Even those parts of the labor movement thought of as the natural allies of the Negro people in their fight for equality were in most instances class collaborationist and had been converted into cesspools of racism.

The absence of a genuine Marxist vanguard deprived the Negro people of a consistently anti-imperialist force which fights the poison of white chauvinism and develops the necessary unity between the freedom struggle and the class struggle *which must be jointly waged by Negro and white workers and their allies.* This absence severely weakens the fight for the leadership of the Negro working class in the freedom movement; it has meant failure to point out that socialism is the only way to gain genuine Negro freedom; it has meant failure to develop the essential intermediate forms of struggle that advance both the movement for Negro freedom and emancipation for all workers.

Imperialism Needs to Smash the Black Liberation Movement

The imperialists are alert to the dangers in the freedom movement, and attempt by all means to contain and emasculate it. The monopolists have been able to control in one way or another the Negro leadership. This middle class leadership has supported the cold war even though the cold war intensifies the problems of the Negro workers, rather than resolving them. If support of the cold war by the Negro leadership was meant to buy them integration in the white man's structure it has proved a dismal failure.

The leadership of the NAACP and the Urban League failed to win even their limited demands. They propounded the concept of gradualism and tokenism, buttressed primarily with court action. Their ideology was not "Freedom Now" for the Negro masses. They preached reliance on the good will of the white ruling class; they clung to its political institutions, especially the Democratic Party. They denied the need for direct mass action, characterizing it as "provocative." They struck out at any militant development among the Negro people while militantly peddling the anti-communist crusade with extreme red-baiting.

The failure of this leadership to win victories of substance, even for middle class Negroes, by 1960, forced the development of the integration movement. The integration movement developed in the South because it was in this area that the greatest oppression existed. It was also in the South that the traditional leadership was the weakest. In the South no reason existed for illusions about the Southern oligarchy.

The integration movement developed around the strategy of non-violent direct action. In the main the movement developed under the leadership of students and clergy. Its goals were solely equal civil rights for Negroes. Unlike developments of bourgeois nationalism occurring in other areas of the world, the integration movement had few, if any, independent demands; it had no program of political and economic demands. It accepted the primacy of the white ruling class in all spheres and sought only to reform some of the worst manifestations of racism. It pleaded with the ruling class to curb racism, because it weakened the "democratic" image the white ruling class tried to establish among the oppressed people of the world. But unemployment ravaged the Negro communities, North and South. Small farming was rapidly being eliminated in a period of mechanization. The general economy provided no new opportunities for jobs.

Despite this limited outlook the integration movement captured the imagination of millions. Tens of thousands of Negroes were brought into sharp conflict with the Dixiecrats. The leaders of the movement displayed great courage and skill in developing non-violent tactics. Many establishments were integrated in the heart of the South. Hundreds of thousands of Negro and white people in the North supported the integration movement. The old line leadership was forced to adopt many of the policies of the integrationist leadership in order to maintain some base among the people. Millions of white Americans were confronted with the knowledge that Black Americans had had enough.

In the course of these limited struggles thousands of young Negro militants emerged as new forces capable of taking the liberation movement forward to new, higher stages. SNCC exists because of this development. For one thing, illusions about the government (the state apparatus) are disappearing. Meaningful programs are resisted by the state, which uses all its agencies and often force and violence. Secondly, while integration is good, you can't eat it. Thirdly, the entire concept of working within the framework of the two-party system is being questioned. A "Freedom Now" Party has emerged in the North, and all strata of the Negro people are probing to determine exactly how to begin challenging the white ruling class for power. All this is leading to a general re-evaluation of the strategy of non-violence, and in many cases armed self-defense (originally proposed by Robert F. Williams) is being advocated and used.

Because the main section of the integration leadership has no far-reaching program for independent power and no anti-imperialist outlook, it is in a bind. It cannot take the Negro masses further. Consequently, sections of the integration leadership compromised themselves with the government. The Negro people are not in the same position economically and politically as were the white workers years ago. They cannot afford the "luxury" of a collaborationist leadership.

The ruling class has been dealing with the integration movement on two levels. On one level it identifies with the movement. By doing this, it tries to create further illusions about its "fairness," hoping that people will continue to believe that racism can be eliminated within the capitalist framework. The ruling class also hopes to change the racist image that it currently has among the colonial peoples. It corrupts elements of the integration leadership, either with direct monetary contributions or with minor posts in the government and some job opportunities for trained Negroes in private industry. At the same time it puts forward meaningless legislation supposedly to curb racism.

On the other level, the ruling class and its Dixiecrat agents step up the terror against the Negro people. The federal government, while mouthing platitudes about the Dixiecrats, allows them to operate at will. The federal agencies, like the FBI, openly collaborate with them. They have yet to capture or stop terrorists.

The Justice Department, instead of vigorously using its enormous powers to indict racists, indicts militant integrationists. The Army is never used to break the power of the racists. The Army is used whenever it appears that the Negro masses are threatening to abandon non-violence. This was the case in Birmingham.

In the North, police terror is being stepped up against the Negro people. No racists are prosecuted by the liberal mayor of New York City, only militants are jailed for fighting racism. The ruling class is the chief racist because it perpetuates the system that demands that profits be produced and it derives the maximum profits that racism makes possible. These actions by the ruling class prove that equality cannot be won under capitalism, and that only power in the hands of the workers, Negro and white, can ultimately guarantee freedom for the Negro people.

Birmingham, which marked a turning point in the liberation movement, is a classic example of how the ruling class functions. Here in this industrial complex the sharpest and most protracted fighting rages. It is here that the ruling class has some of its largest investments in the South. This is where the Wall Street magnates depend on the hard labor of Negro workers. Here it is necessary to have a poorly educated, unquestioning Negro worker to do the dirty work, to stay in line, to accept plantation discipline in a factory environment. It is here that the southern racists did a most thorough job for their northern masters. But it is the main sections of the ruling class that benefit most from this situation. Maximum profits are their goal. The gravy, in the form of managerial jobs, lucrative retail trade based on plant employment and higher real estate values stemming from a great industrial system are the rewards for the local racists.

This two-level strategy of the ruling class has had much success. Despite massive outpourings of integrationists from one end of the country to the other, victories on key questions have been few and slim. Negro workers are unemployed in ever-growing numbers. No key concessions have been forced from the ruling class regarding the democratic rights of the Negro people. Even more dangerous, the open coddling of the Dixiecrats by the Kennedy-Johnson Administration has encouraged racist tendencies among wide sections of white Americans.

Another important development among the Negro people is the emergence of the Muslim movement. This religious, bourgeois-nationalist trend has gained considerable strength especially in the northern cities among Negro workers. This happened because the Muslims vigorously developed the idea of Negro identity and dignity; they advocated a form of independent political power (separation) and no one countered that with any alternative form. In this way the Muslims were able to capitalize on the aspirations of the Negro people.

At the same time, the integrationists failed to produce any appreciable gains. And the Communist Party abdicated the fight for a socialist and nationalist outlook for the Negro people and left the field altogether.

A strength of the Muslims has been their strong position on the government. Some Muslim leaders have been relentless in exposing the failure of the state to act for the benefit of the Negro people. However, the Muslims' plan for separation is in contradiction to their general estimate of the white ruling class. They put forward no specific program to achieve separation or even indicate where their new state would be. They simply asked the ruling class to give them land. Obviously this ruling class will not simply turn over territory on request when it will not even grant the Negro people civil rights. Thus the Muslims create the illusion that the ruling class will set up some kind of "reservation" for the Negro people. It should be noted that in the past months Muslim influence is on the decline, as people cannot find in it a program for action.

Within the Muslim movement there are significant contradictions. The Muslim paper has consistently supported anti-imperialist struggle. Recently they made a valuable contribution reporting the Cuban Revolution, revealing how the Negro people in Cuba won complete freedom and equality in the course of the revolutionary struggle and victory. But the Cuban Revolution was and is led by Negro and white. This contradicts the Muslims' extreme and undifferentiated hostility to all whites. Also the Muslims refer to the Chinese Revolution favorably. But the Chinese have always advocated the unity of all oppressed peoples regardless of color as the means to destroy imperialism internationally.

One of the central tasks for a revolutionary movement is to help coalesce the various dissatisfied elements that make up a growing alternative trend in the Negro freedom movement, elements that embody the most militant forces and concepts, and reflect more directly the interests of Negro workers and farmers.

This re-alignment would serve to isolate those who compromise with the government's policies at home and abroad, and would prevent the dispersal and crushing of more militant forces.

Among the policy implications of this re-alignment would be: development of a bond of mutual support with the world-wide anti-imperialist liberation movements; identification of the ruling class as the wellspring of racist oppression; recognition of the government as the servant of the ruling class; development of a strategy for achieving political power for the Negro people together with all other workers. This should be based upon the eventual merger of the liberation movement with the over-all class struggle–and armed self-defense–to achieve demands.

Only such a program can attract and organize the millions of Negro workers who today are attracted to no group because no group has the program that fits their needs.

But if Leninists are to be able to play this kind of role they themselves must be free of illusions. They must have ideological clarity, at least on fundamental questions. Therefore, illusions about the state must be combatted so as to be able to overcome illusions among the people. The CPUSA long ago lost the ability to understand the implications of the fact that the Negro people are the main source of maximum profits for the ruling class; that this power structure is the main exploiter of the Negro people; that the state is the political leadership of the ruling group.

During World War II the Communist Party abandoned the Negro workers. It did this by distorting a correct slogan: "all out for the war effort." The Negro workers' demands were shunted aside. Browderism relegated the "Negro question" to the status of just another minority problem to be solved by the "enlightened ruling class." The Party more and more ties itself to the gradualist policies mouthed by the ruling class and the reformist Negro leaders. Democratic Party convention platitudes are relied on to accomplish Negro liberation. The CPUSA persists in maintaining the fiction that those representatives of the ruling class who make up the current administration are not the main enemies of the Negro people.

James Jackson, editor of the *Worker,* writing in a magazine calling itself the *World Marxist Review* says:

> The entire trade union movement in our country has been stirred to its depths. . . . There is already a substantial beginning toward wiping out remaining color bars and discriminatory practices

in the unions, and major components of the trade union movement are giving valuable support to the Negro Movement. As a consequence of the mass actions of the Negro people and their white supporters the Federal government has been compelled to exercise its constitutional obligation to uphold the rights of its Negro citizens.[8]

Jackson hails Kennedy's stand on civil rights. He says:

> In a subsequent message to the Congress, the President called for the enactment of a Civil Rights Act of 1963 which would have the effect of nullifying the bulk of the state Jimcrow, anti-Negro laws, and generally outlaw the practices of racial segregation and exclusion in places of public accommodation, in voting and voter-registration, in employment, and in schools.[9]

He characterized the upsurge of the Negro people for justice as a "peaceful revolution" for those measures of democratic rights which white Americans have long since enjoyed. He warned that if the Congress would not act promptly to secure those rights to the Negro citizens there could be no assurance that the Negroes would abandon their struggles in the streets for them, but on the contrary, he foresaw and feared a growth in civil strife. Jackson then refers to remarks made by Gus Hall, Communist Party leader.

> Gus Hall said recently that the relationship of forces within the nation and within the South, as well as within the Federal Government itself, are such that with determined, sustained struggle, and further involvement of the trade unions and masses, victory can be won—"a death blow can be dealt to the whole system of segregation everywhere." This is a time and a cause when a century of history is packed into days, he said.[10]

In an article which refers to itself as *"On the Ideological Position of the Communist Party of China"* reference is made to the role of the Dixiecrats and the ruling class as regard the Negro people.

> The distorted picture of the American scene which the Chinese party presents is especially glaring in relation to the Negro Free-

[8] Jackson, James, Editor of *The Worker,* Published in the *World Marxist Review,* Prague, Czechoslovakia, September, 1963.
[9] *Ibid.*
[10] *Ibid.*

> dom Struggle. The perpetrators of the terror against the Negro people in the South are in the first place the Wallaces, the Barnetts, the Eastlands and the rest of the Dixiecrat racist elements, supported chiefly by the extreme Right in other parts of the country. In its failure to move against these elements and to take resolute action to crush the terror, the Kennedy Administration shares in the guilt, and the Negro people are fully aware of this. The Chinese Party makes every effort to place the *main responsibility* for the oppression of the Negro people on the Kennedy Administration.[11]

Earlier in the article, the C.P. lays bare its position of apologizing for the Kennedy-Johnson Administration and the ruling class on the Negro movement by indicating that the state is not the main enemy of the people. It says:

> One could, as the Chinese leaders evidently propose, apply this characterization mechanically and dogmatically, and conclude that since these things are true of imperialism as a whole, then every section of monopoly capital, and every spokesman for it, must be branded as equally reactionary. Hence one cannot differentiate among them in any significant way, but must direct one's attack at all equally. More, one must conclude that the most dangerous sections of monopoly capital are those which are in control of the Federal Government, and hence the attack must be centered on these.[12]

In an attempt to answer the Chinese, American Communist Party leaders only further expose their class collaborationism.

In the first place they always refrain from, and divert any exposures of the state apparatus. It is never the state, i.e. the ruling class, that is fundamentally responsible for racism. It is always someone else. The Dixiecrats are placed as a force unrelated to the ruling class. Examples of good, progressive and bad, reactionary, unreasonable forces in the State are cited, but no mention is made of the fact that one of the State's functions is to resolve differences in the ruling class without weakening the class or its rule. The labor movement is pictured as seething with activity to overcome racism. This is part of the C.P. policy to cover up for the AFL-CIO labor leaders, who are also tied to the ruling class policies.

---

[11] Communist Party of the United States of America, *On the Ideological Position of the Communist Party of China,* New York, January 9, 1963.
[12] *Ibid.*

To expose the labor leaders on their continued racism would ultimately force the C.P. leaders to expose the government. No one can seriously believe that a movement under the leadership of Meany, Harrison, Dubinsky and Reuther is cleaning out racism, nor is there any evidence to lead anyone to such a belief.

The C.P. apologists for the Kennedy-Johnson Administration are in direct conflict with the newly emerging militant forces in the liberation movement; forces that more and more recognize the class role that the Kennedy-Johnson Administration plays, forces moving into more direct conflict with the main sections of the ruling class. The clearer these forces become as to the class character of their oppression, the better they are able to fight on a day-to-day level against local racists and to cope with the two-pronged strategy of the ruling class. They become capable of fighting the collusion between the state and the local Dixiecrats. At the same time, this exposure and loss of illusions opens up perspectives for far-reaching solutions. It is seen that not only the local racists have to be smashed, but the entire class which nourishes and dominates the southern bourbon.

The need for independent political power is becoming more evident as the Negro people are denied satisfaction on any of their demands. It is also obvious that most white workers are still riddled with the self-defeating concepts of white supremacy. Much of the labor aristocracy sees the onrushing freedom movement as a threat. The Negro worker wants a job. But what jobs? Consequently, many white workers view the Negro as competing for their jobs. While the level of class struggle among white workers is rising, it still is not at the pitch which would objectively force them to seek alliances with Black workers.

White workers must learn that they will never be secure themselves as long as racism poisons their thinking, and disunites the working class. Therefore, it is crucial that the Negro people fight for some form of political power now. They cannot and must not wait for the white workers to catch up. In order to do this, Negro workers must not be sucked into the self-defeating idea that the white workers are the source from which gains can be won. The Negro workers can only win victories of substance from those who control the economy. The economic royalists would like nothing better than for Black workers to view white workers as their principal enemy.

The precise forms of this power must be developed. A program for Negro power will emerge. It will be evolved by revolutionary forces in the liberation movement and Marxist-Leninists. Some tentative concepts being discussed today are: development of an independent political force outside of the parties of the monopolies, which would elect Negro representatives to the various political bodies; coordinated development of self-governing and protective bodies outside the existing political structures wherever Negroes make up a large section of the population.

Some embryo examples of this have developed already. In Monroe, North Carolina, then under the leadership of Robert Williams, Negroes mobilized themselves outside of the state apparatus to defend themselves. They no longer were willing to wait for, or depend on the state to act for them. In doing this, they took the first small steps to take power into their own hands. The failure of the national government to act for the terror-stricken Negro community in Birmingham compelled the people there to move in a similar direction. It is reported that there exists a block-by-block militia organization to defend the people. Once again, the Negro people begin to move to establish, no matter how limited, their own power. While it is not possible to blueprint the extension of this phenomenon, it is quite possible that these formations may begin to exercise greater independence encompassing forms in addition to defense.

Independence and power can enable Negro workers to enter into alliances with other sections of the workers on an equal footing. Such organization can strengthen the revolutionary growth in the country and give real meaning to the eventual and absolutely necessary unity of all workers to achieve state power.

In the final analysis, racism will be defeated only through the establishment of a socialist state where the workers hold power.

Intrinsic parts of the vanguard's role in fighting for Negro liberation in this period are consistent exposure of U.S. imperialism's drive against the colored people moving to freedom all over the world and the linking of the freedom movement in the United States with all other liberation movements in a common world-wide anti-imperialist front. This is necessary because the Negro people's movement is part of the world-wide anti-imperialist liberation movement. If the liberation movements all over the world weaken imperialism, it encourages Negro revolution at home. The defeat or weakening of these movements would allow U.S. imperialism to concentrate more or all of its energies in defeating the Negro people at home. In this sense the C.P. line, buttressed by the revisionist line in the international movement, plays into the hands of imperialism and must be combatted and defeated.

What Kind of Peace Movement Is Needed?

The emergence of a powerful anti-imperialist peace movement in our country is important for all people who desire peace. Peace will not be won by reliance on the so-called "more sober circles" among U.S. imperialists. Nor will it be secured by allowing imperialism to maintain and extend its grip over large portions of the world; that is a peace based on the "status quo" of aggression and expansion. Peace will not be won by calling for peace, nor by presenting the horrors of atomic war, however necessary that may be. Peace will not be won solely through small meetings and working out "compromises," although negotiations and compromises are valuable instruments in the fight.

The way to fight for peace is to bring millions of Americans into sharp conflict with the foreign policy of the government. In order to do this, it is necessary to expose the contradictions between these policies and the needs and aspirations of the people.

In recent years, there has been a sharp battle between the concept of an anti-imperialist peace movement and the concept of a peace movement which wants to "win the peace" by winning the cold war. The latter concept has been, for the most part, the one around which the peace movement has operated. Though this may be hotly denied by some of its leaders and adherents, winning the cold war can be the only goal of a movement which includes the administration as a "factor for peace." In other words it commits the extreme absurdity of including the war makers themselves in the peace camp. The Committee for a Sane Nuclear Policy, a major component of the peace movement in this country, follows this line and has conducted a relentless anti-communist crusade in and out of its ranks. While there have been notable offshoots from SANE, most important the Women Strike For Peace, the peace movement has not been able to emerge as a class force. It has not been able to win the working class (which in the main goes along with the government's foreign policy) because, not being anti-imperialist, it cannot link up and explain the harmful consequences of the foreign policies of the ruling class as these policies worsen the conditions of the workers and stand in opposition to the class requirements of the workers. The peace movement has stuck essentially to the question of ending testing. While this is an important issue, it doesn't deal with the heart of the matter, which is that U.S. imperialism is the source of the war danger in the world.

The objective of revolutionaries would be to move the peace movement to an anti-imperialist position. However, this cannot be accomplished if the "revolutionaries" have the same outlook as the backward sections of the peace movement. Unfortunately, this is the case.

Events around Mme. Nhu's visit to the U.S. graphically illustrate the disastrous consequences of opportunist peace policies. One would imagine that the visit to our country of a rabid fascist like Mme. Nhu would evoke a storm of protest in the peace movement. This movement, on several occasions, has mustered thousands. Mme. Nhu was then an active partner in the war of extermination going on in south Vietnam. Crimes have been committed against the people by local fascists and the U.S. fascists that would make Hitler dance his favorite jig. Their crimes, and her attitude toward the crimes, made even the hard-bitten State Department blush. More important, there are 16,000 troops at war in Vietnam.

But in New York City, the peace movement could muster only a couple of hundred pickets to greet her. Obviously, several factors were at play. If the leadership of the peace movement feels that the Kennedy-Johnson Administration is really not so bad and is really moving in the direction of peace, and if the recent Test-Ban Treaty is a fundamental breakthrough, then it follows logically that the war in south Vietnam is not of concern in the fight for peace. It's just a bit "dirty." After all, it is against bad communists. It's just that it was led by nasty, inefficient people. If only the Buddhists wouldn't burn themselves up and if only the U.S. could hurry up and smash the "Viet Cong," then the awkwardness would be ended. And, after all, the administration would take care of Mme. Nhu.

Secondly, the peace movement is built around the testing issue. Now that "issue" has been removed. "Therefore, we are much closer to peace." At least that is what Kennedy and Khrushchev told us. But where are we?

Every spokesman in the government who has testified indicated that the treaty not only doesn't weaken the U.S. military, but on the contrary, freezes its advantages over the Soviet Union. Underground testing has been legalized by the treaty. Now we find out that the poisoning of the atmosphere, which was the whole impetus behind the peace movement and over which even the imperialists shed crocodile tears, will not be ended. The atmosphere will be poisoned anyway by underground testing. "Radioactive fallout from nuclear weapons tests will continue to plague mankind even after the signing of the treaty." Writing in the *Bulletin of Atomic Scientists* this month, Sloan-Kettering's L.D. Hamilton notes that "explosions of enough energy not far enough underground can produce considerable fallout."[13]

The day the treaty was okayed in Moscow, tests resumed underground. Stockpiling for overkill is being accelerated. More Polaris subs are being built. Since the treaty, West German Nazis are being given more nuclear weapons. After the treaty was signed, General de Gaulle indicated that the French nuclear air force will shortly become operational. After the treaty, Fidel Castro told the world that U.S. provocations were stepped up against Cuba. The U.S. pulled off coups in the Dominican Republic and Honduras. McNamara, returning from south Vietnam after the treaty, said we will guarantee victory over the "Viet Cong." One can see the progress of the treaty.

Dr. Hans Morganthau, of the University of Chicago Center for the Study of American Foreign Policy, told the 130th meeting of the American Association for the Advancement of Science in Cleveland, December 28, 1963, that the treaty was "completely inconsequential" in its impact on great world issues.

Morganthau described the treaty as "merely a formal recognition of Western military superiority."

The principal function that the treaty serves for the Soviet Union, Morganthau said, was a show of the success of Premier Khrushchev's policies over those of Communist China.

"New negotiations [with the Russians] should be seen in this light," he said, "rather than as if a general abatement of tensions has occurred; this has not happened."

The fact is that the treaty makes the threat of war greater than ever. It disarmed the entire peace movement in the United States.

---

[13] *National Guardian,* New York, October 3, 1963.

Thousands of people are led to believe that the U.S. is sincerely following a peace line. After all, if Khrushchev says Kennedy was moving towards peace, who are we to argue? Therefore, the peace forces are momentarily demobilized, and are prevented from being won over to an anti-imperialist position,

In the meantime, the U.S. is stepping up its aggressive actions against China. A purpose of the treaty is to further divide the international communist movement. It attempts to create a situation in which China would be isolated if she tested nuclear weapons. (Obviously, the imperialists knew that China would reject this treaty.) Once having isolated China, they could heat up the campaign, aided by the Soviets, that China is a dangerous warmonger, a danger to peace, and therefore, we must destroy China. This would be a conditioning program, all in the name of "peace" of course, to have the American people accept expanded military action in Asia. Implicit in the whole deal is denial of nuclear weapons to China, thus trying to impose a strategic inferiority on her.

Obviously, Chinese possession of nuclear weapons adds strength to the struggle of the people of Asia. When the Chinese gain ownership of nuclear weapons, it will consolidate the struggle for socialism and peace in Asia, just as the Soviet Union's possession of the bomb strengthened the struggle for socialism and peace in Europe. And this, above all, is what U.S. imperialism seeks to prevent.

Completely abandoning a class position, the Soviet leadership equated giving nuclear arms to China with a presentation of U.S. nuclear arms to neo-Nazi West Germany. Using this false equation, the Khrushchev leadership hypocritically obscured the fact that the U.S. was already giving the West Germans control over nuclear weapons through NATO and the multi-national atomic fleet.

In the October 1963 issue of *Political Affairs* the CPUSA polemic against the Chinese attacks them for opposing this test-ban treaty. They accuse the Chinese of going against "hundreds of millions of people in all parts of the world," who hailed the test-ban "as a welcome initial step in the direction of peaceful coexistence." The CPUSA statement then lumps the Chinese together with Goldwater, De Gaulle and other reactionaries. As a final demonstration of the validity of their line, they call the Chinese "Trotskyites."

These illogical assertions could simply be dismissed as absurd if they were not the same caricatures of China that the ruling class presents in its press. However, it would be more accurate to lump the CPUSA with the Kennedy-Johnson Administration, since in this 20-page diatribe against the Chinese, not one word appears opposing the foreign policy of the administration.

It is impossible to build an anti-imperialist peace movement if you do not have an anti-imperialist line.

Development of Revisionism in the International Movement

The over-riding feature of the growth of socialism in the USSR was its consistent anti-imperialist line. The Soviet Union was a beacon to all workers. In its infancy, relying on the Soviet people, it threw back united imperialist intervention and dared to build socialism; later it bore the brunt of the onslaught of the Nazi war machine, smashed it to bits and turned once more to performing miracles of socialist construction and reconstruction. No words from whatever source can block out this truth. No force on earth can taint this accomplishment. The U.S. imperialists have tried from the earliest days to tar its image in the eyes of the people of the world as a political despotism. Were they really concerned with the Soviet people or did they fear that the example of great accomplishments of the Soviet Union would stir the oppressed peoples and workers of the world to ever greater revolutionary efforts? Those who joined hands in the defamation of the Soviet Union joined hands with imperialism.

While one can point to errors of Stalin and the Soviet leadership in this period, it is generally recognized that there existed a militant revolutionary line. Otherwise, how can one explain how one of the world's most backward countries rapidly became the second producer nation? How can one account for the emergence of millions of technically and culturally-trained people in a country that had been noted for mass illiteracy? Without this recognition of the correctness of its main line, one is hard put to understand why the Soviet party and people were feared and hated by the imperialists, for the very reason that the working people and oppressed people of the world revered and loved them.

Their unyielding anti-imperialist line and their generally correct application of Marxism-Leninism made it possible to defeat imperialism time after time, encouraging hundreds of millions to take the road to socialism and freedom.

Along with Browderism the next most serious post-war manifestation of collaboration in the international working class movement was the emergence of Titoism. The basic motive behind the development of Titoism was the apparent strength of imperialism after World War II. The Titoists put forward the proposition, based on a supposedly "changed imperialism," that there would be a long period of tranquility. They envisaged the development of their own economy, without rapid industrialization, based on long-term credits and imports from the United States. The Yugoslavs advanced the notion that the socialist state is not a new and more advanced type of state; it is not essentially different from a bourgeois state. According to them, the bourgeois state

> is characterized by those attributes that belong to the socialist state during the stage of transition from capitalism to socialism.[14]

Under conditions of "gradual and peaceful integration" of capitalism into socialism, according to them, "state capitalism" is the highest phase of imperialism and at the same time, "the first phase of socialism."

Stalin and the Soviet party met this theoretical clap-trap head on. They re-affirmed that the gradual and peaceful development from an advanced state with a capitalist economy into socialism is a hoax and a rejection of the basic Marxist position that there can be no socialism without the smashing of the state apparatus, replacing it with a new state built on workers' power.

Revisionism in Yugoslavia was used to penetrate the working class movement with the line of the imperialists. It dove-tailed with the cold war policies of U.S. imperialism directed at world domination. In 1951, Stalin expounded the law of "maximum profits," in which he clearly defined the objective process governing imperialism's drive against the peoples of the world.

> The main features and requirements of the basic economic law of modern capitalism might be roughly formulated in this way: the securing of the maximum capitalist profit through the exploitation, ruin, and impoverishment of the majority of the

---

[14] *Problems of Political Economy of Socialism,* Belgrade, Yugoslavia, 1958, p. 138.

> population of the given country, through the enslavement and systematic robbery of the peoples of other countries, especially backward countries; and lastly, through war and militarization of the national economy, which are utilized for obtaining the highest profits. It is said that the average profit might nevertheless be regarded as quite sufficient for capitalist development under modern conditions. That is not true. The average profit is the lowest point of profitableness, below which capitalist production becomes impossible. But it would be absurd to think that in seizing colonies, subjugating peoples and engineering wars, the magnates of modern monopoly capitalism are striving to secure only the average profits, or even a super profit which, as a rule, represents only a slight addition to the average profit. It is precisely the maximum profit that is the motor of monopoly capitalism. It is precisely the necessity of securing the maximum profit that drives monopoly capitalism to such risky undertakings as the enslavement and systematic plunder of colonies and other backward countries; the conversion of a number of independent countries into dependent countries; the organization of new wars–which, for magnates of modern capitalism, is the new "business" best adapted to the extraction of maximum profits–and lastly, attempts to win world economic supremacy.[15]

The 20th Party Congress of the Soviet Union was a crystallization of developing revisionist trends. The Congress was used by Khrushchev and his cohorts as a springboard to elaborate a new policy for the world Marxist movement. The dynamite-packed report, which somehow managed to get into the hands of U.S. imperialists, to this day has never been presented to the Soviet people.

But in content and in the manner it was presented this report had nothing in common with a serious Marxist analysis and evaluation of Stalin's true role. It did not place both his enormous contributions and his serious errors in their historical context, but offered instead a subjective, crude, total negation of a great Marxist-Leninist and proletarian revolutionary. It did not examine the source of Stalin's errors, many of which were matters of principle and others in the course of practical work. Thus, it was impossible to conclude which were avoidable and which arose from the historical realities of the time and the fact that the young Soviet state was the first proletarian dictatorship in history without experience or precedent to guide it.

This is not to say that Stalin's errors were not serious and

---

[15] Stalin, J.S. *Economic Problems of Socialism,* International Publishers, New York, 1952.

without severe consequences. A heavy price is being paid both within the Soviet Union and in the international working class movement for errors contrary to socialist principles.

In the matter of Party and government organization, Stalin did not apply proletarian democratic centralism. He was guilty of abrogating it. There was a great development of centralism without the absolutely essential corresponding growth of proletarian democracy. This fostered a growth of bureaucracy which often resulted in reliance on administrative "diktat" rather than the participation of the party membership and people in making and carrying out policy. Such a one-sided development created the conditions for the growth of privilege among administrative cadre and a weakening of the concept of "serving the people" as the highest reward of a Communist. This had the effect of impairing the ties of Stalin and the Party with the people.

Stalin also erred in confusing two types of contradictions which are different in nature. Thus, he did not differentiate between contradictions involving the Party and the people on the one hand and the enemy on the other, and contradictions within the Party and among the people. Consequently, he did not employ different methods in handling these different types of contradictions. Stalin was right to suppress the counter-revolutionaries. If he had not, he would have been derelict in his defense of the Soviet State. Thus, many counter-revolutionaries deserving punishment were duly punished. But, because contradictions within the Party and among the people were not recognized as something totally different, something natural and even essential to the Party's theoretical growth and development, no Communist method of principled inner-Party struggle, proceeding from unity through struggle to a higher unity, was developed. Many innocent people, or people with differences which could have been worked out in the course of principled ideological struggle, were wrongly killed. Moreover, such a failure to differentiate between these two different types of contradictions and to handle them correctly created an atmosphere which stifled inner-Party debate, inquiry and exchange. This is detrimental to the training and development of Marxist cadre and collective leadership. It has the further negative aspect of encouraging the learning of Marxism by rote rather than through political and intellectual struggle, which is the only kind of learning that endures. This error contributed to a low level of theoretical training and consciousness on the part of many in the Soviet Union, which makes it possible for the present Soviet leadership to go so far along the path of revisionism.

The one-sided emphasis on centralism as practiced in the Soviet Union under Stalin had its counterpart, to a degree, in the relations of Stalin and the Soviet Party with brother parties. This resulted in distortion of true proletarian internationalism which demands the full and equal participation of all parties, large or small, in the making of policy. It is one of the ironies of the current situation that a number of the fraternal parties which unquestioningly acceded to Stalin are in the main blindly following Khrushchev in a disastrous collaborationist line today. Thus, it can be seen that Stalin's errors and their sources are not being seriously studied and corrected, but are only being opportunistically used. Stalin's contributions, which an over-all historical evaluation of his life demonstrate to be primary, are being thrown out. His grievous errors are being perpetuated.

The crude, public attack on the Albanian Party at the 22nd Congress, CPSU (in which Khrushchev openly called for a change in the Party's leadership), and China's exposure of the economic pressure brought to bear upon her as a "persuader" in the ideological dispute, make clear that the present Soviet leadership has not learned the lesson of non-interference in the internal affairs of other parties or the true meaning of proletarian internationalism.

Under the pretext of "combatting the cult of personality" Stalin is ground into the dirt and Khrushchev lauded to the skies. Stalin is "exposed" but no one explains the role of the exposers who themselves participated in the leadership of the Party and the state during Stalin's period. On what basis do Khrushchev and others repudiate responsibility for all errors during this period and shift the blame solely on to Stalin while taking all credit to themselves? Has one of them shown himself capable of self-criticism? If so, it is a carefully guarded "top secret."

In initiating and repeating their violent attacks upon Stalin, the present leadership of the CPSU sought to undermine the influence of this proletarian revolutionary among the people of the Soviet Union and throughout the world. In this way, they prepared the ground for negating Marxism-Leninism, which Stalin defended and developed, in order to introduce their own revisionist line.

Corresponding to this internal development, has been the step-by-step abandonment of a Marxist-Leninist position on imperialism. From the generally correct estimate that the forces of peace, freedom and socialism were stronger than the forces of imperialism and war, Khrushchev drew a series of wrong conclusions. He imagined that imperialism would draw proper conclusions from this changing relationship of forces and learn to live with socialism. The idea was fostered that there were now sober "enlightened" capitalists who wouldn't resort to war to promote their interests. This deduction was based on the concept that nuclear weapons have become so devastating that the imperialists too, could be destroyed, and therefore would refrain from war. Also, embodied in his position was the fear that local wars, however limited, could be the spark that would ignite a nuclear war.

Therefore, Khrushchev says, "local wars in our time are very dangerous . . . we will work very hard to put out the sparks that may set off the flames of war." This position is confirmed in Khrushchev's message of January 3, 1964 to all heads of states and governments, which said "one cannot fail to reckon with the fact that wars that begin with the use of conventional weapons, in our time, may grow into a world war with the use of thermonuclear weapons." This "theory" of Khrushchev's would have maintained the Cuban people, the Algerian people, and the people of south Vietnam in chains forever.

This in effect, whatever words to the contrary, rules out consistent support of wars of liberation, because any war, just or unjust, could ignite atomic war.

> The principle of peaceful coexistence determines the general line of the CPSU and other Marxist-Leninist parties.[16]

This concept means that Marxist-Leninists in the oppressed nations must take a position of co-existing with their oppressors rather than defeating them in revolutionary struggle. Thus, Khrushchev put forward a one-sided position on peaceful coexistence, rather than maintaining the central theory of Leninism, which is the continuous revolutionary process.

Khrushchev's conception of the non-inevitability of war is separated from the material economic contradictions confronting capitalism and rests on the idealist subjective notion that certain

[16] Ponomoraev, *World Marxist Review,* Prague, Czechoslovakia, November 12, 1962.

"reasonable capitalists now recognize the danger inherent in all wars and reject war as a means of solving their contradictions." On January 3, 1964, Khrushchev said "no one except madmen, except political figures blinded by hatred, can resign themselves to such a prospect."

Lenin's teaching that imperialism is the period of wars and revolutions, or Stalin's analysis of what is the motor force (maximum profits) of imperialism today are ignored. The effects of inevitable capitalist crisis are passed over, and the questions of Fascism, and its relationship to imperialist decline, are disregarded. The possibility of preventive war is also overlooked. Indeed, a rosy picture is painted of capitalist intelligence and good will, a very dubious foundation for the basis of a Leninist policy. Khrushchev pictures the U.S. government and its head as resisting the forces of war, and not as representatives of the imperialist forces of war. He includes them in the peace camp in spite of the fact that the 1955 twelve-party statement, and the 1960 statement of the Workers' Parties, clearly stated "U.S. imperialism is the main force of aggression and war."

Khrushchev has praised Eisenhower, "as one who has a sincere desire for peace," and who "also worries about insuring peace just as we do." He praised Kennedy, as one who showed "solicitude for the preservation of peace and who worked to create reliable conditions for a peaceful life and creative labor on earth." As early as the 20th Party Congress he indicated he saw that "symptoms of a sobering up are appearing."

Finally, Khrushchev nowhere deals with war as an extension of politics. His non-inevitability of war thesis does not come from a policy of weakening and smashing imperialism; it is not based on the acceleration of the fight against colonialism and neo-colonialism; and it does not include the concept of workers in the capitalist countries moving towards smashing the capitalist state and establishing their own power. Khrushchev sees the solution of all international contradictions between imperialism and the socialist anti-colonial camp in the cooperation between the U.S. and the USSR.

Gromyko, in a speech to the Supreme Soviet, on Dec. 13, 1962, said:

> . . . if there is agreement between N. S. Khrushchev, the head of the Soviet government and John Kennedy, the President of the

> United States, there will be a solution of international problems on which mankind's destiny depends.[17]

Khrushchev himself underscores this, saying:

> We (U.S.-U.S.S.R.) are the strongest countries in the world and if we unite for peace there can be no war. Then if any madman wanted war, we'd but have to shake our fingers to ward him off.[18]
>
> The inevitable struggle between two systems must be made to take the path exclusively of a struggle of ideas.[19]

Obviously the exclusive battle of "ideas" is in complete contradiction with the Marxist interpretation of the class struggle.

Two other revisionist ideas advanced at the 20th Congress and carried forward to this day were a one-sided placing of the possibilities of a peaceful transition to socialism and a non-class attitude to bourgeois nationalist leaders in governments. In his report to the 20th Party Congress, under the pretext that "radical changes" had taken place in the world situation, Khrushchev expounded the "theory" of peaceful transition. He said that the road of the October Revolution was "the only correct road in those historical conditions," but that as the situation has changed, it has become possible to effect socialism "through the parliamentary road." This is a clear rejection of Lenin's teaching on State and Revolution which thus far has been confirmed in all revolutionary experience.

The second proposition in effect abandoned the class approach to bourgeois nationalist leaders and governments. It does not judge them on the basis of whether their policies support the overall anti-imperialist struggle and is generally in the interest of the peoples. It advocates the unprincipled power politics approach of the bourgeoisie, namely trying to woo them by "aid" and diplomatic maneuvering. A glaring example is the unprincipled "aid" to India.

In succeeding years the bitter fruits of Soviet policy have begun to ripen. What might have been useful and legitimate criticism of Stalin and the Soviet leadership, from which the whole international movement could have learned, instead was con-

---

[17] Gromyko, Andrei, *Speech to the Supreme Soviet,* December 13, 1962.

[18] Khrushchev, N. S., *Report to the Supreme Soviet,* January 4, 1960.

[19] *Ibid.*

verted into an assault on the very heart of Marxism-Leninism. Many communist parties all over the world, in the name of the 20th and 22nd Congresses, have now disavowed the concept of workers' rule. In its place has sprung up non-Marxist-Leninist ideas of reform, wherein a multi-class government, including the ruling class, could shift into socialism.

Gus Hall wrote:

> The state must enter into the realm of our economic developments. But it must be made to do so in partnership with the people, curb the power of the monopolies and not to add to their powers ... the trade unions and the public should be democratically represented in the management of these institutions. But this development puts the necessity to have a state where the working class and the common people have the dominant influence. Such a state can then proceed from private ownership of the means of production to the social ownership of the means of production.[20]

Hall disassociates himself from Lenin's concept of the dictatorship of the proletariat by calling people "dogmatists" who call for "militant revolutionary actions . . . the dictatorship of the proletariat, and smashing the bourgeois state." Hall claims that advancing these ideas would "separate us" from other Americans.

According to the Italian Communist Party it is possible

> to break up and abolish monopoly ownership of the major productive forces, and transform it into collective ownership . . . through nationalization.[21]

At the tenth Congress of the Italian Communist Party, Togliatti, in his address, presented the notion that the state in an imperialist country is a vehicle for revolutionary progress. He said:

> ... In this lies the value of reforms of the economic structure, nationalizations, and attempts at state planning and programs. It is right for us, too, to encourage the state to take this course, provided that democracy is developed at the same time, not merely in the traditional form of public debate, but in the form of dem-

---

[20] Hall, Gus, *The Only Choice—Peaceful Coexistence,* New York, 1962.

[21] *Elements for a Programmatic Declaration of the Communist Party of Italy,* Rome, Italy, Tenth Congress of the I.C.P.

> ocratic control and leadership organs, such as to enable the working class and the workers of all categories to intervene to make of state intervention an instrument of struggle against the powers of monopoly capital, and to deal a blow, limit and break down the domination of large monopoly groups. It is possible thus, to open up the prospect of a new type democracy, of a renewed democracy. . . .[22]

Failing to accept Lenin's concept that imperialism is "moribund, dying capitalism," and that in its final stages the imperialists' grip on the state structure becomes more intense, not less intense, Togliatti then calls for

> . . . starting from the present state structure, on the ground of the democratic organization in which the masses participate today, and imposing deep reforms of structure, to develop such a movement and to reach such results as to modify the present power bloc and create the conditions for the formation of another bloc, in which the working people participate. . . .[23]

These ideas completely reject Lenin's thesis that the bourgeois state must not be reformed, but destroyed, and that the workers must not share in power but *be* in power as the dictatorship of the proletariat. Considering the reality of modern politics, Togliatti's ideas are more likely to lead to the corporate state than to socialism.

By creating illusions about the national bourgeoisie of various countries, communist parties within these countries have abandoned an independent and revolutionary perspective. As a result of policies which lose sight of the class nature of the national leaders, parties have been almost wiped out or sections of them have been won over to the ruling class. The Iraqi experience and the betrayal of a section of the Indian Communist Party are examples.

An example of the depths to which a supposed communist leadership can sink is given by S.A. Dange and his group, which presently dominate the national leadership of the Indian Communist Party. The *New Age,* official Communist Party weekly, on November 1962, carried a banner headline and a statement of the National Council of the Communist Party of India, which for

---

[22] Togliatti, Palmiro, *Address to the Tenth Congress of the Italian Communist Party,* Foreign Bulletin of the I.C.P., p. 34.

[23] *Ibid.*

sheer jingoism, give the Hearst press a good run for the money. The headline reads: UNITE TO DEFEND MOTHERLAND AGAINST CHINA'S OPEN AGGRESSION. A typical example of the statement:

> . . . The Communist Party joins hands with all our patriotic people who stand behind the Prime Minister's stirring appeal for national unity in defense of the country. The National Council pays its humble tribute to the remarkable heroism of our soldiers in the face of extreme odds. . . The last few weeks have seen an unprecedented upsurge of our people against Chinese aggression. . . The Communist Party of India is not opposed to buying arms from any country. . .[24]

Compare this with the testimony of Gen. Maxwell Taylor, former Chairman of the Joint Chiefs of Staff, who was testifying at a secret Congressional hearing. As released by the committee, Taylor told the congressmen, "that India might have started the border fight with China." Rep. Robert L. F. Sikes (Dem.–Fla.) said, "Let me talk about Red China and the Indian operation. Did the Indians actually start this military operation?"

"They were edging forward in the disputed area," replied Gen. Taylor. "Yes Sir."[25]

Worse than this we have the situation where the CPSU supplies the Indian ruling class with weapons to fight and kill workers and peasants of socialist China. In the Congo, where the people fight for freedom, we witness the Soviet Union voting for a resolution in the U.N. July 13th, 1960 which legalized U.S. penetration of the Congo under the cover of the U.N.

This led to the murder of Patrice Lumumba and the subsequent imprisonment of Antoine Gizenga. Neo-colonialism was imposed on the backs of the Congolese people. The Soviet position on the Congo showed a total lack of understanding of the class composition of the U.N. and its continued domination by the United States. It is an example of how Soviet moves have, in fact, placed obstacles in the path of liberation.

This line is in essence one which builds up illusions about imperialism and results in disarming the masses and diverting them from consistent class struggle to wipe out imperialism.

---

[24] National Council of the Communist Party of India, *New Age*, official Communist Party weekly, November, 1962.

[25] *The New York Times*, City Edition, April 18, 1963.

The fact is that in the past several years the imperialists have been able to check the movement for socialism—they have been able to use the incorrect line of the Soviet leaders to split the international movement, and have stepped up their counter-revolutionary activities.

All renegades from Marxism-Leninism have found in the Khrushchev line a confirmation of their own opportunism. Earl Browder, in a recent interview with the FBI said:

> Khrushchev occupies today a position on the big issues in the world that I occupied in 1945. When the Chinese accuse him of revisionism they are merely echoing and elaborating the arguments used against me when I was thrown out of the movement.[26]

Tito, attending a meeting of the Supreme Soviet, Dec. 12, 1962 hailed Khrushchev and said that

> he had followed it with close attentiveness, and that he was generally in agreement with what Nikita Sergeyevich had said concerning the relations between our two countries . . . that our views on the major international issues are identical or nearly so. . .[27]

A Period of Revolution

What imperialism fears most is revolution. Revolution deprives them of profitable areas of exploitation, areas of essential resources and strategic areas for military aggression. Revolution weakens imperialism, although in its fury to repel revolution it may appear strong. One of the most debilitating features of the Soviet line is that it weakens the will to revolution. Hence, the warnings to go slow, "examine the parliamentary process" and depend on Soviet economic supremacy to topple capitalism by example, winning bourgeois nationalists by buying them off with "aid."

> Peaceful co-existence alone is the best and sole acceptable way to solve vitally important problems confronting society.[28]

---

[26] Browder, Earl, *San Francisco Chronicle,* October 7, 1963.

[27] Tito, J., *Speech in the USSR Supreme Soviet,* December 12, 1962.

[28] Rumyamtev, A., *World Marxist Review,* No. 1, Prague, Czechoslovakia, 1962.

And in the program of the CPSU 22nd Congress there appears the remarkable statement:

> . . . when the Soviet people enjoy the blessings of communism, new hundreds of millions of people on earth will say, "we are for communism." . . . the question at issue today is: which system will give the peoples more material goods and spiritual values . . . it is precisely in this field, I think, that the hardest battles between socialism and capitalism will be fought.[29]

Instead of supporting a revolutionary line, the revisionists seek to integrate the socialist and capitalist systems. In an interview with Drew Pearson, Tito said, "Economic and political integration is our perspective."[30] Winding up discussions at the international forum of Marxist scientists in Moscow on problems of modern capitalism, a report printed in *Tass* Sept. 3, 1962 quoted A. Arzumanian as saying, among other things:

> Now at the third stage of the general crisis of capitalism, state ownership cannot be considered an ordinary reform. It is connected with the revolutionary struggle to do away with the monopolies, to overthrow the rule of the financial oligarchies. . . . The state ownership of industries and of banks is now becoming the slogan of the anti-monopolist coalition.[31]

What difference can there be between this notion and the proposition put forward by the Titoists who say:

> The specific form of state capitalist relations can be . . . the first steps towards socialism . . . the ever-growing wave of state capitalist tendencies in the capitalist world is the most eloquent proof of the fact that mankind is heading more and more in an irresistible manner towards the epoch of socialism.[32]

Thus the opportunists tell us the way to socialism is to unite (integrate) capitalism and socialism, "politically and economically" with the state apparatus of imperialism in the vanguard.

Despite revisionism, the past 42 years have witnessed unabated

---

[29] Twenty-second Congress of the CPSU, *Khrushchev Speech,* Moscow, 1963.

[30] Pearson, Drew, *Washington Post,* September 18, 1962.

[31] Arzumanian, A., *Report of the International Forum of Marxist Scientists, Moscow, 1962,* Reported by *Tass,* September 3, 1964.

[32] *Ibid.*

revolution, always under the most difficult circumstances, always confronted by the seemingly impossible. The following events and revolutions demonstrate that when people were organized around a correct line they have been, and can be, victorious. They have shown that they can take everything the imperialists hurl at them and defeat them. They dared to fight back. What is more, they dared to win. Some of the most important examples are:

1. the Russian Revolution;
2. the consolidation of the revolution and the achievement of the first five-year plan;
3. the defeat of Nazism;
4. the reconstruction of the Soviet economy in record-breaking time after World War II;
5. the Chinese Revolution;
6. the defeat of U.S. imperialism in Korea;
7. the defeat of French imperialism in Indo-China;
8. the Cuban Revolution;
9. the Algerian Revolution;
10. the war for freedom in south Vietnam.

All these efforts have won despite the most resolute efforts of imperialism. In the case of Korea, the Koreans and Chinese volunteers won in the face of threatened atomic warfare.

If the international movement were united around a policy of class struggle, it would be an invincible force. Collaboration and accommodation never satisfied the appetite of imperialism. It always grabs for more. The louder some people begged Hitler for mercy, the less they got–the more he took. U.S. imperialism has been engaged in armed conflict since the end of the Second World War. The only thing that slows it down is when it is met by fierce resistance. Does anyone seriously think that the United States would have stopped at the Chinese border in Korea if it had not been turned back by the Chinese volunteers? Does anyone believe that imperialism would not have taken over Hungary and Eastern Europe if the Khrushchev leadership had not pulled itself together under the advice and pressure of the Chinese Party and other communists, and responded to the requests of Hungarian revolutionaries to help crush the counter-revolution? Does anyone think that the U.S. ruling class would have refrained from open invasion of Cuba if the Cubans had not made it clear that they were ready to defend socialism to the last man and woman?

Peace was imposed in those areas only because the revolutionary will of the people was the highest. Often, in order to have peace and freedom you must wage revolutionary war. The history of our country will tell us that.

Experience has shown that accommodation never leads to freedom, nor in the long run to peace. The advent of atomic weapons does not change this truth.

Not only has revolution been successful in this period, but it has for the first time in history made it possible to contemplate peaceful existence. If it is now possible to even speak of preventing nuclear war, it is wholly due to the success of revolutionary struggles. Will the fight for peace be accelerated by slowing down the revolutionary process or vice-versa? Co-existence then, must be imposed on a ruthless imperialism by the force of strength and battle.

It would be a disastrous blow to our own efforts if the freedom movements around the world were slowed down, halted, or crushed. It was the success of these movements which helped spark the militant and inherently revolutionary battle of the Negro people. Socialist revolutions and national liberation movements in other countries act to weaken imperialism at home, because it is the monopolies' power here which oppresses workers in other lands. Their weakening can only assist the workers here. What is more, revolutions elsewhere act as an example to the workers here, enabling them to learn the universal truths of Marxism-Leninism.

The slogan "workers of all countries unite," is not a meaningless platitude, but the heart and soul of a revolutionary outlook. U.S. imperialism must be defeated. If the "paper tiger" has nuclear teeth, it is not for us to recoil, but to recognize it as the fact, and develop the means to pull them.

Contradictions of Imperialism

U.S. imperialism is faced with overwhelming contradictions. Some of them are:

1. between the U.S. imperialists and the USSR (which will continue despite the line the present leadership follows);
2. between U.S. imperialism and the oppressed peoples;
3. between U.S. imperialism and China;

4. between U.S. imperialism and other capitalist countries;
5. between U.S. imperialism and the people of our own country.

U.S. imperialism is becoming more and more isolated from all people. Despite attempts of the ruling class and its ideological puppets to create illusions among the masses, more and more people, including our own, are learning from bitter experience the true nature of imperialism. U.S. imperialists more and more often find that there is a great gap between what they desire and what they are capable of achieving. The overwhelming majority of the peoples of the world are opposed to imperialism. They could probably prevent war if united in a world-wide anti-imperialist front. But can anyone guarantee that the imperialists will never launch a war even if the people do all in their power to prevent it? The answer is no. Only by pointing to both possibilities, pursuing correct policies, and preparing for both eventualities, can we best organize the people to wage battles in defense of world peace.

But capitulation to imperialism only accelerates the war danger. The more imperialism is weakened, the less chance for war.

All serious Marxist-Leninists are ready, willing and able to utilize every form of struggle to prevent a nuclear war. This includes negotiations, concessions that do not betray peoples' basic interests. We recognize the devasting power of atomic weapons, but to show demobilizing fear in the face of them, emboldens even the most "reasonable" U.S. imperialists. Revolutionaries seek the banning and destruction of all nuclear weapons. They reject the approach which makes testing of nuclear weapons the center of the struggle for the peace movement, and above all, they reject illusions about the partial test-ban treaty.

No matter to what degree the Soviet leaders placate U.S. imperialism, the material reality of the contradiction between them persists. The Soviet Union is the second largest producer in the world. As such, it is both a market and a source of competition with which imperialism must deal. If the Soviet leadership feels that it is buying absolution with its present line, it is only deceiving itself. It has forgotten the basic laws governing imperialism. The U.S. is setting the Soviet Union up for the kill. German rearmament, including nuclear weapons, grows unabated. Imperialism continues to aim its nuclear arsenal at the heart of the Soviet Union. U.S. imperialism is moving to dominate the newly liberated countries and areas of anti-colonial struggle, as well as to control its western allies. This is all preparatory to dealing with its main target, the Soviet Union.

Marxist-Leninists must arouse the heroic Soviet people to the plans of imperialism. To equate the Soviet Union with the imperialists would be a bad mistake. The Soviet people fought for and won socialism. The Soviet people will in time defeat the wrong line of its present leadership.

The colonial and national liberation movements threaten the life-line of imperialism. They lessen its ability to amass maximum profits, making the imperialist economy less stable. Hundreds of millions of people are now embroiled in a life and death struggle with imperialism. The imperialists have to spend vast energies to cope with these dynamic movements. The threat of atomic weapons holds little fear to people who have been experiencing a living death all their lives. If the imperialists were to use atomic arms against any of these people, it would bring the wrath of the peoples of the world against them, and would expose forever, their "new look" cultivated for "neo-colonial" ends—of being for "freedom, national independence, self-determination," etc., etc.

Mass revolutionary action is what will decide the fate of these peoples, and to a great extent, the fate of imperialism.

The experience of the Congo and other colonial areas, has taught oppressed people that the imperialists will fight tooth and nail to preserve colonialism. The imperialists are learning to develop new forms to maintain old ways. Neo-colonialism is the form through which the imperialists maintain economic domination of an area by "indirect" political control. For this, the United Nations, the impartial "socialist" Yugoslavia, and peace-minded India are invaluable. These forces combined with the U.S. in the Congo to cheat the Congolese people of their freedom.

Neo-colonialism is at the heart of the foundation of Malaysia, where the British have been able to exploit divisions of the people to maintain their economic and political control.

In the final analysis, when all this hocus-pocus fails, U.S. imperialism will resort to naked force, as in south Vietnam.

The Negro people of our country, who are waging a decisive battle for democratic rights and national liberation, are becoming increasingly familiar with the two level strategy of neo-colonialism. More and more they see that they will never win their full freedom under imperialism. The character of their struggle will lead them increasingly into direct conflict with the state apparatus. And just as the revolutionary struggles of one group of workers tends to spur others on, so will the Negro liberation movement weaken the imperialists, thereby assisting the white workers in their struggle. This will in time lay the basis for a genuine alliance against the common enemy, especially when the white workers are forced to resist the white ruling class, which is increasing their exploitation.

The liberation movements, far from acting as a force to ignite or spread war, are a key force for peace. The Negro freedom movement in our country can also be a decisive force for peace, can weaken the grip of the imperialists on other peoples. Would anyone who considers himself a revolutionary in our country ask the Negro to go slow, because U.S. imperialism might be provoked? We say full speed ahead—we support the national liberation struggles of the peoples of the world including the Negro people. Their victories bring us closer to peace and freedom.

Modern revisionists say that almost all oppressed people are now free. Therefore, don't rock the boat. Those 50 millions or so who are still in chains, will eventually be free. The Chinese Communist Party views neo-colonialism as oppression and sees the national liberation movements as decisive. They say:

> The various types of contradictions in the contemporary world are now concentrated in the vast areas of Asia, Africa, and Latin America; these are the most vulnerable areas under imperialist rule and the storm centers of world revolution, dealing direct blows at imperialism.
>
> The national democratic revolutionary movement in these areas and the international revolutionary movements are the two great historical currents of our time.
>
> The national democratic revolutionary struggle of the peoples of these areas is an important component of the contemporary proletarian world revolution.
>
> The anti-imperialist revolutionary struggles of the people in Asia, Africa, and Latin America are pounding and undermining the foundations and the rule of imperialism and colonialism, old and new, and are now a mighty force in defense of world peace.
>
> In a sense, therefore, the whole cause of the international revolutionary movement hinges on the outcome of the revolutionary struggle of the people of these areas, who constitute the overwhelming majority of the world's population.[33]

---

[33] Hongqi (Red Flag), Editorial Board of, *Two Different Lines on the Question of War and Peace,* November 19, 1963.

Therefore, the anti-imperialist struggle of the people of Asia, Africa and Latin America is definitely not merely a matter of regional significance, but one of overall importance for the whole cause of proletarian world revolution.

"Friends" of the U.S. Fight Back

The general economic recovery of western Europe following World War II has made it possible for western European capitalists to intensify their resistance to U.S. control. No longer are they willing to blindly follow the economic and political dictation of their U.S. masters. This has been dramatically driven home by the differences of opinion between De Gaulle's concept of a united Europe with a Common Market, and the version of the United States and Great Britain. The Atlantic Alliance has been greatly weakened by the failure of the United States' European "partners" to fulfill their end of the bargain in NATO. Within the past year, almost all of western Europe has refused to go along with U.S. ideas about trade with socialist countries. Recently, Great Britain, the most trusted, has dared to enter into trade relations with Cuba. The French have the audacity to enter into independent relations with China. Germany, the bulwark of NATO, often appears to be subservient to U.S. interests, but in fact, is jockeying for its own interests, and ultimately for control of Europe. Within Europe itself, there are deep-seated hostilities and fears. These divisons will not be reconciled, especially as the fight for markets is increased. The continued loss of markets, due to revolution, undermines all imperialist relations and spells imperialism's doom.

Chinese Communist Party Fights for Marxism-Leninism

The great debate, now taking place between two trends—revolutionary struggle or revisionist opportunism—in the international Marxist movement did not spring up overnight. It has been a number of years in the making. Throughout the world Marxist-Leninists, both inside and outside of the official communist parties, were becoming increasingly aware that on the international as well as national scenes, the underlying philosophy of

Marxism-Leninism, dialectical materialism, was, in the practice of the present Soviet leadership and those who followed it blindly, being superseded by opportunistic pragmatism. The concept of the Marxist vanguard was fast turning into its opposite—timid "tail-ism." Class struggle, the dynamo of social change, was more and more being discarded for class collaboration under the general catch-all phrase "peaceful co-existence."

In the CPUSA those with a will to struggle found no means or ideological leadership for it. On the contrary, every move to introduce a fighting vanguard policy was met with contemptuous rebuff. When the Chinese Communist Party began to provide political and ideological leadership for the world Marxist movement, it was warmly welcomed by true Marxist-Leninists, because it accurately generalized and confirmed their own experiences.

Chinese Communist Party Fights for Peace

From the moment the Soviet leadership embarked on a path of opportunism, the Chinese Communist Party took the initiative to fight for a correct line. As early as 1956, in two articles on the *Historical Experience of the Dictatorship of the Proletariat,* it counteracted the gross distortions of Khrushchev's evaluation of Stalin and placed his serious errors in perspective. It upheld the concept of the dictatorship of the proletariat, and reaffirmed the class nature of every state, and the bourgeois state as the dictatorship of the bourgeoisie. It reiterated the basic Marxist truth that only revolutionary class struggle could achieve state power for the workers, that the oppressed peoples of the world must conduct revolutionary struggles for freedom and social progress, and that these two struggles support each other, weaken imperialism and are the path to peace and socialism. It holds not that war is inevitable, but that the only chance for preserving peace lies in exposing and opposing imperialism. It firmly maintains that the general line of foreign policy for the socialist countries cannot be "co-existence" but the strengthening of the unity and the power of the socialist camp and the strengthening of the unity of the world communist movement around the revolutionary line.

The Chinese position on peaceful co-existence, on war and peace, and on negotiations, has been shamelessly distorted by many communist parties. Some have been unscrupulous enough to say the Chinese would welcome and are trying to provoke world nuclear war as a swift path to revolution. Even those who say this know it is the "big lie." It is no accident that the imperialists use these distortions word for word to help whip up anti-Chinese and general anti-communist prejudices. In an article the Chinese said:

> We hold that the oppressed peoples and nations can achieve liberation only by their own resolute revolutionary struggle and that no one else can do it for them.
>
> We have always maintained that socialist countries must not use nuclear weapons to support the peoples' war of national liberation and revolutionary civil wars, and have no need to do so.
>
> We have always maintained that the socialist countries must achieve and maintain nuclear superiority. Only this can prevent the imperialists from launching nuclear war and help bring about the complete prohibition of nuclear weapons.
>
> We consistently hold that in the hands of a socialist country nuclear weapons must always be defense weapons for resisting imperialist nuclear threats. A socialist country must absolutely not be the first to use nuclear weapons nor should it, under any circumstance, play with them or engage in nuclear blackmail and nuclear gambling. The fact is that when the leaders of the CPSU brandished their nuclear weapons, it was not really to support the people's anti-imperialist struggles.
>
> Sometimes, in order to gain cheap prestige they just publish empty statements which they never intend to honor.
>
> At other times, during the Caribbean crisis for instance, they engaged in speculative, opportunistic, irresponsible nuclear gambling for ulterior motives.
>
> As soon as their nuclear blackmail is seen through and countered in kind, they retreat one step after another, switch from adventurism to capitulation and lose all by their nuclear gambling.[34]

The masses of the world are well aware of the Chinese position on relations between states with different social systems. They practice "the five principles of co-existence." China's role at the 1955 Bandung Conference is well-known. The world is familiar with the fact that the Chinese negotiated for a long period with the United States in Korea. It is well aware of China's participation in the 1954 Geneva negotiations on Indo-China, and again in the 1961-1962 negotiations on the neutralization of Laos. The Chinese demand for a complete and universal ban on the manu-

---

[34] *Ibid.*

facture of nuclear weapons, and the destruction of present stockpiles, is a forthright position making it difficult for imperialist demagogy. Important, too, are China's achievements in reaching negotiated border settlements (Burma, Nepal, Pakistan) as well as her firmness in repelling attacks on her rights and sovereignty. The Korean battle prevented imperialism from unleashing a full-scale war in Asia. The Indian border counter-action, disabused, at least for the time being, the U.S.-inspired invasion of China by the Nehru government. These demonstrations of determination and strength are important in the fight for peace. Nor are people unaware of the great restraint China has shown about the occupation of Taiwan, and the continued use of this and other areas by the United States to provoke and plan aggression against China. China has been capable of the widest range of tactics to preserve peace and support revolutionary struggle in Asia. This is a tribute to her skill, firmness, and patience in the face of constant pressures.

Chinese Communist Party Fights for Unity

It is true that the Chinese are conducting a vigorous struggle for Marxism-Leninism in the international movement, but only after and because the Soviet leaders opened the assault on Marxism-Leninism. Is this inconsistent with the concept of maintaining unity in the international movement? We say no. Nothing would be more disastrous than the unity of the socialist camp against world revolution. The Chinese have made great efforts to prevent the splitting of the international movement. At the beginning, their position was not put forward as a drive against the Khrushchev leadership of the international movement, but as an effort to persuade those who had departed from Marxist-Leninist ideas. In this way, they hoped to curb, and eventually defeat, the revisionist line taking shape.

For a time, this policy showed results. The shift of the Soviet position in regard to Tito, after the '55 reconciliation, was an example. The statements of '57 and '60 were others. The general effect was to compel the Soviet leaders to acknowledge revisionism as the main danger in the international movement, and Tito its main practitioner. However, this victory ultimately became a paper victory.

The 1960 Moscow statement of the 81 parties said:

> The Communist Parties have unanimously condemned the Yugoslav variety of international opportunism, a variety of modern revisionist theories in concentrated form. After betraying Marxism-Leninism which they termed obsolete, the leaders of the League of Yugoslav Communists opposed their own anti-Leninist revisionist program in the Declaration of 1957; they set the League of Communists of Yugoslavia against the international communist movement as a whole.[35]

All the world is able to view the Soviet leadership's unprincipled, unexplained flip-flop on Tito. Articles in the *Christian Science Monitor* twit the Soviet leaders:

> In 1958, the major part of the Premier's address was directed against the Yugoslavs, who ten months earlier, had refused to sign the Moscow Declaration of the World Communist parties, and in May had come out with a "revisionist" program of their own. In 1958, Mr. Khrushchev tore into the Yugoslav communists for having collectivized only about 2 percent of their farmsteads.[36]

An article by Eric Bourne said:

> . . . rapprochement between the heretical Yugoslavs and the Soviets has certainly gone further now than at any time since the patching-up in 1955. It is now nearly two years since Yugoslav foreign secretary Koca Popvic found on a Moscow visit that the Soviet and Yugoslav foreign policies were either identical or similar on most major East-West controversies . . . but he did get a firmer than ever confirmation that Yugoslavia is a "socialist state" . . . the Soviet leader also wrote off that part of the 1960 Moscow Declaration which dubbed revisionism (Titoism) the main enemy of the communist movement and enscribed in its place the dogmatism of his rivals in Peking.[37]

If the Chinese were narrow nationalists or mere opportunists, they could have allowed revisionism to go unchallenged. In an immediate and narrow sense, China's challenge to opportunism has been extremely costly to her. The Soviet Union, exerting economic pressure to "solve" ideological differences, terminated aid to China and tore up trade agreements between the two countries.

---

[35] *Statement of the 81 Communist Parties' Meeting,* Moscow, 1960.
[36] *Christian Science Monitor,* January 12, 1963.
[37] *Christian Science Monitor,* November 12, 1963.

The Chinese have moved to open and sharp struggle with the Soviet leadership because they recognize that Khrushchev's policies are rapidly undermining the stability and revolutionary potential of the international movement. They are aware that a disarmed movement is an open invitation to the imperialists to intensify oppression and aggression against all people. In a short time, as previously indicated, we have seen the tragic decimation and disintegration of parties and movements that have followed the Soviet line. This will only be a shadow of events if that line prevails. The Chinese Communist Party has helped other communists to see things for what they are. This is a profound contribution to proletarian internationalism.

Decisive Task Is to Build a Revolutionary Party in the U.S.

Building a revolutionary party in our country could be decisive in the fight for peace and socialism. It has been proven that revolutionary changes do not occur without political organization. If U.S. imperialism is the main enemy of the people of our country and the people of the world, then it can only be defeated by a vanguard party, capable of leading millions directly.

The ruling class is well aware of the potential of such a development and has, over the years, exerted great effort to prevent it. One could say that the defeat of revolutionary ideology and organization is a major internal objective of U.S. imperialism.

It is true that U.S. imperialism is the most powerful ruling group in the world, and to build a vanguard within its very "citadel" appears once more to be doing the impossible. However, U.S. communists have a great deal in their favor.

There is a growing level of revolutionary experience and understanding in the world.

The victory of socialism in Cuba—the combination of flexibility and adherence to a consistent anti-imperialist policy—characterizes socialism in that nation. This, combined with Cuba's closeness to the U.S., makes socialism more understandable to broader sections of our people. Ever growing sections of our people are coming into conflict at various levels with the ruling class. The Negro liberation movement is quickly moving to new levels of battle.

We are part of the world-wide anti-imperialist front that is taking shape. This makes us and our allies–the people fighting for national liberation and progress, the workers throughout the world, a majority, as compared to U.S. imperialism with its handful of supporters. This is not "pipe dream" talk, but an important reality bearing on our daily activities.

The experience of our predecessors is two-sided. On the one hand there are negative features which we expose, criticize, and reject. But we are not interested in exposure per se–but in studying the source of the errors and not repeating them. On the other hand, the communist movement in our country in its militant days created a legacy of dedicated and courageous struggle. There is a residue of positive feeling for communists among sections of the people which can be reactivated by a principled, fighting vanguard. Young radicals can learn from and emulate the devotion to the working class and socialism of such outstanding communists as William Z. Foster.

The defeat of revisionism on a world basis will be a decisive ideological victory of the working class leading to the defeat of imperialism.

Develop Theory and Practice

An effective movement in our country demands the understanding of Lenin's theory of the state. Lack of clarity on this basic point has been the main stumbling-block to the movement over the years. Every state, with all its government forms and institutions, is an instrument of the ruling class. Only under fully-developed communism where classes have completely disappeared will the state disappear.

In an imperialist country like ours, the state is the political arm and high command of the ruling class no matter what "administration" represents it any given time, and no matter whether that administration's tactics are "democratic" or violent–or both. We have in the U.S. a dictatorship of the bourgeoisie. This state apparatus must be swept aside and a new state built reflecting only the aspirations of the workers and their allies. This new state must be a dictatorship of the working class, in order to prevent counterrevolution by the displaced class and other elements hostile to the new workers' state.

It is not written in the stars that a privileged ruling class must hold power. This country was born in revolution, and Abraham Lincoln, John Brown, Thomas Paine, Thomas Jefferson, Nat Turner and many others confirmed our right to revolution. A vanguard must fight for the right to revolution as being in the best interests of the American people. Here, where there is much prattle about "freedom," it is forgotten that those who lose the right of basic change can never be free.

We envision no easy transition to socialism. We say those who promote the notion of voting socialism into existence create illusions. We say that those forces who see an evolutionary path to socialism based on an accumulation of reforms–the last reform toppling us into socialism–live in a dream world. Despite all the hoopla, any serious examination of the reform movement in this period shows no significant gains, despite militant activities in some sectors. The white workers and the Negro people are losing ground. At this moment when thousands of our people are fighting merely for reforms, they are often met by ruling class violence. The miners in Kentucky, the integrationists North and South are but two examples. What would be the response of the ruling class to revolutionary demands? Violence is inherent in capitalism. The more advanced and deeper its fatal contradictions, the greater its violence as it fights against being forced off the stage of history.

Communists do not advocate violence. But they must, in all responsibility, warn the people of the actual character of imperialism, and alert them to what can be expected as the conflict sharpens. We say that the people must be able to defend themselves and their progressive achievements from ruling class terror. Not to do this is not to be revolutionary, to be afraid of the consequences of fighting imperialism. Naturally, communists would welcome a peaceful transition to socialism, and do all in their power to compel the ruling class to surrender peacefully. However, to date, nothing indicates that the U.S. imperialists would even remotely contemplate this eventuality under any set of circumstances. As a matter of fact, U.S. imperialism is becoming one of the most destructive ruling classes in the history of mankind.

The U.S. is rapidly abandoning much of its heralded bourgeois democratic form. The Negro people, especially in the South, are confronted with a judicial structure and police set-up which not only fails to protect their rights but itself is part of, and conspires with, those who break the law. In recent years, repressive legislation has been passed which, in effect, rules out fundamental dissent and curtails the right of the working people to have their own organizations. A whole network of truly subversive agencies such as the FBI and the CIA, lavishly endowed with unlimited funds, accountable to no elected body, rides rough-shod at home and abroad. Sen. Eugene McCarthy writes of:

> . . . its 14,000 employees among whom are specialists in intelligence analysis and espionage, U-2 pilots and assassins.[38]

Events surrounding the assassination of the President and the subsequent murder of Lee Harvey Oswald have only begun to lift the lid on the cesspool of corruption which makes a mockery of our "democratic rights."

The declining "democratic" norms are necessary to prevent the workers and their allies from fighting their worsening positions. Of course, this is not done all at once, but unevenly and in a zig-zag process, depending on the needs of the ruling class and their room to maneuver. Communists believe it is in the interests of the workers to fight for whatever is positive in the Constitution and whatever democratic gains the people have won over the years. Only the people led by a vanguard party would be capable of picking up the banner of freedom and democracy long since abandoned (except in demagogy) by the ruling class.

The essential tactic of the united front has been distorted in recent years to mean that communists should operate in "the mainstream" without identity, and without an independent perspective. Under such circumstances "revolutionaries" have tailed behind or even impeded militant developments. Instead of winning workers to new levels of understanding, they have often pandered to and sunk to the backward tendencies among the people. Communists must achieve tactical flexibility and utilize all forms of struggle. Participation in united fronts should be around a specific program for limited objectives. Participation with other forces should not be a cloak for passivity, or the excuse for the failure to build the vanguard or to obscure its independent line.

While the vanguard recognizes the need to fight for reforms at certain stages in the development of the people's consciousness, it should not create the illusion that reforms, in and of themselves, can lead to socialism, or that the ruling class can satisfy the

---

[38] McCarthy, Sen. Eugene, "The CIA is Getting Out of Hand." *Saturday Evening Post,* January 4, 1964.

needs of the people. It plays a leading role on the day-to-day level, fighting to win victories where possible, and always exposing the actual nature of the ruling class, increasing the class consciousness of the workers, and learning and devising the strategy and tactics for revolution.

The working class is the main class on which to rely to smash the power of imperialism. A continuous fight must be waged for this concept. This is particularly necessary among students, intellectuals, and certain sections of the petty bourgeoisie. They observe many of the present-day manifestations of corruption and misleadership in the unions, the prevalence of bourgeois ideology among large sections of workers, and draw superficial conclusions. Many of them do not understand the historic role of the working class, by virtue of its relation to production, and consequently cannot grasp the dialectics of the class struggle. This gives rise to cynicism, go-it-alone tendencies, and eventually, rationales for capitalism. The aspirations of these groups will never be solved under decadent capitalist reaction. Only alliances with the workers can create the necessary strength for victory, ensuring the conditions for creativity, morality, and the security they seek. Objectively, their future is tied with that of the working class. Weakness within the working class must be viewed not from a defeatist point of view, but scientifically analyzed and combatted.

The fight for a correct policy must be accompanied by continuous criticism and self-criticism. We know that this vital idea was paid lip service in the past, and we know that this simple recognition is no guarantee for improvements in the future. But there is absolutely no way to change policies and people without thorough-going evaluation. It is very plain that those who have attempted to fight revisionism in the past, including many of the leaders of today's Progressive Labor Movement, have been weak in understanding dangers of revisionism. They did not display initiative, boldness, or consistency in this effort. In short, they were not equal to the task. Many of those now attempting to build a new movement have had years of incorrect training based on erroneous ideas. However, some people did attain the political development to break from the corruption of revisionism. It is necessary to build on this development to defeat the intense pressures of the ruling class.

In the coming period the vanguard must educate and re-educate older and new revolutionaries in the science of Marxism-

Leninism with particular emphasis on the philosophy of historical and dialectical materialism. A key weakness of the movement in this country has been the lack of ideological training of members and leaders. "Following the leaders," has too often been substituted for independent scientific analysis based on international and national experience. Revolutionaries have a responsibility to develop the widest discussions and practices as the basis for formulating a correct line.

Socialist methods of inner-party struggle must be developed, and an atmosphere created for frank and open examination of ideas and work. This can lead to unity in struggle–leading to a higher level of unity. It means the step-by-step destruction of illusions and notions of the old movement, in order to create the theoretical and practical basis for a new movement.

We understand that words alone cannot develop the confidence necessary for this achievement. We can only win the confidence of genuine revolutionaries and workers by the actual development of deeds and the advancing of Marxist-Leninist concepts.

Fighting for a revolutionary outlook nationally and internationally, the working class in our country will set the stage for an end to its oppression. Correct Marxist-Leninist theory and practice is the only guide to the triumph of the working class. More than one billion people have found that out. Hundreds of millions more are on the way. U.S. workers will not be far behind.

Road to Revolution—II

DECEMBER 1966

(The following statement by the National Committee of the PLP was adopted on December 17, 1966, after a discussion begun in September, 1966. The statement is a reaffirmation of the basic political position of the PLP. The first comprehensive political statement by the founders of the Progressive Labor Party was issued March, 1963, under the title "Road to Revolution.")

In order for revolutionary socialism to win power, or to hold state power and consolidate it once it is won by its proletarian forces, it is necessary to win the struggle against revisionism.*

This requires a clear understanding of the consequences of revisionism, of its main anti-revolutionary ideas and the manner in which it presents itself in the present period.

Revisionism is the main ally of U.S. imperialism. In fact, revisionism is imperialism and its ideas camouflaged within the ranks of the revolutionary movement. The main goals of revisionism are to crush existing revolutionary movements, to prevent the development of new revolutionary movements, and to subvert socialism and restore capitalism where the revolution has triumphed.

Actually, all the work of revolutionary fighters should be measured by their efforts against revisionism and whether, in practice, they pursue a revolutionary path. Any battle is lost to the extent revisionism is obscured or not fought in an all-out way.

Yet many people within the revolutionary movement, or allied with it, who recognize that revisionism is wrong, do not clearly understand its counter-revolutionary nature. Because of this, the fight against revisionism is partial and is not viewed as a life-and-death matter. Revisionism and imperialism are not equated. Instead, revisionism and revisionists are viewed as "the lesser of

*Revolutionaries welcome the enrichment of Marxism-Leninism when it strengthens its revolutionary content. Revisionism does just the opposite. Under the guise of enrichment it destroys the revolutionary content of Marxism-Leninism. Hence, revisionism is the enemy of revolutionaries.

two evils." Revisionists are considered as somewhat better than imperialists, and the attitude is fostered that you can do business with them.

Only a revolutionary party that resolutely opposes revisionism and practices revolutionary socialism places itself in the vanguard of the revolutionary process. By applying Marxism-Leninism to particular circumstances and developing it to refute revisionism, the party acts in accordance with the aspirations of the people. Only such a party, whether it has already helped the working class to win power or is in the earlier stages of guiding the working class to power, can help consolidate that power, can insure that the quest for the dictatorship of the proletariat is consummated.

Only genuinely revolutionary parties, acting on the basis of proletarian internationalism, can aid the cause of revolution on a world scale. Only they can correctly practice unity in action.

Facts have proven that in the countries where communist parties have succumbed to revisionism, the cause of revolution has been impaired. These parties have been undermined, have degenerated and have become forces of counter-revolution. This has placed the party and the working class at the mercy of hostile forces. And this process has been most striking in the countries which had won socialism and have now reverted to capitalism.

Today the main center of revisionism is the Soviet leadership. But the *source of revisionism* exists in each party and must be dealt with by each party.

The fight against revisionism must be intensified, for no party can succeed in anything while under its influence. A party only partially infected with revisionism is like a lady who is "slightly" pregnant. The elimination of revisionism is the main job within the ranks of revolutionaries. This fight must be carried out ideologically, politically, and by demonstrating in practice the correct way to fight and defeat imperialism. It is no academic effort. The fate of the world will be determined by the outcome of this battle.

How Revisionism Emasculates Marxism-Leninism

The key manifestations of revisionism in this period are the notions that: (1) the overriding things to "fight" for are "peaceful co-existence" and the "peaceful transition" to socialism; (2) the abdication of the dictatorship of the proletariat; and (3) the destruction of proletarian internationalism.

Revisionism "Abolishes" Imperialism's Inner Laws

The revisionists say that imperialism has changed. Khrushchev reduced imperialism to a set of subjective relations. At the 20th Congress of the Communist Party of the Soviet Union, he stated: "The advocates of settling outstanding issues by means of war still hold positions there [in the U.S.] and they continue to exert big pressure on the President and the Administration." But, he added, "symptoms of a sobering up are appearing among them." (*CPSU, 20th Congress*: *Proceedings*.) In other words, the U.S. state apparatus is for peace and is resisting the forces of war. Consequently, either the U.S. Government and its head do not represent the interests of the imperialists, or the imperialists are peaceful by nature.

Gus Hall, the chief spokesman for revisionism in the U.S., constantly applies this deliberately falsified version of imperialism to the war in Vietnam. Hall told a press conference that the war was "waged by the 'invisible government'—the militarists, the CIA, and the FBI." (The *Worker,* October 23, 1966.)

The *Worker* announces that "the truth of the matter is that the decision as to whether there will be peace or war in Vietnam can be made by President Johnson." (Editorial, June 28, 1966.) He doesn't choose to make peace, the *Worker* continues, because he is "reckless, irresponsible" (June 28, 1966), and "obstinate." (July 10, 1966.) This "shocking arrogance" (September 18, 1966) is "pushing [the President] into bed with all the ultra-Rightists, the white supremacists, the anti-Semites, the hate-mongers of every vicious type." (September 18, 1966.)

Of course, the truth is that U.S. aggression in Vietnam and in other parts of the world results from imperialism's need to maintain itself as a system. This system, which is based on the export of capital for the generation of profit through exploitation, is governed by objective laws. These laws, and particularly the law that imperialism cannot exist without expanding its investments and its oppression, determine its actions. The personality of this or that imperialist leader has nothing to do with what imperialism must do to defend and advance its interests as a system, though it may affect the style with which it is done.

(Just one of numberless examples: "Senator Fulbright met with President Kennedy and later told newsmen that he [Fulbright] would support the sending of U.S. combat troops to South Vietnam and Thailand" in accordance with the wishes of the administration. [*New York Times,* May 5, 1961.] At that time the U.S. reportedly had 685 military personnel in Vietnam. Within eight months of the meeting, Kennedy had sent 5,000 troops to Vietnam with more to come.)

Clearly, if the Vietnamese people deluded themselves with this imaginary description of imperialism, they would have given up a long time ago, and the revolution wouldn't exist. Revisionism would deliver Vietnam into the hands of the enemy.

Revisionism "Abolishes" Class Violence

Khrushchev also advanced the notion of "peaceful transition to socialism through the parliamentary road." Claiming that "radical changes" had taken place in the world situation, he said that the October Revolution was "the only correct road in those historical conditions," but now with the changed situation, it was possible to effect the change to socialism "through the parliamentary process."

Gus Hall, ever creative, "discovered" that Marx, Engels and Lenin were wrong when they demonstrated that the state was an instrument fashioned and used by each ruling class principally for crushing its antagonists. Triumphantly Hall proclaims that imperialism controls the state in the U.S. through a conspiracy.

> The government-monopoly conspiracy . . . is directed against the interests of the people. . . . As long as the conspiracy is intact, the extent of [concessions and reforms] will always be sharply limited. . . . Hence, short of socialism the only qualitative change that will open the doors to meaningful social, economic and political progress is the breaking of the ties of conspiracy between the state and the monopolies. This would call for an Administration and a Congress resting on a very different class and political base. . . . But it would not be a socialist government. . . . It would be . . . an anti-monopoly government. (*Report to the 18th National Convention, CPUSA,* pp. 54-55.)

In line with this, revisionists the world over (who share Hall's point of view) have come up with what Pat Sloan (a British revisionist who spent a year training Nkrumah's cadres in Ghana) terms "the non-capitalist road to socialism."

> Ghana . . . was a blueprint for a "non-capitalist" development towards socialism, not through a revolutionary setting up of a "workers' and peasants' state," but by a planned evolution towards such a state after the overthrow of the colonial power. (*Political Affairs,* October 1966, p. 21.)

Poof!—Classes have disappeared altogether.

Since classes have disappeared, violence—upon which class rule rests, and the reason why the state exists—also disappears from politics except as some "unreasonable" and nasty habit.

> Hall spoke of the new quality of political struggle, as distinct from armed struggle, on a world scale.
>
> The imperialists have mis-calculated this new quality. They think they can impose their domination through military means. For 20 years the U.S. has been operating on this mis-calculation. It is on a collision course with the entire world because this new level of political struggle has been underestimated.
>
> On the other hand, we too have underestimated this new quality. We too have sometimes over-emphasized the importance of armed struggle and have overlooked the need for waging political struggles for immediate needs of the masses. ("You Gotta Have Punch, Hall Tells Audience," The *Worker,* June 7, 1966.)

When Herbert Aptheker, the chief American revisionist theoretician, ran for Congress, the incumbent circulated a letter saying Aptheker's activities should be "halted." Aptheker responded that the letter was "an incitement to violence rather than something belonging fairly within the realm of political battle." (The *Worker*, October 25, 1966.)

When the *Worker* office was bombed in September, 1966, the general manager of the newspaper wrote that "the perpetrators of this latest act of terrorism . . . are hoodlums and fascist degenerates. . . . They are the *Daily News*-inspired punks, illiterates, uncultured, half-civilized brutes. . . ." (September 13, 1966.) When James Meredith was shot in Mississippi, the W.E.B. DuBois Clubs immediately organized a demonstration in New York demanding "Get U.S. Troops out of Ky's Saigon and into Dixie." (The *Worker,* June 12, 1966.) And the *Worker* editorialized: "The President must be forced to act now. . . . Let him bring the . . . G.I.'s home from Vietnam and order them to defend freedom and democracy—in Mississippi." (September 12, 1966.)

This vulgar, racist insult to the intelligence of Black people, this lie that the ruling class government which must destroy freedom in Vietnam is able to defend freedom in Mississippi and just has to be nudged to make it willing to do so, this deliberate cover-up of the oppressor-class nature of the state, was first put forward by the Trotskyites, and later shamelessly adopted by the revisionists.

Naturally the result of this complete distortion of reality and total denial of Marxism-Leninism is the revisionists' sly joke, enshrined in the *New Draft Program of the CPUSA,* that socialism will be brought to the U.S. peacefully through a constitutional amendment, just as slavery was abolished.

> We believe this democratic transformation can be effected through the Constitutional process. . . . One Constitutional amendment . . . would abolish the capitalist form of property. . . . Unthinkable? There is precedent for it in the Constitutional amendment abolishing slave property. . . (*New Draft Program of the Communist Party, USA,* p. 97.)

To attribute the abolition of slavery in the U.S. to a "Constitutional amendment" is a deliberate misreading of history. The fact is that tens of thousands of Black people fought and died for centuries in the struggle to emancipate themselves from the slave trade and from slavery. And in the Civil War more people were killed than in any other war in U.S. history—nearly 600,000. In saying that slave property was eliminated peacefully, the CPUSA masks the class violence used against the people when they attempt to break fundamental chains. It thereby disarms U.S. workers now, telling them they shouldn't expect violence from the ruling class in attempting to abolish private property.

Furthermore, it says that the abolition of slave property was accomplished by the "good white fathers" (those who passed the 14th amendment), not by the fight of the people, especially the Black people who engaged in thousands of slave revolts from the time they were forcibly brought to this country right up to the Civil War. Racism is the handmaiden of revisionism and this is racism of the worst order. On such "reasoning" does the CPUSA base its "peaceful road to socialism" in the U.S.

If there were ever cruder and more blatant enemy ideas injected into the revolutionary movement, they do not come readily to mind. To be taken in by these revisionist concepts is to renounce socialism.

Revisionism Renounces Dialectical Materialism

By destroying the fundamentals of Marxism-Leninism, revisionists force the restoration of capitalism in a socialist country. And their interest, the maintenance of their rule, requires collusion with imperialism to prevent revolutionary developments anywhere. The revisionists try to hide this collusion with imperialism and particularly the collusion of the two "super-powers"–the United States and the Soviet Union–with pacifist slogans. As Gus Hall said:

> The deadly logic of the war in Vietnam leads to world nuclear war. It could be the "crime of all crimes." It could be the "war to end all wars" because it could end human existence on the globe.
>
> On this path there is a point of no return. There is a point where all discussions, all exchanges will have no value or meaning . . . war fronts, casualty figures, expenditures for war budgets, or even the debate of who is wrong, who is the criminal and who is the victim. . . . (Speech at Columbia University, N.Y., December 15, 1965.)

But pacifism by itself is insufficient to meet the needs of the revisionists. They require a complete bourgeois ideological system to substitute for dialectical materialism, and pacifism is only a part of this. So, under the guise of being "new" and "creative," revisionists resurrect and perpetuate bourgeois philosophy and ideology.

First they turn Marxism-Leninism into a burlesque. So Gus Hall says:

> Marxism is distinguished from other systems of thought in that it is an instrument of social change. Any instrument must be judged by how effective it is as a tool. An idea may be "true" but that is not enough to make it an instrument to change reality. It must also provide that subjective *punch,* because it is the punch that brings change in reality. ("You Gotta Have Punch, Hall Tells Audience," The *Worker,* June 7, 1966–emphasis in the original.)

When Marxism-Leninism is reduced to that kind of meaningless mumbo-jumbo, it is easy to discard.

Then Herbert Aptheker appears with his contribution:

> Lenin said that the struggle for democracy is the struggle for socialism, and the struggle for socialism is the struggle for democracy. Now we might say–we do say–that in addition, the struggle for peace is the struggle for socialism, and the struggle for socialism is the struggle for peace. And we also now may add: equality is the struggle for socialism, and the struggle for socialism is the struggle for equality, and the struggle for reason and beauty is the struggle for socialism, and the struggle for socialism is the struggle for reason and beauty. This is our banner then, comrades –democracy, equality, reason and beauty, peace–and all together socialism. Marching under this banner, dearest comrades, our victory–that is the victory of mankind–is certain. (Speech to the 18th National Convention, CPUSA, *Political Affairs,* August 1966, pp. 44-45.)

We too are for all good things, but you cannot achieve them by discarding revolution, class struggle and the victory of the working class and replacing these with "reason," "humanism," and the "victory of mankind." With the substitution of the bourgeois philosophy of humanism for Marxism-Leninism appears Waldek Rochet, head of the French revisionists, to defend humanism:

> Thus [humanism] inspires [communists] in the manner in which they approach the problem of war and peace; not only do they proclaim that the peaceful co-existence of states with different social systems is the only sensible policy today, but they fight unrelentingly to make it triumph. . . .
>
> It is a special form of the class struggle in the sense that it enables socialism and communism to win the battle against capitalism by peaceful means. . . . (*Political Affairs,* November, 1966, p. 38.)

And following the triumph of bourgeois ideology comes its development and elaboration. Roger Garaudy, chief theoretician for the French revisionists, proclaims:

> Christians and communists constitute two of the major forces shaking the world today, and there is much they can learn from each other.
>
> In an age when mutual extermination is possible, we must abandon the spirit of the crusades, the urge to convert the world to our own position. Instead we must learn to accept each other as we are.
>
> A Christian can become a better Christian and a Marxist a better Marxist if we can learn from each other how best to develop our own beliefs. ("Christian-Marxist Dialog Urged by Frenchman," *New York Times,* December 1, 1966.)

Garaudy also claimed, according to the *Times*, that "both Christianity and Communism had undergone 'metamorphosis' and both had abandoned the previous claims to possess 'unique, definitive, and absolute truth.' "

Not only does this revisionist throw out the Marxist concept of materialism and substitute for it a mish-mash of "exchange" with idealism (religion), he also libels Marxism, setting up the straw man of "absolute truth" which he says Marxists are "abandoning." It is precisely the science of Marxism which teaches that change is the cornerstone of everything; that truth is *not* absolute (an idea that *idealism* and *religion* have fostered for centuries). No Marxist materialist can become "a better Marxist" by learning to accept idealism.

We who have no fear of pointing out that the emperor's new clothes are figments of his imagination know that all of this is intended to mask the return to the regime of private ownership. Possessions are primary here. Personal success is measured by ownership of TV sets. Khrushchev's "goulash communism" becomes the goal of "communists." Accumulation is society's new motor force, not class struggle. Socialism will triumph everywhere through the example of how many private cars and traffic jams can be produced in the Soviet Union.

> The force of example of the victorious working class following the road of socialism and communism is one of the key factors furthering the development of the world revolutionary process. It would be fully in order to say that the Soviet Economic Plan and successes are the best possible publicity and propaganda for socialism and communism among the millions of working people in all countries. (*Twenty-third CPSU Congress; Results and Prospects,* Moscow, 1966, p. 7.)

For the revisionists, as for all past ruling classes, a mature good society is an unchanging society where men are happy with their stations in life. For them, the most important thing is that those who possess should keep what they possess, and those who don't should wait patiently.

For the revisionists, the revolution must not continue, it must be halted. But life cannot halt—it must flow in some direction. So, like Alice's Red Queen, the revisionists must run as fast as they can to stay in the same place. Their dominance requires active counter-revolution at home and abroad and accelerating regression at home and abroad. Alone they cannot effectively achieve this, so they are forced to turn to the main suppressive force in the world–U.S. imperialism–for help. Their objective needs force them to become the junior partner of imperialism.

Revisionism is a reversal in class domination within the communist movement. The newly dominant oppressor class must substitute its ideology and politics for the ideology and politics of the working class. This is the essence of revisionism. Revisionism is not a series of "mistakes" (although a working-class revolutionary may make a revisionist mistake). But because it is within the communist movement, the class enemy is faced with the problem of developing its ideology and politics using a Marxist-Leninist format. So it must distort the meaning of Marxism-Leninism and turn it into its opposite, so that a new meaning accrues to the old language. This is the form of revisionism.

That is why the key to evaluating revolutionary forces is not the formulations they may use but how well they encourage the revolutionary process at home and abroad, how well they pursue revolutionary thought and action as individuals to transform themselves and society.

Revisionism is the antithesis of that transcendent humaneness with which the revisionists cover themselves. For by opposing the revolutionary process, they attempt to consign countless millions to the sharpest imperalist barbarity. In real life revisionism encourages, enhances and condones the barbarism of imperialism and leads potentially progressive forces to become accomplices of imperialism, thus making a mockery of its noble slogans for peace and all good things.

Thus revisionism perpetuates racism. The economic foundations of imperialism depend on extracting huge profits from tens of millions of oppressed colored peoples abroad and in the U.S.

The people of the world will never have peace and safety until imperialism–especially U.S. imperialism–is destroyed.

Revolution is what is new and creative. Only revolution, guided by the science of Marxism-Leninism, leads to the fullest flowering of society and individuals. Revisionism and imperialism are the old, foul past. They represent the maintenance of the jungle world of dog-eat-dog, endless war and oppression. Marxist-Leninists fight for the full development of the revolutionary potential of the masses in all spheres. Revolutionary socialism places its confidence in people. It is based on the idea that people, not their possessions or weapons, make history.

Revisionism Ends Working Class' Political Control

One of the biggest crimes of revisionism is its betrayal of the basic Marxist-Leninist concept of class dictatorship—the dictatorship of the proletariat.

The dictatorship of the proletariat is the seizure and consolidation of power by the workers and their allies. They use that power to achieve their aspirations and ruthlessly deny those of the old ruling class. The workers proceed to destroy the old bourgeois state institutions and build new ones. Only then can they enforce their domination of society and prevent counter-revolution. This means a new army, police force, court system, etc. are in the hands of the working class to insure its rule. The workers seize the means of production and use all the benefits of their labor to satisfy their needs, the needs of the vast majority of the people in their country and the whole world. Democracy flourishes for the working people but not for the old exploiting class.

Without this concept, there is no Marxism-Leninism. If a party does not fight for the proletarian dictatorship, it is not a revolutionary working-class party. No revolution can fully succeed unless the dictatorship of the proletariat is achieved and consolidated. If the dictatorship of the proletariat isn't consolidated in a socialist country, you can be sure that the old class forces will eventually make a comeback.

In the recent past Soviet leaders have proposed the "new" idea of the "state of the whole people." This phony position is based on the equally false conclusion that there is no longer class struggle in a socialist country after the revolution. This makes unnecessary a revolutionary struggle, in new forms, against the old class forces and the old class ideas. The revisionists argue this way:

> As a result of changes in class composition the Soviet society has become *united and monolithic: it is a society of socialist working people.* It is welded together by the unity of interests of the workers, collective farmers and intellectuals, the unity of their world outlook. . . . The victory of socialism in Soviet society removed the causes of struggle between classes and strata, for there was absolutely no reason for struggle between the socialist working class, the socialist collective-farm peasantry and the socialist intelligentsia. . . .
>
> As a result of the complete victory of socialism class struggle in the USSR was entirely liquidated. The question of "who will

win" was decided irrevocably in favor of socialism, of socialist working people. There is no economic and social ground in the Soviet society for the restoration of capitalism with the class struggle characterizing it. The Soviet state has become different. While there were exploiting classes in the country the dictatorship of the proletariat was needed to suppress them. It also helped to transform the petty-bourgeois peasantry and the bourgeois intelligentsia.

After the liquidation of the exploiter classes, the complete and final victory of socialism and the conversion of the USSR into a single society of socialist working people, the dictatorship of the proletariat ceased to be necessary. The state of the dictatorship of the proletariat has been transformed into the socialist state of the entire people. . . .

Since the complete victory of socialism, the Soviet Union has neither exploiting classes, nor a class struggle, nor have their remnants been preserved. Therefore, there is no need artificially to preserve the dictatorship of the proletariat. . . .

Some individuals retain survivals of the past, some try to live in the old way, through deception and dishonesty. All this is relentlessly combatted by the Soviet people. The struggle against anti-social elements in the Soviet Union is waged by all groups—workers, peasants and intellectuals. The handful of anti-social outcasts—profiteers, idlers and hooligans, etc., are opposed by the united Soviet people. . . . (*Twenty-third CPSU Congress: Results and Prospects,* pp. 27-31.)

The only "new" aspect of this is that it sounds like a commercial for U.S. democracy. For don't "our" capitalists claim the government represents the "interests of all the people," and the economy is run "in the interests of all the people"?

How does this Soviet assertion square with Lenin's estimate of the protracted class struggle after the seizure of power?

The transition from capitalism to communism *represents an entire historical epoch.* Until this epoch has terminated, the exploiters will inevitably cherish the hope of restoration, and this hope will be converted into attempts at restoration. And after their first serious defeat, the overthrown exploiters—who had not expected their overthrow, never believed it possible, never conceded the thought of it—will throw themselves with tenfold energy, with furious passion and hatred grown a hundredfold, into the battle for the recovery of their lost "paradise," on behalf of their families, who had been leading such a sweet and easy life and whom now the "common herd" is condemning to ruin and destitution (or to "common" work). . . . In the train of the capitalist exploiters will be found the broad masses of the petty bourgeoisie, with regard to whom the historical experience of every country for decades testifies that they vacillate and hesitate, one day marching behind

> the proletariat and the next day taking fright at the difficulties of the revolution; that they become panic-stricken at the first defeat or semi-defeat of the workers, grow nervous, run about aimlessly, snivel, and rush from one camp to the other. (Lenin: *Selected Works,* Vol. VII, pp. 140-41.)

The notion of "the state of the whole people" exists to obscure and cover up the return to capitalism. There is no classless society in the Soviet Union. What is more, the masses have never been won over to the ideology of Marxism-Leninism. It is precisely because of the existence of classes and the low level of ideology that the present leaders have been able temporarily to usurp state power. The dictatorship of the proletariat must remain long after the revolution takes power. It must prevail until bourgeois ideology and imperialism have been totally smashed. This stage of the revolution is probably the longest, hardest, and most complex of the entire revolutionary process. Many people think the revolution successfully concluded when the fight to seize power has been won. The fight to hold power has proved far more difficult.

The revisionists, having destroyed the class dictatorship, have peddled varied notions from continent to continent. In Europe, "structural reform" has become the mating call of the old C.P.'s. England and France have their variants of the "constitutional road" to socialism. The Finnish revisionists, a step ahead of their British, French and Italian brothers, are already in the government:

> ROLE IN COALITION IRKS FINNISH REDS
> THEY ARE FORCED TO SUPPORT
> STEPS THEY LONG OPPOSED
>
> Finland's Communists are finding their current role after 18 years in opposition a bitter experience.
>
> Holding three of the fifteen portfolios in the Cabinet . . . they are being compelled to share responsibility for stringent tax and other austerity measures they have battled for years. . . .
>
> At this stage there is no expectation that the Communists will topple the government when the tax and other budgetary proposals come up for decision in Parliament in December. Communist leaders say that although they are faced with "bitter pills," these must be swallowed as part of the processes of joining and governing after 18 years.
>
> These "pills" include proposals for raising the sales tax . . . and for increasing income taxes.
>
> Increasing numbers of workers would be affected.

> Some political leaders say it is clear that the Communists have instructions from Moscow to stay in the Cabinet despite the outcry from their supporters over the fiscal measures.
>
> The purpose, it is said, is to re-establish a precedent for participation in government by the Communists who poll about 22% of the vote in parliamentary elections. The Communists, who entered the government after the armistice between Finland and the Soviet Union in late 1944, were ousted in 1948. . . .
>
> Some analysts suggest that the Soviet Union is eager to see Finland serve as a testing ground for the idea that Communists can be allowed into a coalition without fear that they will seize power. This example is intended as a lesson to such Western European countries with large Communist parties as France and Italy. (*New York Times,* October 30, 1966.)

The revisionists train themselves to play such a role:

> Dick Ethridge, a Communist who is not only the undisputed trade union leader in Britain's largest, but strike-bound automobile plant, but who also enjoys the far-reaching confidence of management. . . .
>
> Mr. Ethridge is a man who combines his contradictions comfortably. . . .
>
> He says that since he has to live in a capitalist system he wants British Motor Corporation to make the biggest possible profit and pass most of it on to the workers; he claims to have prevented a great many more strikes than he has started. Management finds him a good man to work with. (*New York Times,* November 5, 1966.)

In all of this two things are apparent: The seizure of power is ruled out, and the people are denied protection from ruling-class terror. These ideas mean the acceptance of the status quo or "respectability." The concept of "structural reform" presupposes the nonsensical idea that the ruling class, because of an election, will share state power with the workers. It preaches to workers that half a loaf is better than none, and in fact denies them even crumbs. It states that to go all the way is too dangerous and is wrong. In effect, it consigns the working class in Europe to capitalism. Eventually the class struggle will erupt there sharply and the workers will sweep away all the false leaders.

In Africa, the revisionists made a big effort to demonstrate that socialism could be won without the dictatorship of the proletariat. Ghana, with its "non-capitalist road," was the apple of the revisionists' eye. But Africa, and Ghana precisely, have demonstrated how true is the concept of class dictatorship. As long as the army and other repressive instruments are in the hands of the old class, progressive developments are in danger. Unless completely new instruments of power are established during the revolution, the revolution is in danger. Economic independence is key to accomplishing the above. If the economy is still under the control of, or dependent upon, imperialism, even if it's back door control or dependency, the revolution will not succeed and is in danger.

Events in Indonesia have demonstrated the same thing. In the development of any united front with progressive nationalist forces it is necessary to fight for the dominance of the working class. This will lessen the impact of vacillations by petty-bourgeois and bourgeois nationalist forces. This struggle for dominance also provides training and experience necessary for the seizure of power. When the right moment comes in the struggle for power the workers must be in a position to ward off counter-revolutionary terror, or to prevent it by taking power. But if the national bourgeoisie is the leading element in the united front, vacillation will inevitably appear just at that moment and will be the dominating feature. If the working class is dominant, the bourgeois flip-flops will not be as damaging because they are subordinate to the working class' steadfast determination for revolution.

Of course, it is necessary to work with progressive sections of the bourgeois nationalists in anti-colonial struggles. But to rely on them to move the revolution to a new, higher stage leaves the masses open to attack and to defeat. The vanguard party must rely on its own consciousness, its own will, its own strength, and on the masses.

Among the major forces opposing U.S. imperialism today are the anti-colonial national liberation movements in Asia, Africa and Latin America. These forces make up a powerful bloc in the growing worldwide united front against U.S. imperialism.

Obviously, the focal point of this worldwide anti-imperialist uprising is in Vietnam.

In order to carry these progressive movements through to socialism, it is necessary for the working class, guided by Marxist-Leninist parties, to become the dominant force in the alliance with peasants, intellectuals, and progressive bourgeois forces.

The sharper the struggle by anti-colonial and national liberation forces against U.S. imperialism, the better. This will enhance the struggle to transform the national liberation struggles into class struggles.

The overwhelming majority of the world's population is opposed to U.S. imperialism. Their struggle for liberation will go through many stages. But in the final analysis, it will be a fight for the dictatorship of the proletariat.

In our country the fight to win radicals to accept the concept of the dictatorship of the proletariat is long and uphill. The bourgeoisie has enormous influence and endless means to communicate its ideas. Internally the chronic weakness of the American communist movement has been its failure to expose the nature and role of the state apparatus, its failure to fight for the end of the bourgeois state and the building of a new state apparatus based on the power of the working class.

Earl Browder, longtime head of the U.S. Communist Party, who trained all the current top leaders of that group, was a great advocate of class peace with U.S. imperialism to secure peaceful coexistence. He was the vanguard of the modern revisionists. (Let it never be said that the U.S. hasn't made its own unique contribution.)

> We must be prepared to give the hand of cooperation and fellowship to everyone who fights for the realization of this [Anglo-Soviet-American] coalition. If J.P. Morgan supports this coalition and goes down the line for it, I as a Communist am prepared to clasp his hand on that and join with him to realize it. Class divisions or political groupings have no significance now except as they reflect one side or the other of this issue. . . .
>
> Marxists will not help the reactionaries by opposing the slogan of "free enterprise" with any form of counter-slogan. If anyone wished to describe the existing system of capitalism in the United States as "free enterprise," that is all right with us, and we frankly declare that we are ready to cooperate in making this capitalism work effectively in the post-war period with the least possible burdens upon the people. (Browder's Speech at Bridgeport, Conn. in *The Communist,* January, 1944, p. 8.)

Browder's thinking is still the thinking of the CPUSA.

As a result of such erroneous theoretical pronouncements within radical circles there is a great mistrust of theory. There is also strong bourgeois influence in the form of individualism among radicals. Moreover, there is a great mistrust of, and lack of understanding of, the role of the working class in social transformation. A non-class conception of democracy prevails, which really means democracy for the upper class. The idea of involving millions in the development of society is alien and almost unimaginable to these circles. Contrary to their often-professed democratic ideals, they hold elitist concepts. They feel that only the "most knowledgeable" have the right to shape society. They distort even the real errors made in the past by communists, and build fantastic programs based on these distortions. We have a great deal to overcome in fighting for the victory of the concept of the proletarian dictatorship.

The betrayal of the concept of the dictatorship of the proletariat has weakened the international communist movement. It has opened it to penetration, and set it up for setbacks. For either the working class suppresses the imperialists, or imperialism suppresses first the revolutionary movements of the workers and then all the workers.

Revisionism Spawns Reactionary Nationalism

The abandonment of the dictatorship of the proletariat by former communists has encouraged the growth of bourgeois nationalism. As it is developing in this period, this bourgeois nationalism is a manifestation of fear of imperialism, and of the growing strength of bourgeois forces and ideas within a "socialist" country or "communist" party. To avoid revolutionary struggle before or after the seizure of power this new crop of revisionists–as well as the centrists who use a more leftish vocabulary–distort the valid concepts of independence and self-reliance. They advance the slogan of "independence" meaning independence from Marxism-Leninism. They cry "self-reliance" to flee from proletarian internationalism.

The new bourgeois nationalists try to project only the "unique" conditions of their particular country, and do not apply the universal features of revolutionary experience and class struggle. Having distorted Marxism-Leninism in this way they then try to impose this narrow nationalism on the entire world movement. Marxist-Leninists study both the laws of history and their own society, and apply their conclusions to the real conditions of their country.

The new bourgeois nationalists constantly invent "new" circumstances in order to stop fighting imperialism and to co-exist with it. Jay Lovestone, George Meany's fascist adviser on foreign policy, was among the first of this "new breed." As early as the 1920's, when he was a leader of the CPUSA, he advanced the slogan of "American Exceptionalism." He claimed that revolution was all right for other countries but not for the U.S. The U.S. imperialists, he felt, were so rich that they could and would willy nilly hand out unlimited concessions if they were only properly advised.

In the late thirties and forties Browder went one step further. Based on the "concessions" won during the Roosevelt administration and the destruction caused by World War II he advanced the notion of alliance with capitalism (see above). Thus, a benign U.S. imperialism could be lived with and nudged into socialism.

After World War II, Tito also advanced the notion that U.S. imperialism was changed, and that the state apparatus in an advanced capitalist country had no class allegiance. Therefore, it was all right to cooperate with it and obtain huge handouts to subsidize the Yugoslav economy. Because things were different, he claimed, socialist countries didn't have to undergo a long difficult period of industrialization to become independent of imperialism. Instead, he "chose" to be independent of the Soviet Union or, in fact, Marxism-Leninism, in return for U.S. dollars. After the 20th Party Congress, Khrushchev declared "independence" from Stalin, which meant independence from Marxism-Leninism. And, shortly thereafter, Togliatti put forth the idea of "Poly-Centrism." This was a system of relations between so-called socialist states and communist parties which proclaimed "independence" for all. Actually, it meant that everyone who claimed to be a revolutionary socialist could be independent of Marxism-Leninism.

Of course, the imperialists jumped for joy and welcomed with open arms all of these socialist statesmen. Of course, Browder is eulogized and viewed with nostalgia by the ruling class, and Lovestone became the darling of the State Department, the CIA and the labor bureaucrats. Of course, Khrushchev and Togliatti were, and are, extolled by repeated articles in the capitalist press. Of course, Tito received three billion dollars from the U.S.

U.S. imperialism coined a new term–"National Communism." U.S. rulers hailed this as a new creative development, and said they could co-exist with it. U.S. imperialists explain (to each other) that "National Communism" is no longer revolutionary because it doesn't seek to expand the revolution.

A recent Korean Party statement is an excellent example of how the distortion of valid slogans is used to undermine Marxism-Leninism. For example, the Korean statement says, "As regards the actual situation in each country, the party of that country knows well; no one else is in a position to know better." And Kim Il Sung, in a report to the Korean Party in October, 1966, says (referring to the Chinese):

> They say we are taking the road of unprincipled compromise and sitting on two chairs at the same time. This is nonsense. We have our own chair.

If everyone has his own ideological chair to sit on, what happens to Marxism-Leninism as a science?

Of course, it is generally true to say that a party within a particular country knows its own situation better than others. But to assert that *general* proposition within the *specific historic context* of the present struggle against revisionism throughout the communist movement, is to say the following: "Whatever any party says or does concerning its policies and practices is correct as long as that party doesn't try to tell our party (i.e. criticize) about our policies or practices."

This kind of line is obviously anti-Leninist. Lenin dared to "interfere" by criticizing the policies and practices of the opportunist parties, and exposed their betrayal of Marxism. He also dared to criticize those who were making left mistakes. Lenin's entire works (as well as Marx's and Engels') are replete with such examples of "interference." What a sorry state the world communist movement has fallen into to try to cover up revisionism and centrism by such talk of our sacred "independence."

Of course, no party can force another party to change its course. But the power of Marxism, Lenin said, is that it is true. And truth is not confined to national boundaries.

Marxism-Leninism approaches reality from the point of view of science, of dialectical materialism. If every party's interpretation (that is, its policies and practices) is to be regarded as correct whether or not it is revisionist, centrist, opportunist, sectarian or what-not, then of course Marxism has been reduced to subjective idealism.

Yes, one must do one's own thinking, but this is true for all comrades within national parties, as well as between national parties. Doing one's own thinking, however, cannot become a formula–a cover-up–for opportunism, for failing to struggle against revisionism and centrism. One's own thinking can be either right or wrong, or partially right or partially wrong, but whatever it is, it certainly cannot be defended as being correct simply because it is "my own thinking."

Communists have always understood that revolution *cannot* be imported or exported; that the working class of each country has to smash the state power of its "own" bourgeoisie and establish its own working-class state power. It is not new to say that primarily by its own efforts a working class of any one country must defeat its own national bourgeoisie and build socialism. Stalin's historic struggle to defeat Trotskyism was precisely over this question. Trotsky maintained that it was impossible for the Soviet Union by its own efforts to build socialism without the European proletariat winning state power. Yet Stalin, who fought to defend the dictatorship of the proletariat and to build socialism in the Soviet Union, *never* took the position that this was possible without the support of the world proletariat, nor could the victory of socialism be "complete"—"final"—in the Soviet Union as long as the world bourgeoisie was not overthrown. (Read and study particularly Stalin's report to the Seventh Enlarged Plenum of the Executive Committee Communist International–Stalin's *Selected Works,* Vol. 9.)

> Does this mean that such a victory can be termed a full victory, a final victory of socialism, one that would guarantee the country building socialism against all danger from abroad, against the danger of imperialist intervention and the consequent danger of restoration? No, it does not. While the question of completely building socialism in the USSR is one of overcoming our "own" *national* bourgeoisie, the question of the final victory of socialism is one of overcoming the *world* bourgeoisie (page 25).

Again, Stalin indicated that the proletariat in the Soviet Union could overcome its own bourgeoisie by *its own efforts only in alliance with the peasantry and with the world proletariat.* He said:

> Only in alliance with the world proletariat is it possible to build socialism in our country. The whole point is how this alliance is to be understood. . . . The trouble with the opposition is that it recognizes only one form of alliance, the form of "direct state support. . ." (Stalin, *Selected Works,* Vol. 9.)

One's own thinking"—"One's own efforts" or "self-reliance" —"respect for other parties and other comrades"—"the equality of all parties big and small" . . . these are all correct ideas and useful ideas if placed within a specific historic context. The concrete analysis of specific conditions is the heart of Marxist-Leninist methodology. In today's historic battles to defeat imperialism and advance revolution, it is necessary for all parties to wage a struggle to defeat the revisionists and the centrists within their own ranks nationally and internationally.

Thus, self-reliance and independence are valid when combined with the basic slogan of "Workers of All Nations, Unite." Nationalism denies class struggle exists after socialism. Kim Il Sung, in the report mentioned above said:

> In our society there exist no socio-economic and material sources for the emergence of outdated ideas. . . . One may commit a leftist error if one emphasizes class struggle only . . . forgetting that the alliance of the working class, peasantry, and intellectuals constitutes the basis for social relations under socialism . . . this may cause unrest in society.

Consequently, this point of view obliterates the dictatorship of the proletariat, and prevents class struggle against old and new bourgeois forces because of the fear of "unrest"—a nice cozy estimate, in which the stage is set for the restoration of capitalism.

Revisionism spawns nationalism. Revisionism and nationalism split and fragment the communist movement. This corresponds to the needs of the imperialists. Under these new circumstances nationalism becomes ultra-reactionary and paves the way for capitulation to imperialism and the return to capitalism.

Soviet Revisionists Have Already Restored Capitalism in the Soviet Union

Because the Soviet Union is the main and most powerful center of revisionism, we will better understand the nature of revisionism and the real meaning of the destruction of the proletarian dictatorship by examining life there. In this way we will be able to avoid making two serious errors.

The first possible error is to confuse the Soviet people with the gang that now holds power. Millions of Soviet people have revolutionary experience. Millions fought in the Great Patriotic War to defeat Hitlerism.

To be pro-Soviet today requires that you oppose the Soviet leaders and defend the revolutionary traditions of the Soviet workers. It requires confidence that the class struggle continues and will sharpen in the Soviet Union; for no more than imperialism can revisionism halt the class struggle. Because class struggle is a constant development in class society, millions of Soviet people are part of today's anti-imperialist front. It will take more time for this fact to become apparent. But especially because of the earlier socialist developments in the Soviet Union, the class contradictions will intensify between the Soviet workers and the Soviet leaders.

The second serious error would be to have a foggy notion about who holds state power in the Soviet Union, and what forces the state represents.

Which class holds power determines the nature of the state. The character of the state cannot be defined simply by the contradictions that exist within a particular country, no matter how sharp these contradictions are. The nature of the state rests on which aspect of the main contradiction is dominant. The Soviet Union has changed from being a country whose means of production were owned by the working people to one controlled and owned by a new exploiting class whose origins are in the former managerial-technical-professional strata. Profit—the private appropriation of the society's economic surplus—has replaced planning the economy for the benefit of the workers. Profit has been brought to the fore in all aspects of the Soviet economy.

> Economists and business executives wanted the individual enterprise to be given more independence in planning its production and selling its goods. . . .
>
> The state still represents the economic interests of all the people. . . . What is fixed by the state is the volume of goods to be sold; i.e., what should reach the consumer. . . .
>
> A factory has to find buyers for the goods it manufactures. It has to study demand, gauge the market, and make contact with consumers. Some firms have branched out from the production end. . . . They also sell the items they manufacture. This stimulates business. . . .
>
> Profit gives the personnel of a plant more incentive. Higher remuneration for work has a great deal to do with productivity and the quality of the items turned out. The new system of management and planning makes it possible for an enterprise to reward its personnel more adequately for increasing the volume

> of goods sold, for cutting costs, etc. How is it done? Part of the profit a plant makes goes into what is known as an encouragement fund for bonuses, grants, and other such awards. The size of the fund will depend, first, on the rate of growth of goods sold, and, second, on the level of a factory's profitability. . . .
>
> To use the Volgograd Red October Works as an example: Of its 800,000 rubles of additional profits, 720,000 rubles are going for bonuses. . . . (*Soviet Life,* October, 1966, p. 63.)

What is clear is that this scheme puts the workers of any plant in competition—that is, in antagonistic contradiction—with workers at other plants. Instead of society as a whole, that is, the working class as a whole, receiving the economic surplus produced by the Soviet workers, production units privately accumulate that surplus. In the example of the Volgograd Red October Works, 92% of the surplus which should accrue to the entire working class is being kept as private profit and distributed in the form of bonuses.

> Does not the element of profit contradict the fundamental principles of socialism? No, it does not. . . . Profit has survived capitalism. . . . (*Soviet Life,* June 1966, p. 26.)
>
> Anyone but anyone who knows the first thing about it is perfectly aware that profit, price and credit are all categories of commodity production in general, not only of capitalism alone. Under socialism commodity production does continue to exist, therefore, the categories inherent in it also continue to exist. . . .
>
> The output of a socialist enterprise is created by the joint effort of the entire staff. It is therefore quite in order, alongside the material remuneration of each employee in accordance with his personal labor, to secure the material interests of the entire staff in the final results of the enterprise's work. This ensures a fuller combination of personal and public interests. . . . (*23rd Congress of the CPSU: Results and Prospects,* p. 39.)

But "anyone who knows the first thing about it" knows that commodity production is the characteristic of capitalism. Under socialism commodity production is superseded. That is the strength of socialist production.

One of the key economic indicators of a socialist society developing in a progressive manner—towards communism—is the shrinking of the sphere of commodity circulation. While commodity production and circulation cannot be done away with immediately upon the access of the working class to state power, the resolute introduction of measures to restrain, limit, and reduce commodity production and circulation is a prerequisite for the continued existence of a socialist society.

The best example of this is the replacement, on a gradual basis, of wages by social benefits, at first available on a limited basis, but increasing as the society develops. Bourgeois methods of cost accounting, etc. should likewise disappear as the sphere of commodity circulation shrinks. As long as workers work for wages which they must then use to purchase commodities, the economic potential for the "peaceful" restoration of capitalism exists.

The retention of the market economy–the production and circulation of commodities–will inevitably lead to the fostering and resurgence of bourgeois ideology; and in a nominally socialist ideological context, bourgeois ideology is revisionism.

For a long period in the Soviet Union, the sphere of commodity circulation did not shrink but remained pretty much the same. This was not seriously damaging at first because the surplus of the Soviet economy was distributed on a social basis rather than an individual basis.

In the early 1950's, a trend set in advocating the widening of the sphere of commodity circulation (this trend was fought by Stalin; see *Economic Problems of Socialism in the USSR*). This trend was the forerunner of Khrushchev's economic policies and those of his successors.

The present-day transformation of social surplus into private profit is the unconditional victory of commodity circulation over socialism.

As Lenin wrote:

> Any direct or indirect legalization of the possession of their own production by the workers of individual factories or individual professions or of their right to weaken or impede the decrees of the state power is the greatest distortion of the basic principles of Soviet power and the complete renunciation of socialism. (Lenin, *On the Democracy and Socialist Character of the Soviet Power.*)

In a socialist society therefore, commodities exist as a hangover from the past and in time their production will cease altogether. If "profit survives capitalism," consequently, it is as the afterbirth survives the womb. Socialist society transforms profit by socializing it. But the Soviet revisionists have done just the opposite. They have turned a remnant of the capitalist past into the hallmark of the present. In a socialist society it is quite out of order, and not in the public interest, for the staff of an enterprise to keep the surplus that the workers of the enterprise have produced. This is theft from the working class. It is a form of private appropriation of the social surplus and therefore is a form of capitalism. Victor Perlo, the main American revisionist economist, describes the Soviet plan as "labor-oriented profit-sharing with a vengeance." (*The Worker,* July 3, 1966.) He goes on to say that "Soviet economists consider it desirable that ultimately bonuses should account for one-fourth of all workers' earnings and one-third those of leading personnel." (ibid.)

Of course, profit-sharing is regressive under socialism. But of greater interest is the fact, which Perlo points out, that this theft of the working class' production is in the interest of the "leading personnel."

Evsei Lieberman, author of the *Pravda* articles that ushered in the new economic system, tried to deny that the Soviet economic managers are new capitalists.

> And where in the U.S.S.R. will you find managers who would be living off anything but incomes derived from work? Maybe you know they own plush villas? Or perhaps luxurious yachts? Or maybe they have private swimming pools? Quite the contrary. ("Noted Soviet Economist Sets the Record Straight," *The Worker,* May 19, 1966.)

Just how well do the managers live? Reports from the Soviet press about growing corruption and individual officials living high off the hog–legally and illegally–have been widespread. Lately, a more-than-individual pattern–a portrait of a class–has begun to emerge. A recent detailed study gives many examples of the conditions and class outlook of the "10% of the Soviet population" which has achieved overlordship. Here are just a few:

> The neo-bourgeois of Russia longs for more elegance, better pastimes and better manners. . . .
>
> But the greatest passion of a middle-class family is to own a house of its own.
>
> Soviet law says that you cannot own any *lot* . . . but a *house* can be privately owned–if it does not exceed five rooms. . . .

Wonders can be done even within these limits. An aroused correspondent described in *Izvestia* "a kingdom of private enterprise"—a bourgeois suburb of a new West Siberian industrial town:

". . . As we pass, people are on guard as they stare at us from their windows with curiosity, and angry watchdogs bark."

Watchdogs, ever-present in such communities, . . . no less than the high fences around these private houses. . . . Some houses acquire yet more singular guardians. In Kiev a scientist bought a bear to waddle and growl along a wire between his gate and his house. In Magnitogorsk a metallurgical engineer planted a mine under his apple trees, and elsewhere a major of engineering troops rigged up a detonating device at his private garage door. . . . More frequent are . . . the owners who patrol their houses and orchards with guns and have shot trespassing fruit-pickers, usually young men or boys, sometimes fatally . . . an executive in charge of building materials illegally erected two houses for himself and his family, one of which had a reinforced-concrete bomb shelter. . . .

At meetings of the cooperatives, high-sounding phrases about Socialism and Communism reverberate, but as a woman journalist asked bitterly in *Literaturnaya Gazeta*:

"What worth have these phrases . . . side by side with this real phenomenon of one's own plot of land, this sharply felt matter of one's own irrigation ditch behind the fence, this asphalt-paved path to one's own privy? . . . This is real, this can be touched and felt with one's own hands, and it is precious also because it can become a durable guaranty of some future prosperity, such as one's own car . . . and you can never tell what else may yet be installed on one's own land."

. . . When a party zealot got up at one meeting of a gardeners' cooperative and urged that the cooperative ideal be restored by taking down all the fences and merging all the gardens and berry patches into one big commune, the answering cry (as reported in the Soviet press) was: "Burn it! We'd rather burn everything! So that nobody would get it!"

Some party leaders . . . explain away the discrepancy between the Communist ideal and the bourgeois reality by saying that the founding comrades never actually opposed *personal* property, that what they forbade was *private* property. Ah, but not *property*, the neo-bourgeois says triumphantly, so I will continue to collect and it will be I—not you, comrades—who will decide where "personal" stops and "private" begins. ("Russia's New Bourgeois Grows Fat," *N.Y. Times Magazine,* June 5, 1966.)

This article is just one of many which have recently appeared on this subject—usually with a tone of great approval for the new Soviet capitalists. And the new exploiters act the part:

Leonid Brezhnev, General Secretary of the Soviet Communist Party, told Hungarian workers today that the Soviet road to communism was going to be filled with private cars. . . .

To his factory audience this appeared to be a welcome echo of Nikita Khrushchev's speech in praise of "goulash communism" on his visit here as Premier three years ago.

It was also Mr. Brezhnev's way of saying that his Party and the Hungarian Party remain committed to the building of a better life for their people instead of violent revolution as preached by the Chinese communist leaders. . . . (*New York Times,* December 2, 1966.)

SOVIETS ADJUST PRICES TO INCENTIVE SYSTEM

Wholesale prices of heavy industry products in the U.S.S.R. are to be raised an average of 11-12% beginning the middle of next year as part of a reform by the state prices committee of the U.S.S.R.

The committee chairman . . . wrote that the need for reform of wholesale prices stems from the introduction of new principles of planning and material incentives, which increase the importance of profits as a standard of efficiency. . . . (*The Worker,* October 23, 1966.)

SOVIET BIDS ALLIES PAY FOR TECHNOLOGY

A Soviet demand that other communist states pay for advanced Soviet technology has introduced a new element into the relations among members of the Council for Economic Mutual Assistance, the East European Economic Alliance.

In the past, Soviet and Eastern European propagandists have often emphasized the "brotherly" character of the free transfer of technology among communist states.

An earlier Soviet demand for Eastern European capital to develop Soviet raw material resources is already being implemented.

Soviet demands for payment for Soviet technical knowledge were published in the Soviet magazine *New Times.* It said that "licenses, patents, and technical specifications" must be sold among socialist countries at world prices, on the same basis that capitalist countries deal in technology.

If the Soviet Union has its way, only technical knowledge covering obsolete machinery will henceforth be given away free of charge. (*New York Times,* November 27, 1966.)

The Soviet leaders, under the guise of the "International

Socialist Division of Labor," have tried to stifle the economic development of the other socialist countries. The concept was first put forward by Khrushchev. It has run into serious opposition from the East European countries. This is the background to Rumania's disaffection with the Soviet Union. Under the "International Division of Labor," the Soviet Union's allies supply food, raw materials and capital to the Soviet Union and, in turn, the Soviet Union forces manufactured items on her allies.

RUSSIANS SEEK TO RAISE PRICES ON GOODS THEY SELL TO EASTERN EUROPE

. . . To hear the Russians tell it . . . they have been supplying East Europe's critical requirements for fuel and raw materials for years at lower-than-bargain-basement prices, slowing Russia's own economic growth and damaging its "national interests."

So the Russians are bluntly demanding that their Communist partners shell out more for the supplies they buy.

They also are insisting on advanced payments for such supplies . . . when meeting the demand requires an increase in Soviet capital spending. . . .

Now, Russian pressures are forcing each of the Comecon nations to define a new economic relationship with the Soviets. . . .

The Russians clearly view their trade relationship with East Europe as an economic drag, and they wish to expand their own dealings with the West considerably.

Russian economists have become more and more intrigued lately with capitalistic methods of cost accounting.

O.T. Bogomolov, a leading Soviet economist, recently calculated that the Soviet Union could earn much more on its investment by exporting manufactured goods than by exporting the raw materials it has been supplying to its allies. An investment in production of manufactured goods like machines, his calculations showed, would return five to eight times as much in foreign-currency earnings as an investment of equal amounts in production facilities for such raw materials as iron ore, fertilizer or coal. "In drawing up the 1966-70 Economic Plan," he wrote, "the Soviet Union even overrode its own national interests in order to meet the requirements of the other Comecon countries."

The other Comecon countries haven't agreed to such conclusions. In fact, the Soviets have long been accused of charging their partners more than prevailing market prices for supplies. . . . (*Wall Street Journal*, August 17, 1966.)

How the scheme is applied is graphically illustrated by Perlo in an article from Havana.

Economic relations with socialist countries will require careful readjustment. Increasing economic aid to more and more socialist and developing countries involves significant sacrifices for the people of the U.S.S.R., Czechoslovakia, etc. As Cuba increases output, it will want gradually to reduce its negative trade balance with these countries. Thus, the Cuban people themselves will not derive all the benefits from their increased productivity. Cuban planners will have to work closely with their European socialist friends to divide the increased output so as to noticeably improve Cuban living standards while simultaneously reducing the burden on the U.S.S.R. and other socialist countries. . . .

. . . With full employment and wages fixed, a large proportion of the population are not working normal hours or with normal intensity. They neither fear hunger from taking it easy nor look forward to much gain from working harder. While being paid for an 8 hour day, many workers put in only 5-7 hours. But the key to realization of Cuba's economic goals is higher labor productivity, which requires that workers observe elementary labor discipline.

This can be obtained temporarily through moral or patriotic stimuli. During the October, 1963 crisis, despite the partial mobilization, production increased notably. But, as European socialist experience shows, in the long run moral and material stimuli must be combined. Ways must be found to reward people in proportion to their effort and productivity. The European socialist countries are striving to improve their performance in this respect. Inevitably, this is closely connected with cost accounting and attention to profitability in industry and agriculture. . . .

Some industrial administrators I talked with had an excellent grasp and control over the economic factors of their enterprises. Despite theoretical de-emphasis, significant practical use is made of economic incentives. In construction, a group of workers contracts to complete a specified job in a given time at the regular wage rate for that period. If they complete it ahead of time and it passes quality inspection, they get the agreed amount of money anyhow. In effect, that increases their daily wage.

Cane cutters at a farm I visited in Matanzas Province are paid $1.90 per 100 arrobas. At the quota of 300 arrobas, they would make $5.70 per day, a better-than-average wage. Outstanding cutters can earn up to $20 daily, approaching the salary of cabinet ministers.

While I was in Havana, papers published the names of scores of cane cutters who won new houses as a reward for cutting 100,000 arrobas last season. I visited the excellent home of such a winner in Matanzas Province. Hundreds of outstanding farm workers win all-expenses-paid vacations at Varadero Beach for themselves and their families. A sizable block of buildings has been erected at this resort just for them.

. . . As planned increases in consumers' goods output become

> available, it will become possible to distribute them more in accordance with the individual's contribution to production. If this is done, a real increase in labor productivity and diligence should be realized. . . .
>
> Cuba is irrevocably building socialism. If it fails to overcome the obstacles discussed above promptly, the road will be slower, there will be more setbacks, more opportunities for imperialist provocation, and less of an incentive for other Latin American countries to follow Cuba's course.
>
> If Cuba does overcome these obstacles, progress will be rather swift. There will be better possibilities of defeating finally the U.S. Government's aggressive economic and political warfare. And, by the 1970's, Cuban reality will be a more powerful stimulus to Latin American anti-imperialist revolution than the most militant verbal propaganda. ("Cuba Builds Human Resources to Meet Tasks of the Future." *The Worker,* October 2, 1966.)

This all has a familiar ring. You could substitute the United States for the Soviet Union and Latin America for Eastern Europe (or Cuba).

Within the Soviet Union the essence of capitalism has been restored. Everything from Lieberman's plan to the ability to will complete personal fortunes to heirs gives the game away. Within the Soviet Union a crop of millionaires has arisen complete with the problem of dealing with their corrupted offspring. The capitalist spirit has swept the Soviet hierarchy and the overlords of industry which it represents.

The class position of a state is reflected by its foreign policy. Soviet policy is reactionary in every sense. It acts to betray revolution all over. It is propping up a series of open fascists and thinly-disguised reactionaries as in India and Indonesia. If we viewed the United States doing these things we would have no trouble characterizing it as imperialism.

No more can there be a good LBJ at home and a bad LBJ abroad than there can be good revisionists at home perpetuating socialism while practicing counter-revolution abroad. The revisionists must mask their policies at home and abroad in the name of socialism. They must try ever harder to hoodwink the Soviet people because the contradictions in Soviet life are growing sharper. We have confidence that the Soviet workers will win back state power. But we cannot obscure the fact that the state apparatus in the Soviet Union is in the hands of capitalist forces, and this is what characterizes the system today.

Revisionism, Having Destroyed Proletarian Internationalism, Merges Its Foreign Policy With Imperialism's

Emboldened by the spread of revisionism to a majority of the parties of the old international communist movement, U.S. imperialism is accelerating its efforts to halt the tide of revolution. The U.S. is making a determined but futile effort to change the course of history. In previous articles in *Progressive Labor* we have pointed out that the focal point of the confrontation between the forces of revolution and counter-revolution is in Vietnam. The outcome of this struggle will be important for the future of Asia and the world. It is here, where the struggle is so sharp, that revisionist and revolutionary ideas and actions can be more clearly evaluated.

A vital part of U.S. imperialism's strategy for world domination is the philosophical, ideological, economic and, if all else fails, military defeat of People's China. U.S. rulers know that it is the Chinese people, led by the Communist Party of China, which bars them from a more sweeping victory over the international movement. Additionally, the Chinese stand is a formidable obstacle to U.S. imperialism's efforts in Asia, Africa and Latin America. China is a mainstay to all forces fighting U.S. imperialism.

But revisionism, especially revisionism in the Soviet Union, helps U.S. imperialism by allowing the U.S. to shift most of its guns to the East. U.S. troop reduction in Europe corresponds with the growth of Soviet revisionism.

Of course, the revisionists and the imperialists would prefer to have revisionism triumph from within the Chinese party. They are making every effort to achieve this. Naturally they would like to win the easy way. They would like to see capitalism restored in China peacefully. The Soviet model of restoration is a model imperialism would like to duplicate wherever revolutionary forces have triumphed.

Were this revisionist-imperialist scheme for the destruction of revolutionary leadership in China to bear fruit it would be a paramount victory for imperialism. It would have a negative effect on the revolutionary process in the world for a long time. At the moment this scheme of the Soviets and the United States is gathering more and more steam. They are growing desperate because the Vietnamese people refuse to succumb to imperialist terror and imperialist blackmail. And the Chinese revolutionaries are organizing in a revolutionary manner to defeat imperialism and, if need be, to repel armed attack by revisionism and imperialism.

U.S. imperialism is counting heavily on Soviet cooperation for both the ideological and military penetration of the Chinese party and country. China is too big a job for U.S. imperialism to take on without the full cooperation of the Soviet Union. Imperialism is unable and unwilling to do all the expensive and dirty work itself. On November 22, 1966 a *New York Times* article exposed the game:

> SOVIETS TELL U.S. OF CONCERN ON CHINA BORDER.
> GROMYKO STRESSES PEKING'S NUCLEAR ARSENAL IN TALKS WITH JOHNSON AND RUSK
>
> The Soviet Union has become so concerned with increasing tensions in its relations with Communist China that it has taken steps to bolster their frontier and to discuss the problem with Washington. . . .
>
> According to some high American officials, the Russians have transferred some special intelligence units and equipment to monitor Chinese tests of missiles and nuclear warheads. These units were said to have focused previously on U.S. military activities. The Russians are also reported to have moved additional troops, both border guards and regular army divisions to the frontier area. . . .
>
> One official with access to details of the conversations described them as "the most honest, direct, objective and non-ideological in years. . . . Mr. Gromyko made clear that the break with China is quite fundamental, and that Russia is more interested than ever in settling other outstanding issues."

The next day the State Department, in an attempt to cover up for its partner, issued a statement disavowing the *Times*' article:

> The State Department denied today a report that the Soviet Union had discussed in high level talks with Washington officials concern over problems along the Soviet border with Communist China.

But, the same article went on to say:

> In answer to questions, a State Department spokesman said he was not denying that the recent discussions had dealt with Soviet-Chinese relations, China's development of nuclear weapons and prospects for a treaty to prevent the spread of atomic arms.

Another indication of how advanced the collusion is between the U.S. and the Soviet Union appears in a story in the November 26, 1966 *New York Times*:

> U.S. VIEW ON CHINA LINKED TO SOVIET.
> WASHINGTON IS SAID TO AVOID DRASTIC POLICY
> SHIFT LEST MOVE DISTURB MOSCOW
>
> . . . The two-Chinas formula might be regarded by the Russians as making mischief in the communist world, which is deeply divided by the ideological conflict between China and the Soviet Union. . . . A change in America's China policy, it was thought, might also weaken the impact in Eastern Europe of President Johnson's speech of October 7th in which he sought a far-reaching improvement in relations between East and West.

Naturally cultural togetherness flowers along with the political and military machinations of the Soviet Union and the United States. While the United States is busy leveling as much of Vietnam as possible Yevgeny Yevtushenko, foppish Soviet poet and model of what is new and creative, is busy touring the U.S. He is ardently spewing counter-revolutionary ideas. He is attacking China and apologizing for U.S. genocide in Vietnam. He has spent hours with Bobby Kennedy. And Kennedy found him "most interesting." He was up till 4 A.M. with his pal John Steinbeck, who defends U.S. aggression in Vietnam. Yevtushenko's biggest kudos came from none other than Robert McNamara, mass murderer of Vietnam, who is hated by millions of Americans. The following article appeared in an early edition of the *New York Times* of November 22, 1966 and then was quickly pulled to avoid further exposing the Soviet beatnik.

> Secretary of Defense McNamara turned out Monday for a poetry recital by Yevtushenko. The Soviet poet made an eloquent appeal for better Soviet-American relations.
>
> Mr. McNamara joined the audience on numerous occasions in lustily applauding Mr. Yevtushenko.
>
> Most of the poems, which were read in an English translation as well as in Russian, were among the poet's new ones and were sprinkled with political allusions. In impressions about American cinema, he joked about espionage and poked fun at the Chinese Communists.

This is no isolated expression of the latest Soviet-U.S. collusion. It is rather the logical, obvious result of the merging of revisionist and imperialist politics. Of course McNamara cheered.

Recently the Soviets have stepped up the attack against the Chinese. One of their Bulgarian stooges has called for a new conference of revisionists to read the Chinese out of the international movement. This has been coupled with the Soviet's latest attack on the Chinese party and its leadership, especially Mao Tse-tung. The Soviets are complaining that Mao and those who follow an unswerving revolutionary path are in the leadership. They bemoan the fate of the opponents of the correct Marxist-Leninist policies of the Chinese party. But their call for another conference to attack China has been coolly received by fellow revisionists. Many of the revisionists, apparently, fear that the hatred they show to revolutionary China, contrasted with the growing love-match with U.S. imperialism, will further open the eyes of millions of oppressed people. Hence the noticeable lack of enthusiasm and the "leave well enough alone" attitude. But the Soviets have their task cut out for them by U.S. imperialism and they are faithfully carrying out their assignments.

Nor are the Soviet leaders simply busy trying to isolate and betray the Chinese revolution. These are busy counter-revolutionaries who don't limit themselves to only a single goal. After attacking Indonesian revolutionaries and patriots for attempting to prevent the fascist counter-revolution, they are now supporting the fascist butchers all the way.

During the fascist army coup the Soviet leaders promised Suharto's personal emissary that they would continue to supply the Indonesian militarists with ammuntion, replacement parts and other military equipment. (The Indonesian armed forces, completely outfitted with Soviet materiel, are totally dependent on the Soviet Union.) After the blood bath, in which hundreds of thousands were slaughtered by the generals' putsch, the Soviets quickly recognized the new government. Now they are out to consolidate it.

SOVIET DEBT MOVE BUOYS INDONESIA
RESCHEDULING ACCORD SPURS HOPE FOR BALANCED BUDGET

> Indonesian hopes of achieving a balanced budget for the first time in 16 years of inflationary deficits took new life today from an announcement that the Soviet Union had agreed to rescheduling payments of part of Indonesia's debt.
>
> . . . The Western nations agreed to a delay in principle during a meeting in Tokyo in September. . . . (*New York Times*, November 24, 1966.)

The large arms shipments to Indonesia continue. These arms can only be used against–are only intended to be used against–the Indonesian masses who eventually will move (if they haven't already moved) to armed struggle.

There has been a constant and growing rapport between the Soviet leaders and the Indonesian butchers. Adam Malik, the Trotskyite foreign minister of Indonesia, comes and goes from Moscow as if there were a subway between the two countries.

What can be the nature of Soviet leaders who support and encourage fascism? What can be the character of a leadership that, seeing tens of thousands of their ostensible comrades exterminated, rushes in to assist their executioners? What can be the morality of a leadership which attacks its Indonesian comrades at the very moment they are being slaughtered by counter-revolutionaries? There is only one answer: the Soviet leaders are counter-revolutionaries of the basest type.

This flows quite logically from the Soviet leaders' policy of arming the Indian reactionaries so they can attack China, and so they can hold power over the ever more rebellious masses in India.

In Vietnam their treachery knows no bounds. When Khrushchev was in the leadership, the CPSU brazenly sided with the U.S. It opposed and undermined the revolutionary action of the Vietnamese people. They claimed that "any local war might spark off the conflagration of a world war." (Khrushchev, press conference in Vienna, July 8, 1960.) Using this concept to intimidate revolutionaries into submission, they openly refused to support the Vietnamese people. However, when the efforts of the Vietnamese and Laotian people against the U.S. grew stronger, Soviet policy in Southeast Asia was officially designated as "disengagement." In July, 1964, the Soviets indicated their desire to resign from their post as one of the two co-chairmen of the Geneva Conference. Shortly after this, when the U.S. engineered the Bac Bo (Tonkin) Gulf incident, Khrushchev claimed it had been provoked by China. In other words China, not the U.S., was escalating the war against the Vietnamese.

Despite the Soviet betrayals the Vietnamese people won victory after victory. Khrushchev's policies of open betrayal in Vietnam and elsewhere became a liability to the Soviet leaders. The revolutionary masses of the world branded U.S. imperialism as their chief enemy and hailed China as their mainstay. Soviet influence was rapidly receding. Revolution in Vietnam was mercilessly exposing Soviet revisionism. Khrushchev was dumped.

This demonstrated the vulnerability of revisionism. The lopping-off of the main architect of revisionism was an important tactical victory for revolutionaries. It proved the validity of our position that, since the overwhelming majority of the masses of the world are opposed to imperialism, anyone who helps imperialism will sooner or later be crushed.

The new Soviet leaders tried to learn from this experience. They retreated from open, brazen betrayal to covert, insidious treachery. They changed their policy in Vietnam from "disengagement" to "involvement," for they knew that if they were to undermine the tremendous efforts of the Vietnamese people they would have to worm their way into the confidence of the Vietnamese leaders.

The policies of "involvement" and "disengagement" are fundamentally two forms of one policy. The policy, in both forms, meets the needs of U.S. imperialism. U.S. imperialism desperately needs the revisionists to undermine the revolution in Vietnam. They need them to force the Vietnamese to concede in negotiations what they have not lost in war.

The U.S. rulers need the Soviet clique to mask imperialism's hideous nature. And imperialism's junior partners are willing to do this job. But the greatest amount of toadying by the revisionists will only postpone but not prevent the day when sharp contradictions, having an objective basis in their economic rivalry, arise between them and the imperialists. And then the imperialists will turn on the Soviet clique. The unity of exploiters is a sometime thing.

In the meantime we have the spectacle of the world's biggest "socialist" country improving relations with the U.S. at the moment the U.S. is slaughtering thousands of the Soviet Union's allies. The Soviet absolves the U.S. rulers and blames the war of genocide on some "lunatics in the Pentagon." Thus the Soviet leaders are used in every manner to help achieve the goals of imperialism.

Additionally, "involvement" is designed to overcome the Soviet Union's growing loss of influence in Asia. Its concern for these interests is shown by its role in Indonesia, India, and by its meddling in the India-Pakistan border war. The Soviets want to build up a sphere of economic and political domination which they can exploit more fully at a later date. Like any other nation which is developing an economy based on private profit, the Soviet Union needs areas to exploit.

Soviet "involvement" is designed to undermine the unity of the Chinese and Vietnamese. "Involvement" is being used to stop the revolutionary process in Vietnam and isolate the revolutionary forces. This is the real meaning of the statements:

> The scientific and technical revolution of the second half of the 20th century and its subsequent revolution in military science have fundamentally changed the nature of war, aggravated its aftermath and engendered the possibility of turning what at first glance would seem to be an inconsequential conflict breaking out in some remote corner of the world, into the detonator of a universal rocket-nuclear war. In present conditions a threat to peace, wherever it appears–in Africa, Asia, Latin America or Central Europe–is equally dangerous for the peoples of all countries and imperils their national and social gains. (*23 CPSU Congress: Results and Prospects,* p. 59.)

This is the real meaning of the Soviet policy of "peaceful coexistence" applied to the focal point of revolution in the world today.

Soviet "Aid" Is a Trojan Horse Used by Imperialism

Now the Soviet Union is giving "aid" to the Vietnamese. The reason for this "aid"–its essence–is to undermine the revolutionary struggle in Vietnam, and to weaken the political struggle around the world in support of the Vietnamese.

Coupled with the "aid" is a call by the Soviet Union to all "socialist" countries for "unity of action." On the face of it, these two steps seem fine. However, Marxist-Leninists cannot simply view the superficial aspects of things but must delve deeper.

Certainly Marxist-Leninists stand for and welcome all genuine expressions of proletarian internationalism. Aid and unity of action designed to help the revolution are to be lauded. But aid and unity of action designed to betray should be rejected.

How can one unite with revisionism? The real unity in this situation is between revisionism and imperialism. No one understands this better than the imperialists. As the *Christian Science Monitor* noted:

What might have been considered another "silly" proposition in the Chinese text–the one referring to a presumed collaboration between Washington and Moscow in sabotaging "the revolutionary struggle of the people of various countries"–is widely accepted by some diplomats here as an obvious truth.

The imperialists welcome Soviet "aid" to Vietnam, for they understand its purpose. They know the Soviets are trying to drag the Vietnamese to the bargaining table to fritter away the revolution in south Vietnam and socialism in the north. U.S. imperialism, which has a clear class outlook, sees all this without trouble. As Drew Pearson wrote:

> For the first time in years in which the State Department has chased down every peace feeler coming out of Hanoi, Moscow, Paris, Algeria or the U.N., it looks like something solid is in the works. Reason for optimism is two-fold. The Russians are really putting the heat on North Vietnam for peace. Since they supply MIG fighter planes, anti-aircraft guns and even train North Vietnamese pilots, their influence can be decisive. . . .
>
> In private talks with Secretary Rusk and Goldberg, Gromyko has appeared highly interested and quite conciliatory. This is why the President took the unusual step of inviting the Soviet Foreign Minister to dinner. . . .

And in the October 24, 1966 column by Marquis Childs appears the following:

> President Johnson sees the Russians, since his conference with Foreign Minister Gromyko, as anxious as the Americans to find a solution for Vietnam. This confirms the cautious optimism expressed by British Foreign Secretary George Brown following his meeting recently with Johnson in Washington.

The U.S. press is replete with instances documenting the treachery of the Soviet leaders. Here are more examples of the Munich-style efforts of the revisionists:

> UPI, Moscow, November 13, 1966–Foy Kohler in his farewell talks with Soviet leaders raised the Vietnam issue. The Soviets indicated to Kohler that an end to the bombing would produce a better atmosphere and possibly lead toward progress in Vietnam.

A *New York Times* article dated November 13, 1966:

> The Soviets were reliably reported to have demanded an end to U.S. bombings in North Vietnam. . . . The Soviets did not specifically mention the issue of withdrawal.

A UPI report from London, dated November 7, 1966:

> Top American and British leaders are becoming increasingly convinced that Russia wants to see the Vietnamese hostilities ended. . . . The Soviet leaders have indicated cautiously . . . they may yet play an active part in a settlement.

Drew Pearson, writing in the second week of November, 1966:

> Lyndon Johnson acting as his own salesman for his peace talks did some selling with Foreign Minister Gromyko. Since then some noises have come out of the Kremlin indicating that Mr. Johnson's sales effort was not in vain . . . a development of recent diplomatic events is a tacit agreement of the U.S. and the U.S.S.R. to pull together for peace.

The November 7, 1966 issue of the *U.S. News and World Report* gave a full roundup of the reaction of U.S. allies to Washington-Moscow collaboration. It began by saying that a "deal" was beginning to be cooked up between the U.S. and the USSR. The deal arose from the fact that "the U.S. wants the tacit aid of Russia in de-escalating the war in Vienam," while the Soviet Union was "interested in shelving the Cold War so that they might concentrate on opposing China."

It cited Western observers as saying that:

> There is growing evidence that the Soviets are moving gingerly to press for a political settlement in Vietnam. . . . The Russians want peace in Vietnam almost as much as the U.S. does because Vietnam was a handicap to its plan for peaceful co-existence with the West. . . .

Despite Vietnam, there is

> a noticeable thaw in the diplomatic climate between the United States and Russia. Cautious probing is under way for agreements. . . . All around the world, in Western Europe, America and Asia—diplomats are signalling that something big is stirring in relations between the U.S. and Russia.

At the recent Bulgarian Party Congress:

> A high Bulgarian official, commenting on the Soviet bloc's attitude on the war, said the main objective was to bring about a peace conference. Pre-conditions, such as a halt in U.S. bombing raids, are of no great importance. . . . He voiced concern over the intransigence of powerful groups in Hanoi, that he said, were

> closer to Peking. . . . The nations of the Soviet bloc must bring pressure on Hanoi to counteract the influence of the pro-Chinese forces (*New York Times,* November 15, 1966).

A week after the Bulgarian Party Congress, the main task of which was the launching of a proposal for the convening of a conference of "communist" parties to attack China and her revolutionary policies, the United States rewarded the Bulgarians for services rendered by improving diplomatic relations, raising its representative in Sofia to the rank of ambassador and permitting a Bulgarian ambassador in Washington.

Clearly, the U.S. and the Soviet Union are trying to entrap the entire revolutionary movement into uniting with imperialism in opposition to the revolution in Vietnam. By a combination of expanded terror by the United States and "aid" with political pressure from the USSR, the Vietnamese are being pushed to make a deal, a deal they have rejected over and over again. What sort of friends of the Vietnamese would enter into this collusion? What kind of friendship is that?

Commenting on the quality of this "friendship," I.F. Stone wrote:

> Let us try to see what is happening in a fresh perspective. What if Japan were again a great military power, and it was bombing a small country in Latin America allied with the United States? What would we think if our Secretary of State paid a friendly visit to the Prime Minister of Japan under such circumstances and began to negotiate favors from him, like landing rights for a New York to Tokyo airline? Imagine how Latin allies under Japanese bombardment would feel if they saw pictures of their supposed American protector in a friendly confabulation with Tokyo? This may help us to see what Johnson has already achieved in his talks with Gromyko. Whatever else comes from them, the moral effect is debasing. Johnson debases the Russians, and he debases the American people. (I.F. Stone's Weekly, October 17, 1966.)

The Soviet Union is trying to subvert the principles of people's war. The Soviet leaders would like the Vietnamese to become dependent on weaponry rather than to rely primarily on their own strength, which has been proved invincible time and time again. The Vietnamese are winning because they have developed the art of people's war to new heights. The forces of revolution grow stronger as U.S. imperialism becomes more isolated. People's war in Vietnam can't be coped with by the U.S. If the revisionists, by increasing the doses of their "aid," were to seduce the Vietnamese into de-emphasizing the main concept of people's war—that it depends in the first place on the efforts of the entire people—this would result in undermining the revolution.

We recognize that the comrades in Vietnam are on the horns of a serious and complex dilemma. Taking "aid" from the revisionists may bring some momentary help in their battle. And it may give the appearance of unity. But the imperialists are not fooled.

To the extent that people are confused about the real nature of revisionism, revisionism is perpetuated. The cleverer tactics of the Soviet leaders have tended to lull and confuse many honest people. After all, they say, "whatever way you cut the cake, the Soviet Union is helping the Vietnamese."

The point is that there have been instances, and there will be more instances, in which different class forces work together in temporary and unstable alliances. But if each case is examined, it will be seen that a progressive aspect dominated the partial unity of purpose. For example, during World War II the Soviet Union was in an alliance with the U.S. Both wanted the defeat of Hitler but each for a different reason. Since the defeat of Hitler was critical for mankind's progress to socialism, there was a basis for partial and temporary unity. And the result was that the socialist revolution did advance.

But in the case of Vietnam, things are quite the opposite. Both the Soviet Union and the U.S. want the revolution crushed now! Therefore, there is no basis for partial and temporary unity with the revisionists. Revolutionaries should not enter into Soviet-inspired alliances. They are traps to thwart the revolution.

It's not really a new trick—this Trojan Horse. Less than two years ago, LBJ himself offered (on behalf of U.S. imperialism) to provide a multi-billion dollar program of "aid" and "development" to North Vietnam. Some might argue that the North Vietnamese leadership should have accepted Johnson's offer ("take aid wherever you can get it!"). But the strings on LBJ's "aid" were too obvious—the Trojan Horse was too transparent.

So the anti-revolutionary forces fixed up a new Trojan-Horse "aid" program and re-routed it this time via Moscow.

But the essence is the same. You can't take increasing "aid" from the revisionists and fight revisionism at the same time. That is the nub of it.

The struggle against revisionism and for unity around Marxist-Leninist principles is the responsibility of all true revolutionaries.

If some comrades believe it's possible to take "aid" from the revisionists "without strings," let them test it. Let *all* who claim to be revolutionary parties publicly call upon the revisionists to renounce their collaboration with U.S. imperialism, their phony test-ban treaty, their constant "peace" conferences, their repeated anti-China activities, their support for U.N.-U.S. aggression in the Congo, Middle East and Latin America, their applause for such reactionaries as Popes John and Paul, their military aid to the counter-revolutionaries in India and Indonesia, and abandon their attempts to deal away the Vietnamese revolution in phony "negotiations." Let *all* who claim to be revolutionary parties *publicly* call on the revisionists to *really* aid the Vietnamese revolution by renouncing their own revisionism. And see how long the revisionists continue their material "aid" to Vietnam—supposedly "without strings." (How long did Soviet material "aid" to China continue when the Chinese party publicly maintained its revolutionary position?)

In a recent interview Fidel Castro unwittingly hammered the point home:

> *Question:* When the U.S. and Russia came to an agreement that the missiles would be removed, did Cuba have any influence by which she might have kept them?
>
> *Castro:* It would have been at the cost of a complete break with the Soviet Union and that would have been really absurd on our part.
>
> *Question:* Wasn't there great popular sentiment in Cuba for keeping the missiles?
>
> *Castro:* All of us were advocates of keeping the missiles in Cuba. Furthermore, the possibility that the Soviet Union would withdraw them was an alternative that had never entered our minds. (*Playboy* magazine, January, 1967, p. 70.)

In our own country, people are learning with whom to make alliances and from whom to accept aid. While the situation isn't as much a military confrontation as in Vietnam, it is quite sharp in the Black Liberation Movement. Haven't Black militants learned what "unity of action" with the liberals means? Haven't they learned what it means just to take money from the liberals? It means, in essence, working with the Establishment. To take their "aid" means to accept their domination. To unite with liberals means to abandon Black Liberation. Liberals do not give "aid" without conditions. Only to the extent that Black Liberation forces rely primarily on their own resources and unite with genuinely radical and revolutionary forces, can they hope to achieve self-determination.

In the final analysis, the Vietnamese comrades may reject Soviet "aid." They may characterize Soviet "aid" and its so-called "unity" for what it is. This would be a sharp blow to revisionism. It would demonstrate that the road to victory is reliance on the strength of the masses coupled with genuine aid from really revolutionary forces.

Of late, some previously anti-revisionist parties have attacked the Chinese for being opposed to the notion of unity with revisionism. The Chinese party has been called "dogmatic and sectarian" for this. We believe that the Japanese and north Korean parties have been sucked in by the revisionist slogan "unity in action." They define their "independence" from the Chinese party by declaring that they are ready to work with the revisionists. Inasmuch as they were always organizationally independent, this new-found cry has a false ring.

The Koreans in particular chastise the Chinese for not doing more in Vietnam. They say the socialist countries ought to be sending troops to Vietnam. But the Chinese have made it clear that if the Vietnamese ask for more aid or men, they will supply them. Certainly U.S. imperialism remembers how the Chinese honored their commitments in the Korean War, if the Koreans have temporarily forgotten.

If the Korean party leaders really believe that the revisionists want to mend their ways and conduct a real struggle against U.S. imperialism, in particular against its aggression in Vietnam, then why don't the Korean party leaders address their statements to the revisionists? Why don't they call upon the revisionists to repudiate their policies of collaboration with U.S. imperialism, to utilize their political, economic and military power throughout the world to expose, isolate and defeat U.S. imperialism? No one is tying the hands of the revisionists if they are really anxious to build a genuine struggle against U.S. imperialism.

We believe the proposal to send volunteers to Vietnam now, as advocated by the Koreans and Cubans, is a bluff. Why don't the Koreans send troops? Who stops them? (Or why don't they make a start by preventing the South Korean puppet troops from being sent to Vietnam?) The truth of the matter is that the Vietnamese haven't asked for troops and don't want them now. The people of Vietnam are quite a match for U.S. imperialism.

The sight of the cream of U.S. armed strength being ground up by people's war in Vietnam is the greatest political lesson in the world today. It proves that oppressed peoples can take on imperialism and defeat it by relying primarily on their own efforts—even in a war.

This lesson exposes the arguments of U.S. pacifists and revisionists who use the "horrors of war" to urge phony negotiations with the U.S. aggressors—just another way of saying "lay down your arms and abandon the revolution."

What we believe is the problem with parties like the Korean and Japanese (and with many elements within revolutionary movements around the world) is their unclear estimate of revisionism. Is it counter-revolutionary or isn't it? A group of students at the University of California in Berkeley recently indicated that even non-communist radicals are becoming more and more alarmed by the revisionist position. In a leaflet calling on students to picket the First Secretary of the Soviet Embassy (who was speaking in Berkeley), they declared:

> Moscow tilts Westward. This news disturbs us. We fear that the "Soviet tilt" could not come at a worse time. . . . By tilting towards the U.S. at this time, the Soviet Union encourages the most adventurist and militaristic U.S. leaders. . . . We are concerned that actions and statements of the Soviet Union give U.S. policymakers the view that the Soviet Union is prepared to sell-out China and Vietnam for a big-power division of the world into "spheres of influence."

We hope that parties like the Korean and Japanese will withdraw from the anti-China campaign which, in its essence, is a campaign for revisionism and against revolution.

Success for China's Cultural Revolution Is a Defeat for Imperialism

The Communist Party of China recognizes the serious counter-revolutionary efforts of U.S. imperialism and its revisionist allies, and is preparing itself and the world revolutionary movement to fight back and win.

There are similarities between this preparation and the period in which the Soviet Union prepared itself politically, ideologically, economically, and militarily to defeat Hitlerism. If the Soviet Union had not taken stern measures in the face of the greatest imperialist danger of that time, it would have been smashed. Instead, the greatest menace to the world, up to that point in history, was defeated. But the Chinese communists are going one big step further than the Soviets.

Revisionism received a qualitative boost at the 20th Party Congress of the S.U. It was at this Congress that the process of restoration made the "great leap." However, the roots of revisionism in the Soviet Union go deep. The ideological transformation of the masses didn't nearly keep abreast of the material development of Soviet society. Given the enormous difficulties of a backward country surrounded and under continuous attack by world imperialism, and a lack of previous socialist experience to draw from, the Soviets placed a one-sided emphasis on material development.

Stalin recognized the rightist danger and its consequences early. At a speech to a Plenum of the Moscow Party Committee in 1938 he said:

> A victory of the right deviation in our party would mean an enormous accession of strength to the capitalist elements in our country. And what does this mean? It means weakening the proletarian dictatorship and multiplying the chances for the restoration of capitalism. . . Hence, a victory of the right deviation in our party would add to the conditions necessary for the restoration of capitalism in our country.

However, in fighting the rightist danger the stress was put on eliminating the small commodity producers (soil for capitalist ideas) and replacing them with new advanced techniques. Ideological struggle was limited even within the party, and certainly not developed to transform the millions.

The Chinese communists are making a thorough-going effort to transform the thinking and develop the ideology of hundreds of millions of people. Under the leadership of the Communist Party of China, led by Mao Tse-tung, the Chinese people are demonstrating that people determine the course of history.

The CPC is not making material incentives the primary motivation for the transformation of China's masses. It is really elevating ideas, man's dialectical and creative thought, into an invincible force. And this force, the revolutionary ideology of hundreds of millions of people, is becoming the key force in shaping the future as these people join in active battle to carry the revolution through to the end.

It is in this struggle that Mao and the Chinese party are implementing the essence of Leninism. The revisionists claim that the cultural revolution is anti-Leninist. They claim that it is perverting and making a mockery of Leninism. From the outset, Lenin and Stalin warned about the possibilities of capitalist restoration. They warned that the class struggle goes on fiercely long after the smoke of revolution has died down.

Lenin wrote:

> The abolition of classes is a matter of long, difficult, stubborn *class struggle* which, after the overthrow of the power of capital, *after* the destruction of the bourgeois state, *after* the establishment of the dictatorship of the proletariat, does not *disappear* (as the vulgar people of the old socialism and of the old Social-Democracy imagine), but only changes its forms and in many respects grows fiercer still.
>
> The proletariat must maintain its power, strengthen its organizing influence, neutralize those sections which are afraid of parting company with the bourgeoisie and too hesitatingly follow the proletariat, by waging the class struggle against the resistance of the bourgeoisie, against conservatism, routine, indecision, and the waverings of the petty bourgeoisie. It must consolidate the new discipline, the comradely discipline of the toilers, their firm ties with the proletariat, their rallying around the proletariat, this new discipline, the new basis of social ties, which is replacing the feudal discipline of the medieval ages, the discipline of starvation, the discipline of "free" wage slavery under capitalism.
>
> In order to abolish the classes a period of the dictatorship of one class is necessary, namely, of the oppressed class which is capable not only of overthrowing the exploiters, not only of ruthlessly suppressing their resistance, but also of breaking with the entire bourgeois democratic ideology, with all the philistine phrases about freedom and equality in general (in fact, as Marx has long ago pointed out, these phrases mean the "freedom and equality" of the *commodity owners,* the "freedom and equality" of *the capitalists. . . .* (V.I. Lenin, *Collected Works,* Russian Edition, Vol. XXIV, pp. 314-315.)

The strength of the overthrown bourgeoisie rests in the fact that:

> . . . for a long time after the revolution the exploiters inevitably continue to enjoy a number of great practical advantages: they still have money (since it is impossible to abolish money all at once), some movable property—often fairly considerable; they still have various connections, habits of organization and management, superior education, close connections with the higher technical personnel (who live and think like the bourgeoisie), incomparably greater experience in the art of war (this is very important) and so on, and so forth. (V.I. Lenin, *Selected Works,* Vol. VII, p. 140.)

Further strength of the overthrown exploiting class lies

> in the *force of habit,* in the strength of *small-scale production.* For unfortunately, there is still very, very much of small-scale production left in the world, and small-scale production *engenders* capitalism and the bourgeoisie continuously, daily, hourly, spontaneously, and on a mass scale; . . .
>
> . . . the abolition of classes means not only driving out the landlords and capitalists—that we accomplished with comparative ease; it means also *getting rid of the small commodity producers,* and they *cannot be driven out,* they cannot be crushed, we must *live in harmony* with them; they can (and must) be remoulded and re-educated only by very prolonged, slow, cautious organizational work (V.I. Lenin, *Selected Works,* Vol. X, pp. 60 and 83).

Thus, Lenin wrote:

> The dictatorship of the proletariat is a most determined and most ruthless war waged by the new class against a *more powerful* enemy, the bourgeoisie, whose resistance is increased *tenfold* by its overthrow . . . the dictatorship of the proletariat is a persistent struggle—sanguinary and bloodless, violent and peaceful, military and economic, educational and administrative—against the forces and traditions of the old society. (V.I. Lenin, *Selected Works,* Vol. X, pp. 60 and 84.)

China has seen the Soviet experience. The Chinese have witnessed the persistence of bourgeois ideas in many sections of their own population, especially among the intellectuals. They have seen that the institutions of higher education have, to a great degree, remained as training grounds for the children of the old middle and upper classes. Until recently, 50 per cent of the students at universities were of non-proletarian origin. To allow this to continue would indeed give great help to U.S. imperialism's cherished hopes that capitalist restoration will become possible after the death of the original revolutionary leaders. U.S. imperialism bases its hopes for restoration (or collaboration in the event of armed struggle) on the youth. Imperialism feels that the youth, who have not gone through actual revolutionary struggle, are good targets for bourgeois ideology.

The Chinese have also seen the dry rot of intellectual corruption in Hungary and Poland burst into the flames of counter-revolution. They see its current insidious effects. A recent article in the *New York Times* (November 7, 1966) showed the sickening effect of revisionism on the youth of a so-called socialist country:

> POLISH STUDENTS ADMIRE KENNEDY
> LATE PRESIDENT FIRST CHOICE IN POLL TO NAME HERO
>
> JFK was the choice of a great majority of students at the Cracow Metallurgy and Mining Academy, an advanced technical college, when asked to name their hero.
>
> The inquiry was not a banal popularity poll but part of a sounding of the state of political and ideological awareness of Poland's future elite. . . . Only 45 per cent of 734 first-year students gave correct answers about the political organization of Poland, whereas 80 per cent were informed as to the main political parties in the United States.
>
> Not only did President Kennedy head the list of "heroes," but no Pole placed among the first five. Following the late President were Yuri Gagarin, first man in space, President de Gaulle, Pope John XXIII and Karl Marx.
>
> On the other hand 18 students were unable to say what job Mr. Gomulka had, and two gave wrong answers. 43 did not know that Edward Ochab was President of Poland, and 24 others said he held a different post.

Communist Party officials felt that this was a "serious matter." In the same article, further indications of the general corruption in a revisionist-controlled state are given:

> Another problem that is provoking grave misgivings among Communist leaders is the progressive transformation of the party from a body held together by principles and ideals to an association of freeloaders and careerists. The same is true of student organizations, according to *Zyzie Literackie,* the literary weekly that took the poll. The article accused the leadership of the Union of Polish Students at an unidentified college of devoting its efforts to forming cliques, arranging agreeable free vacation trips for themselves and their girl friends, and above all, "impudent belittling" of learning.

These manifestations of revisionism are characteristic of all the countries dominated by the counter-revolutionaries. And just as their imperialist friends wail about the degeneration of their youth and are powerless to rectify it, so too the revisionists cry bitterly and fruitlessly. The degeneration to careerism and perversion is the logical consequence of bourgeois ideology.

Should the Chinese Communist Party sit by and twiddle its thumbs and allow China's youth to become corrupted in the guise of "liberating man's inner nature"? This corruption is not "liberating" but is one of the oldest enslavements known to man. The Chinese know that the socialist development of youth requires the destruction of individualism, of egoism, and the fostering of an unselfish approach to society. It means the end of "what's-in-it-for-me?" and the substitution of "what can I do to build socialism and make myself better in the process?" This is truly liberating. This would unleash real creativity, the real flowering of the individual and the actual development of millions of youth into an invincible revolutionary force.

Knowing that the Soviet Union has betrayed the cause of revolution in Vietnam and everywhere else; knowing that the Soviet Union and the United States are sharpening their ideological and military knives to destroy China, should not the Chinese move vigorously to defeat revisionist elements in their own ranks? Should not the Chinese prepare themselves to rely fully on their own resources? Or should they make themselves dependent on aid from revisionism? We say no! To lay themselves open to revisionism would guarantee the defeat of China, the defeat of the bulwark of world revolution.

Edgar Snow wrote in the July 30, 1966 issue of the *New Republic*:

> Apart from revamping the economy to devote a major section to defense industry, great questions face Peking's leadership. What would be the character of China's military strategy against the United States? If war was unavoidable, would it not be prudent to mend fences with Russia? China's own defenses were not adequate to protect her urban industrial bases against heavy American air attack. What would be Russia's price for providing an air defense umbrella? To submit to Moscow and revisionism was unthinkable; to subject to American destruction the results of nearly two decades of sacrifice to modernize China was also unthinkable. Yet both had to be thought through.
>
> Acceptance of the Russian line would mean a compromise

> in Vietnam which would leave the United States firmly planted in Southeast Asia. If Vietnam were surrendered, why not Taiwan? And if Taiwan were abandoned why not concede American dominance in general, accept a secondary role for China, and also seek aid from the United States, like India. This reverse view of the dominoes collapsing inward on China could lead to the conclusion that capitulation to Russian pressure was synonymous with capitulation to the United States, abandonment of the revolution as well as vital national interests: and suicide for the Chinese party leadership. . . .
>
> Marshal Lin Piao has emerged as the spokesman for the dominant view, which simply invokes all the experience of the Chinese revolutionary wars to prove Mao's old thesis, man is more important than weapons; the only kind of war China could fight and win, alone, is a protracted war dependent essentially on manpower, space, and resolute social revolutionary leadership based on unrevised Marxism-Leninism. The presence of large American armies in Asia makes Mao's kind of war possible, and the more Americans the better. China would suffer, there could be no doubt about that, but there could also be no doubt (according to Lin) about the ultimate victory.

In China the long range effort to fight the revolution through to the end is called "The Great Proletarian Cultural Revolution." This is a decisive class struggle. As Chou En-lai explained:

> After the socialist revolution on the economic front had been basically completed the socialist revolution on political and ideological fronts was started. This revolution in its present stage of development has become the dynamic mass movement of the great proletarian cultural revolution which has stirred up the whole of society and in which hundreds of millions of people are consciously taking part. (*New York Times,* December 6, 1966.)

As the objective situation is sharpening, class sides become more distinct. Erroneous viewpoints, which might have been dealt with in a less sharp manner under different conditions, must now be dealt with quickly, thoroughly, and sharply. Now they are a dire threat to the Chinese people's ability to withstand the onrushing efforts of revisionism and imperialism, whose new "grand alliance" waits for no one. This struggle is no Sunday picnic.

In the Chinese cultural revolution, the main criteria are deeds, not words.

> What counts above all in their eyes is the conduct of one's daily life. A good communist is someone who lives in complete austerity and who on all occasions shoulders the heaviest burden.

Every official, every intellectual, who takes advantage of his position to make his life easier immediately unveils his "revisionist nature." (K.S. Karol, *New Statesman,* September 9, 1966.)

The defeat of revisionism in China involves the future of the entire world. Upon that defeat depends the freedom of hundreds of millions of workers to live as free men in a socialist state. They are fighting in China to eliminate the class base from which a return to private accumulation of society's wealth could spring because, as K. S. Karol points out, "China, over and above Vietnam, remains the main target of American aggression, and by virtue of this fact alone, she is the vanguard of the resistance to the Pax Americana."

The imperialists and revisionists spread mountains of lies about the Cultural Revolution. They know it is aimed at them from a class point of view and they are trying to defeat it at all costs.

When have the revisionists and imperialists ever based themselves on the truth? Are they really concerned about the people of China? Imperialism still prattles about the "good old China" where millions of people died from hunger, where children were sold into prostitution and any imperialist could make a buck. They openly discuss plans to "bomb them back into the Stone Age."

Revisionists and imperialists spout about their love of the Chinese masses. But the only love they have is for their lost opportunities to oppress and exploit them. In fact, the revisionists have contempt for and fear of the Chinese masses. They hate the Chinese Communist Party and its great leader Mao Tse-tung. Their hate is born of the fear that the Chinese Communist Party and people are the most powerful revolutionary force in the world, the chief obstacle to carving up the world into "spheres of influence."

All revolutionaries have a vital stake in the outcome of the Cultural Revolution. 700,000,000 Chinese steeped in revolutionary ideology would be an invincible force. It would be the first time that Marxism-Leninism became the ideology of an entire population. Heretofore, ideology was the "property" of only a few, the special province of intellectuals and a relatively few party leaders. A powerful revolutionary China is a tremendous boost to the emerging forces of revolution all over the world. Their example of proletarian self-reliance, ideologically and materially, is an inspiration to all. We wish the Cultural Revolution every success. Its every success is a key defeat for U.S. imperialism and modern revisionism. We have great confidence that by utilizing the thought of Mao Tse-tung the experienced and tested CPC will succeed in its new historic endeavor.

The thought of Mao Tse-tung is the summarization of the experiences of the Chinese revolution. It points the way for the revolutionary process everywhere.

Therefore, the Cultural Revolution assumes historic proportions. The development of the world revolutionary movement will be immeasurably strengthened by its success.

Defeating Revisionism Internationally Is the Basis for Revolutionary Advance

The fight against revisionism must be one of the main tasks in the international communist movement. The history of the emergence of Marxism-Leninism is a history of consistent battle against all deviation. Even though Marxism-Leninism is now a minority position in the international movement, it will eventually triumph. Marxism-Leninism is invincible because it is in accord with the aspirations of the people. Revisionism, like imperialism, runs counter to the tide of history. The danger of modern revisionism is great. We cannot simply take the position that Marxism-Leninism is true and therefore it will all come out right in the end. Revisionism can only be defeated by struggle based on reality. Some of the newer features that make the struggle against revisionism difficult and complex are:

(1) Today a series of states is held in the grip of the revisionists. This is the first time in history that revisionism holds state power.

(2) The revisionists have covered up their tracks considerably. They no longer build open platforms as the Bernsteins and Kautskys did. Everything they say and do is in the name of Lenin. They claim they are bringing Leninism up to date. As they move to greater defeats they may well claim that they are bringing Stalin up to date.

(3) They play upon the fears of the world's people because of the advent of atomic weapons. Instead of demonstrating that peace can only be secured through sharpening the class struggle, they resort to the deceit of bourgeois pacifism. They try to terrorize and blackmail people to keep them from aspiring to revolution.

Because of the spread of revisionism, the imperialists have been given some short-term tactical advantages. Revisionism in power in the Soviet Union and in other countries means defeats for the international working class. Revisionism prolongs the fight against imperialism. Specific battles against imperialism will be successful to the extent they overcome revisionism. It is important for all revolutionaries to learn from defeats as well as successes. Unless revolutionary forces learn from their errors they will not be able to exploit the generally favorable conditions for revolution.

Revisionism cannot be underestimated. In the long run it will be smashed. In the short run it can cause considerable harm. What makes Marxism-Leninism powerful is the ability to learn from failure and change. Imperialism cannot do this. At best it can make tactical, but never strategic, changes. Sometimes imperialism is so pragmatic and subjective that it can't make even tactical adjustments.

History has shown that Marxism-Leninism has emerged stronger from each major struggle with revisionism. But the struggle against revisionism isn't won on the pages of a magazine, but in life! Real struggles have to be carried on against the enemy. His forces must be sapped until he can be defeated.

Our party, like scores of groups around the world, has sprung up to carry forward the banner of revolution. All these groups will be judged by their ability to wage struggles with the enemy and win. Only those that learn over a long period of time to apply Marxism-Leninism to their particular circumstances will earn the confidence of the people and stand the test of life.

It is useful to look at Stalin's description of revisionism in the Second International. Revisionists appeared to have dominated the movement.

> I said above that between Marx and Engels on the one hand and Lenin on the other lay a whole period of domination by the opportunism of the Second International. To be more precise, I must add that it was not so much a question of the formal as of the actual domination of opportunism. Formally, the Second International was headed by "orthodox" Marxists like Kautsky and others. Actually, however, its fundamental work followed the line of opportunism. Because of their petty-bourgeois adaptable nature, the opportunists adapted themselves to the bourgeoisie; as for the "orthodox" they adapted themselves to the opportunists in order to "maintain unity" with the latter, to maintain "peace within

> the Party"! As a result, opportunism dominated, because the links between the policy of the bourgeoisie and the policy of the "orthodox" were joined.
>
> It was a period of relatively peaceful development of capitalism, a pre-war period so to speak, when the disastrous contradictions of imperialism have not yet so obviously revealed themselves, when economic strikes and trade unions developed more or less "normally," when in the electoral struggles and parliamentary fractions "dizzy" successes were exalted to the skies, and when it was hoped to "kill" capitalism by legal means. In other words, it was a period when the parties of the Second International were becoming gross and stodgy, and no longer wanted to think seriously about revolution, the dictatorship of the proletariat and the revolutionary training of the masses.
>
> Instead of a coherent revolutionary theory, they propounded contradictory theoretical postulates, fragments of theory isolated from the actual revolutionary struggle of the masses, and which had been transformed into threadbare dogmas. For the sake of appearances they always, of course, referred to the theory of Marx, but only to rob it of its living revolutionary spirit.
>
> Instead of a revolutionary policy there was effete philistinism, practical politics, parliamentary diplomacy and parliamentary scheming. For the sake of appearances, of course, "revolutionary" resolutions and slogans were passed only to be pigeon-holed.
>
> Instead of educating and teaching the Party true revolutionary tactics from a study of its own mistakes, we find a studied evasion of thorny questions, which were glossed over and veiled. In order to keep up appearances they were not averse to talking about these awkward questions, only to wind up with some sort of "elastic" resolution.
>
> Such were the features, the methods of work and the armoury of the Second International. (J.V. Stalin, *Foundations of Leninism.*)

Despite the opportunism in the Second International the mighty communist movement was born.

Today, even though Marxism-Leninism is not the majority in the old communist movement, Marxism-Leninism is a much more powerful force throughout the world than in Lenin's time. It is becoming the dominant trend in all the newly-emerging revolutionary forces, and for all the revolutionary peoples of the world. In the final analysis this is more important than whether or not revisionism will be defeated within the old C.P.'s.

Also, the current struggle against modern revisionism, led by the Communist Party of China, has raised Marxist thought to new heights. The thought of Mao Tse-tung is proving invaluable to revolutionaries all over the world. In this debate revisionism is being challenged to a degree that it was never challenged before.

A far more fundamental approach is being taken by millions, *not just a few*. And backing up this titanic struggle is the powerful Chinese Communist Party which gives the revolutionary movement a courageous example.

Only the development of a new, powerful, united revolutionary movement can halt the increasing possibility of World War III. Revisionism has increased the danger of World War III and has made a vast Asian war probable! Revisionism has split the solid front of struggle against U.S. imperialism. The split has only emboldened U.S. imperialism. It is true that only a world communist movement united around a revolutionary line, and developing the widest front against U.S. imperialism, might be powerful enough to prevent World War III.

But whatever difficulties revisionism has imposed on the revolutionary movement, and despite the apparent strength of imperialism, great possibilities exist for waging varied revolutionary actions. The political and economic base of imperialism is dwindling as contradictions upon contradictions arise and sharpen.

Combat Revisionism Within the Progressive Labor Party

It would be most naïve of us not to recognize the danger of revisionism in our party. We function in the center of the strongest imperialist power in the world. The ideological pressures on us are extremely strong. The ruling class has a million and one ways of undermining our commitment to Marxism-Leninism. Corruption is a big aspect of American life. We all bring some into the party. Therefore our efforts have to be complete and not partial. Only the most diligent exemplary efforts can maintain our initial positive efforts.

Even though we have embarked on a more consistent educational program the results are still limited. It will take a long hard effort for our study to bear fruit. We must learn how to overcome laziness in thought. After all, this is a bourgeois trait. Studying by rote, instead of by struggle and practice, is a very dangerous tendency in our party. It limits our ability to apply universally true Marxist-Leninist ideas to the conditions in which we are working. The mere recital and memorization of "truth" leads only to passivity on our part and "leftist" errors. It prevents us from struggling in a constructive and creative way and winning over the people with whom we are working.

Moreover, the object of our study must be to learn Marxism-Leninism. As our struggles develop, the Marxist classics will take on a new and more profound meaning. They will become far more relevant and will be invaluable in guiding our work. We must time and time again study, restudy, think and rethink so as to understand the fundamental question of the dictatorship of the proletariat. Imperialism has been partially successful in undermining communists' understanding of this valid and essential concept. In our country, because of the non-class ideas about democracy, much more work and study must be done to solidify ourselves, and be able to win others to this idea.

The main manifestation of revisionism inside our party at the present time is the continued isolation of too many members from the working people. We have made some progress here in recent months, but not enough.

It's important to recognize this, because we usually view isolation simply as a sectarian or "leftist" error—which it is—but we seldom attack it as a reflection of revisionism. Yet revisionism is fundamentally the substitution of individual bourgeois interests for the interests of the working class, and that is precisely what happens when members refuse to join the people. Examples are numerous in every area of work:

One member spends his time running around from one internal meeting to another, usually giving advice, so he is "too busy" to get a job. Another member manages to get a job but manages also to quit or get fired from each job after no more than two months. Another member finally manages to hold a job for six months but spends all his free time getting as far away from his fellow-workers as possible. Another member does pretty good political work on his job, but when his wife—who is doing community work with workers in the neighborhood—asks him to come to a party at the home of a local tenant, he refuses, saying he would rather spend his Saturday nights at another party with students. Among student members the idea of a worker-student alliance is advocated on paper, but to get some people to actually go out and meet the workers is like pulling teeth. Still other members know workers (either on the job or in the community) but make no real effort to become friends, and are unable to have political discussions with them except in the most patronizing and missionary manner.

Essentially what these members–most of whom come from middle-class backgrounds–are saying is that working people are a drag. You have to spend time with them (because that's the line) but mainly others should do it. ("As for me, I agree but I'm too busy.") It comes down to: spend time with workers if you have to–but spend as little time as you have to. On paper, they say the working class must lead the revolution, etc., but their lives say they don't really give a damn about working people. One who is not willing to devote a Saturday night to workers is hardly likely to devote his whole life.

These people really wish that some way could be found to make the revolution without bothering with the working class. And after the revolution, if they do not change their ideology, these people would be the first to abandon the working class.

That is revisionism. It takes the form of "leftism" in day-to-day work. It not only comes from a bourgeois outlook, it leads (through continuing isolation from the working class) to a more bourgeois outlook. If it is not fiercely opposed and overcome by our party, our party will never lead the working class. And no matter what these members might secretly wish, socialism cannot be achieved without the leadership of the working class.

Of course, there are other examples of revisionism, mentioned above, and at different stages of development one or another of these might be the main danger to our party's work. (It's possible, for example, to have a party whose members have close ties among the working class yet which follows a reformist, "peaceful struggle," line or some other revisionist policy.) But at this stage, we must fight isolation.

Because of the tactical strength of U.S. imperialism we must develop an impregnable, unshakable class position. The revolution will succeed in this country only to the degree that it has a base among large sections of the working class. Bourgeois ideology is particularly strong when it comes to undermining confidence in the working class. The enemy likes nothing better than to hear radicals talk about the "corrupt workers," and to hear self-professed "independent" socialists wail about the "utter hopelessness of white workers." The United States is a modern industrial country. It has millions of workers. Without them we can throw in the towel.

It's funny how the ruling class is becoming less smug about the ability of their current labor lieutenants to keep the workers in line. Hence the spate of articles in *Life, Fortune* and other magazines promoting new "leaders" better able to mislead workers. In this sense Gus Hall's apparent idiocy that "every honest trade union leader will welcome our help in mobilizing and educating his members—if he feels it is not directed against him" (*Labor, Key Force,* Gus Hall, p. 31) takes on a real and ominous meaning.

Our party must become the party of the working class in every sense. We have made progress in this effort. Obviously, we have a long way to go.

We can best measure our efforts to combat revisionism by measuring the results of our work. Are we growing in our ability to bring people into struggle with imperialism? Are we developing a base among key sections of the people for the party and its line? Do we fight to do this in a serious way? Do non-party forces with whom we work view us as serious in our outlook? Have we overcome pragmatism in our work? Do we have a long-range perspective? Is our performance the best we can do? Are we self-critical about our work, or are we content and satisfied with everything? Is the party the most important thing in our lives? Is the party, the working class, the fight for revolutionary socialism the main thing in all that we think, in all that we do? We believe that on all those matters we are learning to improve and have improved. But we are far from satisfied. No partial effort can defeat U.S. imperialism.

U.S. imperialism and revisionism are determined to destroy the revolutionary process. They hate revolution. They hate revolutionaries. History past and recent has shown us their hatred–the hundreds of freedom fighters murdered in our country, the hundreds of thousands of Indonesians, the hundreds of thousands of Vietnamese–all murdered by imperialism and its junior partner, modern revisionism. Do we ardently hate them? Can we match them in determination to win our class goals? We must if we want to win.

To win means to defeat revisionism. Revisionism is imperialist ideology in our midst to prevent our victory. The enemy will never let up, so long as he has a breath in him. Nor can we!

Criticism and Self-Criticism

JUNE 1966

Deepening Roots

The seed of revolution has been sown again in our land, and our Party can feel some sense of achievement in the part we have taken in this planting. We are still young and small but we have made a strong start. We have done more than scratch the shiny surface of the U.S. ruling class; we have begun to rip away its mask, to expose its ugliness—and to get under its skin.

It's not for nothing the ruling class has decided to make our Party its number one target in the U.S. In a relatively few months, we have set up a national communist party with a wise and firm foundation of friends, readers, supporters and members among working people, black and white, as well as among the students, in the forefront of today's battles.

Also, we have begun to overcome the main internal weaknesses which had been holding us back. First and foremost we have corrected certain sectarian policies which had isolated us from too many people and organizations in the growing people's movement against the war, slum conditions, high prices, wage-squeezing and other fat-profit Government policies. We know now that in our early stages we underemphasized united front work, neglected the labor movement, and expected too much too soon. Since our founding convention a year ago we have begun to combine with large numbers of people and to take united action with many groups, while maintaining and advancing our Marxist-Leninist principles and actually expanding our advocacy of socialist revolution.

To some extent our early sectarianism was inevitable as we fought to avoid the right-opportunist errors of the old Communist Party which had followed (and still does, if anyone cares) the "three secrets" policy: keep the Party a secret (except from the FBI), keep the activities a secret (even from Party members), and keep revolution and socialism a secret (from the masses of people).

Our members had to fight hard to put forward publicly the principles of socialist revolution. We had to let people know what communism really means, that yes, there is a way finally to solve our problems–socialism; and that a Party exists which is not afraid to fight for that solution. We had to, and still must struggle to make the idea of revolution popular.

It's not surprising, then, that in our early activities many members tended to go overboard and ignore or even reject people and groups who were not yet ready to join us. This early sectarianism hurt us, and it's a tribute to our correct overall political line, and to the energetic, youthful spirit of our members, that we were able to attract so many young radicals, in spite of this weakness.

Sectarianism and isolation remain problems for us today, but they are not primarily problems of policy. On the whole we have corrected our policy, and our significant influence in the current anti-imperialist upsurge reflects this change.

At the same time, we have begun to conquer the lack of seriousness which once thrived in our ranks. Here, the enemy has been most helpful. The arrests, subpoenas and physical attacks on us have made every member think twice about why he is sticking with this Party, and understand that the revolution is not to be achieved quickly, but through *a lifetime of struggle,* continuing, in new forms, even after the working class takes power. Some have chosen to leave, of course, but those who remain are stronger for it.

Here, too, our early policy was wrong, dominated by liberalism and carelessness in recruiting new members. We often placed quantity above quality. Perhaps this, too, was inevitable at the outset. Also, we didn't always sit down and explain to people what they were getting themselves into when they join a communist party, what the risks are, the long-range commitment that is a necessary part of the revolutionary ideology. We even had cases where young people with virtually no understanding of what was happening were brought into a club and made voting members.

We have learned from these errors, and changed our membership policy. In general, our members and leaders have been forced to begin thinking about long-term strategy both for their own lives and the life and growth of the Party.

As a result, we can already see an increase in both the quantity and quality of our work, our membership, and our Marxist-Leninist study. Last summer's cadre school was a big step up this hill. Naturally, there remain a few who still have their heads in the clouds, who are still playing at revolution, but we can rely on the ruling class to thump them down to earth.

These successes are only the beginning, and it is easy enough to say that none of the changes has yet gone far enough. But an honest evaluation of our recent growth must emphasize our success and achievement. Our Party has stood like a young sapling in a windstorm of howling attacks, sometimes swaying a little but holding firm and deepening its roots as it grows.

Our Main Obstacle Today

We cannot, of course, just sit and admire ourselves in the mirror of achievement. As the situation sharpens we must ask ourselves, will we be prepared? As we expand our circle of friends and relations, will we be able to avoid the opportunist "Hamlin" approach of trailing after every reformist pie-eyed piper in town? And will we at the same time avoid sectarian isolation? Will we continue to struggle as we unite with other people and groups? Will we know how to struggle? *Are we perfect or can we improve our work?*

If we ask this question, and ask it again and again every day in every way then we are halfway improved already. If we do not ask the question, then we will surely become smug and complacent and flabby, and we might as well join Gus Hall and Norman Thomas.

To improve our work means, first, to look for the main weakness or obstacle to our progress. We should not look far. Those who run to Palomar to scan the skies in search of dangers may see many interesting phenomena but they will miss the main point. "It is not in our stars, but in ourselves . . ." that the main contradiction, and the main obstacle to our continued success, lies. The main cause of failure—like the main cause of success—is contained within any revolutionary party or movement, not outside it. Those, like the old C.P., who blame the ruling class for their failure are only diverting attention from their own weaknesses or betrayals. Of course, every party must reckon with the real conditions of life around it, but the party's internal strength or weakness will determine how well it reckons.

Our Party's main obstacle is the influence and ideology of bourgeois society within our ranks. Our most decisive struggle today is between revolutionary and bourgeois ideology, and particularly between revolutionary morality and bourgeois individualism, between complete dedication to the working class and middle-class self-interest, which is the moral and material basis of modern revisionism.

The existence of bourgeois ideas, attitudes and habits within our ranks is hardly astonishing. At this early stage, our Party, like most new-born revolutionary parties, has a large percentage of intellectuals and members of middle-class background. Moreover, every revolutionary party has internal struggle reflecting the class struggle in the society around. And the society around us in this case causes some pretty weird reflections.

The U.S. capitalist class is not only the richest, most powerful ruling class in history, it is also the most corrupt, most brutal, most degenerate and most egoistic; and the ruling class tries to impose its own morality on the whole of society. It's not just "getting and spending" that is too much with us. Books, newspapers, comics, teachers, philosophers, politicians, psychiatrists, movies, and especially television all give subtle daily indoctrination in the basic elements of capitalist, and fascist, morality: Might-makes-right (the tough guy is the good guy) and Me-before-every-one-else ("Don't trust nobody").

From our first breath we breathe this stuff. How could we possibly be completely free from it? The history of the left in the U.S. shows one group after another surrendering to this bourgeois self-interest, first slowly, then completely abandoning the difficult struggle against the ruling class and ending up in the comfort-corner of class collaboration.

Yet it need not always be so. The bourgeois ideology in our ranks can be a good thing, too. If we recognize and know how to deal with it, we can grow stronger as a result of having purged it away. This experience can be a valuable lesson for the future. When the working class takes power, bourgeois influences do not automatically disappear, as we can see by looking at the countries ruled by revisionist parties. If internal contradictions are mishandled in a socialist country the result may be disastrous, as we can see by looking at these same countries.

Once we recognize that bourgeois influences are inevitable in our ranks, then the whole question becomes how do these influences crop up, and how should we handle them. If we fail to handle correctly the problem of bourgeois ideology, then the Party itself, and particularly the leadership, must accept responsibility for the consequences. We cannot blame it on society.

> The source of such incorrect ideas in the Party organization lies, of course, in the fact that its basic units are composed largely of . . . elements of petty-bourgeois origin: yet the failure of the Party's leading bodies to wage a concerted and determined struggle against the incorrect ideas and to educate the members in the Party's correct line is also an important cause of their existence and growth.
> (Mao Tse-tung, "On Correcting Mistaken Ideas in the Party," Dec. 1929, *Selected Military Writings,* p. 51.)

Overcoming these ideological obstacles is not easy. New revolutionary forces all around the world are currently discovering that setting up a new organization is only the first step in building a new communist party.

> To break politically is not so difficult, for the disasters into which modern revisionism is leading the workers are not so difficult to see. That something different is needed is fairly obvious. But the problems of fundamentally altering our ideology and building not only a new organization but an organization on entirely different lines are far more difficult. (E. F. Hill, Chairman of the Australian Communist Party, Marxist-Leninist, *Looking Backward, Looking Forward,* p. 2.)

The ideological struggle is the primary struggle. Its outcome, in the long run, determines the political line and the organizational form. This struggle includes understanding and developing the ideology of the working class as well as battling against bourgeois ideology.

At the same time, we must know how to conduct this struggle. Here, it is particularly important to distinguish between antagonistic and non-antagonistic struggle; we want to wipe out antagonistic bourgeois ideas and habits, not the individuals who display, often unknowingly and usually without antagonism, those ideas and habits.

But before discussing how to deal with the problem, let us look more closely at the problem itself.

Bourgeois Individualism

The corrupt influence of capitalist morality crops up in many ways. The contradiction between this influence and our Party's collective, revolutionary spirit and goals takes many forms.

Sometimes there will be an open ideological dispute between two lines. A few of our members wanted to support Johnson against Goldwater in the last elections, arguing that Goldwater would expand the war, bomb north Vietnam, draft hundreds of thousands of U.S. boys, and other such things. In the course of discussions this position was clearly exposed as an opportunist abandoning of the working people's interest. Later Johnson helped make it even clearer.

That was a case where one line was revisionist and the other was Marxist-Leninist. That is the best form of contradiction for our Party. It is open and clear cut. The debate is political and the revisionist or other incorrect position is exposed and eventually rejected. Such debates should be welcomed and carried to the end. At this stage in history, the struggle against revisionism is the main struggle within the revolutionary movement.

Thanks mainly to the consistently negative example of the U.S. revisionists and social democrats, our Party has not had too much difficulty with these policy disputes. However, we must be continuously alert to bring such disputes out in the open when they arise.

We intend to deal mainly with those aspects of this contradiction which are more concealed; with the struggle against bourgeois habits and ideas, which are often little understood by those who harbor them. Here, the two main conflicts are between bourgeois individualism and revolutionary dedication, and between pragmatism and Marxist-Leninist analysis and planning.

Bourgeois individualism is a fancy term for selfishness. That is, capitalist selfishness, selfishness for personal gain, prestige, power, comfort or material goods—usually at the expense of others. People with this approach have an amazing variety of rationalizations.

"The heads of such people are stuffed with the ideology of the exploiting classes. They believe that 'Every man is for himself'. . . 'Man is a selfish animal' and 'No one in the world is genuinely unselfish unless he is a simpleton or an idiot.' They even use such exploiting class rubbish to justify their own selfishness and individualism." (Liu Shao-chi, *How to Be a Good Communist,* Feb. 1964 edition, p. 58.)

The conflict or contradiction within our Party, and often within an individual member, is between the individualist tendency, which is the authentic Golden Rule of capitalism, and a dedication to the working class and the vast majority of the world's people, a dedication that makes socialist revolution and the achievement of communism more important than personal gain. It might be more accurate to say that through this dedication our *selves* become one with our class, and personal gain is achieved only through a gain for the entire class.

In other words, how much do we want this thing, this revolution? That's what it all comes down to. Is it more important to us than ourselves, our personal comfort, prestige, money, or life? Are we willing to remold ourselves into integral parts of a revolutionary party, to subordinate and eventually transform the old self into the new self which exists only through our Party and our unending fight for revolutionary change?

At this point a cry of protest will no doubt arise from many a radical heart. "No," they will exclaim, "we cannot live only through the Party! That is denying our humanity! Our individual essence! Our goal of full and free and creative expression for each! We will sacrifice our time, our energy, our money, but never our minds, never our hearts!"

Some may say these things having been sincerely repelled by the unfeeling bureaucracy of the old C.P. And it is crucial that we avoid any repetition of that Gus Hall-itis.

But it is intriguing that those who argue so long and loud about feeling and thinking often do amazing little of either.

It is self-evident to anyone who dares to look that we do not want an unfeeling, unthinking party. Such a party could not last two days as a revolutionary force. A party whose members don't feel pain and suffering could hardly burn with a desire to wipe out the rats and slumlords who are eating away at the flesh and blood of our ghetto children. A party whose members do not care for their fellow men could hardly care whether or not coal miners can afford to send their children to hospitals. A party whose members cannot love the people cannot hate the ruling class. A party which does not know trust and confidence in humanity could never build a society based on that trust and confidence. And as for thinking, the entire science of Marxism-Leninism requires thinking, a science which enables us to understand–only through hard thinking–the rules of reality and change, to develop new thoughts on how to make life better for the vast majority of people, and to fight effectively the long war against those who fear ideas. Without creative, individual thinking, there is no Marxism-Leninism. Automatons will never make a revolution, and any automatons within our ranks are useless at best.

The question is: What is the aim of feeling and thinking? For whom and to what end? Are we grumbling about going to a meeting because we would rather sit home and watch TV, or because it may be keeping us from selling newspapers to working people in our community? Do we worry—when making a public speech or writing an article—about our individual prestige, how we will look, or about how people will respond to the ideas we express? When deciding for or against a demonstration do we consider the best interests of the Party or are we more concerned with staying out of jail?

In other words, don't stop thinking and feeling, but change the purpose for which we think and feel if the purpose is wrong. Use our minds and hearts–as well as our time and energy–for the working class. The statement, "I'll give my time and energy for the Party but not my heart" reveals a person whose time and energy are as empty as his emotions. It is like the artist who says, "I will gladly support the movement, but when it comes to painting, that I reserve for myself." The movement gains little from his support, and even less does the world gain from his painting.

Bourgeois individualism takes many forms, all bad. Some of the most common are:

Personal fear

This is the most direct form of placing one's own physical comfort above the interests of the Party and the working class, and in a sense it is the most basic form.

Sometimes fear is obvious and even admitted by the individual member: "I won't take part in that street meeting because I don't want to go to jail, I don't want to get hurt." Of course, we don't argue that anyone should be reckless or that it's good *per se* to go to jail. But sometimes it's necessary. The old C.P. made—and makes–its first rule of operation, to stay out of jail. Usually, a good way to stay out of jail is not to cause any trouble for the ruling class.

When a member openly admits his personal fears, that is good. We all have personal fears, and there's no shame in that. Will we dominate them or will they dominate us, that is the question. If I am willing to talk about my fears with my club, I will not only be helped in overcoming them but I will most likely express thoughts troubling other minds as well as mine. In this way, the collective, as well as individuals, will be strengthened. Occasionally, someone may decide not to remain in the Party, but if there's honest discussion such a person will stay a good friend.

The bigger, more common problem is the member who is afraid to admit he's afraid; sometimes he may not fully recognize his own fear: "I'm not afraid; I just don't enjoy selling newspapers, and I'm not very good at it, anyway."

Sometimes fear becomes a kind of automatic reaction, a near-instinct that rejects any initiative from members or leaders. The slogan of such fear is, "Don't rock the boat." This attitude shows about as much revolutionary zeal as Calvin Coolidge.

Such a member will often develop a mask of "differences" with the Party over what he calls policies, i.e. we shouldn't publish a newspaper, we shouldn't publish a declaration advocating revolution, we shouldn't run a candidate, we shouldn't publish a criticism of the Soviet revisionists; we shouldn't organize a new branch, or a new project, or a demonstration, or speak out as communists. Of course, not every opposition to a new proposal is bad or comes from fear, but we should watch for the pattern.

Such a member will tell himself that his only, or his main problem is his "policy difference" with the Party. The renegade Phil Luce confided privately that he was afraid of going to jail. Yet when his fear led him to heroin and the *Saturday Evening Post,* he told the press, "I'll never inform on anyone, I just have a political disagreement with PL."

The ruling class has the power to jail or kill each of us. That is a fact, and jail or death is a real possibility facing every revolutionary. Shall we therefore not be revolutionaries? Some may answer "Yes." They are the ones who won't cross the street because they're afraid they might be hit by a car. It is wrong to try to convince these people that the chances of being hit by a car are not very great, that it's safe to cross the street. If you cross *this* street, you may very well be struck down.

The chicken crossed the road to get to the other side. And people, no matter how chicken, will cross *if they want to get to the other side badly enough.*

The enthusiasm of our members—organizing tenants, mobilizing demonstrations, speaking at street meetings, collecting signatures—has generally been one of our strong points. But excitement over an immediate issue will wane over the long, hard, zig-zag road of life-long revolutionary work. Our enthusiasm must be strengthened with deep-going understanding. This means day-to-day work on the job and in the communities. And it means thorough study of Marxism-Leninism.

In opposing fear, then, we must not just expose it. We must increase the desire for revolution, and the understanding of revolutionary ideology. What would we do with our lives, after all, if we weren't revolutionaries?

Even as we argue, we should recognize that fear, especially concealed fear, will be a big problem in our work. Moreover, fear usually plays some part in other aspects of bourgeois individualism.

Comfort corruption

This is the ruling class carrot that accompanies the stick that causes fear. It is a gimmick as old as the class struggle itself. The old higher-paid workers in the "aristocracy of labor," with a few exceptions, did not *consciously* sell out; they were simply softened into forgetting the majority of their class brothers.

For years, the AFL-CIO has been running its CIA-controlled "school" in Washington for promising (potentially militant) Latin American labor leaders. In the same way, Kennedy's Peace Corps and LBJ's War on Poverty take the cream of the young idealists in the civil rights and peace movements and put them to work selling, instead of fighting, U.S. capitalism. The former SNCC worker who used to worry whether or not his $20 would be coming every week, now gets a $150 LBJ-check without fail each Friday and is finding that middle-class life is not so bad.

Most of these people are not bad. They do not intend to sell out. Often they are simply discouraged by the slow, unromantic pace of progress. But they are bought off just the same.

For those, and they are many, who won't take the bait, there are other ways of getting hooked. Every pore of the U.S. of A. oozes with the syrup of "success" stories, soft living, soap operas, and, above all, comfort–no real struggle–and escape. "Honest" opportunities for easy living are not hard to find for the middle-class intellectual, no matter how radical he may have been. If your parents can't come through in a pinch with a house in the suburbs or a soft job, there are always scholarship funds, foundation grants, and trips around the world–in some worthy cause.

The vast majority of working people in this country and the world have no escape from the day-in day-out discipline of hard labor for someone else's profit, or from the constant gnawing insecurity. Their only way out is the grave–or taking power. But for the more "advanced" forces, including many of those who inevitably make up a communist party such as ours, the "opportunity" for comfort is always around. Like some colorless, odorless gas, slowly suffocating its victims.

To resist this comfort-corruption requires a serious commitment to revolution.

Lack of seriousness

As we said, significant progress has been made since our founding convention. Yet, despite the ruling class attacks on us, some members still think they're playing games. They think they can call "time out" whenever they want. They are as sloppy in their work as in their dress and personal habits. They live in a dream world. They just can't quite understand or believe that our Party is really out to make a revolution, and that making a revolution takes a lifetime, which means as long as we are alive, and then some. You can't really blame these people too much. After all, the U.S. Left has been non-revolutionary for so long that revolution is a brand new thought to most newcomers.

The lack of seriousness first crops up in a lot of "little" day-to-day ways: The student PLer who sleeps late instead of getting out on the campus early to talk with more people; the member of a neighborhood club who never thinks of writing a story for our newspaper on PL or other community activities; the "organizer" who never stays after a meeting to talk informally because he's always rushing, no matter how late at night, to meet his latest girlfriend; those who just never seem to sell any PL literature, but have seen all the latest movies; those in study groups who read assignments as if they were carrying out the hardest job, or don't bother to read at all.

These habits and dozens of others—lazy, degenerate attitudes —are simply self-indulgence. They grow out of a society which makes work a burden and loafing a goal. But they are directly related, as is fear, to the lack of desire for the revolution and lack of understanding of, and commitment to, the working class.

Some members who come from middle-class comfort seem to seek a safe little living room to crawl back into from time to time, just as water seeks its own level.

True, revolutionary struggle is often taxing, and everybody needs enough rest to maintain adequate physical and mental health. But racism is a strain on the Black people in our country, napalm bombs are taxing to the Vietnamese, and trying to feed a family when you don't have a job can be downright exhausting. The ruling class permits its enemies few vacations.

Many techniques are available to help enlarge our commitment. Study history! John Brown and Sojourner Truth can be teachers as well as examples. Films like "Salt of the Earth" or "He Who Must Die" and "The Organizer" can also give both inspiration and understanding.

But at the same time, let's look closely at the real conditions of this world we tend to live in so complacently. Let us remind ourselves of the napalmed children of Vietnam and the Congo. But that may be somewhat distant, although distance should not be a measure of importance. Let us take ourselves through the ghetto communities of our big cities where we have begun some work, or the Kentucky miners' homes, or the Mississippi croppers, or the Puerto Rican "migrant serfs" of New Jersey, or their brother-migrants in the Salinas Valley—the rat bites, the TB, the hungry bellies and the soulful eyes, the living death that constitutes the casualty list of the class struggle. Let us make every member understand that war is not a sometime thing.

The leaders of our Party must constantly set an example by hard work, commitment, and willingness to sacrifice. At the same time, we should call attention to Party groups and rank-and-filers whose consistent activities and courage can inspire us all.

Here we should not seek out those who are simply "devoted" to the Party—as a blind man is devoted to his seeing-eye dog.

When we praise dedication we should praise dedication to revolution, to the working people of our country, and *therefore* to the Party, as the leading part of–but always part of–that revolution and that people. No blind men here! Each of us dedicates his eyes to all the rest, and so each of us can see better.

To be dedicated, of course, does not mean to be dead. In striving to overcome carelessness we must avoid the deathly grimness which pervades those few pseudo-radical groups which have virtually declared laughter counter-revolutionary. The laughter of our Party is healthy and a sign of great basic strength. In general, individuals who take themselves too seriously, besides being overstuffed with their own importance, are no fun to be with. Most people laugh even through hardship; if we are people, we'll laugh, too.

Unfortunately, a few of our people don't yet understand that we are also revolutionaries, which means that underlying our laughter must be a basic resoluteness. In due time, of course, the enemy will teach these people. But it may be a costly lesson for all of us if we wait till then to learn.

Isolation

The most serious immediate problem facing our Party is the isolation of too many members from non-Party people, especially working people. This problem persists despite changes away from some early sectarian policies and despite the fact that a significant number of Party members have begun to establish important roots for themselves, particularly in the labor movement.

Too many members still have no real friends outside the Party. A few members still shun getting a job.

This is not a policy problem today, but a problem of ideology in every one of us.

Some members seem to think that developing friendships with new people is some sort of burden. On certain evenings they'll force themselves out of a sense of duty to visit non-Party contacts, and some won't even do that much. But every free moment they get they'll drop in for a relaxing bull session, cup of coffee, and rest with one of the in-group or "real friends" who are usually in the Party.

This elitist snobbery reflects fear and lack of resoluteness. After all, it takes an extra effort to make a new friend in the neighborhood, in school, or on the job. It may even mean going out of the way, crossing the street to say hello to a neighbor, inviting co-workers over for supper or organizing a party. And why strain ourselves to visit new people's homes when we have such a comfortable "home" here in the social-political clique which, in cases where it applies, we call our Party club?

Another side of this anti-social attitude is the member who has just read the above and said to himself most righteously, "I've got friends outside the party–lots of them!" but who somehow never discusses political questions with any of these friends. He patronizes these non-Party friends by systematically, though not always consciously, excluding them from the supposedly most important part of his life–his commitment to revolution. Not that they have to agree politically, but this patronizing member never even discusses politics with his friends. The result is they are not genuine friends, and they don't develop politically even if they should want to.

No one is arguing here that every friendship and tie outside the Party should be purely or even mainly political. Not at all. The member who can't discuss anything but politics is going to have a rough time when the World Series rolls around. A few of our members still seem unable to say anything but "Will you come to the demonstration?" when they meet people in the street.

But anyone who divides his political comrades from his friends, who keeps one set of ideas for one and another for the other and never the twain shall even overlap, is just as useless as the person with no friends outside the Party.

The whole question of mass work requires an analytical article on its own. But it is basically an ideological question. What do we really want? If we want to make a revolution in this country, we have to win new people and work with people even when we won't win them. We cannot do it alone. Alone, we can make ourselves as snug, and useless, as the cue ball in a corner pocket.

In our written work, too, we still tend to be too narrow. Clichés come quick, and some members enjoy attacking everybody and anybody who doesn't agree with us 110 per cent, and everybody is attacked with equal venom. A few members still flinch at the thought of working with other, less "pure" organizations.

Of course, polemics such as the recent exchange with *Studies on the Left* are very useful and should be conducted. But in general, our writers and editors should consider carefully how much space is spent on criticizing—and what is the tone of the criticism—various weak and/or negative tendencies. Let us fire most of our shots, and our most explosive ammunition, at the main enemy—U.S. imperialism and its front men, modern revisionism.

Anti-discipline or ultra-democracy

This is the attitude which seeks every way of rejecting leadership decisions *for the sake of the rejection itself.* Moreover, it usually includes a rejection and sometimes even a sabotaging of democratic centralism. It often crops up among members who have joined the Party mainly out of a personal rebellion and who consider that personal rebellion above the class rebellion. Liu Shao-chi describes this phenomenon:

> There are other comrades who do not understand that democracy inside the Party is democracy under centralized leadership. They therefore divorce their actions from the Party's centralized leadership and from the Party as a whole. They pay no attention to the overall situation or the long-range interests of the Party as a whole. They act freely within the Party and without restraint, guided solely by their own interests and views. They neither closely observe Party discipline nor execute the decisions of the Party's leading bodies. They indulge in all kinds of unorganizational, non-political, and unprincipled utterances and actions. They either deliberately resort to exaggeration in order to spread dissension within the Party or engage in unlimited idle talk or debate, never taking the trouble to see whether or not there is a critical situation or an emergency. They even take advantage of the Party membership's temporary ignorance due to ideological unpreparedness, to take votes on their own proposals and to fulfill their own designs in the name of the "majority." (*On the Party,* Jan. 1951 edition, pp. 86-7.)

And Mao Tse-tung points out that this attitude is "objectively, a kind of counter-revolutionary ideology. Those who embrace it will surely land in the counter-revolutionary groups if they allow it to develop instead of checking it energetically." (*Resolution of the Kutier Conference.*)

This kind of member is usually found sitting around someone's house making snide digs at various leaders or members who are not present. He spreads his complaints almost compulsively in a gossipy way to other members and non-members, too.

He is always criticizing the leadership in a factional manner, with overtones suggesting intrigue. Even when his criticism is valid (and the leaders should always listen objectively), the member gives it for bad reasons. He considers the whole Party, and especially the leaders, to be in some kind of grand conspiracy to boss him around. And he will not be bossed! The content of decisions, discussions or policies is reduced to tactical handles in his private war.

Ironically, this same individual almost always want to be a boss himself, and behaves like a boss every chance he gets. He will even organize his own coterie of followers on the job or around the neighborhood, and instead of developing these people politically and integrating them into the Party, he'll try to keep them on the side–to himself, so to speak.

Naturally, such a member almost by definition will not easily accept criticism or be self-critical. His attitude will not change easily. Part of the change process must be the thorough study of Marxism-Leninism.

Note that Mao calls this undisciplined attitude "objectively" wrong. The member who expresses this attitude is not an enemy, at least not unless he turns himself into one in a course of degeneration. This is a critical distinction which will be dealt with more extensively later.

Employee mentality

This attitude says, "I will do what I'm asked to do and no more. I will follow orders. I will question nothing. I will not think. I will not criticize. And of my sacred, inner self, I will give nothing." Often, if criticized, members with this attitude will simply withdraw. Basically, this attitude resists change because to change would mean to give of that sacred, inner self which is held above and beyond the Party and the working class.

Members with this attitude almost always try to select or somehow manage to get jobs which require the least responsibility. When they are not doing "Party work," they don't think about making revolutionary changes in anything. They are "off the job" until the next meeting or assignment.

If they ever have a new idea it scares the hell out of them, and they quickly smother it as unbefitting a "good" Party member. They are revolutionaries in a rut, which is an impossible contradiction. Sooner or later, usually sooner, the revolutionary must destroy the rut or the rut will destroy the revolutionary, no matter how regularly he attends Party meetings. Even when they work efficiently and devotedly, such members work dully and without initiative. "Initiative is for the leadership." Presumably if the leadership disappeared tomorrow, these members would stop political work because they wouldn't know what to do. Isn't that just what happened in the fifties with so many Communist Party members?

Paradoxically, such people often harbor resentments against one or another of those they consider to be their "employers," usually some among the leadership. In fact, it is sometimes hard to figure out what stubborn streak of personality keeps such people in the Party. Yet if they could only see that it's not so horrible to try something and fail, that failure is in fact a necessary prerequisite for every success, these members usually have great political potential and sometimes even brilliant minds buried beneath their employee mentality.

In a sense, this attitude appears to be just the opposite of the super-critical anti-discipline. But essentially it is simply another collar on the same dog of individualism–some members may simply alternate between the two collars–but even more dangerous because it keeps to itself and may not be noticed.

Bureaucracy, commandism, arrogance

This is most common among "leaders," and often in those who have many strong points.

> But many comrades very often exaggerate one-sidedly their own strong points to the neglect of their weak points and the strong points of others. Thus they easily become arrogant, look down upon others and cannot stand others' criticism. . . . (Liu Shao-chi, *On the Party*, p. 110.)

Instead of looking for new and better leaders, bureaucrats will actually try to hold back the development of others out of fear of "competition."

These people are always pushing or wangling themselves into the spot-light. They will make loud claims even when they're not sure of the facts, as long as they think those around them are even less sure. They seem to feel compelled to make some self-assertive, emphatic comment about any conversation going on around them.

Often they will make stupid political statements (usually in a pompous manner) just because it goes against their grain to keep their mouths shut until they learn all the facts. Arrogant people don't know how to say they don't know. They will sometimes quote at length from Marx, Engels or whatever "authority" is most convenient rather than investigate the particulars of a case in point. They love to give orders. In their egotism, they will even boast and show off.

If not corrected, sooner or later they will be arrogant in their relations with non-Party people as well as with their more understanding comrades.

Those of us who were in the old C.P. know the bureaucratic animal well, and could detail example after example of tired old men and women who love their desks above everything and call themselves leaders.

But it's always easier to point to others, especially when there are so many to point to. The trouble is bureaucratic attitudes can develop—and our American Way of Life breeds them—in any one of us. Usually, they are not conscious at first. The club chairman who is sincerely critical of another Party leader for being bureaucratic may in turn adopt quite arrogant and bureaucratic attitudes towards members in the club.

These attitudes are particularly dangerous because they are usually bolstered by the prestige of the organizational rank of the bureaucrat involved. People are afraid to criticize a "leader." In some organizations, like the old C.P., people may be afraid they will be disciplined if they criticize the leadership. But even where this is not a danger, people still sometimes hesitate to raise criticisms because "it doesn't look good" to criticize a "leader." Therefore, arrogant people often go uncriticized—to their faces, at least—for long periods of time.

Perhaps the worst part of it, this attitude by leaders feeds the ultra-democracy and employee mentality described above, providing fuel for the anti-discipline fire and at the same time praising and promoting the unquestioning "employees." More easily intimidated members may decide it is better to take no initiative—to do nothing—than to be "blasted" by arrogant "leaders" for making a mistake. When a party stops taking the initiative it stops being a revolutionary party.

Ironically, the same individual who is arrogant as a leader is usually either subservient and unthinking as a follower—after all, that's how he thinks followers should be—or super-critical of those in higher leadership positions—he assumes all leaders are as self-centered as he himself is; or both.

The arrogant person doesn't mean to be arrogant. He is usually very sweet and gentle "underneath"—at least in the beginning. Just as the other weaknesses described above, arrogance is a reflection of bourgeois individualism. In criticizing and dealing with arrogance, commandism, and bureaucracy, it is important to keep this in mind.

Combat Liberalism

How shall we react when our weaknesses are pointed out? Unfortunately, it is easy to pick out weaknesses which obviously apply to others and shrug off or ignore our own. That attitude, of course, reflects the very individualism of which all these weaknesses we have mentioned are only different forms.

These weaknesses often reflect a lack of involvement in the daily struggles of the working people. At the same time, they always reflect a low level of revolutionary ideology. To the extent that individualism dominates any individual, to that extent Marxism-Leninism is subordinated. The weakness, in other words, consists of both the existence of bad traits and the non-existence of revolutionary ideology. We must understand this in order to struggle against these shortcomings. When we criticize, and when we suggest ways of improving, we must emphasize Marxist-Leninist study.

To the extent that any of the above-mentioned tendencies exist in a member, to that extent personal concern and personal loyalty have taken the place of class concern and loyalty. But that is precisely the moral—and material—foundation of modern revisionism. "Don't fight the imperialists because you might get killed." So we can see that bourgeois individualism, if it is unchecked, if it is not consciously opposed in our ranks will lead to revisionism. The struggle against it therefore, must be sharp, and it must be ideological. This can't be said too many times.

> We stand for active ideological struggle because it is the weapon for insuring unity within the Party and the revolutionary organizations in the interests of our fight. Every Communist and every revolutionary should take up this weapon.
>
> But liberalism rejects ideological struggle and stands for un-

> principled peace, thus giving rise to a decadent, philistine attitude and bringing about political degeneration in certain units and individuals in the Party and the revolutionary organizations. (Mao Tse-tung, "Combat Liberalism," Vol. II, *Selected Works,* December 1965 edition, p. 31.)

We have often been too liberal in the past. We have tended to avoid sharp criticism. We didn't want to hurt feelings, or get someone angry at us. True, there is a place for tact in criticism. But tact is one thing, liberalism–avoiding ideological debate–is something else.

Our criticisms have tended to be too general–always, "a lot of us made a wrong estimate of the neighborhood situation" or "this club hasn't functioned collectively." Rarely have individual members been criticized sharply by their clubs, co-workers or others in the organization, or given sharp self-criticism, in a face-to-face discussion where ideological weaknesses were pointed out. On the few occasions when this *has* happened, it has been quite helpful.

Unless our Party consciously takes up the job of remolding and involves every member on all levels, then simply writing about weaknesses will do little good.

Of course, we all have weaknesses. And to say that is to say that we all need to deepen our ideological understanding and revolutionary commitment.

But while true, it is also untrue to say, "well, we're all guilty, and we should all improve." If that is all we say, then it's a dodge. Some members are more influenced by bourgeois ideology than others. Some have been more successful in struggling against it, while in some, bourgeois individualism is so pronounced it virtually negates the positive aspects of the members and threatens to disrupt the work of the Party in the particular unit.

"Active ideological struggle" is not easy. It means painful and drawn-out transformations of individuals. It means criticizing friends. It means criticizing ourselves. It sometimes means being criticized by three or four or even ten people, and paying careful attention to what each one says. It means asking for criticism instead of avoiding it. It means honestly admitting fears. It means constantly studying the political, economic and philosophical concepts which make up the ideology of revolution, and then thinking about them and trying to apply them. It's not easy.

Making a revolution isn't easy.

Criticism

Good criticism *means* self-criticism. If one does not consciously seek out his own weaknesses and attempt to improve, one cannot give consistent constructive help to others. The approach to criticism by a member of a club or a leadership body should *begin* with self-criticism. Unfortunately, many of us have built-in defenses, refined by years of middle-class rationalization.

One member who is particularly guilty of selfish, anti-collective attitudes read an early draft of this article and responded by saying, first, "It's good." And then, almost as an afterthought, "I disagree about selfishness being caused by bourgeois society," and continued along the lines that "man is a selfish animal" and the whole pattern described by Liu Shao-chi (cited above) as "exploiting class rubbish to justify . . . individualism." Naturally, this member diligently avoided self-criticism—and change.

Criticism and self-criticism constitute the main process of inner-Party struggle to resolve the contradiction between revolutionary and bourgeois ideology within our ranks.

How shall we criticize our comrades? Here, the word comrade is used not just in the formalistic sense of Party member, which is, by the way, a definition quite alien to most people in our country, but in the truest sense—friend, class brother and fellow-revolutionary. As we said above, most of our comrades who display tendencies of bourgeois individualism do so without bad intention. Their ideology, their attitudes, are enemies. They, as people, are not. Therefore, our criticism must be aimed at changing the comrade, at eliminating his wrong ideas and attitudes, not at driving him away. Our criticism must be aimed at reaching unity—unity based on better understanding of Marxism-Leninism, but unity.

That is the key. Both the comrade offering the criticism and the one receiving it should begin with a clear desire for unity. If either lacks this desire, if either is out to knock the other down or preserve and defend his own position, the criticism may well be wasted. Still, it's important to try. Even if the criticism is not received or given constructively, the discussion may in time lead to an honest re-evaluation with positive results.

There will always be a few who cannot, will not, improve, who refuse to change, who sink deeper into their own selfishness, who break with the Party. But we must make those as few as possible. Even in those cases, the correct handling of criticism may determine whether such persons leave the Party as enemies or as friends with whom we can continue working. We must work hard to improve every comrade. Let those determined to abandon the struggle make that decision for themselves. Sometimes the process of criticism and improvement may take a long time, during which the outcome of the struggle is in doubt. In such cases, it's necessary to reserve final judgment on the comrade in question. But let us not be anxious to write anyone off.

Here, the revolutionary movement has a great need for sensitivity. With the enemy we must be ruthless, as they are with us. But with ourselves, our comrades, our potential comrades, our allies, we must be understanding. Che Guevara says "the true revolutionary is guided by great feelings of love." Can that love be just for humanity in general, as an abstract thing, without including understanding of and sensitivity to the fears, doubts, and feelings of individual friends? That kind of love would be as phony as Natalie Wood's "love" in technicolor and cinemascope.

Actually, all of us are capable of real understanding and friendship, and all of us would like to share these qualities with our comrades. But for one reason or another many of us are embarrassed, ashamed or afraid of our feelings. Battling the grinding machinery of a society based on cynicism and hate, we tend to become as metallic as the machine we battle. Look at all the "organization men" on the Left, as well as everywhere else in our country, who have ended up as lonely and bitter old bureaucrats.

In relations with our comrades, we might keep in mind Keats' plea: "Men should bear with each other more. There lives not the man who cannot be cut up, aye hacked to pieces on his weakest side."

Let us not forget that criticism includes positive as well as negative evaluation. Praising a particular member or unit for worthwhile achievements can be a big factor in improving the whole Party. Those members and groups who usually stay in the background, who do consistent, un-glamorous, day-to-day work selling papers, sealing envelopes, talking to people in the community, should be especially singled out for recognition whenever possible. Such positive examples of dedication to the working class may help our members overcome weaknesses more than negative criticism. Inter-club visits should be arranged to help members learn from the best Party groups. Appreciation for positive work must be included in the overall process of criticism.

Criticism, like everything else, contains two opposing aspects. In this case, they are the giving of criticism and receiving of criticism. Both of these opposite positions are essential to the process of criticism or self-criticism, but in determining the outcome of the process one of these is decisive: in almost every case, the receiving of criticism, or the way in which criticism is accepted, determines the success or failure of criticism or self-criticism.

No matter how badly, angrily, or subjectively criticism may be given, if the person receiving the comments has a constructive self-critical and unity-seeking approach he will be able to listen carefully, and draw out the legitimate criticism–often unexpressed in words–from the emotion. On the other hand, no matter how constructively criticism may be presented, if the one being criticized has a bad attitude, does not want unity and does not want to change, the criticism will be useless. Of course, the way in which criticism is given may affect the attitude of the receiver–a little human understanding and self-criticism will make it much easier for others to accept the criticism you offer; but in the final analysis it is that attitude of the receiver which is decisive.

Therefore, let us consider some of the most common wrong ways of receiving criticism, all of which reflect bourgeois individualism:

Some members pay little or no attention to criticism from anyone who happens to be below them on the organizational ladder. They feel it will compromise their prestige and authority. In reality, of course, it is just the opposite. By ignoring honest criticism they lose–and rightly so–both prestige or authority. When leaders have this attitude towards rank-and-file criticism they are bad leaders or even misleaders; if they maintain this attitude they have no business in leadership positions. There is no such thing as rank in the realm of criticism.

Some members will seize on the wrong *manner* of his critic to evade the content of the criticism; they take advantage of the weakness or inexperience of their critics, and immediately turn upon them and accuse them of "subjectivism" and other such terrible things.

> Sometimes people raise criticism in the heat of a situation and they don't put it forward in the best way. Of course, this usually turns people off. But even when criticism is not given in the best way, we should try to hear the criticism, evaluate its merits, and then later discuss with the person the manner in which it was given.

Some members adopt the approach of "retaliation" to assuage the wrong they think has been done them. They will listen to criticism only if the person giving it includes an equal amount of self-criticism or if they are given a chance to criticize back. The sharper the criticism of them, the sharper they plan to make their retaliation. They are usually so obsessed with measuring the "equality" of the exchange that they pay only the most superficial attention to the content of the criticism. If they are denied the "right" to retaliate they consider it an undemocratic plot against them. This attitude, of course, makes a mockery of the critical process. It is especially a danger during formal criticism meetings.

Then there are the sulkers. They consider it a grave tragedy to have a weakness uncovered and criticized, and they usually adopt a very grim look and go off in a corner and brood for a few days or weeks or even months. They don't understand that the purpose of criticism is to improve the Party through improving its members, and it's not a game of hide-and-seek where you hide your own weaknesses and seek those of others. Sulkers, for all their sulking, usually do little improving. No one can ever be quite sure whether they're trying to change themselves or just to find better hiding places for their flaws in the future.

Then there are the wrigglers and squirmers, the "lawyers" who will try to turn honest criticism into courtroom maneuvers. They will challenge some minor point in the criticism in order to obscure the essence of it: "I never used exactly those words!" They will make their statements as general, and as vague, as possible. They will claim they didn't intend to do what in fact they did. And in general they will talk about anything and everything except the concrete point of criticism which is raised. They are so desperate to salvage their selves that they often actually convince themselves they are being maligned, and sometimes even that a conspiracy exists against them. They are like the six-year-old boy who is criticized for throwing a stone at his little brother. "It wasn't a stone, it was just a piece of dirt. Besides, I didn't mean to hit him, I just wanted to scare him. Besides, I didn't throw it at him, I just wanted to see if I could throw it that far." That may be a normal childish response. But how often have we found it in our own members!

Of course, everyone should defend his views as long as he honestly believes them, but the key point is that the aim of this defense–as well as the aim of the views–must be to improve the work of the Party and the working class.

Criticism will only work if everyone has confidence in the group; if the *aim* of the criticism and self-criticism is to help the group. In such a situation each person will honestly admit all weaknesses and errors, even those not apparent, not try to protect himself by legalistic maneuvers or "what I really meant was . . ." or obscuring his ideas so no one will be able to tell what he really meant. Why should you be so afraid of criticism? Whom are you afraid of? Your comrades? If you are so afraid of your comrades that you will go to such lengths to avoid being honest with them, and yourself, then how will you react to the enemy? The likelihood is you will react like a leaf reacts to a hurricane. On the other hand, confidence in each other and in the group will give us each the strength of our entire Party and enable us to withstand any enemy storms.

What form should criticism and self-criticism take within our Party? Here, flexibility must be the key. The form must be subordinate to the content and the spirit of the criticism. Many forms are useful.

Formal criticism meetings, or what Mao Tse-tung calls a "rectification campaign," in which the entire Party holds unit meetings to deal with a particular weakness such as bourgeois individualism, offer many advantages. First, when such meetings are announced in advance, people will spend time thinking critically about each other, about themselves, and about the ideological weakness. This is especially important when we are not–as too many of us are not–in the habit of thinking critically. Second, when the entire Party launches a "rectification campaign," members will concentrate attention and suggestions on overcoming the main weakness or obstacle to the Party's progress at a given moment. This may avoid scatter criticism, in which everything, big and little, important and unimportant, is discussed at once, and which can often be more confusing than helpful. Third, formal sessions will encourage those members who are more shy to speak out and express their views, which are often extremely valuable. In the process those more withdrawn people may begin to emerge, get more confidence in themselves, and take on more responsibility.

Of course there are dangers in formal criticism sessions. The thing can be abused. We can demand too much from people too soon. Even when we try to improve, and even when we make some headway, we tend to slip back, and need constant help from our comrades. Remolding a human being first molded by 20 or 30 years of U.S. capitalism is a long process. The most we can ask is that everyone sincerely try to slowly improve.

Then, too, criticism sessions can be overdone and institutionalized into empty forms. People can begin to think of Tuesday night as Criticism Night, and beat their breasts for a couple of hours, often with incisive criticism and self-criticism, and then go home and forget about it. The Sunday morning sermon with left-wing cliches! Frankly, a good hell-and-brimstone preacher is more fun.

Finally, formal sessions may sometimes embarrass a particular person who is criticized, and make it more difficult for him to accept criticism or to criticize himself. Such attitudes are wrong and we should struggle against them. But we should understand them, and be sensitive to them. Sometimes a private informal chat or series of chats between two or three members, or between some of the leadership and a particular member produce better results than formal meetings.

Still, on the whole, a "rectification campaign" would be most useful for us at this time, if it is conducted constructively and with common sense. Many types of criticism meetings are possible. Sometimes each member may take turns criticizing himself and the others; or the discussion may center on one particular member; or everyone may evaluate a particular event and each member's role in it; or a particular weakness which is prevalent in the group; or a leading member may be criticized by everyone, at least as the first step.

Whatever the forms, our Party and every member of our Party should recognize *the need now for criticism and self-criticism within our ranks, especially aimed at bourgeois individualism.*

We must study and learn how to conduct what has come to be known as the "inner-Party struggle." In the process, we must concentrate on the basic cause of weaknesses and avoid personal squabbles and mechanical criticism. We have to find ways to keep the discussions as much as possible on an ideological level, and encourage members to express and explain their policy differences whenever possible. The aim of these discussions must not be to "knock" a particular person or to remove anyone from a particular post, although occasionally such action may be necessary. As we said before, the aim of all our criticism and self-criticism must be a new unity of the Party, a unity based on more and deeper political understanding, and a firmer commitment to revolution.

Through all these weaknesses in every aspect, the overriding danger is revisionism: abandoning the international working class, substituting reform for revolution, trying to negotiate the class struggle until you negotiate yourself over to the other side. This is the enemy of the working people of the world, and those who spout this line are as dangerous as their buddies, the Washington war-makers. We must expose them and attack them at every turn, and constantly guard against this ideology within our midst.

We might just mention here the personal inner feelings involved in remolding oneself. It seems paradoxical because most of us cling so desperately to our individualism. Yet no one enjoys fighting the whole world all by himself. And anyone who has gone through discussions where he was criticized, where he recognized his weaknesses, and then improved himself, even partly, knows an exhilarating feeling of freedom—freedom from his internal self-aggravation and fear—and a new self-confidence and confidence in his comrades and in the collective composed of all of them. In that feeling we may get just a glimpse of the man of the future, the communist man, we are working to create.

No criticism, no matter how carefully presented and constructively phrased, should be expected to bring about significant transformations in anyone who is isolated from political activity. Any club or group which spends so much time in criticism sessions that it never leaves the meeting room should be sharply criticized. *Participation in the struggles of working people, students, farmers and others for a better life is essential in remolding our members.*

Within this environment, if we can develop correct criticism in our Party we will see that our errors and weaknesses are not just bad things, but, in fact, can be transformed into good things. We will learn that without mistakes there can be no progress, and discover how to turn weakness into strength.

Lack of Planning

Planlessness and pragmatism are inherent in the every-man-for-himself capitalist economy. And what leads in economics follows suit in politics and even in military action.

In practice, of course, the ruling class does its best to plan ahead, and we must not underestimate their ability to scheme. But successful planning is against their inhuman nature. So they plan for years to wage a remote-control war in Asia without involving U.S. land troops, and they wake up one morning with a quarter of a million soldiers sinking in the quicksand of aggression in Vietnam. This doesn't mean they are "irrational" or "crazy," just that their original plan couldn't work and they were forced to make new plans–which also can't work. Even in the conduct of their military operations they find themselves, for all their computer-brains, with such chaotic situations as too many ships in one place and not enough ships in another.

Traditionally, the U.S. working class and its leaders have been just as pragmatic as our enemies–if not more so. "But there is no time," we constantly declare in excusing ourselves. "There is so much to do." And so we rush from meeting to meeting and picket line to picket line, wearing ourselves out like the proverbial headless chicken and using just about as many brains.

In our "personal lives," of course, we are capable of great planning, no matter how busy we are. Individuals develop the most intricate schemes for "getting ahead." In school, a student will know exactly which courses he needs to take over a period of years, and which teachers are the "best" in order to achieve whatever degree he has decided upon in order then to get whatever job he is aiming at. On the job, a worker can tell you just what has to be done to achieve a promotion. And housewives are constantly preparing, and applying, the most careful plans not only to get by on inadequate incomes, but often even to save a little bit for hard times. Yet we say we are too busy to plan for our class.

The result is we run the risk of drifting along from day to day following the easiest path, which is usually the wrong path. We don't see problems or dangers which lie ahead, or if we see them we do nothing about them. In the past, faced with unforeseen developments, so-called working class parties have swung back and forth between adventurism and retreat. If the police suddenly attack a demonstration, for example, the demonstrators without a plan either fight wildly, causing needless injuries and extra arrests, or simply run away, dragging their tails behind them. Even if a plan is made for a given demonstration, no plan is made to follow it up, to consolidate the gains, to raise the protest to a higher level, etc. More often we hear, "Well, let's see how it works out and then we'll decide what to do next."

Our Party's founding convention took a big step towards meeting this problem and provided our members with the beginnings of a realistic long-range outlook for the development of the revolutionary movement in our country. But it was only a start.

Pragmatism in our ranks is mainly an ideological problem and cannot be overcome at one meeting or by one report. We fail to plan because essentially we don't *believe* in planning. Also, it seems easier not to plan, and those who suffer from laziness will do the least planning. We do not really *understand* the necessity for planning. We thoughtlessly adopt the bourgeois approach that only God can make a plan.

It's like a football team coming out of a huddle without a play. "Just snap the ball back and we'll see what happens," says the quarterback. What happens is that you can't gain much ground with the other team piled up on top of you.

There are three main ways to overcome this lack of planning in our ranks:

1) *Marxist-Leninist study.* To plan for change without understanding dialectical materialism, the science of change, is like planning a trip to the moon without understanding rocketry, or even basic physics.

Every single member of our party—no matter what his position—needs to study Marxism-Leninism consistently. A few have already done a great deal of reading of Marxist works. Too often, however, these few do not relate what they have read to real life. One former member used to act as if Marxism-Leninism were a series of magic words which need only to be repeated enough times to solve the problems of the world. Therefore, he would repeat the words as often as possible, usually quoting the exact formulation—and only the exact formulation—written in the Book, and showing polite toleration for those younger people who didn't know the Word. The result is he actually discouraged honest study and created a cynical attitude among some people towards Marxism-Leninism, which became identified with his clichés. Not all those who have studied Marxism behave in this way, of course; some can give and have given valuable assistance to our younger members.

The main obstacle to overcome in organizing the study of Marxism-Leninism is the lazy and basically contemptuous attitude towards study—all study—which is one of the few things most of us learned in high school or college. "What will it get me?" is the unexpressed question behind most members' resistance to study. One way to deal with this problem might be to start handing out cash prizes to those who read the most pages per hour. If we run out of cash, we could offer free goulash. But perhaps we can find a better way.

Numerous good techniques are available to "enliven" the study of Marxism, and nothing's wrong—everything's right—with trying to make study as provocative and lively as possible. Such creative forms as special schools, films and debates can and should be used. Classes or study groups can be organized in which each student writes an essay on his experience in reading a particular Marxist-Leninist work, his reactions, his understanding, his questions. The subject of how to study Marxism-Leninism merits a separate article; it should deal with, among other things, our positive and negative experiences, including cadre schools.

But whatever methods are added, *there is no substitute for reading basic Marxist-Leninist works* including the writings of Mao Tse-tung. Here, our members should give special emphasis to studying contradictions, the kernel of change, and understanding the two aspects—emerging and declining—of every phenomenon, and the struggle between them.

Study of conditions in our country

The encyclopedia of errors committed by well-intentioned students of Marxism who mechanically tried to apply strategy and tactics based solely on experiences of revolutionaries in other countries fills many volumes. Mao Tse-tung writes again and again of the need to study "living ideas," real-life conditions in each country. In the U.S. we have an advantage because the ruling class has already organized a vast research network and publishes endless statistics, many of which are extremely valuable. These must be studied systematically. Of course, no government statistics should be accepted blindly.

In any case, no book research, no matter how thorough, can be useful unless it's combined with study-through-experience, examining conditions with our own eyes. This means living with the people–workers, students, farmers, and everyone we want to influence. We must be a part of the people, not just at meetings but on the job, on the campus, and on the farm. If we don't live with the people we can't learn from the people. And if we can't learn from the people we can't teach anybody.

We should try to study one or two typical samples of a phenomenon and then generalize from them. For example, if we want to learn how big cities in our country operate, we might pick Baltimore and Denver, or any two we think are typical, and study their economies, their politics, the racketeers who run the local business interests, their connections to the national syndicates and big political bosses, monopoly interests, composition of working class, main immediate problems, wage scales, unemployment, etc., and then see if we can draw general conclusions about all or most big cities, and how to conduct the revolutionary struggle there.

Of course, no one should use "study" as an excuse for inactivity. Our day-to-day political work must be a source of and a test for our studies, as well as the reason for which we study. Study without political work is like a menu without food.

The study of concrete conditions has two main aims: to know ourselves, our class and our allies and the contradictions within us; and to know the enemy and the enemy's contradictions. If this article serves any purpose, it may help us to understand ourselves a little better. However, we have been sorely lacking so far in thorough-going studies of the enemy. In his military writings, Mao Tse-tung says that in learning the laws of war "what has to be learned and known includes the state of affairs on the enemy side and that on our side, both of which should be regarded as the object of study. . . ."(*Selected Military Writings,* p. 86.) Whether during a relatively peaceful period, such as the present, or otherwise, what we are studying–or should be studying–are the laws of war, class war. Understanding and taking advantage of the contradictions in the enemy—we don't mean phony contradictions such as the "protect-Johnson-from-the-ultra-right" garbage of the revisionists—at home, and within the international imperialist camp, is essential if we intend to plan ahead.

Systematic summarizing and evaluation of experiences

In our short history, we have already lived through several struggles. We have made mistakes. That is not so important. The question is, have we learned from the mistakes? Do we summarize our experiences, good and bad, our work in the South or in ghetto communities for example, and attempt to draw lessons for future work? Do we analyze our publications? Sometimes we do. But not enough. Our Party must make time for regular and systematic evaluations. Otherwise, even Marxist-Leninist theory and a study of concrete conditions in our country will not help us win. Only practice can put our programs to the true test, only the reactions of the working people and intellectuals around us.

Summarize our experience, evaluate, draw lessons, make new plans, carry them out, summarize, evaluate: on and on. But when we say summarize our experience this must be mainly experience among non-Party working people. And here we cannot be like that fat-headed politician whose only contact with the masses is looking down from a platform at a street corner meeting.

It's worth repeating several times: every Party member must have close friends outside the Party. And if a person is a friend, naturally we will share ideas on what is important to us, politics as well as baseball. Without this base at the job, the school, in the community or on the farm, no meaningful evaluation of our policies is possible. The "mass line" is the basis of effective planning.

We must consciously plan to plan. We must assign ourselves time to summarize and evaluate. If the day-to-day rush of "business" appears too hectic to permit such meetings, then certain leading members or bodies should take a period of time together away from the big city's hustle-bustle in some area where they can spend as long as necessary—even up to a week or two or three —to summarize, evaluate, study and draw up new plans. The Party's daily functioning can continue for a while without physical presence of these individuals (it will even give some of the newer people valuable experience in self-reliance), but the Party's long-range functioning will flounder without such sessions from time to time.

In planning, the leadership should pay careful attention to individual assignments. However, planning can not be seen as the responsibility of the leadership alone, any more than thinking. Every member should give careful thought to the Party's perspectives, take part in summarizing and evaluating experiences, and insist on a thorough understanding of his own assignment.

No member should wake up in the morning and wonder what he's going to do that day. Every member should have a daily plan, which in turn is part of a weekly and monthly and one-year and five-year and ten-year perspective; each individual plan should be part of a club plan and the club plan part of an overall Party strategy.

Here it should be useful to organize the perspective by stages, setting clear-cut minimum goals for each stage, and devoting most attention to what is determined to be the major objective of each stage. For example, if the objective of one stage is to build a base in a community, we should analyze the neighborhood forces, their relative strength, stability and class outlook, then set some simple concrete goals for working with the forces we seek to develop.

Naturally, we can't make a blueprint for every minute of the day or predict exactly what will happen in the next ten weeks, let alone ten years. Our plans must be realistic and flexible. More important, we must be flexible in carrying them out, changing them when necessary, adapting to new situations, raising questions and proposing new plans. Above all, we must never plan away our boldness and enthusiasm; we must never reject initiative because "it's not in the plan." On the contrary, we must always have the initiative, launch new projects, and stay one jump (at least one) ahead of the ruling class. But none of this negates the need for planning. Revolutions don't appear magically any more than skyscrapers do.

Some Objections

Some members reading this may complain that the points raised, while not completely worthless, are inappropriate at best and perhaps even harmful. They may raise a number of objections.

First, they may say, this is not the time to get so introspective, to turn so much of our attention inward. We've made great strides recently; the tide of struggle is rising; the class war is sharpening; the people are on the move. If we devote all of our attention to ourselves, we will miss the boat.

The last point is obviously true. But no one proposes that we devote *all* our attention to ourselves–or even most of it. This is not basically a plea for more time, for a new quantity of agenda-space to be spent on self-improvement, although that should be one result. It is an argument for more consciousness, for a new quality of understanding of ourselves in order to improve our work. And it is precisely *because* we are currently moving forward that we must worry about our weaknesses. When we suffer defeats and failures, everyone will be sitting soberly with head in hands trying to figure out what went wrong and what to do next. That will be the time to emphasize our strengths, to fight against pessimism and defeatism. But now, when we are "rolling along," we may tend to overlook or minimize serious weaknesses, to overestimate our strength and underestimate the enemy. Everybody knows what happened to the hare in his race with the tortoise.

Let no one underestimate the effects of bourgeois ideology. What may begin with a few private dachas in a Moscow suburb very quickly becomes the restoration of Russian capitalism, complete with unemployment and official anti-semitism. Who would have imagined that the land of Lenin would one day let itself be represented by slick vodka ads in Madison Avenue magazines paraphrasing Ian Fleming's CIA story with the slogan "From Russia With Ice"? In the same way, Gus Hall's private Westchester dacha is part and parcel of the whole shameful policy under which a once-communist party mobilizes its feeble forces to help elect the most blatantly reactionary President in U.S. history.

If bourgeois ideology is permitted to get a foot-hold, if it is not constantly opposed in our ranks, it can spread as quickly as cancer with just as deadly results. Of course, we must keep struggling on the front lines of demonstrations, strikes, and mass movements, but we must keep improving ourselves, too.

Second, some will say these remarks are too negative. If we have all those faults we ought to give up! Here, there is a real weakness in this article. It doesn't deal with all the positive qualities which our membership and our leadership possess. It doesn't detail all the tremendous gains we have made in the past few years, and especially since the founding of our Party. By leaving those things out, it presents a one-sided picture, or it would present such a picture to those who don't know the whole story.

All right, the article is guilty of one-sidedness. But if we recognize that–and we who know the full story of our Party's development surely don't need to read self-praise to know that we have done fairly well–then we can approach the questions raised here with a constructive attitude. It is patently ridiculous to say that if we have all those faults we ought to give up. If we have those faults and we don't try to overcome them *then* we ought to give up. In other words, if we give up we ought to give up.

Third, some will argue that all this may be true, but there is a war on and a danger of a much bigger war at any moment. It's a crisis! An emergency! When bombs are dropping is hardly the moment to consider bourgeois individualism!

If bombs are exploding around you as you are reading this, please be sure you have good shelter before going any further. If bombs are not exploding where you are then surely it can't be much of an unusual crisis. Even where U.S. bombs have been dropping every day for years–in Vietnam–the people don't stop their work, their studying, their discussions, their criticism, or their evaluations. That is one of their great strengths.

Our organization has been in a state of crisis every day of every week of its short life. And if we are true to our revolutionary principles we should expect crisis upon crisis for the rest of our lives. By that standard, we would never get to consider bourgeois individualism. This argument is precisely the kind of lack of planning referred to above.

Actually, the sharper the crisis the better from one point of view. People are forced to face their weaknesses in time of emergency. Some, the weakest, will retreat from the revolution, a few will betray. Many who have managed to conceal or ignore their inner doubts and fears will be forced to grapple with them, and some will overcome them. For those, strikes, arrests, battles, wars add steel to the makeup. There is no room for revisionism at such moments. There are only two sides and it is life or death; when you come out to fight you leave your goulash behind. The essence of the class struggle emerges to the surface.

In such a situation, the conditions of battle will do more than this or a dozen better written pieces could ever do to improve the quality of the work of those who survive. Nonetheless, if we don't prepare before the battle, most won't survive. It's as simple as that.

Can We Succeed?

By this time, not so many people as a few years ago feel the revolutionary struggle in the U.S. is hopeless. Our people have begun to show their potential. Our Party has never doubted that we can succeed.

But it won't be easy. Those who think it's a snap are going to wake up one day and find themselves snapped flat on their backs. We are fighting a rich and powerful enemy; this enemy is not going to permit a peaceful change; this enemy cannot win in the long run, but it can kill a lot of people in the meantime.

And we cannot succeed alone. We must join forces with every possible ally among the working people, black and white, students and intellectuals, farmers, and small businessmen—in other words, the overwhelming majority of our population. This cannot be done overnight, but this must be our goal. It is a necessary prerequisite for revolution. This means united fronts, united work, alliances both temporary and long range, using the contradictions in the ruling class, distinguishing the main enemy from secondary enemies, and concentrating all forces possible against that enemy. It means we must utilize many organizational forms for mass action. In a ghetto area, for example, in addition to a PLP club, we might have a Tenants' Union, a part-time nursery school run by a committee of mothers and older sisters, cultural workshops, a health and welfare action committee, a youth defense league, etc.

This in no way means that we abandon our independent communist position, our ideological leadership of the revolutionary movement, or adopt the old C.P.'s "Hamlin" tailism in so-called united fronts. Everything in this article presupposes the continuing of our basic line, our socialist education and our open advocacy of socialist revolution as the only solution to the problems which plague our people. We are simply saying that to win we must eventually find ways to unite the above-mentioned potentially progressive elements behind the working class. At the same time, to succeed we must ally ourselves with the world revolutionary forces, especially in Latin America, Asia and Africa.

Even with this, we won't succeed automatically. Better than the question "Can we succeed?" would be "Do we dare to succeed?" Do we really want to make a revolution? Are we willing to go all the way? That question underlies all the other points in this piece.

Can we fail? Yes, it's quite possible for us to fail, although the working class eventually must succeed. Without struggle–all kinds of struggle–without allies, without deep personal *and* political roots among the working people, without remolding our ideologies, without long-range planning, without constant study and dedication, we'll certainly fail.

But with these elements, the enemy for all its A-bombs, H-bombs, chemicals, gases, and even computers is nothing but, yes, a paper tiger.

The enemy can never defeat us. Defeat or victory is up to us, ourselves, to decide.

We have already begun to overcome some of the obstacles described here; we must continue. Our achievements are growing with our experience. As we suffer some defeats and make some errors, and it is inevitable that we do, we must avoid defeatism. It's going to be a long war. If we rely on our class, the working class, and our Party, and ourselves, we cannot lose. In the end, the U.S. working class will dig the grave of U.S. imperialism.

Actually, there is no final "success" for a revolutionary. Achievement means constantly finding new goals to achieve. After the victory of the socialist revolution will come the job of building the new society, and after that something new. Each goal leads to the next. As we reach each peak, we discover one still higher, set our sights on it, and struggle upward again. Through it all, the new man is formed, the free man.

> It is not a matter of how many pounds of meat one consumes, nor how many times one is able to go to the beach, nor how many foreign luxuries can be bought. On the contrary, it is a matter of the individual feeling his complete existence, his inner resources, and understanding his responsibility to man. (Che Guevara, "Socialism and Man," *PL,* Dec. 1965, p. 93.)

This is the Man we conceive–billions of different men and women of hundreds of colors, cultures and countries united in universal labor, both mental and manual for everybody, with no exploitation. But not without struggle–researching, experimenting, probing, creating and enjoying the ever-new worlds of science and art. This man shall control his destiny. His children will learn to share and love their differences; the grasping private profit system which starves and strangles the spirit as well as the body will be an almost incredible chapter in the communist text-books on "prehistoric times."

From here to there is a long march. The graspers and stranglers will not step aside to let us pass, and they have strong arms. We will need a well-disciplined, dedicated force. Within our ranks, no one will be perfect, and all of us will be influenced to some degree by the sick society we struggle against. Yet even as we march, and even as we hate and fight the enemy, we must strive to remold ourselves—as much as we can—into that image we cherish of our communist children and grandchildren who will surely "inherit the earth."

Program for Black Liberation

FEBRUARY 1969

The struggle of Black people for their liberation has reached unprecedented heights. Beginning with the 1964 Harlem uprising, millions have engaged in open–and frequently armed–resistance to ruling-class oppression. Black rebellions represent the most advanced aspect of class struggle in the U.S. at the present time. They have shaken the ruling class as have no other events in the past 30 years.

Despite government claims, conditions of life for most Black people have worsened over the years. This is true for the entire working class, but because of the special oppression of Black people it is worse for them. They bear the brunt of the contradictions of U.S. imperialism.

U.S. imperialism has received many important setbacks around the world. Two in particular have created enormous problems for the U.S. ruling class: the People's War in Vietnam, and such increasing competition from other imperialist countries that the U.S. can no longer completely dominate Western Europe and Japan.

The resulting loss of profits has forced this country's rulers to bear down even harder on their workers, as they must if they are to continue to make the maximum profits necessary to maintain capitalism. For that system can only survive by seeking not just the average but maximum profits. This is the reason for the oppression of Black workers at home and the oppression of the people in Asia, Africa and Latin America. Nor is such oppression an aberration of capitalism or the work of particularly deranged imperialists; it is the normal and necessary operation of imperialism.

Exploitation and systematic robbery of Black workers at home is the most profitable and most vital domestic business of U.S. imperialism. By discriminating against Black people the ruling class is able to force on them a per capita income of $1,000 less per year than that of white people. When that figure is multiplied by the 22 million Black people it becomes clear that racism earns the bosses $22 billion each year. Because the ruling class is able to depress Black workers' wages, it forces down wages of all workers. Who can calculate the billions amassed by bosses each year by this method? Additional billions are saved each year by bosses who limit the life-giving social services available to Black people. Then there is the robbery of higher food prices and higher rents for inferior housing, all of which shows the enormity of Black oppression.

The cruel meaning of this for Black workers is more unemployment, lower wages, and worse living conditions. It means worse schools, worse medical facilities, more garbage on the streets, little or no decent low-rent housing, more and worse slums, high infant mortality, lower life expectancy and more police terror to prevent or contain the inevitable resistance to this state of affairs.

Such has been the treatment meted out to Black people for over 350 years, first as slaves, then as wage slaves. If one could calculate the hundreds of billions in profits derived from the super-exploitation of Black workers during the last three and a half centuries, one would see that imperialism relies on these profits for its vigor. Similarly the plunder of colonial nations in Asia, Africa and Latin America is the most profitable external business of U.S. imperialism, which explains the fierceness of the Vietnam War and the lengths to which the U.S. will go to retain its influence and control there.

The imperialists use racist ideas to justify their brutal exploitation of national minorities at home and workers and oppressed people abroad. They do this in order to set one group of workers against another and so cover up the fact that the basic and common enemy of all workers is the class of big businessmen and the imperialist system of private ownership.

Only when this imperialist system is eliminated, the government* that protects it smashed and the working class in absolute control will all the workers, for the first time, be able to lead a decent life. This means building socialism, because imperialism can only be replaced by socialism.

Imperialism exists to the degree that it can continue racist exploitation. Three and a half centuries of drumming home to

---

* By "government" we mean the entire state power—every repressive force on every level of government that can be used to blunt and defeat the workers' fight for their class interests: the army; National Guard; state, county and city police; courts; jails; laws (injunctions, martial law, etc.).

Black and white workers the myth of Black inferiority enables the ruling class to continue its oppression; and unless the working class learns to reject racism it cannot end that oppression. No worker, Black or white, should have any illusion that U.S. imperialism can ever grant full equality to Black workers. To do so would end the maximum profits made possible only by Black exploitation.

Black rebellions are currently the most advanced expression of class struggle. They are a serious threat to the ruling class, which, after the Harlem rebellion, prepared a massive effort to suppress future Black rebellions. It well understood that Black working people were not going to take their worsening conditions lying down. Though the ruling class acted to pacify some leaders and militants with the "War on Poverty" programs, it realized the limits of its economic resources. It could bribe a few leaders and co-opt many others, but 95 per cent of the 22 million Black people are part of the working class; and you can't buy off that many people! So the ruling class moved a massive police and army apparatus into action to prevent or smash the Black working people's rebellions. Ruling-class strategy, as always, was to use the dual tactic of bribery and, ultimately, terror.

In each city across the country and in many rural areas the ruling class has mustered a huge army of police, National Guard and regular Army units to suppress the forces of ever-threatening Black rebellion. In addition, the ruling class, finding itself weak, feels it necessary to augment these agencies of state power with "unofficial" vigilante groups. This serves the purpose of diverting Black and white workers from fighting the ruling class to fighting each other.

U.S. imperialism, therefore, is faced with a serious second military front at home. This limits what it can throw against other oppressed people in Asia, Africa, Latin America and socialist China and Albania. Black rebellions help the fight of all people who try to free themselves from U.S. domination. And, in turn, the efforts of any people around the world who fight the U.S. rulers help Black workers at home, since U.S. imperialists must weaken themselves trying to put down these rebellions.

Unquestionably, the heroic efforts of the Vietnamese people inspired the battle of Black workers at home. Millions of Black workers now identify with the struggles of the Vietnamese people, and many recognize that U.S. imperialism is their common enemy.

Recently, in response to the statement of Mao Tse-tung in support of the Black Liberation Movement, revolutionary forces all over the world added their voices in support of Black liberation.

The revolution in Vietnam has exposed the myth of U.S. "democracy," thereby spurring millions around the world to organize against U.S. imperialism, weakening and isolating it politically. Even a U.S. deal in Vietnam made with the help of revisionists in Hanoi and Moscow cannot perfume the stench of U.S. democracy.

Shatters U.S.A. Myth

Because Black worker rebellions occur in the heart of U.S. imperialism, they directly affect both the class struggle at home and the international class struggle. Because of this simultaneous attack on its maximum profits, U.S. rulers repress them violently, despite the political consequences. But this repression by the U.S. rulers is another blow to their phony democratic image. Black action exposes the actual character of the U.S. imperialists. This political awareness will eventually lead to even sharper efforts against the U.S. bosses at home and abroad.

The action of millions of Black workers is also a shattering blow to the myth of U.S. invincibility. Black rebellion destroys the idea of "American exceptionalism"—the idea that U.S. imperialism is "enlightened" and can master its internal contradictions. Black rebellions have pointed up the possibilities for revolution. They show the ruling class is not omnipotent, and easily panics in the face of sharp struggle. Black rebellions finish forever the racist notion that Black people are docile, servile, trained by their circumstances to endless passivity.

A life free of exploitation and oppression is only possible when the capitalist state has been smashed, capitalism outlawed, the country ruled absolutely by the workers, and socialism is being built. Capitalism and imperialism, the bosses' private ownership of industry, can only be replaced by its opposite—socialism, the workers' public ownership of industry. The most important point to be concerned about in fighting imperialism is political power. Either the imperialists have political power and use it to protect imperialism by repressing the workers, as in Vietnam, or the workers have political power and use it to repress the imperialists, outlaw capitalism and build socialism, as in China and Albania.

This workers' political power is called the proletarian (or workers') dictatorship (which means dictatorship over the imperialists).

Countries that checked imperialism but did not establish a dictatorship of the workers halted imperialism only momentarily; they are again controlled by the imperialists. Algeria, Egypt, Guinea, Ghana, India, etc., are all controlled by some imperialist or by all of them. The U.S., Britain, France and the USSR really run these countries. What has changed is the position of the national bourgeoisie (the "home-grown" bosses of the colonial country) who used to be oppresed by imperialism and now front for it.

In these countries the masses of people are in desperate straits. Their rulers call themselves socialists merely as a concession to the people's socialist beliefs and sense of international solidarity. In none of these countries do the workers hold political power. And since there are only two classes capable of holding state power–the working class or the capitalist class–it is the latter that continues to rule. The working class is still exploited and does not own or control the means of production and the state power that is needed to enforce that control. That, too, is the state of affairs, in countries once socialist, like the USSR, where the dictatorship of the workers has been overthrown and turned into its opposite–the dictatorship of the bourgeoisie.

In the supposedly "liberated" colonial countries and in the former socialist countries, the ruling bourgeoisie spreads the idea of loyalty to "our nation." But since only one class can hold power in any nation, "loyalty to the nation" can only mean loyalty to the class that holds power in that nation–which means to the bourgeoisie, in all countries not ruled by the workers' dictatorship. Such "national loyalty," which really means loyalty to imperialism, is expressed in the United States by supporting reactionary, racist, fascist and anti-working-class groups.

The ruling capitalist class urges on the workers a nationalist ideology to replace their loyalty to the international working class. The latter loyalty–internationalism–is a fundamental Marxist-Leninist idea that runs exactly counter to nationalism. Consequently it is in the class interests of U.S. imperialists to promote nationalist ideas among workers since it diverts them from loyalty to their own class. Nationalism is a bourgeois idea, which infects workers and prevents them from winning their freedom from the capitalist class.

Although Black workers today are usually consciously propelled into struggle because of their nationalist beliefs, this nationalism has its material base in the fact of special class oppression of Black workers by the ruling class. The initial reaction of Black workers to this oppression may take the form of a proud affirmation of the "blackness" which the bourgeoisie uses to set them apart for special oppression. Unless the fundamental, but usually ignored, working-class content of the Black workers' struggle becomes the conscious basis for action, the ruling class will co-opt the movement. The imperialists can always turn the initial nationalist reaction to class oppression into a reactionary movement if the nationalism is not transformed into conscious loyalty to the entire working class and to the class struggle.

In the course of the fight against class oppression, Black workers put forward special demands to meet their special class oppression. They understand these demands to be nationalist demands. There are three types of such demands: (1) the demand for more Black supervisors; (2) the demand for an end to oppressive working conditions such as speedup (which may even take the form of saying "speedup is an attempt to destroy the Black workers"); and (3) the demand for preferential hiring and upgrading.

The first type of demand will not help end special class oppression of Black workers. On the contrary, it will intensify it; it is a bourgeois demand. It creates a group of Black straw bosses who will be more effective than white straw bosses in running the factories and overcoming Black workers' resentment against the bosses. This must be opposed.

The second type of demand is clearly in the interests of the entire working class; we support it. The fight against such conditions as speedup is a fight against oppression of all workers, even though some Black workers may see speedup merely as a special attack on them.

The third type of demand is in the interests of the entire working class, although this is not always clearly understood by white and Black workers. Such demands are in opposition to the special class oppression of Black workers. Imperialism requires this special oppression to maintain itself. The struggle against this special oppression, to improve the conditions of Black workers, is a struggle against the imperialist system that is responsible for the common oppression of all workers. White workers must therefore support such demands.

The real answer to the ruling class' nationalist ideology, which corrupts the struggle for class demands, lies in Marxism-Leninism, which rests on internationalism and loyalty to the working class and is the only serious enemy of imperialism. It is only Marxism-Leninism that can take the imperialists' state power from them and place it in the hands of the workers.

Therefore, it is decisive for Marxist-Leninists to be actively involved in all aspects of the class struggle in our country and through these struggles learn how to win millions of people to the fight for the workers' dictatorship. All history proves conclusively that no people can determine its own destiny without the dictatorship of the workers.

Black Workers' Key Role

Black people in our county are overwhelmingly workers, with almost two million in the organized labor movement. Many are in basic industry, often in the most decisive sections. Therefore, the essence of Black liberation is working-class liberation. And a correct revolutionary strategy must be working-class struggle based on the needs of Black workers.

A worker-led Black Liberation Movement, however, will not easily spring up. The revisionist (anti-Marxist-Leninist) notion of "all-class unity" is still the prevailing idea of Black militants within the movement. For years the Communist Party pushed this idea. It claims that since all Blacks are oppressed by being Black, and since all Blacks are equally oppressed, it is irrelevant to differentiate them into classes. Rather, the common bond provided by ruling class oppression unifies all Black people; and if Black people are not unified they are weakened.

This theory contains a fundamental error: It disputes the pre-eminence of Black workers, thereby requiring and justifying the leadership of the petty bourgeoisie. And this means accepting the reactionary bunk of middle-class Black nationalists.

All-class unity means obscuring class demands and accepting ruling-class ideology. First it meant encouraging the non-violent integrationist leadership. As the various Rev. King types lost their footing among large sections of militants, they were replaced by Black Power advocates. Their aim was not to defeat imperialism but to reform it and get "in" using more militant tactics than their predecessors.

The ostensible goal of the "all class unity" theory was the "completion of the bourgeois-democratic revolution." Although the C.P. and others occasionally mouthed the idea of Black workers being in leadership, what they actually had in mind was gaining equality under capitalism for Black people. But this is impossible. The outlook must be to smash capitalism, get rid of the existing state apparatus and replace it with the dictatorship of the proletariat. And this can only be done under the leadership of the working class–Black and white.

Later, demands of Black Power advocates were outlined as Black capitalism. This has been further refined to demands for "community control" or "decentralization." Most leaders of these movements were virtually bought off. This was done through the various government anti-poverty agencies, private foundations like the Ford Foundation, or simply working for the government.

Many petty-bourgeois forces used the militancy and national feelings of Black masses to bargain for a place in the bourgeois sun. Obviously, ruling class strategy is not reduced to terror. To contain Black liberation, the ruling class works to impose on Black people a phony leadership. They have already succeeded in doing this to white workers.

A Black bourgeoisie never developed in the U.S., although many people talk about one. Black people do not own any significant portion of the means of production. They are not a factor in the basic economic ownership of the country. There is no national Black bourgeoisie in the United States; and even if there were there would be no justification for its leadership of the Black Liberation Movement.

In many colonial countries the national bourgeoisie often struggles against the imperialists for a larger share of the profits. At some stage in this struggle the national bourgeoisie may attempt to enlist the support of workers. However, the national bourgeoisie will always betray any workers with whom it has formed a temporary alliance. This occurs when workers begin to rid themselves of nationalism and adopt working-class struggle attitudes and practices towards imperialists and towards the national bourgeoisie. In other words, when workers of an oppressed country fight for class leadership, for the dictatorship of the proletariat, the national bourgeoisie will unite with the imperialists to stop it. For example: In Egypt the national bourgeoisie, under Nasser's leadership, with the USSR as its main economic and military backer, has been murdering communists and militants for years while mouthing an anti-imperialist line. In Indonesia when the national bourgeoisie felt the power of the communist movement and of the workers and peasants was too strong, it slaughtered 500,000, using Soviet and U.S. imperialist aid. And the bloodbaths and jailings aren't over. The Indian ruling class has wiped out each electoral victory of the people with killings and jailings. There, too, the military arsenal is furnished by the Soviet Union and the U.S. All this proves that the national bourgeoisie is the implacable enemy of the people. And you surely can't vote them out.

As long as the Black Liberation Movement remains under the leadership of fake radicals, basing themselves on the petty bourgeoisie, it is no threat to the ruling class. Within the Black community there is a tiny group of small businessmen who want a monopoly market in the Black community. There is a larger group of offspring of this small middle class and of other relatively privileged families who want to "make it" in the white capitalist world. These petty-bourgeois forces, often reactionary "intellectuals" like LeRoi Jones, demogogically identify with the militancy of the Black masses. They are articulate and, with the cooperation of the bourgeois publicity media, they emerge as the "leaders" and "spokesmen" of the Black masses. After they get a little footing among the people–when they have 40 or 50 followers–they demand that the bosses give them jobs. One could fill the pages of a book with the names of Black "leaders" who now work for the government or the Ford Foundation.

The burning militancy of the Black masses impels the ruling class to engage in this farce because it is in the ruling class' interests. It slows the development of working-class leaders thoroughly dedicated to the defeat of imperialism. It slows the development of long-range strategy and planning. It limits unity of Black and white workers. These Black middle-class elements manipulate the understandable anti-white feeling in the Black community in order to share the plunder of racist imperialism. The sight of leader after leader selling out reinforces cynicism and defeatism already found among sections of the Black community.

The idea of "all-class unity" under petty-bourgeois leadership must be replaced by a Black Liberation Movement that is a workers' movement. It will be led by workers and compel support from the Black middle class. Gradually, the ideology of nationalism must give way to Marxism-Leninism. Only the ideas of Marxism-Leninism can liberate the working class from imperialism. Furthermore, only such a development can save the petty bourgeoisie from vacillation and corruption, for it is only this development that can pull the petty bourgeoisie out of the arms of the ruling class and unify it with Black workers. When working-class leadership emerges from factories to organize the ghetto, the shackles of nationalism will begin to fall away.

If the Black people are to play their historic role in the defeat of imperialism the Black Liberation Movement must be a workers' movement. It must have workers' leadership.

Black workers are equipped to lead the fight for the workers' dictatorship. They are disciplined and organized by conditions of work. The enemy is clear to them since they are at the point of production and they see more easily that the enemy is the boss. Black workers have to fight on the job. This means taking on the boss, his foremen and flunky union misleaders. And because of their special oppression within the working class they understand now how the boss uses the state apparatus to hold power. Open repression by the police, the National Guard and the Army are now a part of their life conditions, especially since 1964.

Studies of Black rebellions have proven that stable Black workers were thoroughly involved. Black workers are trained by life conditions to shoulder the job of leadership. They are involved in the class struggle on all fronts. They have the best experience for building solid class organizations in the shops and communities, and can give active, correct leadership to the struggles in the ghettoes. This is what the ruling class fears.

Black workers work side by side with white workers. They are more aware of the need for unity to win the smallest demand. All the demands that are in the interest of Black workers correspond to the needs of white workers. This creates the possibility for future unity. Their common struggle is the arena in which racism, an extreme form of nationalism (and after anti-communism the main internal danger in the working-class movement), can be defeated. As fighting unity grows between Black and white workers, Black nationalism, a reaction to racism, will recede.

Just as the Black workers can use their experience in fighting the ruling class in the shop to give leadership to the whole Black Liberation Movement, so, too, do the Black workers—specially oppressed in all aspects of life—bring a special militance and class understanding to the working-class movement at the point of production. In many instances using the form of Black caucuses, they have advanced class demands against the bosses (and fought their "labor lieutenants") in a way that has drawn tens of thousands of white workers into militant class struggle.

Black workers in the auto industry, reacting specifically to racist oppression, have organized wildcat strikes at Dodge in Michigan, at Ford's Mahwah (N.J.) plant and elsewhere throughout the country after the assassination of King. Most of these walkouts have occurred over oppressive working conditions on the assembly line and most have inexorably drawn the white workers into the action, for they too feel the implacable tension and harassment on the line. These are actions that worry Reuther and partially explain why he is organizing a "dynamic" second labor federation. Just another attempt to cover up the racist character of the top leadership of the labor movement.

The strike of 1,300 Black sanitationmen in Memphis against the ruling-class structure of the anti-union and unorganized South was a milestone in stimulating trade unionism and class struggle all over that region among Black and white workers. The sanitationmen brought not only the militance of the Black Liberation Movement into a trade union struggle but organized the active mass support of the whole Black community. Without both that militance and backing they never could have won. The ruling class in Memphis fought tooth and nail against the sanitationmen because they feared the thrust of the militance and class understanding of the Black Liberation Movement in setting an example for unionization all over the low-wage South.

The rebellion of 15,000 shipbuilding workers in Newport News (Va.) in July 1967 was sparked by the refusal to work compulsory overtime by 200 Black workers in the transportation department. Actually that issue was but the latest of a long list of grievances suffered at the hands of the biggest employer in the state (and the biggest shipbuilder in the world) and his helpers in the sellout company union. What began as a departmental walkout quickly spread to become the first shutdown of that company in its 81-year history. When the white majority saw that the Black workers' demands were on behalf of all workers, they united to fight the company, the union misleaders, the courts, the governor and the full power of the state cops and state troopers. A two-day rebellion ensued in which white and Black workers smashed the pawnshop and finance company loan sharks that fed like leeches on the workers' paychecks across the street from the plant. "They fought us like brothers," said the police chief.

Examples such as these are becoming even more numerous: the 1968 summer's wildcat strikes in Chicago involving drivers for the city's bus company and for Railway Express, both sparked by Black caucuses and both supported by white workers; the walkouts and threatened walkouts of New York hospital workers, overwhelmingly Black and Latin, which have set the pace in militance for all low-paid workers; and the titanic battle of 800 garment workers against a world-wide imperialist outfit, Kayser-Roth, as well as their sweetheart partners-in-crime, the International Ladies Garment Workers Union sellout misleadership. This fight, too, was supported by white workers wherever the issue was brought to them.

The growth of a working-class Black Liberation Movement under the leadership of workers will be a powerful stimulus to the class struggle in the country. It will sharpen it and will clarify for all workers the problem of who the enemy is. The development of a worker-led Black Liberation Movement is a pre-condition for the unity and victory of the working class, a pre-condition for Black liberation.

Elements of Program

White chauvinism—the idea that being white makes one superior—is rampant among white workers. The struggle of white workers lags behind Blacks. Certainly white workers have not begun to grasp the Marxian truth that the worker in the white skin can never be free until the worker in the Black skin is free. Consequently at this stage the Black Liberation Movement is developing as national in form and working class in content.

The organization of a national network of Black caucuses in shops across the country would be a most welcome development. For many years Black caucuses have existed in basic industry, with particularly strong roots in steel and auto. Though most have been short-lived, they are once again springing up. The most notable of these are in auto. In the past year there have been major walkouts by Dodge workers, mainly Black, under the leadership of a Black caucus. Their program is a working-class program and includes more jobs, better pay, an end to speed-up, no compulsory overtime, shorter hours and an end to abuses from foremen. And there are also good demands based on the special oppression and needs of Black workers, such as equality in hiring, upgrading and job training. Of course, when boss-inspired nationalist ideology stimulates such demands as Black foremen and stock options, they must be resisted and defeated. These caucuses could amalgamate locally and eventually lead to the re-birth of a new powerful nationwide Black workers' organization.

One element of a program based on a caucus movement in the shops would be to fight against the special oppression of Black workers. This would include equal pay, upgrading, preferential hiring in all industries (especially the ones that exclude Black workers), special training and rank-and-file representation in unions.

The following have been demanded by Black caucuses and can immediately unite all workers: higher wages, shorter hours with no loss in pay and demands dealing with problems of speedup, automation and safety.

A second area in the program of the Black Liberation Movement is anti-U.S. imperialism. An important aspect of this is how the ruling class tries to make mercenaries of Black workers to suppress colonial workers and peasants. The main demands today would be for the U.S. to get out of Vietnam now, organization of Black troops against the war, utilization of skills learned in the army by Black troops to defend whatever gains were won by the Black Liberation Movement and to protect the community from police terror, and U.S. out of Puerto Rico, Dominican Republic and other occupied countries.

Within the community a program is needed to prevent the pacification of the ghetto by placing in its midst huge bourgeois institutions, like the State Office Building in the middle of Harlem. A fight must be made for funds to improve and build more schools, hospitals, parks, for improved garbage collection and more and better housing. This program should include plans for low-rent housing and punishment for slumlords.

A key aspect of any program for Black liberation is armed

self-defense, a concept in opposition to the liberal-revisionist clamor for more Black cops or for decentralization of the police. Decentralization of police control would still keep the police under the control of the ruling class because they would pick, train and pay the new Black policemen. But more important, the Black policemen would still enforce the laws of imperialist private property. In fact, many in the ruling class feel this can now be done better by Black cops. This would be another slick maneuver to prevent the people from organizing their own protection and would reduce their fighting capacity by creating the illusion that they controlled the police.

The essence of a program for Black liberation is anti-imperialism, and is based mainly on working-class demands. It would steer clear of "democratic" demands for decentralization, more Black representation in legislative bodies, and federal money and foundation funds to support Black organizations. It would shun and resist bourgeois demands for Black foremen or Black bosses and businesses. This immediately distinguishes it from any other program. Its particular significance is that it is based on, and is led by, Black workers.

This program could create the basis for a united front between Marxist-Leninist revolutionaries and the broadest stratum of the Black workers, as well as with a significant section of the middle class.

Black Students

During the past few years Black students in Black colleges across the country have rebelled, in many cases going far beyond the militancy of SDS demonstrations. Through a few of the actions reached the level of armed confrontations with the police, students' demands were generally limited to improving their education.

In addition, Black student groups have come forward at many of the major white institutions all over the country. These groups have fought for more Black student enrollment, improved curriculum relating to Black history and culture and, at Columbia and San Francisco State, elements of an anti-imperialist program.

The major weakness of these movements is that they don't have a working-class orientation. Nationalism is strong, sometimes leading the struggle into the dead-end of "Black student power." Basically the goals of the Black students are limited to securing a better deal for themselves from the schools and from the ruling class. They are not aimed at defeating the system.

Within these movements attempts should be made to promote alliances with Black workers. Almost all major labor action includes large sections of Black workers. The Newport News shipyard strike of Black and white workers could have been a great rallying point for all militant Black students in the South. Suffice it to say there are no shortages of similar battles taking place, or soon to occur.

Black students–as well as white–must start the long process of determining with whom they are going to ally. Will they fight the ruling class for crumbs but support the framework of capitalism, or will they ally with workers? Helping workers win immediate demands, as well as their own at school, creates the basis for a political transformation of students and workers. This alliance will speed the growth of political consciousness.

Racism is an essential part of the liberal apology for imperialism disseminated by universities; it must be fought by white students as well as Black. Alliances should be formed between Black students and anti-racist white students based on a principled fight over this issue against the campus administration. In fact there is no way to build a radical movement on campus and a worker-student alliance without a strong fight to defeat racism.

Such a united front between Black workers, including communists, and a section of the middle class will exclude those who rely on the ruling class, which includes those few who still parade under the slogan of integration or those pushing "community control" and "decentralization." And because this movement is aimed at the bosses and their government it will limit the indiscriminate "hate whitey" bunch. Though we can expect considerable antagonism against white workers, they are not the enemy and must be criticized with the aim of winning them. A serious Black leadership must have the outlook of fighting racism among white workers to help gain strength for specific and long-range battles.

This will be a Left-Center coalition with varying points of view within it. It must include communists, who, together with their closest allies, must defeat anti-communists within the Black Liberation Movement–or that movement will fail. No movement can win if it is saturated with anti-communism. The anti-communism of Roy Wilkins has given way to the more subtle anti-communism of Black clerics like King. And now there is an extremely bellicose "revolutionary" anti-communism produced by so-called militants like Stokely Carmichael. Anti-communism, no matter how much it is covered over with verbal militancy, is still imperialism's primary ideological weapon against any people. You cannot win with the ideas and tools of the master.

For years the ruling class has harped on the idea of the "outside agitator," with the specific aim of excluding communists from the Black Liberation Movement. Men like Roy Wilkins and King dedicatedly carried out this line. Communists not only threatened their leadership but more important, threatened their bosses. The ruling class tries to exclude communists from all movements by creating the notion that Marxism-Leninism is a foreign idea and alien to our people. It knows that it can only retain control if it keeps revolutionary ideas and organization out of the people's movements.

A Left-Center coalition will provide an effective cutting edge against the ruling class and be the vehicle to defeat right-wing Black forces like the Muslims, cultural nationalists like LeRoi Jones, the various successors of Rev. King, phony radicals like Carmichael, and Black-capitalist spokesmen like McKissick.

The Ford Fraud

The growing militancy of Black workers and the corresponding drop in influence of Rev. King's successors have compelled the ruling class to take a more flexible attitude to Black Power advocates. It has not always been skillful in using them. At one time the ruling class felt that between the praying of Rev. King, the general bribing of the middle-class leaders and the guns, clubs, dogs and police, they could keep the Black people in line. But the eruption of armed rebellion forced the ruling class to reevaluate its team of frontmen. One could say the limited outbreak of sniping forced this. Guns are a dangerous business. So, within a short time everyone was for "Black Power." All the politicians became "soul brothers."

It soon became obvious that the anti-poverty programs could only buy off a relatively small number of militants. The ruling class knew it would have to do better. Recognizing that education was a burning issue within the ghetto for millions of Black working-class families, the ruling class decided that this was a good place to harness the new nationalism and buy off the new nationalists. In "reorganized" schools the ruling class could continue the miseducation of millions of children with the full cooperation of the Black Power nationalists. The Ford Foundation, the leading bourgeois ideological and management center outside the government, was chosen to do the job. It adopted the slogan "community control."

The Foundation devised a plan by which the Board of Education would create local governing boards. The local board would have some paid staffers and some parents elected by a few people in the community. The plan also called for introducing aspects of Black history and culture into the curriculum together with more Black teachers. The more ardently nationalistic the teachers, the more anti-communist and anti-working class they were. What could be the big danger to the ruling class? The children would be in school and presumably more interested in the new curriculum. The parents would be happier, because it would appear that they had some say in the schooling process. And the nationalists could have all their psychotherapeutic name-calling of "whitey" institutionalized. They would get pretty good pay. And some of the administrators would have the "privilege" of embezzling from the Foundation like their white counterparts.

Applying this scheme in New York City, the ruling class received some fringe benefits. Setting up local boards deflected the mounting criticism of the central board and the city administration. The city, state and federal government still controlled all the money, still controlled the entire teacher-training apparatus. However, by skillfully manipulating the teachers' racist ideology, which led them to be controlled by racist union leadership, they got Black and Puerto Rican parents to fight the teachers as the main enemy. This let the government off the hook and obscured the key issues of anti-communism, the Vietnam war, ruling-class control of the school system, and the poor working and learning conditions of teachers and students. The ruling class, by creating the illusion of community control, has manipulated the teachers into fighting the parents instead of the Board of Education, thereby laying the basis for the destruction of any decent type of union.

The two hundred thousand dollars the Ford Foundation will spend in New York, and the tens of millions it will spend around the country, is a cheap price to pay to continue the miseducation of Black children with anti-communist, anti-working class ideas. It is a cheap price to pacify some Black people. It is a very cheap price if it keeps Black people within the framework of the system, creating the illusion that the system is flexible enough to be forced into meeting them part way. It is even a cheaper price if this slows down the class struggle in the auto shops and in all industry.

Unfortunately, many people are taken in by the Ford Foundation, and especially by its money. They rationalize the money grab: "Now we're getting a little of it back." But by now we should have learned the lesson that the enemy gives nothing for free. If you take his money or his "aid," you are working for him, no matter how well-intentioned you are.

The school decentralization plan is reaping quick returns. There is now a move to do something similar with the police. Isn't it better, the ruling class reasons, to have Black cops drawn from the ranks of the most militant, having respect in the community? Let them maintain the ruling-class interests. The ruling class has a great opening here. And most Black nationalists, having no understanding of the class structure of society, greedily see a way to get some jobs and money. Most call for more Black cops in the ghetto.

The ruling class reasons well when it recognizes that the current advocates of Black Power "want in" on imperialism's spoils, like the integrationists. There are only some differences in form and tactics between the integrationists and the Black Power advocates. They are both the same in content. Having a Ford in your future means having capitalism in your future. Having Ford's better idea means not having working-class ideas and never winning your freedom.

Within the ruling class there are tactical differences about how to handle the new Black nationalists. But as the Black masses keep up the pressure all the ruling-class factions will eventually make greater use of nationalists.

Revisionism Means Slavery

Over the past 25 years the Communist Party has lost its base among Black people primarily because of its consistent selling-out of the Black people's struggles. During the past decade it pinned its hopes on the integrationist leadership. It slobbered over Rev. King. However, it should be noted that at the beginning of the integration movement the C.P. branded it "adventurous." It considered the first Freedom Rides a "provocation." But when the integration movement became established and politically conservative, the C.P. hopped on the bandwagon, reasoning that the Black people were in ferment and King could put his non-violent, pro-imperialist ideas over on the people without running afoul of the imperialists. By supporting him the C.P. hoped to curry favor with the base of his movement.

When the rebellions broke out in Harlem in 1964, the C.P., King and the rest of the ruling class attacked them. They attacked the masses and called on police power to put them down. The C.P. attacked the PLP, accusing it of fomenting disorders with "Chinese money," and got the Kremlin "leaders" to attack the Black masses. The District Attorney used the C.P.'s lies and opportunism in court against the PLP.

But as the tide of rebellion became irresistible the C.P., like the ruling class, had to hedge its bets. Since it could no longer rely completely on King & Co., the C.P., like Ford and the U.S. Government, began to hail "Black Power." It became a "soul brother" and like the Ford Foundation hopped on the community control bandwagon. Petty bourgeois nationalism posed no serious obstacle for this "Communist" Party. Because the C.P. has no base among Black workers it is not visible in the movement. Consequently there is a tendency to underestimate its influence. Like the Ford Foundation, it buys its way in, often with lawyers who are always willing to "help" a Black victim out.

Because of the C.P.'s financial resources, it is able to co-opt some of the nationalist leaders in the community. Probably some of the community control bureaucrats are on two or three payrolls. They get paid by the C.P., the Ford Foundation and the Government. Fortunately, the C.P.'s consistent record of betrayal and its support of the shameful imperialism of the Soviet bosses isolate it from the people.

But because there is so much corruption at the top, money turns the trick. The C.P. does influence some nationalists to push community control or whatever new nationalist gimmick that comes along. It has gotten the Black Panthers to institute court actions for police decentralization in New York and California, and has influenced them to meet with Lindsay and the New York police commissioner to discuss "mutual problems." The C.P. role is one of guaranteeing the leadership of the liberal bourgeoisie, which in New York means the Lindsay administration. It is no accident that the C.P. is one of the biggest boosters of community control of the schools in New York. Unfortunately it is doing a lot of damage to the development of the Black Panthers. C.P. lawyers have persuaded some Panther leaders to rely on court action rather than mass action. The current actions for decentralization of the cops are C.P. inspired.

Anti-communism was given a big boost among Black workers because of the sellouts they suffered at the hands of the revisionist C.P. from World War II until the present day. The C.P. either never fought anti-communism or denied its existence.

Unless anti-communism is met head-on and defeated, it will cripple and destroy revolutionary movements. Only communist organization and ideology, based on class analysis and the need for workers to seize state power, can lead to victory over imperialism. Thus, those who tolerate or advocate anti-communism are advocating the continued exploitation and suppression of the Black as well as the white workers. Nationalism and anti-communism are inseparable.

About Our Party

In the past we in the Progressive Labor Party have been guilty of creating illusions about Black nationalism and nationalists. In our early period we were one-sided; because we supported the resistance of nationalists like the Muslims and Robert Williams, we viewed them as generally good. We failed to understand that nationalism is reactionary, and that this is its main aspect. We made similar errors internationally. We were wrong in evaluating Ben Bella, and then Boumedienne. We were wrong in our evaluation of Sukarno.

The political and economic basis of nationalism is capitalism. It is bourgeois ideology. Often we tried to understand the Black Liberation Movement through the experiences of other countries. We believed nationalism here would play the same role that it has appeared to play in other countries, where a national bourgeoisie often resisted complete foreign domination.

Loyalty to one's class and the international working class

must replace narrow allegiance to a nation or a grouping within a nation. As long as oppressed people are limited to defending the nation—that is, the ruling class of that nation—they will remain enslaved. As long as people remain loyal only to themselves as an oppressed national minority, they will fail. Unless they aim to liberate all of oppressed mankind they will be unable to liberate even themselves. Although the nationalists may win some small initial gains, even these will be lost unless the strategy of the dictatorship of the proletariat emerges, for this is the only strategy for victory. The outlook of Black Power advocates today narrows down finally to "get what you can," a form of Black capitalism.

In any event, there is no national bourgeoisie here. There is only a relatively small Black petty bourgeoisie. We have been guilty of spending too much effort with them and failing to work sufficiently among Black workers, especially in the shops. We made these errors because we did not fully understand that Black liberation could not be won without the dictatorship of the proletariat. By making these errors we limited our base-building among workers and left the petty bourgeoisie open to co-option. Without a strong working-class leadership, the petty bourgeoisie will always vacillate and limit its efforts against the ruling class.

When the special oppression of a particular group among the masses becomes the initial stimulus for action, the capitalist class attempts immediately to saturate that group with nationalist ideology—loyalty to the bourgeoisie. Unless that initial stimulus is transformed into conscious class struggle it is co-opted by the ruling class, which has learned from experience that it can quickly turn such an initial progressive response into its opposite—into nationalist loyalty to capitalism.

An even more significant error is that we have not fought vigorously against white chauvinism among workers and students. This is because we are still weak in understanding how racism is used to maintain ruling-class power. Though we have singled out nationalism as the chief internal weakness in the Black Liberation Movement, we dare not fail to understand that white chauvinism is, after anti-communism, the main weakness within the entire working class. Nationalism can never be defeated without defeating white chauvinism and its foundation, U.S. imperialism.

The working class will eventually unite into an unbeatable force as Black and white workers become more politically conscious. This can only be achieved by sharpening the struggle.

Future unity is a goal, but this should in no way imply the slowing down of the Black Liberation Movement. On the contrary, the path to unity is through increased struggle on all fronts. Naturally there will be struggles between different groups of workers, but this is an inevitable feature in the process of developing greater political consciousness.

Unity will be achieved by the creation of centers for Black struggles, especially in the shops. Virtually all actions of Black caucuses can be aimed at the boss. This fact of life will create the condition for the unity of Black and white workers, as communists in the workers' movement give political leadership.

The next important moves for our Party are to step up the struggle against nationalism and to focus our work among Black workers. As the political consciousness of the workers grows under the leadership of Black caucuses and the work of communists, organizational unity of the workers will be realizeable. Even today wherever there is the possibility of unity between Black and white workers that form should be used. In every case a study of the situation must be made to find the form that best advances the class struggle.

Though we still use the concept self-determination we believe that the dictatorship of the proletariat is the only solution for Black workers and the Black people generally. In the future, however, the petty-bourgeois tendency for separation (Black capitalism) may grow strong and come into sharp conflict with the ruling class. If the imperialists acted to physically destroy this movement we would support it against imperialism. We would support it by fighting for the dictatorship of the proletariat as the only solution.

This is our attitude in regard to Vietnam. Though we no longer believe that the Vietnamese leadership is fighting for the dictatorship of the proletariat, we support the efforts of the people against imperialism and demand that the U.S. get out now, regardless of what type government the Vietnamese wish to set up. We also call upon the Vietnamese workers and peasants to fight for the dictatorship of the proletariat as the only way they can determine their own destiny.

We regard this as a principled concession to nationalism because it is within the framework of a serious fight against imperialism. If not for the anti-imperialist struggle there would be no reason for the concession.

The Question of Black Women

Women have always been a specially-exploited section of the working class. U.S. imperialism has maintained and extended this special exploitation by barring women from certain types of work, paying lower wages for work similar to men's, and by using them as a special "reserve" force against militant male workers. There has always been, too, a systematic ideological campaign to place women socially, politically and economically beneath the status of the male population in general. As Engels said, "within the family, he is the bourgeoisie, and she is the proletariat."

While this special exploitation of women is true in general, it is more brutal when applied to Black women; they must face super-exploitation as workers who are Black, together with the additional burden of being women. The super-exploitation of women and the triple-exploitation of Black women workers can only end with the destruction of imperialism and the construction of a workers' dictatorship.

It is precisely because of the special position of women and the brutal exploitation of Black women that they therefore are the most potentially revolutionary section of the working class; they are the most oppressed and therefore will fight back the hardest. Recent history has shown that Black women have taken leading roles in the fight for better housing, welfare, against police brutality and drug addiction. As a result, U.S. imperialism, attempting to use its "divide and conquer" technique, is attempting to utilize the old male supremacist standby to split Black women from Black men.

Ruling-class "scholars" and press are telling Black men to regain their "rightful male position" in their lives and "not permit their own emasculation." And, at the same time, the so-called "revolutionaries" in the ghetto, the "cultural nationalists," preach that Black women should stand behind their men and play a supporting role. Some even claim that this is in the historical "African tradition." It is much the same argument that the ruling class uses when it tells Black Americans that their forefathers on the Southern plantations "liked the warm, leisurely way of life."

In seeking to find African roots for the ruling-class inspired campaign of oppression, the Black nationalists distort the feelings of internationalism that Black people have for their brethren in Africa, and the other colored peoples of Asia and Latin America. In line with this insidious plot, they foist drugs, which were forced upon the people of Latin America and Asia, as a "traditional Asian experience" and even prostitution of Black women, in the name of the "traditional polygamous forms of marriage" in Africa.

These ruling-class inspired plots to split Black men from women will not work in the long run. As Black and white workers will fight to defeat the common class enemy, so Black men and women will defeat the splittist tactics of the enemy. As the working class generally will be led by communist Black workers, leaders among these Black working-class revolutionaries will be Black women.

While racism is the greatest source of profit for the ruling class, it is also its Achilles Heel. Racism has created a huge politically advanced force for the working class. Black people have shown the greatest persistence and courage against imperialism. This advance force of fighting Blacks is having the same effect in the U.S. as the Vietnamese are having in the world. The ruling class can buy up some of the loudmouths, but it can't buy off 22 million fighting Blacks—any more than it can buy off tens of millions of other workers and students.

Black workers are beginning to see that to achieve their liberation the only answer lies in Marxism-Leninism—the science of class struggle and proletarian revolution. This is the science of the international working class of which Black working people in the United States are an integral part.

Black Workers: Key Revolutionary Force

FEBRUARY 1969

Imperialism has one primary need—to amass maximum profits. Therefore, the oppression of Black workers at home and the domination of oppressed peoples in Asia, Africa and Latin America is not merely an aberration of deranged imperialists, but the necessary operation of imperialism.

Racism is the political expression of imperialism; it organizes and justifies such brutal exploitation at home and abroad that the exploitation of Black workers is the most profitable domestic business of U.S. imperialism.

Wage differentials between Black and white workers each year amount to $22 billion. In addition, billions more are saved by denying Black Americans the vital social services necessary for survival; this is the enormity of Black oppression.

Imperialism as a system must perpetuate racism in order to thrive; it must continue to reap the super-profits derived from the "racial inferiority" thesis it has drummed home into both Black and white workers.

Consequently, the ability of the working class to reject racism is crucial to its ability to end class oppression. U.S. imperialism cannot exist without the brutal super-exploitation of Black people and, therefore, will never grant equality to Black workers.

The fact of this $22 billion of super-profits raked in by the bosses in this country permeates every aspect of life. It leads us to the conclusion that unless an all-out fight is made against the racism that permits this robbery—a battle waged by revolutionaries in the first place and by the working class in general—then (1) the workers will be unable to make any basic advances in their class interests and establish a Left-Center coalition to lead their fight against the bosses; (2) the danger of fascism will increase; (3) the hacks who serve the ruling class at the head of the trade union movement will continue to ride roughshod over the interests of the rank and file; and (4) no Marxist-Leninist revolutionary party will succeed in the United States.

The basic industries on which the U.S. ruling class depends for its very existence are increasingly using Black workers as a source of labor power. In the auto industry, which affects one out of every seven jobs in this country, there is a growing Black minority. No longer limited to 10 or 20 per cent of the work force, it now makes up 35 to 50 per cent, and in many plants Black workers are in a majority. In the steel mills the Black work force has reached about 35 per cent of the total. In the next 8 to 10 years the present 500,000-man work force in basic steel is expected to dwindle to 200,000 if the $2 billion annual capital investment plans of steel bosses produce their planned results. Since the preponderance of Black workers are among the unskilled—those most likely to be affected by such plans–a fierce struggle involving tens of thousands of Black workers is looming.

The transportation industries are gaining increasing numbers of Black workers, since this is another area that hires many unskilled workers. In many metropolitan mass transit systems, Black workers form a majority. This is also true in other "vital city services" such as sanitation where Black workers compose from 30 to 70 per cent of the work force.

Thus, though Black workers compose only 10-15 per cent of the population, their presence–and militancy–in such vital areas of the economy as basic industry, the key unionized sectors, and key industries in big cities, gives them a far greater importance than their numbers suggest; in fact, a decisive importance.

Consider New York City, for instance: Black and Latin workers make up 25 per cent of the population but are a majority, or near it, in mass transit, sanitation, garment, post office, welfare department, and are sizable minorities in teamsters, railroad, longshore, distribution and city government. Though New York's white workers form majorities in some of these industries, most of them are in the skilled crafts and in the white-collar sales areas. Black workers, therefore, being either a majority or sizable militant minority, can bring the city's politicians and their bosses to their knees.

The above example can be repeated in other large cities where Black workers make up an even larger percentage of the population–up to 40 and even 50 per cent in places like Chicago, New Orleans, Newark, and Detroit.

Since capitalism as a system creates racism, there is more to the problem than just the effects within the working class at the point of production. The ruling-class-created ghetto so permeates every area of life that white workers–and the middle class–can no longer escape its growing effects. During the New York school shutdown, a racist fight affected every neighborhood in the city as Black parents demanded better education for their children.

But the effects of the ghetto spread far beyond education: super profits to banks grow from mortgages on ghetto housing; rebellions begin to shape the uses of the army and national guard as well as local police forces; the flight of whites to surrounding areas makes Black people a greater force within the cities and creates sharper contradictions about "who pays" for the running of the city, since the remaining Black workers are the lowest paid; the hopelessness of ghetto life leads Black youth to enlist in the armed forces or await the draft, making for a less stable military to depend on in foreign imperialist wars and in domestic rebellions. The increasing revolts among Black servicemen in Vietnam and here at home attest to this instability. The special oppression also leads to a greater resistance to being drafted by many Black youth. Both types of opposition to the military creates a greater need for the ruling class to figure out ways to put more pressure on white youth to "serve their time," resulting in all kinds of new gimmicks to maintain a standing army. Again the special oppression of Black people sharpens the contradictions for the whole population.

Of course, the ruling class has many "answers" for these problems: "community control"; breaking up present slums with middle-class housing and relocating Black people in new slums; making welfare clients into case-aides and eliminating caseworkers, who cost more money; hiring more Black cops and national guardsmen, as well as turning militant Black youths in the ghetto into local police forces over Black workers ("community control of the police").

Though it's been said that fascism will come to the U.S. in the guise of democracy, it is more important to say that racism will be the main tool the ruling class uses to turn white workers and the white middle class to fascism. The bosses will try to present the Black workers as the main enemy in every one of the situations already cited, thereby preventing the specially oppressed Black workers from leading the whole working class in revolution against the bosses.

Recent Experiences in Labor Movement

The central importance of the fight against racism—and the potential for working-class victory if the fight is successful—is reflected in the fact that it is fast becoming the burning question in just about every major trade union and community struggle now taking place.

In the New York City school shut-down, the Shanker leadership of the United Federation of Teachers has done the bidding of the bosses by calling a racist walkout directed essentially against the Black and Latin working-class parents of the city. The split between white and Black workers in New York has not only hurt any common class struggle against these bosses, but has set rank-and-file white teachers fighting ghetto parents, and generally taken the heat off the main enemy—the ruling class' Board of Education.

In a recent major rank-and-file led strike in New York's largest industry, garment (see *PL,* October, 1968), racism was the tactic the bosses tried to use to split the Black and Latin workers. This was a particularly important gambit for the garment bosses because these workers were setting an outstanding example to the 250,000 workers in the garment center and could become of decisive importance in breaking the boss-banker-ILGWU-Mafia-police hold on those workers. Nor did the ruling class lose sight of the fact that half of these quarter-million workers live in the ghetto and could bring it special organized leadership because of the experience gained in their struggles against the bosses at the point of production.

In recent auto wildcats, the issue of racism assumed an increasing importance. First there were the King assassination walkouts, led by Black workers, which shut down the plants; in some cases the companies tried to forestall the movement by voluntarily closing down "in memoriam" before the Black workers walked. Then there were disorganized attempts by white workers to walk after Kennedy was killed, but these were racist reactions. (If "they" could shut it down for one of "their own" why can't we do the same for one of "ours.") For the most part these failed to shut the plants.

In two wildcat strikes in Chicago—Railway Express and bus drivers—again it was Black workers in the lead, with the bus strike contributing to the disruption at the Democratic Convention.

And there have also been welfare client demonstrations. Since these were generally led by government anti-poverty forces, the caseworkers were on the spot. They had to find a course of action that would neither be directed against the clients nor seek out the cops as allies but would, at the same time, help build the union against the city, not against the clients, and also defeat the racism existing among both white and Black caseworkers.

These struggles–involving either the leadership of Black workers, the fight against racism by Black and white workers or the use of racism by the ruling class to divide and weaken the working class–follow many battles of a similar nature in the past year: a wildcat at Ford's Mahwah (N.J.) assembly plant when Black workers walked out with the support of white workers after a white foreman called one Black worker a "Black bastard" (see *Challenge,* May, 1968); the historic Memphis sanitationmen's strike, which fought the whole ruling-class structure of that deep Southern city for union recognition and decent pay and conditions, setting a fighting example for unorganized workers all over the South (see *PL,* June, 1968); the wildcat strike and two-day rebellion of 15,000 Black and white workers at Newport News (Va.) Shipbuilding and Dry Dock Co., initiated by 200 Black workers over oppressive working conditions and discrimination, and joined by the rest of the workers, a majority of whom are white (see *PL,* Oct.-Nov., 1967). No doubt still more examples both inside and outside the trade union movement could be cited to prove the point that racism and the fight against it, especially when led by Black workers over class issues, has become the all-pervading issue in the country.

Ruling Class Reactions

That the ruling class recognizes the importance of maintaining racism is evident from its latest actions. A two-pronged drive has unfolded, raising racism among white workers to new heights and also pushing anti-working-class Black nationalism to an unprecedented degree.

The ruling class made "law and order" (meaning shoot Black people) the main issue in the recent elections; it gave Wallace tremendous publicity to bring out the worst racism among white workers; under the guise of "community control" it provoked a school shut-down in New York City designed to weaken and destroy the teachers' union as well as whip up racism among white people; it is attempting to use professional workers such as teachers and welfare workers—people with middle-class backgrounds, aspirations and ideology—as a base from which to launch strong attacks on Black and Latin workers and the class consciousness of workers generally; and it is using every anti-working-class Black nationalist it can create or buy as a target for white people to vent their racism on.

And that is the other side of the ideological coin: the capturing of the Black movement by anti-working-class nationalism, using the very increase in Black consciousness itself as a weapon against both Black and white workers. The ruling class is afraid of the class leadership Black workers in Black caucuses can give to white workers, setting them in motion against their sellout leaders. Thus, the big pitch for "Black capitalism" (a major plank of Nixon's campaign), or "sitting down with the Black Panthers," or "making contact" to keep things cool—meaning buying off any Black militants, an approach increasingly used by mayors such as Aliota of San Francisco and Lindsay and his "urban task force" in New York, and "community control"; in other words, anything to prevent Black workers from developing a revolutionary, Marxist-Leninist outlook.

The ruling class "lieutenants" in the labor movement are busy, too. It is no accident that Reuther is forming a second labor federation at this time. In addition to the unions considering joining (UAW, teamsters, chemical workers, rubber workers—all with large numbers of Black workers), it will probably include unions such as District 65, the drug and hospital workers' Local 1199 and the UFT in New York, as well as many ex-left-led unions that are having plenty of trouble keeping their increasing Black memberships in line. Reuther, himself, sees the handwriting on the wall in the UAW, with Black workers increasing in membership and in leadership of rank-and-file actions.

Therefore, what better way to create the illusion of action than to set up a safety valve for more militant workers to "fight the Meany old guard," which, of course, includes the "fight for civil rights." As things stand now, the Alliance for Labor Action may have four million members. It will be looking for—and feeding—Black nationalists and sellouts to join the payroll and become the leaders of the militant Black workers. In other words, the main feature of this new federation will be to contain the rising rank-and-file militancy in the labor movement, of which the Black workers form a crucial part. The organizers are even "sponsoring" (unofficially, of course) Black caucuses in their own unions (Reuther in the UAW, Shanker in the UFT) to steer the workers down the wrong road.

Fighting Racism: Principled Struggle

In PLP's Black Liberation Program we stressed the necessity of organizing Black workers in the shops and at the "point of production." Here, we have emphasized the role of Black workers in certain key industries and the all-pervading influence of racism and the fight against it in every important people's struggle now occurring. From this it must be concluded that unless an all-out fight is made against racism within the working class (which, of course, includes our own members), a Marxist-Leninist party cannot grow or succeed in the United States. Furthermore, the ability to defeat a ruling-class move to fascism will be seriously weakened. We will not even be able to construct a Left within the trade union movement, let alone a real Left-Center coalition.

It is not only crass racism to conceive of building this Left and this coalition without major emphasis on the role of Black workers in leadership of it—it is also impossible. In the past, many of us have coupled the correct idea of the Black Liberation Movement being the "vanguard of the revolutionary process" in the U.S. with the false notion that this meant the Black people as a whole were in advance of the white workers, especially in basic industries. And, further, that while the Black people could not wait for the white workers, at some time the white workers would catch up and assume their rightful place (being the majority, after all) in the leadership of the working-class movement. It is time to bury this theory, for it is now clear that the trade union movement—and any budding Left-Center coalition within it—will be smashed unless it decisively includes Black workers in its leadership as well as, of course, in its rank and file. Therefore, the Black workers (not the "all-class" Black population) are an essential part of the revolutionary potential of the U.S. working class and in a quality and quantity far exceeding their percentage in the population. Without the Black workers, no rank-and-file movement of workers in any key area of the trade union movement can succeed for long, if at all.

The fight against racism is inseparable from the fight for rank-and-file-led unions and from working-class solidarity. We can thus define the New York school shutdown as a racist action, not a strike in the class interests of workers. And we can oppose "solidarity" in the abstract by asking "solidarity with whom and for what?" In New York it was solidarity with the teachers' bosses, the administrators and principals, to say nothing of the cops necessary to "protect" teachers' "job security" in the schools. That's about the last place to look for job protection–to the police whose job it is to break the class actions of workers.

Contradictions such as these are going to increase. We must prepare to analyze every action led predominantly by white workers from a class viewpoint that considers racism an anti-working-class factor. We must carefully determine if the action is building solidarity against the ruling class or "solidarity" for racism.

From all this we must conclude that the question of fighting racism is a principled question, a question of strategy, not tactics. Building a base for revolutionary ideology and for a Marxist-Leninist party, rather than a base "for the union" or a personal base for ourselves, can only succeed if the fight against racism is made a central task of the Marxist-Leninist party.

This problem is most clearly revealed among teachers in New York because the class struggle is a lot hotter, at the moment, on the school issue than it is in many other trade union situations. But when the battle heats up in other industries and areas of working-class struggle, we will be faced with the same ruling-class drive to raise racism to a fever pitch. We could then easily give in to it (since to fight it "isolates me") the way some teachers did.

Such behavior stemmed from the confused idea that the struggle was for solidarity in a trade union class struggle, rather than a racist action; therefore, any opposition might lead to isolation from one's fellow teachers. Yet, in nearly every instance where the class analysis of the action as racist was put forward, some teachers—and parents—were won over to that understanding, and won over on a higher level than ever before. This is building a base for a Marxist-Leninist party, for a revolutionary idealogy. To "defend the union" under any and all circumstances, without examining the class content of that defense, is economism, not Marxism; and in this case was also racism. Such a defense will have the opposite result: It will destroy the union as a viable weapon of class struggle for rank-and-file teachers. In such a situation Black and white workers (in this case, Black parents and white teachers) who see "going into school or staying out" as a purely tactical question are thinking of racism itself as a tactical question. Here we see, in sharp relief, the inseparability of class-conscious trade unionism and the fight against racism, since in not fighting racism in a principled way the union, as an organization that is supposed to fight in the class interests of its members, is being destroyed.

We cannot adopt an approach that says: "Racism is a tough question; it splits workers if you fight on it too soon. Therefore, fight on other not-so-tough economic questions first." With racism staring us in the face now in just about every situation we encounter, the "too soon" approach will tend to make the fight against racism a tactical question. This would be a disaster for a Marxist-Leninist party. We must make the fight against racism a cardinal principle. Of course, this doesn't mean that the first time one meets a particular racist white worker he should be fed the entire Marxist-Leninist analysis in one swallow. But it does mean that the plan of how to—and the necessity to—fight racism every step of the way is laid in concrete discussions in our PLP clubs, in caucuses, and in all organs of people's struggle.

For our part, in PLP, we must re-emphasize the struggle to win over the white workers, away from racism and to a class line. Not to do this would be to fall into the trap of: "All white workers are racist; therefore develop relations with only Black workers." It is possible to make progress among most white workers, as we have found from our own experience. Even more important, we must develop the kind of mutual trust and confidence among workers that goes into their understanding of us as communists. Such a relationship will go a long way to helping us get listened to and break down racism among white workers. The main concentration for white communists is still among white workers.

Black Communists Reflect Anti-Racism

A real measure of whether we're fighting racism among the masses is whether we're recruting Black workers to a Marxist-Leninist party, which in turn is a reflection of how well we're fighting racism among white workers. No Black worker can be expected to join such a party unless it is actively fighting racism among white workers who are racist. Thus, recruiting Black workers becomes a key question and forces white communists to measure up to what they're doing among white workers as well. For instance, are white workers being recruited to a line that doesn't include fighting racism as a principled question?

There are, of course, many special aspects to the fight against racism. For example: People who come from middle class or student backgrounds acquire a special brand of racism over and above the brand developed among white workers, a certain class snobbishness that is directed against all workers but that becomes a racist attitude when it involves Black workers.

Another problem concerns teachers. Teachers have a particular problem in fighting racism because they are involved not only with their fellow workers but also with the children and parents in the large cities where a high proportion of the population is Black or Latin. Though an auto or garment worker may not like his work, this doesn't necessarily reflect itself in racism towards his fellow workers. But if a teacher doesn't like children, he will inevitably adopt racist attitudes toward the ghetto children similar to the racism of his fellow teachers. Teachers deal mostly with the children of the working class and in a high percentage of cases with the children of the specially oppressed Black and Latin workers. Under these circumstances, to dislike children will inevitably result in anti-working-class and racist attitudes. If the cornerstone of any strong teachers' union is an alliance with parents, and if these parents are part of specially oppressed groups —victims of racism—certainly a dislike of children that becomes racism will defeat the aim of any teacher attempting to fight in the class interests of his fellow teachers or of the working class as a whole.

Racism is the main tool the ruling class has to divide the working class. In every instance where its use has been successful, all workers have been set back, no matter how much a privileged group of white workers think they've gained, because the united struggle of workers as a class has been weakened. And in all the instances cited in this article, where racism has been forced to take a back seat, the class interests of all workers—Black and white—moved forward.

To root this cancer out of our Party and the working class is a first order of business. We must make a qualitatively renewed effort to study the questions of racism and nationalism as they reveal themselves in our everyday relations with white and Black workers. We must oppose racism whenever and wherever it bursts forth, in the smallest incident as well as the biggest strike or working-class struggle.

The fight against racism is a life and death matter in the United States. To succeed means to bring the militant and revolutionary leadership of the specially oppressed Black workers to the working class as a whole in the total fight against the same exploiter—the bosses who own and run this country. It means to build a base for socialism within the trade union movement, and a Left-Center coalition that will toss out the present sellout misleadership and work in the class interests of the rank and file. And it means that a truly revolutionary Marxist-Leninist party will be built in the U.S., one that will not in any way accommodate itself to the ideology of the class enemy.

Therefore, for the working class to emancipate itself and all oppressed people, for it to eventually seize state power as a class, with a Marxist-Leninist party in its vanguard, the racism that splits the working class must be buried.

Revolutionaries Must Fight Nationalism

AUGUST 1969

> *Sometimes the bourgeoisie succeeds in drawing the proletariat into the national movement, and then the national struggle externally assumes a 'nation-wide' character. But this is so only externally. In its essence it is always a bourgeois struggle, one that is to the advantage and profit mainly of the bourgeoisie.*
>
> —JOSEPH STALIN, Marxism and the National Question

People all over the world are lashing out against U.S. imperialism. The war in Vietnam is the sharpest expression of this. The Vietnamese people have exposed U.S. imperialism as never before, and prior to the ill-conceived Paris negotations were exposing the inherent weakness of U.S. rulers. U.S. bosses were forced to go to extreme lengths in Vietnam to maintain strategic military, political and economic investments in Asia. But they could not hold on in the face of People's War.

The heroic actions of the Vietnamese people have considerably weakened the U.S. military machines, isolated the U.S. around the world, encouraged the revolutionary process everywhere and, significantly, intensified the internal contradictions in the U.S.

Summing up of the Vietnamese situation, until the negotiations, is not merely idle talk. What we are saying is that U.S. rulers can be taken. They are, really, strategically weak. Revolution is the mortal enemy of imperialism, and the flames of the Vietnamese revolution, if spread correctly, would lead to defeat of U.S. imperialism.

Facing a great weakening of the imperialist system the U.S. was forced to rely heavily on revisionism and nationalism. This discussion is designed to stress the fact that the fight against revisionism is intertwined with the question of nationalism. And we think it is our duty to point out that socialism can't be won without a perspective of the Dictatorship of the Proletariat. The stakes in this battle are enormous. It is a question of whether or not imperialism can be defeated or whether the imperialists can hold on for several more centuries.

It is worthwhile noting what happened in Vietnam. This issue is crucial to the world revolutionary movement. The lessons of the great Vietnamese battle affect revolutionary developments in our country. Vietnam has been at the heart of all U.S. politics for several years. New radicals have cut their teeth on building an anti-imperialist movement in the U.S. Lessons from this battle are significant in our country as well. Revisionist politics of Soviet "aid" and negotiations with the U.S. are opposed to revolutionary politics of rejecting Soviet "aid" and standing firm on U.S. Get Out of Vietnam Now.

The Vietnamese people could have driven out the U.S. and established socialism. But because many of their leaders have stopped halfway, the U.S. will be able to thwart both possibilities. Most important, the U.S. will still be able to remain in Asia to protect its rapidly growing investments.

In addition, the coming conference of so-called socialist states in Eastern Europe, and various communist parties, is actually a nationalist potpourri. Virtually every state and party is at odds with one another. Some want to be tied to the U.S., others to the Soviet bosses. The Soviets don't really want cooperation but want complete domination. The other states are in sharp competition with Soviet bosses. Nationalism in the once communist movement has not only led to capitalist relations in the country but to capitalist relations between the once socialist countries. Russia's aggression against the Czechs, Rumania's alliance with the U.S., etc., are expressions of these contradictions. The contradictions inherent in all capitalist relations must erupt and lead to the undermining of the coming conference. Past conferences of this bunch were a farce, because you can't cover up nationalism-capitalism behind a wall of quotations from Lenin or anyone else.

National struggle instead of class struggle must lead to imperialism. National struggle denies class struggle. And national struggle does not automatically lead to class struggle. Communists must intervene and put forward a Marxist-Leninist line. This gives the workers and oppressed people the correct and only alternative to capitalism.

Revisionists Use Nationalist Tricks

Looking around the world we see the disastrous results of nationalism and revisionism. In Indonesia this tragic blend resulted in the slaughter of over 500,000 of the best fighters. The Indonesian masses continue to live in poverty and under the heel of brutal fascism. The Indonesian masses will eventually reverse this. But we can't call fascism and the slaughter of militants a victory.

In countries like Egypt, Guinea and India the national bourgeoisie holds power under the guise of establishing socialism. These countries are imperialist and revisionist pawns. The rulers of these countries are able to organize the masses and hold power based on a nationalistic appeal. The essence of their battles against the U.S. is over the share of the national profit for the national bourgeoisie.

Algeria was an example of protracted war, involving millions. The Algerians forced the French to capitulate militarily. But all this did not lead to socialism. Certainly, socialism was the alleged perspective of the leadership. Socialism was surely the hope and goal of many of the people. At present, the Algerian people are still extremely poor and have little or no hope for improvement under the system. The economy staggers under the burden of a large army, an army not involved in building the country, and in no way a people's army. Though the French army was driven out, France still controls the dominant section of the economy. The Algerian bosses are busy haggling with the French over their cut from Saharan resources. The Russians control the army through their "aid," and are busy worming their way into the Algerian economy, trying to supplant the French. This is not the Dictatorship of the Proletariat! This is not socialism! This is capitalism, where the rich get richer and the poor get poorer.

In the Congo the people forced Belgium to grant "independence" and established the Lumumba government. The small national bourgeoisie in the Congo fell out with the Belgians over their share of the economy. Lumumba represented the more militant section of these forces. Under Soviet tutelage he pressed his case at the U.N.–and was murdered by the Belgians and U.S. imperialists. Today the Congo remains "independent." It is run by other nationalists for the Belgians. The only real change in the picture is that the U.S. bosses, especially Rockefeller, grabbed a good piece of the action from the Belgians for their assistance in putting down the incipient national revolt. Because there were no forces with a real Marxist-Leninist outlook the people were not organized to fight and win. The Soviets and even Che Guevara tried to stir up a little fight for their interests. But their efforts only led to the murder of more Congo militants. Che's Congo adventure was transported to Bolivia, where he and his group ended up the same way. Dead and Defeated!

Russian Nationalism in Soviet Culture

In the Soviet Union workers' political power has been overthrown. It is true that revisionism has momentarily triumphed in the Soviet Union. It is true that a new national bourgeoisie has arisen. It is true that the Soviets are a new imperial power, who collude with the U.S. to prevent revolution. Simply to ascribe this development to past bureaucratic practices in the Soviet Union begs the question. Any serious study of the development of the Soviet Union will show that a fervent nationalist bent was involved in Soviet culture and thought. The development of a new culture after the revolution did not incorporate a real working class and international outlook. Soviet culture could be best characterized by the Moiseyev dance troupe that was eagerly imported to this country by Sol Hurok. This fine dancing brought forward bourgeois national culture. No doubt, aspects of this culture were suppressed by some czars. But suppression does not license bourgeois culture under socialism. For all who have forgotten the program of this troupe it merely was a demonstration of glorious Russian culture under various czars.

The Soviet movie "Alexander Nevsky" was a fine technical achievement. Bourgeois film makers still try to imitate this classic. However the content of the film was pure nationalism. To rouse the Soviet masses to the danger of Hitler's attack was fine. But showing Prince Alexander flushing the peasants out of their holes to fight the Knights of the Teutonic Order was bad. Prince Alexander was the great hero. The masses were a dull bunch of sheep that needed rousing. In other words, the old rulers weren't so bad. The people? They weren't so hot. This type of thought leads one to the inescapable conclusion that bourgeois society can't be so bad after all. Obviously we should all be like Prince Alexander.

Nationalism was the preeminent factor in Soviet art. Working-class culture was never developed. Certainly the Soviets were masters at maintaining and improving the ballet. But it was not developed from a class point of view. The czars' ballet was perfected. Unfortunately, this was another "communist" contribution to the development of nationalism–hence capitalism.

It is no accident the Cultural Revolution in China is called just that. Centuries of bourgeois thought and culture continued to be widely propagated by the new communist regime. After almost twenty years of state power the Chinese Communist Party decided that bourgeois nationalist culture was a big factor in undermining Chinese workers' power. It is significant that the Chinese began attacking some of the Soviet sacred cows. Suddenly, Sholokov, Shostakovich, Katchaturian, etc., were attacked by the Chinese as nationalists or pacifists or both. Obviously the Chinese felt state power could be reversed by not fighting these bad ideas and trying to develop a working-class approach to culture. The party then attempted to show how these wrong ideas directly entered into the political field. The attack on the Peking Opera was not a simple critique of opera.

All culture has a class content. The main problem has been that once socialism has triumphed in a particular country a new working-class culture has not automatically taken the place of bourgeois culture. And while Marxists-Leninists have tried to wipe out imperialist culture, which has often been imposed on another country, they have not always succeeded. Local bourgeois culture is not an answer to imperialist culture.

To sum up some developments of nationalism in this period:

1. There are the open right-wing nationalists, like Nasser, Kenyatta, Ghandi, etc., who use nationalist and socialist elements in their country to fight the outside imperialists for a bigger share of the profits. Some of these profits may trickle down to the masses, but the overall condition of the people is poverty and no power.

2. There are the Lumumba, Toure, and Nkrumah types, who have a more militant veneer. They espouse socialism but are really out to strengthen the national bourgeoisie of their countries. In these countries the masses are still destitute and still lacking political power.

3. There are the Boumedienne and Ben Bella types, who have been involved, at least peripherally, with a significant war against an outside imperialist. After the war they open up the country to neocolonialism from Europe, the U.S. or the new Soviet imperialists. The masses are still hungry, out of work and powerless.

4. There is nationalism that has flowered in a socialist state and helps turn socialism into its opposite or tries to. (U.S. rulers are quite fond of referring to this development as "national communism.") The Soviet Union and Yugoslavia demonstrate this. And the Lius of China show the rest.

Various national forces in Yugoslavia are at one another's throats today. The Serbs are fighting the Croats, etc. This type of bitter national fighting can only occur in a situation when socialism is not being built. The idea of maintaining national states received a big boost in the early days of the Soviet Union. Having independent or autonomous republics in the Soviet Union was a concession to nationalism. The Union of Soviet Socialist Republics is an expression of nationalism. Though it wasn't incorrect to make it, this nationalist concession didn't wither away under a full-scale ideological fight after the revolution was won. It is now clear why Soviet bourgeois culture has been so persistent.

Nationalism flowers in a situation where self-determination means something other than socialism. We say that self-determination can only be accomplished under socialism. Socialism is the only road away from imperialism and toward workers' power. The slogan "all-class unity" is a cover-up for perpetuating capitalism. Obviously, if workers or oppressed people were leading the revolutionary battle it would have to be for socialism. Workers can't be liberated under capitalism. Unfortunately some of these ideas are at play in Vietnam and in the Black Liberation Movement in the U.S. The only way to incorporate the petty-bourgeoisie and even some small section of the national bourgeoisie in the movement, and prevent them from subverting it, is to make sure workers are in the leadership of the movement and that the movement is clearly for socialism. The petty-bourgeoisie in the U.S. and some sections of the national bourgeoisie in Vietnam can only end their oppression from imperialists by changing their class outlook.

Two Types of Nationalism?

We say if the Vietnamese people follow any of these examples the people will be robbed of their only hope for self-determination, socialism. For many years we in the Progressive Labor Party held to the idea of two types of nationalism: revolutionary and reactionary. But a look at world reality shows there is no such thing. Nationalism is either the path to oppression by an outside imperialist or the road back to capitalism from socialism. Any form of nationalism is bad! Events speak more clearly than words!

Nationalism, whether it develops overtly as in Egypt or covertly as in the Soviet Union, means capitalism. Defeats in the past ten years in the international arena are serious. It is hard to turn defeats into victories if we don't try to see why defeats occur. Nationalism has helped wipe out a good portion of the international communist movement and threatens growing revolutionary action all over. If Asia, Africa and Latin America are the main areas of contradiction today, a Vietnamese leadership surrender is a big setback to revolutionary forces. Unless the forces of revolution understand it is a defeat (and Soviet revisionism is not the only danger) they may fall into the same revisionist-nationalist trap.

If one wants to "serve the people"–to prevent starvation, exploitation, unemployment, the reversal of socialism; and to promote revolution, etc.–one must oppose nationalism. If we want to be on the side of the people it is important to oppose revisionism and nationalism.

There is the tendency among revolutionaries and radicals to believe that any struggle which seems to be against imperialism is good and must be uncritically supported. The "Communist" Party still tries to have us march behind the banners of the so-called liberal bourgeoisie and their stooges in the mass movement. After all, they have reasoned, Adlai was against Ike; JFK was against Nixon; LBJ was against Goldwater; and Humphrey was against Nixon. This was the negative choice put to the people by the C.P. It was called the "lesser of two evils." Nonetheless the "choice" was posed as a "struggle" between two forces: the good and bad capitalists. In the mass movement the C.P. is more positive: Support Rev. King; support Walter Reuther, etc. After all, they are fighting the system. We can now easily see that if we followed this line we would still be fighting to seat Blacks at lunch counters in the South and supporting Reuther's sellouts in the North. Despite good intentions we would be on the side of reaction. Of course a good portion of the developing Left rejected these sellout ideas.

Today the C.P. and the U.S. Government support negotiations in Vietnam and Black studies at the universities. Unfortunately, it is not clear to all that these positions are as false as the old ones. We must judge the merits of any struggle by seeing if it is in the interests of the workers and oppressed people. The more sophisticated sections of the ruling class don't have this trouble. The lead articles in the *New York Times*' "News of the Week" section (May 4) analyzes the battles on the campuses from a class point of view:

> But while the Left-radicals seem to pick their issues with a view to maximum damage to the "Establishment"—often with the bluntly stated goal of destroying the university as the brain of the power structure and as the prelude to bringing down the power structure itself—the black students generally fight for limited objectives which they consider of importance to their own cause and education: open admission of the minorities to college, protection of black tenants against "university expansion" into their neighborhoods, student-run black studies programs. Far from wanting to destroy the university, the blacks aim at making it more responsive to their own needs as they see them.

There are two main trends within a ruling class. Though both are fundamentally united in the aim of holding state power at all costs, there are often sharp divisions and battles over tactics between them. The essence of the difference between the liberal and conservative wings of the ruling class is the amount of terror and coercion to be applied at given points. One group would retreat to full fascism sooner than later. The other group is more anxious to preserve the mantle of bourgeois democracy as long as possible. But when workers are in sharp class fight against bosses, both sections unite to smash workers' movements. Around the country many thousands have been killed and wounded in ghetto battles during the past six years. Thousands more are in jail or face imprisonment.

The main aspect of ghetto battles is that they are primarily working-class efforts. Jobs, wages, housing, equal opportunity in employment, sanitation, schooling, police terror, rent gouging, are the main issues. These demands and actions are intensified by racism. Black workers are a victim of special exploitation and their economic grievances are far more intense than most white workers. Racism acts to aid the bosses amass maximum profits and split the working class.

It is in working-class battles that capitalist terror is brought forward most ruthlessly. Battles that are fundamentally aimed against the capitalist profit structure invoke the ruling class' greatest wrath. National struggle—for Black foremen, bosses, administrators, open school admission, Black study groups, etc.—can be dealt with and eventually co-opted.

This point is beginning to be seen on the campuses today. Demands that have a working class and anti-imperialist focus cannot be tolerated. The bourgeoisie certainly does not even want national struggle and tries to head it off. But when struggle becomes the fact of life there are the kinds they can live with and those that threaten their existence. We believe bosses view struggle from this point of view. Class struggle followed to its logical conclusion means the end of imperialism. Hence socialism. National struggle means imperialism survives, and is forced to use a token of its take to buy off national leaders. In countries where a national bourgeoisie exists, imperialism uses some of its loot to increase local bosses' profits.

In the past we have made the serious error (that is being made today by others) of supporting struggle–any struggle. We were confused by the concept of the two-stage struggle, which claimed that first there is the battle for national liberation, and then communists transform it to the battle for socialism. This theory received a big boost from the Cuban experience. The masses were aroused against the Batista Government and U.S. imperialism. The July 26th movement and leadership was a mixed bag. It was alleged that Raoul Castro and Che were communists. Castro's political philosophy was supposed to be an unknown quantity. The July 26th movement seized power. Castro and his closest allies consolidated their power within the July 26th movement. Castro expropriated the property of outside imperialists. Castro proclaimed socialism. The masses seemed to go along with this because of Castro's enormous prestige and power. The new government made popular and sweeping reforms. Subsequently, Castro proclaimed himself to be a Marxist-Leninist and a disciple of Khrushchev.

It all seemed good to us and to other radicals. Here was an example of winning socialism without telling the masses anything about it. All you had to do was succeed in organizing an anti-imperialist movement and at the zero hour convert it to a socialist movement. Without going into the whole story now, Cuba became a tool of the Soviets. Because there is not a real Marxist-Leninist party and leaders in Cuba, Castro & Co. are busy screwing up revolutions in Cuba and all over Latin America. (Che Guevara's experiences in Bolivia are one example.) And what is worse, the Cuban masses are not being won to Marxist ideology. Cubans are beginning to sour on the Castro leadership. They are becoming increasingly cynical about socialism and are part of the pressure pushing Cuba into the arms of the U.S. Economic conditions in Cuba are lagging badly and add fuel for this move. Eventually there will be two outside "benefactors": the Soviet bosses and the U.S. bosses. (At the moment the Cuban economy is reliant on the Soviets as the Cubans abandoned the concept of a diversified self-sustaining economy.)

Nationalism Bails Out U.S.

Cuba seems to us to be one type of national-anti-imperialist revolution that ends up in the arms of one imperialist or the other —or both. A variation on this theme is at work in Vietnam. The Vietnamese people won enormous battles. They had succeeded in beating U.S. armies to their knees. Victory became a distinct probability. But underlying weaknesses became apparent as the U.S. began to shift its emphasis from the battlefield to the political arena. The U.S. cleverly began to exploit the Vietnamese leaders' political weaknesses. It was the Kennedys, McCarthys and others who realized that Vietnamese nationalism in North and South could help bail the U.S. out. This was in addition to relying more heavily on the Soviets.

The Vietnamese leadership, at least in large measure, became emeshed in Soviet "aid." They were passively on the side of the Soviets in the China-Soviet struggle. The Vietnamese enthusiastically supported Soviet and other revisionist parties' policies that didn't directly involve China. As you recall, the Vietnamese were the first to hail Soviet aggression against the Czechs. We have always been puzzled by never reading about or seeing any statement from the South Vietnamese communists. What was the communist role in the NLF? We did see the ten-point program of the NLF, which was hailed by the Soviets. This program didn't speak of socialism. It proclaimed "neutrality" as the aim of the NLF. The program was typical nationalist propaganda: vaguely anti-imperialist, neutralist, and advocating a vague coalition government when the U.S. was out of Vietnam. What is wrong with this? The U.S. is quickly coming to terms with a variation of this program because it has learned from experience that it can live very nicely with such a formula.

The ten-point program is a variant of the Dimitrov "popular front" theme of the 7th World Congress of the Communist International. It envisions the peaceful transition to socialism. The theory is first to win the victory of the popular front and then move somehow to socialism. The line of peaceful step-by-step reunification of South and North Vietnam through means of negotiations is also variant of the peaceful-transition-to-socialism theme. Is it any wonder that the ten-point NLF program is everywhere hailed and supported by the revisionists? How is it possible for revisionists and Marxist-Leninists to unite behind the same program? Only by sacrificing the Dictatorship of the Proletariat, which is the very heart of Marxism-Leninism.

The U.S. rulers are learning to distinguish between so-called national liberation movements and socialist movements. Nationalism doesn't have to be taken head on. And taking a revolutionary movement head on is used to force it into a revisionist and nationalist path.

The only thing the U.S. can't stand in Vietnam is a Vietnamese alliance with the world revolutionaries and the outlook of the Dictatorship of the Proletariat. A socialist outlook would prevent negotiations or impose on the U.S. negotiations that would actually reflect U.S. military and political defeat in Vietnam. The NLF's program is a nationalistic program that ignores the international situation and looks only to Vietnam. The day has long passed, if there ever was such a day, when this type of program could be of real value to the oppressed people of any country. Any development that leaves the oppressed people or workers of a country far short of liberation or denies that socialism, the Dictatorship of the Proletariat, is the only way to achieve liberation, opens the door to the maintenance or return of capitalism. The fight for liberation is the fight for socialism. It is wrong for communists to advocate two-stage struggle. Communists have no business advocating national liberation movements that do not openly proclaim socialism as a goal. There is overwhelming evidence from Soviet to Algerian experience to prove that nationalism is the road to capitalism.

Communists must try various ways to win a position of leadership among the workers and guide them to socialism. Nationalism won't lead to socialism any more than any other fight for bourgeois reforms. When communists work in a nationalistic movement, or national liberation movement as they are sometimes called, they must put forward the goal of socialism. If national forces are fighting to drive out imperialist forces there is a basis for limited unity.

But Marxist-Leninists must preserve their independent role within the united front. The united front has two important aspects: unity against and struggle against. The notion that everything must be subordinated to preserving the united front is wrong. How can you be a communist and actually fight for capitalism in your country as opposed to the rule of outside imperialists. Naturally, imperialism is bad and must be defeated. And of course outside imperialism imposes its will on native capitalists. We expose this type of contradiction. However, to preserve or not to fight against local capitalists is wrong. Communists should win workers and oppressed people to the party's leadership. The way to defeat imperialism is not to build your own brand of capitalism. The way to eventually defeat imperialism is to build the Dictatorship of the Proletariat.

Nationalism Won't Bring Socialism

Therefore there are two main errors to avoid. One is to remain isolated from the nationalist movement; there can be a tendency not to work in it for fear of a battle over ideas. And of course there is the danger of not advancing working-class ideas, not fighting for working-class leadership, and forgetting that Marxist-Leninist ideas cannot, in the long run, coexist with nationalist ideas. This will lead to a host of tactical problems within the mass movement. And while we don't intend to try to anticipate them all now, we must say that this battle of ideas (or class struggle) within the movement must lead to splits. Unity for the sake of building local capitalism is a bad unity. Communists can never accept this. Unity that obscures the perspective of the Dictatorship of the Proletariat from the masses is equally bad. As we have said, the workers can win state power, but without a mass struggle for ideology they can lose it.

It is no accident that the Trotskyist movement (the SWP) and the C.P. are united in hailing one or another or all stripes of Black nationalism and nationalists. The SWP is still playing Malcolm X records to garner a few dollars and curry favor with various Black forces. The SWP still hails Robert Williams, one of the most divisive forces. Williams' hate-whitey line would perpetuate and widen the split in the working class. The main aspect of Williams' line is to build a Black bourgeoisie. Williams is the nominal head of a new Black state. The group in Detroit that advocates Williams' line is made up of various Black professionals who advocate a separate state and capitalism.

It is a hollow joke when some forces refer to the PLP as

Trotskyist for rejecting SWP-C.P. idols and ideas. Unfortunately, we were saddled with many of these bad faults for some time. To be against the C.P.-SWP axis, which exists in some movements, is to fight their wrong ideas. If we were to follow their line in the mass movement we would be supporting or keeping our mouths shut on the consequences of the Vietnam negotiations. And we would be hailing Malcolm X, Robert Williams, LeRoi Jones, and uncritically supporting the Black Panther leaders. In other words, Marxism would not exist in the U.S., and reference to class struggle would remain a ceremonial exercise as it is among all pseudo-Marxists.

We are not in a popularity contest. The Dictatorship of the Proletariat cannot be won by tailing after right-wing forces in the mass movement. If we hailed and supported any struggle we might be more widely "liked." But we are not in the numbers game. We feel that by acting this way we would be creating illusions about events. The fight for socialism in the U.S. will probably take a long time. In the course of this struggle the workers will recognize socialism as the only course to their salvation. Workers and oppressed people have always rallied to Marxism-Leninism. Marxism-Leninism doesn't need a veneer of nationalism or dilution to suck workers in. In our limited experience, going to workers with our line is proving to be the best work we can do.

We want to make it clear that we can win to a socialist perspective 99 per cent of the forces who hold nationalist ideas. In the U.S., it is fair to say, overwhelmingly large numbers of Black people hold nationalist ideas. Not only Blacks are influenced by Black nationalism; many white radicals are. Despite the old American adage, "if you can't lick 'em–join 'em," we feel nationalist ideology can be defeated. But you can't defeat it by advocating it, or by saying nationalism is a "good thing." We believe two significant strategies must be advanced to win: class struggle ideas –the Dictatorship of the Proletariat–and the idea that communists must be in the forefront of the fight against racism.

Too often we have been one-sided and sectarian. Some people tend to equate the rank and file with the leadership. All too often we see every leader of national movements as an enemy. Some leaders can be won to our ideas. There are enough enemies; but we don't have to manufacture new ones. We must be very careful at sorting out enemies from friends. We must avoid glib and hasty evaluations. If some people don't agree with us now they are not our enemies. Even after a struggle in which feelings run high we should try to win people to our point of view. Why let the ruling class consolidate themselves through the people's victories or defeats? We should try and maintain relations with people over a long period even if we disagree. It is all too simple to break things off.

One of the reasons Black nationalism holds sway on some campuses is because PLP has not energetically and creatively seized the ideological and tactical leadership of the fight against racism. Many people find it is easier to conduct an attack against people who have nationalist ideas. After all, they reason, the fight against nationalism is the fight for socialism. Many times a fight against nationalism without a serious anti-racist battle is a cover-up for racism. White students must be in the forefront, first, in the fight against racism. When white communists or Black communists fight nationalism it will be exceedingly hard for the opposition to brand their effort racist if it is clear to one and all that communists are leading fighters of racism.

One of the reasons many Black and white workers and students get involved in the nationalist scene is they think the nationalist outlook is the way to solve racism. Of course, many students become involved in Black student unions for very selfish reasons. Many want to improve their lot in society, and they don't care how they do it. They don't give a damn for Black workers except how to use them as leverage to win middle-class demands. But almost all these people are against racism and could fight racism from a working-class point of view. They get sucked into a selfish attitude in the absence of something else. All of us are selfish too! We are trying to correct our selfishness. Why don't we let someone else try to correct theirs? Aside from a very few clear, articulate national spokesmen, most people are open. Obviously, these broad sections of the population can and must be struggled with and won if socialism is to triumph.

National consciousness can be the spark that stimulates struggle. And this struggle enables communists to reach and transform this spark to class consciousness. If we don't, the bourgeoisie will quickly transform this national feeling to full-blown nationalist ideas. Black people know they are being screwed additionally because they are Black. And because their oppression is sharpest they are often the first ones to fight back and fight hardest. Why should wc allow the ruling class to misdirect this militancy? Militancy is exactly what all workers need on their side. The ruling class has two tactics which they use to mislead oppressed people: It isn't only killing and coercion. Their arsenal of tactics includes the bribe. The reality of life is that Black workers and students are in the process of rebellion. The ruling class doesn't like it. But not liking it won't stop it. The bosses use the carrot and stick to force the movement into their framework. This doesn't have to work. And it won't, if we recognize that "all that glistens isn't gold."

"Revolutionary" Nationalism

Sometimes we hear the statement that to be a revolutionary one must be a revolutionary nationalist. Or to be a revolutionary nationalist one must be a socialist. Let us digress for a moment and take a capsule view of a leader in another country—Indonesia. Former President Sukarno was the most advanced spokesman of revolutionary nationalism. He was for socialism. He was against U.S. and Dutch imperialism. He even made war on the Dutch bosses. He included communists in his government. He spoke of peoples' power. He spoke of armed struggle. Indonesia was the only communist or non-communist country that pulled out of the U.N. He preached undying hatred toward U.S. imperialism. He even attacked the Soviets as revisionists. When the more overtly right-wing nationalists felt the masses were going too far leftward, they moved in. Sukarno went over to their side. He tried to, and did, save his ass. He didn't care how many people or colleagues he fingered to save himself. As long as he had his palace and his nine wives he spoke of a communist plot to take over Indonesia.

It's hard to imagine any nationalist leader going further than he did. But as Stalin once mentioned, in regard to other national leaders, they run to the imperialist camp when they are threatened by their own people. In other words, when the Indonesian people were getting too close for bourgeois comfort, Sukarno, like other nationalists, betrayed the workers to the imperialists. At the moment, Indonesia is tied to the U.S. and Russia. The people are in dire straits. Millions are dead or dying. The masses are learning the hard way the results of "revolutionary" nationalism. When the Indonesian people fight their way back to political power it won't be by relying on the nationalists, no matter how big they talk or even seem to act sometimes. And no fake national program will lead to their rise to political preeminence. NLF-type liberation programs will take radicals right to the graveyard. They will be next to the heroes of Indonesia who have paid a stiff price so others won't make the same mistake.

The point is that nationalism is the political rationale presented to workers by one group of capitalists to fight outside capitalists for profits. And this fight is never in the basic interests of workers. That is why these capitalists call on the imperialists for help when they feel their own workers see through the nationalist mist. If you had asked Sukarno if he was a capitalist he in all sincerity would have denied it. He would have claimed he was a religious, revolutionary nationalist. The essence of the question is not what you say. It is what you think and do. There are only two sets of political ideas in the world: Marxist-Leninist ideas and capitalist ideas. Nationalism lies in the second category. We conclude from our experience that it is a mistake to believe that being a revolutionary nationalist means you are for socialism. We are sure many people sincerely believe this, and we impugn no one's integrity here, but show us one revolutionary nationalist that built socialism. . . .

It is interesting that many forces who espouse the idea of the good and bad nationalists and that nationalism is progressive, do so under a barrage of quotations from Lenin and Stalin. If you hunt through Lenin and Stalin you can always dredge something out of context to support almost any point. We suppose it is widely known how the Soviet bosses do everything behind the protection of Lenin. As a matter of fact, these bosses are busy seeing how they can use Stalin's image and words to put over capitalism. The Soviet bigwigs palm themselves off as the best Marxist-Leninists in the world.

We have read Lenin and Stalin on the national question. And we would like everyone to consider all ideas that they expressed on this question, because we feel that the essence of their position was the Dictatorship of the Proletariat. We readily admit that it has been difficult for us to grasp this idea because we ourselves have been weakened by revisionist ideas. We thought of the national question as a gimmick. And we found it hard to grasp the complexities of Lenin and Stalin on this question. We don't pretend that what we do or say is necessarily what they meant or did themselves. And we don't feel that the quotations we read are the final authoritative answer on the national question. We simply ask you to consider these ideas and see how they apply to the American and the world scene.

C.P.'s 1930 Line Wrong

The important thing for us to see is how liberation can be accomplished. We should not consider Marxism-Leninism as a collection of ossified rules, but rather apply it creatively to present political circumstances. During the Chinese Revolution there were those who said that you couldn't skip stages and go from feudalism to socialism. They said China had to have capitalism first. It was claimed there were very few workers, and China, of course, had very little industry. One of the great contributions of the Chinese communists was to smash this idea. By leaping from feudalism to socialism they speeded up the revolutionary process and greatly intensified imperialist contradictions. Actually, a similar argument is being advanced today. There are those who claim local nationalists must first defeat the imperialists. Then this nationalist revolution can be transformed to the socialist revolution.

Naturally a movement can go through many stages. But it doesn't have to. And communists cannot advocate anything else but socialism. To do so confuses the issue. Lack of advocacy doesn't serve the masses, as socialist thought and education is hidden from the people. Communists can eventually lead the workers to state power because of the great confidence the masses have for them; and the objective situation cries out for socialism. However, without a long and sharp ideological struggle among the masses for working-class thought (Marxism-Leninism) conditions are created for counter-revolution.

The world has undergone 50 years' more experience since the Russian Revolution. One must consider these years. People are putting forward the C.P. line of the nineteen-thirties on the national question. They are carrying this caricature even further.

In those days the C.P. called for two things: Complete the bourgeois democratic revolution and fight for a separate Black state in the Southern Black Belt. In the light of world experiences, oppressed people cannot achieve their aspirations under any form of capitalism. Even if the bourgeoisie were really to grant the Black people many of the rights that they are granted on paper, they would still be very oppressed. The Black people have the right to vote. What if they all got the full opportunity to register and vote in the South? The Kennedy's and other assorted liberals are for that. They feel this would strengthen the system by expanding bourgeois democracy. The essence of racism is economic exploitation. The U.S. needs maximum profits from racism to impose its will on all countries. No extension of the bourgeois revolution is going to change that fact of life. Many groups in the bourgeois democracies have the right to vote. The people in Harlem have been voting for a century. What has it gotten them?

Black separatism in the South would only split workers further. Black capitalism in the South would not solve the problem of Black workers. You see, there are two things at work at the moment: the drive for maximum profits by U.S. imperialism, and the evaluation of how the U.S. has absorbed nationalism over the past 50 years into its framework.

Demands have to be evaluated from a class point of view. Years ago we would have been big boosters for the right to vote. Now we realize it was a bunch of baloney. This demand was referred to as a revolutionary democratic demand. Similarly, the current demand for open enrollment is not the kind of reform demand that will actually sharpen the class struggle. It will only divert Black kids from a working-class outlook into the capitalist mold. Graduates from the big universities are trained to keep bourgeois enterprises going. Of course, we will try to exploit the contradictions in these situations. But worker-boss relations provide for sharper contradictions, leading to socialism.

At the moment the C.P. has dropped one of its strategems. It still retains the goal of completing the bourgeois democratic revolution, however. It is no wonder that the C.P. can easily make alliances with seemingly militant nationalist groups. In reality these groups reduce themselves to reformers because they don't want to achieve the Dictatorship of the Proletariat. Without a Marxist-Leninist perspective it can't be done. This perspective must be how to win all workers to socialism. Otherwise you are left with the outlook of getting a little more for yourself. And the ruling class is busy seeing how to use and is using nationalism to split the movement. In a recent speech Prof. Hayakawa of San Francisco State College spoke of how radicals use Black nationalists for their own ends. The main thrust of his point is to stir up more hatred between Black and white kids. In an atmosphere charged with a lot of racism and oodles of nationalism this is pretty good strategy.

In summary: Nationalism has been a big factor in the reversals suffered by those countries that were once socialist. The U.S. rulers never stop crowing about the beauties of national communism. As you recall they coerced and pleaded with the Soviets to be national communists like the Yugoslavs. The U.S. likes the Rumanians because they're nationalists and don't support the present Soviet position hook, line and sinker. In short, the socialist process in Eastern Europe has been reversed to capitalism. The U.S. imperialists tried to and succeeded in making each Eastern European country think of its own salvation.

Nationalism has been a big factor in wiping out movements in Algeria, Egypt, Guinea, Ghana, Venezuela, Guatemala, Cuba, Korea, Japan, Indonesia, etc. Even in China the Cultural Revolution was aimed at bourgeois national ideas and leaders. These ideas and leaders almost succeeded in reversing state power. One aim of the Cultural Revolution was to prevent the color of China from changing from Red to White. In other words, nationalism has played a big role in helping to almost wipe out the communist movement. Why should we continue to encourage nationalism? Our conclusion from 50 years of experience is that nationalism and revisionism are intertwined. Both must be combatted.

It seems to us that nationalism is the antithesis of internationalism. We don't think you can have your cake and eat it. Primary concern with "our country," "our people," "our community," "our block," "our family," etc., is selfishness. Selfishness is a capitalist idea. And, after all, you can get more goodies for yourself under capitalism. These ideas cannot today be incorporated into love for and loyalty to the international proletariat and oppressed people.

The victory of socialism in Russia was an enormous breakthrough for the international proletariat. This colossal event proved that socialism could triumph and work. Socialist leadership in the war against Hitler showed that socialism was not only powerful but was the most progressive force in the world. The Chinese Revolution proved you could skip stages, that socialism could triumph in a country without a significant industrial base. To go further, much further, we have to try to learn from all negative developments as well to speed up the socialist advance.

Right now it seems the masses are more than ready to grasp and develop socialist ideas. Why keep pushing the dead-defeatist ideas of nationalism!

U.S. Workers: Key to Revolution

AUGUST 1969

The Progressive Labor Party believes that the fundamental answer to the problems besetting this country's 77 million workers and their families is the elimination of the capitalist system and its replacement by socialism, a society in which the working class will rule on behalf of itself and all exploited people. To achieve the goal of a workers' state the capitalist ruling class* and its state must be smashed. The present dictatorship of the bosses—a tiny minority—must be replaced by a dictatorship of the workers, who, with their families, are the overwhelming majority of the population. The working class must have absolute power to guarantee democracy for itself and to prevent the bosses—who until now have exercised a dictatorship of exploiters over exploited—from regaining power. The dictatorship of the proletariat is our ultimate goal.

We believe that only the working class is capable of leading such a fundamental revolution. To accomplish this task its organized section must break the grip of misleadership and ruling-class ideology that now heads the labor movement and serves the bosses' class interests. We must fight for a united front within the present system—a unity between the mass of workers, who are prepared to battle the bosses, and communists immersed among the workers and equipped with the ideology of revolution against those rulers.

The great majority of workers—the Center—can be won to active class struggle against the ruling class; but a revolutionary communist party is necessary to help lead that struggle beyond mere trade union action, to the defeat of capitalism. Therefore we believe that a Left-Center coalition to lead the working class is

* By ruling class is meant those who own and control the mines, factories, banks, utilities, and transportation of the country, concentrated in the largest 500 to 1,000 companies, in whose interest laws are passed to protect their control, a class whose sole basis for existence is to make as much profit as possible.

the main strategy in the coming period necessary for eventual fundamental change in the United States.

In this trade union program we will attempt to show why the working class is the key force for revolution and why it can win state power only under the leadership of an organized revolutionary communist party committed to working-class ownership of the means of production and control of the state.

U.S. Capitalism's Contradictions

Profits before taxes of U.S. corporations since 1948 totaled over one TRILLION dollars, the sharpest rise in history, and are now approaching $100 billion a year. This profit increase is the result of such factors as speedup, automation, shifting payment of the costs of running the cities onto the workers through higher taxes, higher interest rates, prices rising faster than wages and increased foreign investments that exploit workers through starvation wages.

Although total profits have risen, the amount of capital invested to make these profits has risen at a higher rate, meaning the rate of profit has tended to fall. The drive to lower the cost of production requires the introduction of more and more machinery in place of workers; but workers are the sole source of profit. This insoluble contradiction impels the bosses to intensify their exploitation of the working class.

War is one way the capitalist class attempts to solve this contradiction. It tries to protect its foreign investments against revolution as well as to prevent socialism from spreading–and overturn it where it has succeeded. However, in Vietnam imperialism met its match: People's War waged by a guerrilla army one-fifth the size of its own. This war only intensified the contradictions at home; the system more people have begun to oppose as one not in their interests. (This forced the U.S. bosses' government to try to win diplomatically what it could not win on the batlefield. Unfortunately the Vietnamese leaders believe they can "outmaneuver" the U.S. at the bargaining table and agreed to negotiate over an issue–the Vietnamese people's liberation–that should not be negotiable.)

The Vietnam war has increased the workers' problems. Real wages (purchasing power) are steadily going down: factory workers' real take-home pay in Feb. 1969 was $1.18 per week below a year earlier. (*U.S. News & World Report,* April 14, 1969.) Household debt is up to nearly $400 billion, a jump of 1,000 per cent in 20 years. Taxes of all sorts are taking one-third of workers' wages. Twenty-two cents of every take-home dollar is paid to banks and finance companies. (*Wall Street Journal,* March 11, 1968.) Working hours are longer to make ends meet. The health and education of the working class is deteriorating. Industrial accidents are rising: More than 100,000 workers were killed and over 14 million injured since 1960. In 1964, 22 million workers were either unemployed, in the armed forces or working part time—69 per cent more than in 1948. (These figures don't include those on welfare or those who have been out of work so long they have given up looking for a job.) The problems in the cities—where most workers live—are far worse: congestion, air pollution, slums, dilapidated mass transit.

These burdens weigh even more heavily on Black workers. Because of boss-inspired racism, their annual per capita income is $22-billion less than that of whites—a source of superprofit for the bosses. The differential is reflected in twice as much unemployment, substandard housing, higher infant mortality rates and longer hours at lower-paying, harder jobs.

Other sections of the working class also feel an extra whiplash from the bosses' drive for maximum profits. Women workers—one-third of the work force—receive 40 per cent less wages than men on full-time jobs, a differential of $30 billion annually; and they get the brunt of the worsening conditions in the communities. Certain national minorities—Mexican-Americans, Puerto Ricans, Indians, Asian nationalities (Chinese, Filipinos, etc.)—are also special victims of racism. Young workers are squeezed into a special category by the ruling class. They form the largest section of the unemployed (17-24) or are drafted into the armed forces to fight and die in colonial countries to protect the bosses' profits there.

One-fourth of the population—50 million—lives below the poverty level, $3,000 per year (*New York Times,* Feb. 18, 1968). Seventy per cent earn less than $8,000 annually, below the $8,000-$10,000 level that the Government says is necessary for a minimum adequate standard of living for a family of four.

To all this the workers have answered with a terrific fight-back. Whenever given a clear choice of either fighting in their class interests, for their jobs, or bowing to the (bosses') "national interest," they have invariably chosen the former. In basic industries such as steel, auto, mining, longshore, electrical, railroad they have gone out on wildcat strikes, defying the bosses, the Government and their own misleaders. Black workers have rebelled in the ghettos against insufferable conditions; women workers have been particularly militant in electrical, telephone and government worker strikes; government and farm workers have fought for union conditions as never before; and youths have rebelled in and out of the Army against fighting the bosses' war in Vietnam.

The ruling class hasn't taken this resistance peacefully. It has repeatedly used Taft-Hartley injunctions and passed state legislation–like the Taylor Law in New York–to break strikes. It has locked out workers, sponsored arbitration and intervention by biased "neutrals," jailed union officials and used troops to preserve the bosses' law and order, escorting scabs past picket lines and clubbing workers in innumerable mass walkouts. It has called out the Army against Black workers in the ghetto. All this adds up to a democracy on paper that masks a dictatorship in fact–a dictatorship of the bosses, of the ruling class. (For articles detailing this class struggle and analysis of conditions, see various issues of *Progressive Labor* magazine.)

Until the working class develops the long-range outlook of eliminating the ruling class' state apparatus and replacing it with a workers' government, the bosses will continue to have the power to cut down, sidetrack or crush the workers' struggles. We believe that this past and present history of inevitable class struggle demonstrates conclusively that the overwhelming majority of workers can be won to active battle against the ruling class, and for socialism, and are destined to consign that class to the scrap heap of history. How we can begin to achieve that goal is the essence of the program that follows.

Marxism-Leninism: Science of Class Struggle

U.S. history demonstrates the inherent contradictions of capitalism. Workers engaged in social production suffer under a system of private ownership based on the extraction of surplus value (roughly, profits) from their labors. Their labor creates all value added in production but the bosses rob as much of this value as they can. The class struggle is the constant battle over wages and working conditions, and the social conditions that flow from them. Workers organize trade unions in self-defense to fight their side of this struggle.

Because of its strategic position in the economy, its size, and the ceaseless necessity for it to fight back against its deteriorating material condition, the working class is the only force capable of overthrowing capitalism. This must be a fight to the end because the contradictions of capitalism cannot be resolved unless the system is smashed and a new one built, without bosses or profits: what we call socialism. But although this contradiction is always present under capitalism, the working class will not automatically move forward towards a revolutionary solution. At one point workers were moved to the Right–to fascism–in Germany, Italy and Japan. The key to which way the workers will go is their ideology: What is their class understanding of the role of the state and of the necessity and method of achieving emancipation.

The state,* or government, stands between the working class and its true class interests. The state is not neutral in the class struggle but is the instrument of the ruling class; it always has been and always will be, as long as a state exists. This can be seen in almost every strike or workers' struggle.

When the chips are down, the dictatorship of the bosses comes out in the open. In certain ways most workers recognize this; it is revealed in everyday expressions like "you can't fight City Hall." No matter how hard you fight, no matter how high you go, "they" will always stop you before your demands and needs are fully satisfied. Despite all claims of democracy in the U.S., many workers realize that there is a force that somehow always manages to stop them from achieving the most immediate goals: a living wage, job security, job equality. The working class cannot look to the government for its salvation any more than it can look to the bosses.

Nor is there any such animal as labor's "friend in the White House." The Democratic and Republican parties are both con-

---

*By state power is meant every repressive force on every level of government which can be used to blunt and defeat the workers' fight for their class interests: the army; national guard; state, county and city police; courts; jails; laws (injunctions), etc.

trolled by the ruling class. The only "choice" they offer is a negative one—the so-called lesser evil. John Kennedy was a lesser evil than Nixon (or than Johnson in the Democratic Convention). Then Johnson was the lesser evil to Goldwater. Robert Kennedy and Eugene McCarthy were the lesser evils to Johnson, and Nixon and Humphrey were "not as bad" as Wallace. They only have tactical differences about how to keep the workers down here and abroad—and there's not too much difference even there.

Johnson, elected as the man who would keep things cool in Vietnam, continued the war policies and escalated that U.S. war of aggression. He also attempted to break every strike that came his way—longshore, maritime, General Electric, airline, copper and so on. In addition, he tried to continue Kennedy's "national interest" wage freeze, which the workers are increasingly rebelling against.

Lesser evil Robert Kennedy helped his brother write the Kennedy-Landrum-Griffin anti-labor law and directed the "get Hoffa" drive. "Liberal" Senator Morse was Johnson's right-hand man in arbitrating longshoremen out of wage increases and job security. "Dissenter" Fulbright represents a racist, segregated system in Arkansas. You name it, the ruling class has got it; what looks like sweet syrup is castor oil in brightly-colored jars. When their class interests are threatened they all tend to close ranks; the facade drops; the carrot is put away and the stick—always there as a threat to make the carrot look sweeter—is used unmercifully to club workers into line.

John Kennedy was for civil rights while his FBI watched Southern sheriffs beat down Black people fighting for their rights. Johnson was "pro-labor" while state police jailed striking shipbuilding workers in Newport News, Virginia or miners in Pennsylvania. Nixon allowed local cops to run over striking oil workers as long as they could "handle the job." All this is a clear division of labor. When the "locals" can't control it, the "feds" come in.

Some might think that electing workers' representatives to Congress and the Presidency would be a way of voting the working class into power and thereby changing the state. But what will the rulers of this country do when—and before—they see this happening? Twiddle their thumbs? They have called out the troops when workers were just fighting for simple economic demands—against a wage cut or against rent gouging by slumlords. Think of what they would do when their entire system is at stake!

Although it might be possible to elect some working-class representatives to office, it is naïve and misleading (and for some, like those in the U.S. "Communist" Party, downright dishonest) to think that the capitalist class could be voted out of its state power and socialism voted in. No ruling class has ever yielded power without an armed struggle. Even at the lowest levels of struggle it is necessary to fight the state every step of the way, defending strikes against scabs, cops and injunctions. It is near the point where it has become difficult, if not impossible, to win strikes without fighting bosses' violence. Certainly, as the working class advances to still higher levels of power it will have to be prepared to defend against the most violent counter-attack by the ruling class and take the offensive—go one step further to smash the bosses' state and create a workers' state. And, as is the case with all classes holding state power, the workers must be prepared to repress the old ruling class and prevent its return to power.

Dictatorship of the Proletariat

To end permanently the dictatorship of the bosses, the working class must install its own class rule, that which Marx and Lenin called the dictatorship of the proletariat. Such a state is infinitely more democratic than what exists now since it allows for the greatest sharing of the fruits of labor. It will eliminate bosses, profits and the "right" to exploit others; the police, the Army, the courts, the laws will all represent, and be controlled by, the working class.

The Chinese Communist Party has carried the concept of the dictatorship of the proletariat still further. Chairman Mao Tse-tung and the Chinese revolutionaries have demonstrated that the bourgeoisie (the bosses) must not only be driven from power but that a ceaseless struggle against their ideology must be carried out among the people. Otherwise the former ruling class will desperately fight its way back into state power.

Unless those who want to defeat the bosses' dictatorship have the long-range strategy of establishing a workers' dictatorship, somewhere along the line of struggle we will be trapped into some ruling-class scheme or "reform" program that will give us something with one hand and take it away with the other (just as they concede wage increases—after a fight—and then raise prices and taxes).

Understanding the necessity for the long-range goal of a dictatorship of the proletariat indicates a class understanding of the state. It will enable workers to fight the concept of the state's "neutrality" and prevent them from getting embroiled in capitalist party politics or ruling class-controlled "anti-poverty" programs. While there can be honest differences over tactics, based on varying estimates of the relationship of forces at a given moment, the abandonment of the dictatorship of the proletariat as a principle will lead inevitably to the wrong tactics and deliver the workers into the arms of the bosses. The lack of this understanding was a fundamental weakness of nearly every working-class leader—Debs, Haywood, Foster—and the trade union movements they led. Because of it these were smashed or not consolidated after victory (which amounts to the same thing—it just takes longer) and the victory turned into its opposite. This happened with the communist-led CIO, which degenerated into the business unionism it had replaced.

The concept of a dictatorship of the bourgeoisie is not confined to national boundaries. The ruling classes of all capitalist nations, in order to extract a maximum amount of profits, seek to exploit workers in all nations. History shows that countless times the capitalists of one country have formed alliances with capitalists of other countries against the interests of the majority in the respective nations, all for the sake of profits and maintaining a dictatorship over the working class. History also shows that the biggest capitalist countries have extended their dictatorship over the working class of other countries with or without the help of local capitalists.

Thus the working class of every nation finds itself in conflict not only with the home-grown capitalist exploiter but with the foreign capitalist as well. Therefore the workers of every nation have in common with the workers of all other nations the need to fight against the exploiting capitalist classes of all nations. Workers' state control is not confined to any single country. Whether as a goal pursued or as power already won and exercised it is the weapon of all working classes who would fight for or defend their freedom and class liberation against the attacks of all exploiting capitalists, domestic or foreign.

Today it is U.S. imperialism*—the attempt of the U.S. ruling class to extend its dictatorship over the entire globe—that is the enemy of workers everywhere. Whether through the machinations of the CIA or through naked aggression the U.S. ruling class has intensified the exploitation of hundreds of millions in Asia, Africa and Latin America. It has murdered and continues to slaughter hundreds of thousands in these countries, particularly in Vietnam.

Anything that weakens U.S. imperialism in one area weakens that same ruling class elsewhere, just as, for example, the defeat of strike-busting legislation by transit workers will help the next group of workers facing the same law. Oppressed peoples all over the world are rebelling and inflicting sharp defeats on the same bosses that exploit U.S. workers here at home. By tying down hundreds of thousands of U.S. troops in Asia and elsewhere they put still more pressure on a ruling class that may need to use these troops against workers in this country. International unity of the working class is an immediate need. Without it the ruling class is able to use the strength gained from any victories against colonial peoples to reverse the tide of workers' battles here in the U.S. It is in the class interests of U.S. workers to support their brothers and sisters abroad who are weakening the same ruling class we must fight to gain our own emancipation here at home.

Can Unions Make a Revolution?

When modern industrial capitalism developed in the United States in the 19th century, it produced what its predecessors had produced elsewhere—hundreds and thousands of workers together under one roof, each performing his individual task, all contributing to the final product that the owner (capitalist) then places on the market to realize his profit.

The capitalist was not then, and he is not today, concerned with the condition of the worker. Concern meant less profit, and less profit meant defeat by his more successful competitors, and bankruptcy. Therefore, he was forced, as he is today, by the very nature of the system to extract as much production from the worker as possible while paying him as little as possible.

---

* Bosses always look for new areas to invest their capital. As they export it to other, generally weaker, countries they make an even greater profit than at home. And as the people in these countries rebel against foreign exploitation, what we call imperialists move their troops in to defend their "right to make" profits.

The workers, brought together in the factory under intolerable conditions, had no choice but to use their newfound social relationship to fight back. They formed trade unions to demand higher wages, shorter hours, and improved working conditions. The trade union is the only workers' organization that fights the boss at the point of production, where exploitation is the sharpest. It is there that they organize for a greater share of the surplus value their labor produces.

Trade unions are open to all workers to join, whether militant or not, advanced or backward. They fight for certain immediate demands on which all workers can agree. Their goal is not revolution; they do not have common goals that go beyond the system (although some members among them may). Trade unionism only reflects the short-range needs of all workers, no matter what the level of their understanding, operating within the confines of the system's ground rules; it cannot possibly develop the long-range outlook of going "all the way," exposing and smashing the capitalist state and establishing a workers' state, a dictatorship of the proletariat.

This dual character of U.S. trade unions–tremendous class struggle alongside an inability to move beyond the capitalist system–has marked the last 100 years. From the 1877 national railroad strikes to the 1892 Homestead Steel strike; from the Haymarket demonstrations for the 8-hour day to Debs' Pullman strike of 1894; from the Western Federation of Miners led by "Big Bill" Haywood to the IWW organizers; from the Great Steel Strike of 1919 to the industrial union drive and organization of the CIO in the 1930's–through all this the U.S. working class has stood up to the most violent repression the ruling class could offer, fallen back temporarily, and come back to fight again. In all these struggles the massive class fight waged by the workers was eventually either crushed or undermined by the state power of the bosses, which neither Debs, Haywood nor the IWW leaders thought it necessary to deal with strategically. At one time, in the late 1920's and early 1930's, Foster and the CPUSA did recognize the nature of the state and the necessity to ultimately wipe it out and set up a workers' state, but he and his party only paid lip service to this need.

One good example of both the inherent strength of the working class and its ideological weakness was the 1968 general strike in France. Here the workers overrode their own sellout leadership (who call themselves "communists") and shut down the entire country. But because the ruling class held state power, and because the workers had no counterforce to that power, no goal to smash it and no leadership except those prepared to work within the capitalist electoral framework, the workers' fundamental power to immobilize the economy was dissipated in calls to replace the de Gaulle regime with some other ruling-class flunkies. Meanwhile, de Gaulle and the French ruling class he represented had all the repressive arms of state power to break the back of the general strike, with aid from the phoney leaders, and force the strikers back to work.

Something more than trade unionism is needed to lead the battle against the ruling class all the way, to a new system.

Role of a Communist Party

To build a socialist society a science of class struggle is required, one that embodies many of the principles described in this section—a class analysis of society, surplus value and the contradictions it creates, the class struggle as the moving force of history, the role of the state, the need to smash the bosses' state power and establish workers' state power and the goal of a socialist reorganization of society. These principles compose the science of Marxism-Leninism. To practice this science and apply it to the conditions of a particular country, a disciplined group is needed that believes in these principles and is organized to carry them out. That is the role of a communist party.

Such a party functions at every level of struggle, always attempting to move the fight to the next highest level. It attempts to unify all those involved in the struggle at every level, not just in trade unions but within every section of the people fighting the ruling class and between all sections. It pays attention to the smallest fights and attempts to relate them to other battles and win allies to each.

A true communist party is merciless in destroying the bosses' ideology in the ranks of the working class. To do this it has to be in constant interaction with the people, deeply immersed in their struggles and completely dedicated to serving the people not the selfish interests of individuals.

The concept of serving the people, not one's self, is the direct opposite of the idea fostered by capitalism among workers:

"What's in it for me?" A communist who serves the people is demonstrating the kind of leadership that will be required to defeat the ruling class. As long as the idea of self permeates the working class it will remain divided. Within the trade union movement the idea of serving one's self has led to the acceptance by workers of the notion that labor leaders must be corrupt and self-seeking—"otherwise, why become union officials?" The concept of serving the masses will point the way to another kind of leader, one who cannot be bought by the ruling class. Such a concept helps to steel people for the kind of struggle that will be necessary to smash the ruling class' state power.

To enable the working class and itself to carry out an effective program and advance to a revolutionary position, a true communist party must function on the principles of democratic centralism—democratic in that those expected to carry out a policy must determine that policy, and centralized in requiring all members to carry out the policy once decided by a majority. In this way a communist party can be democratic in determining policy but not so "democratic" that it violates the decision of the majority, destroys democracy and splits every time there is a disagreement. Democratic centralism is particularly necessary in fighting a capitalist class that wields economic and state power and is prepared to use force against the working class.

The practice of criticism and self-criticism enables a communist party to correct its own mistakes and prevents them from destroying the party. This runs counter to the ruling class idea that it is a sin to admit one's weaknesses, much less correct them. This central feature of communist work enables the party to constantly test its theory among the masses and change it where proven wrong in life. People must root out weaknesses engendered by capitalism by looking for the main obstacles within themselves and their co-workers and subject them to searching criticism, but always with the aim of better serving the people and the goal of working-class emancipation. Such a constant cleansing process fights the ideological influence of the class enemy within the ranks of the party and prevents it from degenerating into just another reform organization.

Only a communist party that functions in these ways can supply the kind of leadership and organization to the working class necessary to defeat the present ruling class. Though capitalism's contradictions create the basis for a working class and a working-class party, the ability of that party to master and develop its science will determine whether it can actually change the world. And though workers learn about the class struggle from day-to-day encounters with the boss, history has proven that this is not enough to fundamentally alter the system. To make a revolutionary change, revolutionary consciousness is required. This is the product of a science that cannot be learned on an assembly line but must be studied outside the point of production, although drawing on the experiences within it. It is the job of a communist party to bring this revolutionary consciousness into the working class, while immersed in the workers' struggles, so that the party can become the working class' general staff in the class war.

Most U.S. workers do not accept the goal of socialist revolution but do fight for immediate demands; they are at a point of increasing class struggle. We must deal with how U. S. workers can move from their current reform struggles to a revolutionary overthrow of the system that oppresses them.

Strategy and Tactics to Defeat Ruling Class

The key to winning the workers to a revolutionary consciousness is exposure of the state as a bosses' instrument at every step of the struggle. The bosses keep the workers divided among themselves and separated from their allies by pretending the state is "above classes," through the confines of the two-party system and by dulling the consciousness of the class struggle with a democratic façade.

The biggest obstacle to the workers breaking out of this bind has been the capture of their main class organization—the trade union—by the Meanys and Reuthers, who ably serve as lieutenants of the bosses in the workers' ranks. Their sellout over the past 20 years (with roots still further back than that) has served to crush left-wing influence in the labor movement.

In the 1930's the Communist Party's membership played an outstanding role in organizing and leading struggles that culminated in the formation of the CIO—a great vehicle of struggle for industrial workers in their daily fight against the giants of monopoly capitalism. They were part of the leadership of a movement that embraced five million workers in all the basic industries, and had an excellent opportunity to lead masses of workers away from reactionary trade unionism and towards a class understanding of the state under capitalism.

They attempted to establish a coalition of forces–a united front –between themselves (the Left) and the vast majority of workers (the Center) who wanted to engage in militant struggle against the bosses but didn't necessarily agree with the ultimate goal of socialism. The aim was correct but the communists displayed a fatal weakness that led to their own downfall as well as to a great defeat for the working class. The flaw was one of both form and content.

The mistaken content was an attempt to unite with (or "use") the "good" capitalists–represented by Roosevelt–against the "bad" capitalists (the reactionaries and fascists) even though they had had first-hand experience with the use of state power against them, of the actual class nature of U.S. democracy. They didn't really see the state as an instrument of the entire capitalist class. They viewed it as something that could be "pushed" or "swayed" in a progressive direction if enough pressure were exerted by the working class. They failed to understand that the ruling class ultimately would never yield power peacefully, that there was no such thing as a "good capitalist," and that there were only tactical differences among bosses over the best way to keep the working class in check.

The C.P. fell into the trap of supporting Roosevelt and the New Deal on the grounds that the workers had won many gains under it, rather than seeing that the gains were wrested from it and could be lost at a moment's notice. Thus the ruling class, through its spokesman in the White House, pointed to these victories as having been "given" the workers by democracy or the Democratic Party (and "don't go any further because you might rock the boat and lose the little you've gained").

The form of the united front followed from this view: In the name of "unity" to defeat the "most reactionary" forces, the communists would not criticize reformist CIO misleaders like John L. Lewis, Philip Murray or Sidney Hillman. They were ready to follow the leadership of the Democratic Party and Roosevelt in order to defeat the "ultra right." They did not fight the bad ideas of the reformists who operated within the system and whose goal was to preserve it, not defeat it. They feared such a struggle would "split" the united front. Instead, the Left became submerged within it and gradually assumed a reformist position.

Instead of using the victory of industrial unionism and the bosses' reaction to that victory to raise the struggle of the working class to a higher level—pointing out that we will never make any gains permanent until we eliminate the bosses' state—the C.P. became mired in the swamp of ruling-class politics. It was just a short step to selling out the workers altogether.

This was borne out during World War II when the communists went all out in support of a just, anti-fascist war but glossed over the class antagonism between bosses and workers, who were fighting fascism for different reasons. The C.P. actually led the way in many practices that were hated by the workers—no-strike pledges, compulsory overtime, etc.

Throughout this period the communists did not help the working class understand the necessity to defend communists; nor did they fight for a political view that went beyond reform demands to simply make capitalism better. Because of a faulty political position and a faulty concept of the role of communists in a united front, the left-wing leadership that did exist in the labor movement had no revolutionary political base.

The ruling class was thus able to launch a post-war offensive that wiped out left-wing influence in the trade union movement. This was necessary to a U.S. ruling class that saw as its primary post-war task the prevention of the spread of socialism. It needed a secure home front to pursue its drive for maximum profits abroad. Militant communist leadership in the labor movement had to be smashed because it contained the germ of the answer to the post-war imperialist onslaught.

The Taft-Hartley Law was passed, making it illegal for a Communist Party member to hold union office, and hundreds of communists were hounded out of their jobs amid the cold war anticommunist hysteria. Red-baiting was the order of the day. Red-baiters like Walter Reuther and James Carey moved in and either took over the once-proud CIO unions or set up dual unions to raid the remaining left-led groups that had either withdrawn or were expelled from the CIO.

Some communists stood and fought but were overwhelmed. Others stayed on but sold out their principles completely. Very few, if any, pointed out how necessary communists were to the working class. The failure to follow a real Marxist-Leninist line, to politicalize the working class and to expose the fakers in the CIO leadership and the Democratic Party, all took its toll. The right-wing leadership that had controlled the AFL for so many years was now firmly in the saddle in the CIO, too—all the more decisive because the CIO had unionized the basic industries.

The rank-and-file democracy that had permeated the CIO, and spread to other sections of the labor movement, was no more. A fighting shop steward system was virtually destroyed. Planned organizing drives in the South and other open shop areas were abandoned. The CIO, begun as a vehicle for struggle against the capitalist giants, had turned into its opposite—a vehicle of control by the bosses through their labor lieutenants. This defeat proved that the working class needs communists with a political position that goes beyond the confines of "unity" with the "best" under capitalism, one that combines an understanding of the class struggle under capitalism with the necessity to overthrow it.

The biggest step towards that long-range goal is to throw out the bosses' servants in the trade union movement and fight to establish the unions as class instruments in the workers' interests. The latter strategy will become a major tactic in attaining the still longer-range strategic goal of smashing the system. Neither can be accomplished without the full participation and leadership of communists. Also essential is the full participation and leadership of those militant workers who are ready to actively fight the class enemy and who begin to understand, through struggle, the absolute necessity of working with communists.

Left-Center Coalition: Toward Rank-and-File Control

The trade union movement contains three broad groupings—the Right, the Center and the Left.

The Center is composed, either actually or potentially, of the vast majority of workers; its leadership is militant, class-oriented but non-communist. Though Center forces are ready to fight for immediate demands, they do so under rules established by the ruling class. Their struggle, therefore, is contained within the system and does not challenge it. They cannot learn of the need to overthrow capitalism from these struggles alone.

The Right is composed of the Meany-Reuther misleadership and their flunkies in the districts and locals of each international union. They collaborate with the bosses to secure their own cozy positions in the labor hierarchy, living off the workers although frequently assuming a militant-sounding front. They generally choose arbitration and legislation over militant struggle and oppose strikes unless membership pressures make them unavoidable. They make deals with some workers at the expense of the vast majority, work with the bosses' two political parties (mainly the Democrats), bar rank-and-file participation in decision-making and refuse to mobilize the strength of the rank and file. They sign sellout contracts behind the workers' backs and run the unions in an arbitrary, sometimes dictatorial way through a machine well-oiled by money from the union treasury, maintaining themselves in power election after election. They depend for their base on that small minority of workers who consciously and deliberately choose to serve the boss instead of their own class interests in exchange for a few crumbs.

Within this framework the Left plays a decisive role. It is composed of communists following a path of revolution, not reform, based on Marxism-Leninism. The Left understands the long-range necessity to smash the ruling-class state and erect a working-class state. It knows the workers must seize the means of production on behalf of the overwhelming majority, to make their gains permanent. Therefore, the Left does not limit itself to the ground rules laid out by the ruling class but leads the struggle in a revolutionary direction. Because the Left can point out the class nature of the state it is able to combat some of the political pitfalls that trap the Center, which is guided by a reformist policy.

A Center Without a Left . . .

The Center does not need the Left to launch struggles against the boss. Most of the class fights occurring in the U.S. today have begun without a Left within them. But as the Center becomes more militant in fighting for its immediate (mainly economic) demands, the ruling class uses many methods to halt or reverse that fight. It attempts to buy off some and corrupt others. It splits workers along racial, craft or national lines; and it sabotages the struggle particularly through the use of union misleaders, or demoralizes the workers into thinking their cause is hopeless. It tries to co-opt the successes achieved through working-class unity and strength by claiming they are "gifts" from the ruling class. Through this pretense of benevolence it establishes its own base among the workers. Meanwhile, it presses the workers not to fight if they want to keep their gains won through struggle.

Workers frequently accept partial economic gains (which the bosses can regain through higher taxes and prices, for instance), and cut short their struggle because they fear—or are unable to deal with—state power. When they refuse to accept the "carrot," they feel the full weight of the "stick."

Since the Center has no long-range strategy, and is constantly fighting within the system's ground rules, it inevitably falls prey to a bureaucratic leadership that faithfully serves the bosses. It is inevitably unprepared for the political and class attacks the bosses will launch; it inevitably allows the core of rank-and-file leaders, so necessary to future battles, to be destroyed. The results of short-range Center fights intensify the feeling that "you can't fight City Hall" and that the law is all-powerful. The actual power of the working class remains hidden.

A Center With a Left . . .

It is the task of the Left to maintain and advance the Center forces, to sharpen the struggle even for immediate gains and to "raise the stakes." The Right constantly attempts to blunt the struggle, to either smash or mislead the Center away from a militant, revolutionary direction and to empty it of class content. The job of the Left is to forge a coalition with the Center to defeat the Right.

The Left must politicize at all levels of struggle, not just the highest. If not undertaken at the lower levels, the higher ones won't be reached. Even at the lowest levels the role of the state appears: Workers say, "Let's go to the labor board"; or a departmental walkout, if it lasts, will send the boss into court; or workers will propose to hire an "outside lawyer" to fight their grievance rather than depending mainly upon their own unity and strength in the shop; or the foreman will mount a red-baiting campaign against the "unpatriotic reds"; or a strike will be broken by cops and scabs. The ability, and necessity, to deal with political attacks at the lowest and at each succeeding level will lay the basis to deal with them at higher levels, such as when the ruling class calls out troops to break a national movement.

In all struggles, at every level, the Left must point out to the

Center: (1) that a political fight must be waged against the state, many times in defiance of laws, to win demands; (2) the significance of a particular workers' struggle and what it takes to organize against the state and the ruling class; (3) the potential power of the working class; (4) why the movement was unable to go any further in a particular struggle and what is needed to advance the level of struggle the next time; (5) the necessity for developing additional leaders through each struggle; (6) that the core of people leading a particular fight must be maintained and strengthened; and (7) the role of the Left–why it was necessary (not just "useful")–strengthening the workers' resolve to defend against the inevitable ruling class red-baiting attack that will be launched to split the Left from the Center and move the latter to the Right.

The ability of the Center to fight the enemy depends on the Left. If the Left fails in its responsibilities, or tails the Center, then the Right or a Right-Center coalition will take over. This lowers the level of struggle and may wipe out the Left–as happened in the 1940's and 1950's. Therefore, the Left must lead the Center into greater confrontation with the "ground rules" of the capitalist system in order to avoid the path the ruling class chooses and the consequent movement to the Right.

If the Left fulfills its role it helps raise the level of struggle to the next step, isolates the Right, forces the ruling class to drop another aspect of its democratic façade and recruits some Center forces into the Left, into the revolutionary party. It also enables the mass of workers to win more of their demands, hold on to them longer and learn more about the fundamental nature of the ruling class.

The development of the Left-Center coalition is not a static goal. It is a process in which the character of the Right, the Center and the Left is constantly changing, depending on the level of the struggle at a particular time. The fight of the Center usually begins as a reaction to the pressures of the inherent contradictions of the system–a fight for immediate economic shop demands. (It may very well be composed of anticommunist forces, although still engaged in militant class struggle.)

Of course, the bosses do not take a Left-Center coalition victory lying down. Their chief ideological weapon to break up such a united front is red-baiting. Therefore it is vital for the Center and the Left to fight red-baiting all the way. Here the Left leads by making the Center aware of the existence of the Left, although not necessarily all of its members, from the earliest moment possible. It consciously and openly brings to the mass of workers in the Center the lessons that the Left understands about the struggles under way–and mutually fought for by Center and Left.

This achieves two goals necessary for the further development of the working class' revolutionary potential:

1. It enables the Center to overcome its anticommunist attitudes by making it aware that red-baiting is a weapon used by the bosses and right-wing trade unionists to bring down the Center. As a result, the Center's class understanding goes up.

2. It enables the Left to remain and grow as a force within the working class and trade union movement because the Center, having increased its understanding of the battle, becomes a defender and protector of the Left. Members of the Center who recognize that the Left provides the long-range answers required for liberating the working class once and for all from capitalist exploitation then become recruitable to the Left. In this way the Center replenishes, helps build and continues the Left movement among the working class.

While it may be useful at certain times to have some communists openly in the leadership of the Left-Center coalition, the long-term influence of the Left in the coalition depends more on its ability to secure itself from destruction by the class enemy and its ability to recruit workers to its ranks. Such a qualitative advance of both the Center and the Left allows for continuous political struggle (the presence of communists) under any and all conditions, including the most severe capitalist repression–fascism.

But if the Left is unable to show that red-baiting is a bosses' weapon, by not playing its correct political role, and is therefore unable to bring the Center to a higher level of struggle, it will find that workers in the Center will either drop out of the struggle —as defeats follow on the divisions caused by red-baiting—or move to the Right. Meanwhile the Left's own forces will move to the Center, drop out or even move all the way to the Right, as happened in the 1940's and 1950's when some former communists became, and are still to this day, labor misleaders as underhanded and autocratic as any of those who began as flunkies or opportunists in the labor movement.

In evaluating whether or not workers are potentially part of the Center, one must be careful to relate their actions to the level of struggle at the time. For instance, in the absence of any militant force fighting in their class interests many workers seek their own individual way out in so-called "private deals" with a foreman or a boss. This does not necessarily place them in the enemy's camp. However once a militant antiboss movement emerges to fight in all the workers' interests, if they do not drop these "private deals" but intensify them, it would indicate they are consciously choosing an alternative that represents the boss' interests, not the workers (who now have organized themselves to fight in their class interests).

Just as there are forces within the Center who may move to the Right, so also are there those in the Right who may be affected by the class struggle and moved to adopt a militant, class position. And it is important to win such forces away from the Right. This is more true at lower levels of trade union struggle than at higher ones. There the Right is so hopelessly bought off (Meany and Reuther) that they can never be expected to defend the workers' class interests. They are the confirmed "labor lieutenants of the capitalist class," who eventually must be defeated.

As the level of struggle moves upward the Left becomes more revolutionary and the Center more class-oriented, more militant and less reformist. As the coalition moves towards greater confrontation with the class enemy, the Right will generally become more ruthless. In effect, the character of the Center, the Left and even the Right will change every time the level of struggle changes. To be equal to the task at any level the Left must politicalize its base in the Center; the Center, as a result, will become more class conscious. The Right will then expose itself as it becomes more desperate, move further to the Right and become openly allied with the ruling class.

Building the Coalition: The Caucus

Just as the Center cannot move forward without the Left; the Left cannot operate at all without the Center. The mass of workers in the Center are not ready to adopt the revolutionary position of the Left. Granted, of course, the latter has such a position, it still would be unable to give leadership to the Center without a BASE within it. To win such a base it must participate fully and wholeheartedly in the struggles for immediate demands of the

Center. But if it restricts itself to this alone the revolutionary potential of the working class will never develop. If no organized Center force exists the Left must build such a Center as one of its first tasks–if it is to establish a base.

A caucus is a stable group of workers united around a common set of demands. While many times it grows out of a situation in which workers are close socially, a caucus form implies something more than a social club. It must be an organization that will fight those opposed to its demands.

A caucus is not necessarily a group that represents the best interests (or class interests) of all workers. It can be narrow and reactionary, a vehicle for a power play by those not in union office to displace the present officials. It can also be a Center group that honestly wants to do something in the interests of all workers and is trying to get itself elected to office. But unless a Left is present, sooner or later this Center caucus will become the kind of group it has displaced, through bribes, harassment, threats, and a lack of understanding of how to face the boss and the higher echelons of union misleadership when they "up the ante" of struggle.

Following the general principles already outlined the Left-Center caucus will be able to counter higher-level attacks by the boss, or at least maintain its existence on principles representing the workers' class interests. Where the Left builds such a caucus from scratch, the more quickly can the caucus emerge as a Left-Center one, provided the existence of the Left as an organized force is made known fairly early in its development to workers forming the group.

But before even organizing such a caucus one must learn as much as possible about the past history of the company and the union, what are the chief gripes of the workers and which workers show the most militance and potential for leadership (not necessarily the "loudest mouths"). The issue selected over which to launch a fight should be one the workers feel deeply about and also one that holds some promise of minimum victory. The short-range strategic goal becomes one of carrying on a series of struggles that will create the basis for workers to understand the necessity of having an organized force to fight all the time, not just from issue to issue. If the Left points out all the lessons in a particular struggle, depending on specific conditions sooner or later a caucus will emerge, probably at a departmental level, to be spread to other departments; this will be an organized Center force. If the Left has begun to point out the longer-range class lessons to some workers, and therefore has become known as a Left or communist force (a gradual development), a Left-Center coalition will emerge, even at this lowest rung of the ladder.

It is important that the Left become identifiable simultaneously, if possible, with the organization of the Center, because it is hard to predict when the enemy will choose to launch his first red-baiting attack. If the Center is unprepared and has no knowledge of the Left working with it (nor of its importance), the Left will be cut off.

Once achieved, this most immediate strategy becomes a tactic toward reaching the next strategic goal, which could be for the caucus to launch a struggle against the boss throughout the union local, resulting in leadership being given to a wider circle of workers. After a series of such battles, some won and some lost, the workers will begin to see not only that the present leadership is bad (which is usually–but not always–the case) but that there is an alternative that can change things. Eventually–in most cases, depending on the size of the local, this takes several years–the Left-Center caucus can be elected to the leadership of the local. This should be attempted when the basis has been laid for the coalition to win decisively. If it wins by a narrow margin, it will be heading a union split down the middle, making it easier for the boss and his friends among the former union leadership to reverse the victory with the slightest attack.

Before running for office the coalition must recognize that it is one thing to defend against attacks when fighting on relatively small localized grievances. It is quite another to face attack because of a threat posed by a rank-and-file led, local-wide leadership, for such an attack will come from both the boss and the sellout leaders above the local level–in the district and international. Neither wants to see this victory repeated in other locals. Therefore, the coalition that runs for office should have tried beforehand to make contact with rank-and-filers in other locals as well as with workers in allied unions or in the immediate area with whom solidarity can be built around common issues. Usually a common employer is a natural basis for unity.

Some preparation will thus have been made for allies to help fight the inevitable attack of the boss and higher union officials. Since the boss usually prefers to work through the higher union officials, that relationship must be exposed so that the battle does not develop into one solely between the local and a higher union body.

Once elected, a Left-Center caucus should not disband. In order to fight the inevitable attacks of the class enemy it is essential that an organized core of workers continue to give disciplined leadership. This group could conceivably be the new officers, constituting the union's executive board, but more often than not it can't include all the officers. It definitely should include some of the more militant rank-and-filers, stewards, committeemen, etc., throughout the local. As new struggles are begun by this group and more intensive attacks result, well-thought-out proposals should be put before the membership. This can't be left to chance but should be organized by the very group that the workers respected enough to put into leadership. Leadership still has to be exercised once elected, and the maintenance and expansion of the Left-Center caucus is even more necessary than it was at a lower level. This principle can be extended to even higher levels of leadership and struggle.

As the new leadership launches local-wide struggles, consolidating its base in the entire local, the process of seeking allies must be intensified—"vertically" among other locals within the international and "horizontally" among workers within the labor movement of the area. In the process, the Left in the coalition should be able to begin giving advanced leadership to others outside the particular local. It should also consider transferring members of its coalition into other plants to assist similar movements in sister locals. As national, regional or city-wide struggles develop between the entire company and the international, the advanced leadership in the one or two locals, with its allies in others, will begin to assert itself.

In this way the intermediate strategy of the rank and file winning control of several locals becomes a tactic leading towards a national fight for the whole union and industry. And if this has been happening simultaneously in several unions and industries, the Left-Center coalition can become the new leadership of the labor movement—or of a sizable section of it.

Of course, it would be naïve to think that the ruling class would allow such a Left-Center leadership to win even one national union, much less the whole labor movement, without a terrific struggle. No doubt there will be violent and armed mass attacks against the workers by the bosses' state apparatus to prevent such a victory. The workers' leaders must foresee that and prepare measures to deal with it. It is possible that decisive battles for state power will have to be fought before a Left-Center coalition can assume the leadership of the trade union movement. The capitalist class may try to smash such a coalition before it gets to such a high level. But the workers and their leaders must strive for complete control over their class interests nonetheless.

The key to the advance of the working class and its ability to meet such attacks is the development of the revolutionary Left. The recruitment of communists from among the working class is the guarantee that eventually the workers will be able to take state power, with or without the leadership of the entire trade union movement. And it is precisely out of the class struggles for a Left-Center coalition that the Left will grow and the Center will move towards the revolutionary position necessary to defeat all attacks by the ruling class.

The Left-Center leadership must estimate beforehand what level of minimum demands its base can sustain. At this point the bosses might try bribery to blunt the struggle, while always threatening to force agreement. The Left must expose both tactics, pointing out that the ruling class' use of force is a sign of weakness not strength. The bosses do not like to drop the democratic facade because that exposes them in the future. If the workers can maintain their ranks with this level of leadership, they can stick to their demands and achieve a greater victory. The Left could then teach the lesson for even greater struggle next time—a sit-down strike that would occupy the bosses' property, or winning control of several locals or more in order to allow the fuller use of the workers' power. Such a fight is an uneven one and requires allies on a still higher level in other unions in order to maintain and consolidate rank-and-file control approaching the national level. The rank and file cannot gain control of one international isolated from action in other unions, since if allowed to get that far they will be picked off by the ruling class.

The Left-Center's attitude towards the union contract is an important one in maintaining and expanding its influence. Most workers feel enforcement of the contract is the only way they can gain some measure of job security. The contract is the heart of the union's existence. It is why most workers join the union initially. It is over the issue of the contract that workers conclude that their leadership is either representing them or selling them out. A Left-Center leadership must persuade the workers that the contract is only as strong as the workers who are ready to defend and improve it. It is not the contract itself that brings gains to workers—the boss will break the best contract if he thinks he can get away with it—but the readiness of the workers to defend it. To do this they have to be mobilized and unified to back up even the smallest grievance of the newest worker. Any union leadership that represents the class interests of the workers must recognize this basic fact. Many times demands not provided for in the contract can be won on the strength of a united effort to enforce provisions in the contract.

Even as a Left-Center leadership pursues this path it must also point out that contracts do not guarantee the workers' long-range security. If the boss is not strong enough to break the contract in just the normal daily relationships on the job, he will resort to antilabor legislation, court injunctions, police escort for scabs during a strike fighting to enforce a contract, etc. It is the Left's special role to point out—beforehand—what to expect, beyond the in-plant relations, when the union is strong enough to enforce the contract. In these contract struggles, which many times go beyond just the simple fight over a grievance, the Left can begin to show the political implications of the class relations involved—how the boss resorts to use of the state to protect his interests against those of the workers. In fact, caucus members begin to earn the respect of their fellow workers and prepare for larger battles ahead precisely on the issue of enforcing the contract at the lowest level—departmental grievances. Contract struggles, whether in a crew of 25 workers or in a national, industry-wide strike, are a test of strength between the two classes. So it is important for a Left-Center group to see all the long-range implications in such struggles.

Racism is another important issue that can determine the success or failure of any caucus movement. This is true not only in locals with numbers of Black and other minority-group workers but also in all-white locals being pressured to abandon their discriminatory practices.

A caucus in a local that contains Black workers that starts out on an all-white basis and does not offer a program dealing with the problems of Black workers is doomed to degenerate into a power bloc that will support the bosses' interests in maintaining racism as a divisive weapon. Since unity is a central goal of any caucus striving to represent the class interests of the whole local, Black workers must be involved in any caucus organizing effort. Then when a caucus is formed a program can be developed that will serve the interests of the Black workers also.

Even if Black workers were not to join the caucus immediately (for instance, they might already be part of an all-Black caucus) the basis for unity between Black and white workers would exist—unity on class issues against the same boss. If white workers take such a stand and involve themselves with Black workers in these immediate struggles in the class interest of all, then should a Black caucus exist it will invariably gravitate towards uniting with these progressive white forces. Where Black workers are not already organized, the potential exists for a caucus of Black and white workers to be organized from the very beginning.

In locals where few or no Black workers exist because of long-time discrimination begun by the boss and aided by the union, a caucus formed around class issues and composed of only white workers must eventually try to break down this boss-inspired discrimination. If it does not it will always leave itself open to the threat by the boss either to replace them with Black workers if they get too "demanding" or to move away to a low-wage area like the South. And it will never get the support of the Black communities, which are becoming of key importance in the large urban areas, sometimes composing 25 to 50 per cent of the population. In fact such all-white caucuses formed to protect narrow craft interests as in the building trades, will be fought by the Black community while the boss "makes hay" over the division. More will be said about the role of Black caucuses and their relation to white workers in a later section.

No one can predict if the present sellout leadership of the labor movement can be replaced by a Left-Center coalition representing the rank and file or how long that might take. But as that goal is approached the bosses and workers will be battling on a much higher level and certainly closer to the biggest stakes of all—the system itself. The drive for a Left-Center coalition with a well-defined communist leadership within it thus becomes the "tactic" (among several necessary ones) for launching a final assault for state power itself—one that will be led by the communists with their base within the coalition. And unless this coalition has sought allies outside the trade union movement, other forces in society might be used by the ruling class in the last-ditch fight they will certainly make. So this process does not unfold solely within the trade unions.

In summing up this strategy it can be seen that the Left-Center coalition and its basic organizational form, the caucus, is a major stepping stone to the long-range goal of the working class—defeating the old state power and creating one to serve its interests. This intermediate strategy towards ultimate revolution can help bridge the gap between the present level of the workers and a revolutionary goal.

Build a Base for Revolution

In any struggle the following points should be considered: (1) short-range, partial demands and long-range demands, with a minimum level that one estimates the base is strong enough to win; (2) expand the base; (3) additional leaders; (4) qualitatively strengthen the core of leadership; (5) the leadership and the rank and file should learn as many political lessons as possible from the struggle; (6) lay the basis to fight on a higher level next time by sowing the seeds in each lower level. All these factors affect the kind of base being built.

"Building a base" is not an attempt to see how many workers one can get to support him- or herself individually; it is the development of support for a set of principles. A communist base indicates support for some element in the communists' program. It means that workers are ready to defend a communist because of some of the principles he stands for. A political base is not static but must advance as the level of struggle advances.

History shows that revolutionary movements that have established political bases through struggle have had the strength to withstand ruling-class attacks. A striking example is China: Communists there gave steady attention to winning masses of people as a political base. This led to victory over the domestic ruling class and the foreign imperialists who had invaded the country—some with armed force and all with finance capital. When "revolutionaries" shun bases among the people and "go it alone," they play right into the hands of the rulers and are inevitably wiped out, corrupted or forced to give up the struggle altogether.

Building a political base requires constant examination of the relationship of class forces, knowing the next level of struggle and having a program that will give leadership to the group involved in the particular battle without isolating one from the group. No blueprint is possible because base-building always takes place in particular circumstances. But the history of the trade union movement offers some general guidelines.

Pitfalls in the Movement

The main subjective weakness that has plagued the left-wing movement in the trade unions has been the sacrifice of long-range goals for the short-range struggle. This weakness is expressed as opportunism and appears within communist movements as economism and revisionism.

As has been discussed, the Communist Party led the fight for the immediate demands of the working class in the 1930's but failed to relate that to their announced long-range goal of socialism. Because of either fear of isolation from the workers as "too radical" or lack of confidence in workers' ability to advance politically or fear of ruling-class attack if they espoused long-range communist goals, most C.P. members in the working class set aside long-range aims; they reduced their activities to those of other reformers. Seeing the immediate struggle as everything they failed to raise the political, class and socialist understanding of the workers in those struggles, failed to expose the relation of the trade union misleaders to the bosses and ended up tailing after the misleaders for fear of "splitting" the workers. This is rank opportunism: allowing workers to be abused without pointing out the real enemy and how he must eventually be destroyed. They thus abandoned all their fundamental principles of class struggle and wound up in the very position they most feared—isolation. By failing to build a revolutionary political base with the excuse that "socialism was not the order of the day," the communists left themselves unprepared to meet the ruling-class red-baiting attack in the late 1940's. The result was that the workers could not understand the political nature of the attack and the communists were therefore isolated.

Since anticommunism and red-baiting are still the bosses' main ideological weapon to prevent revolutionary leadership of the working class, it is particularly important for the Left to deal with this problem in any base-building process. If workers do not learn what communists are from the communists themselves, there is only one other source they will learn it from—the ruling class.

Communists must deliberately plan to give communist—not just militant—ideas to at least some of the more advanced workers. These ideas should include a class understanding of the state and, most important, the necessity for the dictatorship of the proletariat.

The best way for workers to understand communists and their ideas is through joint participation in struggle. Although past experiences that parallel present struggles may be stepping stones to the importance of communist ideas, even then communists must be in the thick of working-class struggles if workers are to realize fully how necessary they are at all levels of the fight against the bosses. Only when the working class understands this will it be ready to defend communists and their ideas.

When the Left in a rising Left-Center coalition stops learning and teaching the political lessons of the class struggle, it often uses the opportunistic excuse that the immediate economic demands for which they are fighting form the essence of the class struggle and therefore are actually political. While there are elements of truth in this (which will be analyzed below), in reality they substitute economic demands for a political fight; Lenin called this theory "economism." They abandon the long-range fight for workers' power and eventually fall prey to ruling-class bribery or repression.

Economism can be defeated not by abandoning economic demands but by relating them to the political truths about the state, the ruling class and the need to establish a workers' government. Economism appears when one stops trying to raise the level of struggle to the next highest level and makes the current level the highest one, rather than maintaining as paramount the long-range goal of the dictatorship of the working class. Economism can even be revealed at that high level. Witness the contrast between the Soviet Union and China. In the former, though the workers won state power by smashing the Russian bourgeoisie, they allowed their workers' state power to be usurped by misleaders who introduced economic "reforms" that have brought back capitalist relations of production. In China, the revolutionaries realized that the workers' state power can be reversed and embarked on their cultural revolution to prevent capitalist ideology from seeping back in to destroy the revolution. Until the bosses are destroyed all over the world, the workers' state power in any one country is not completely secure; it must continually be fought for.

When militant but noncommunist workers fight only for immediate demands they do so out of ignorance of a longer-range solution. Their economism is not deliberate and can be overcome by learning Marxism-Leninism. But when those who call themselves communists and revolutionaries abandon the goal of workers' state power for "fear of isolation" or of being "too Left," or because this goal "doesn't apply" to this country, then they are revising Marxism to suit opportunistic purposes. Revisionism is historically the major weakness plaguing the left-wing movement in the U.S. It is the abandonment of revolutionary long-range goals and adoption of a program of class peace or class collaboration.

Another form of revisionism in the U.S. is exemplified by the communists in the 1930's and 1940's in the CIO, and is still advocated by the C.P. We refer to the primary reliance on the bosses' two-party system to win political power. At the heart of this reliance is lack of confidence in the workers' ability to understand the connections between immediate and political interests—in this case the ability to translate their class interests into new and revolutionary political forms. Also at work here is a lack of confidence that workers can be welded into an antifascist force.

This gives rise to the "lesser of two evils" theory. The net effect is always to be saddled with an evil—that is, with a representative of capitalism. As recent elections have shown the people get a lesser evil who is always more reactionary than the lesser evil of the election before and sometimes more reactionary than the greater evil of the previous election. If this theory continues to hold sway, given credence by revisionism, our choice will soon be between fascists one of whom is "not as bad" as the other. In the economic field such principles carried to their logical conclusion would advise New York's transit workers not to strike against the bosses' antistrike law in 1966 but rather to write letters to their state representatives, to elect new ones who would vote for a change in the law—as if antiunion legislation depended on the "differences" between certain supporters of capitalism and not on the character of the system itself. These are the absurdities revisionism leads to and the dangerous traps it sets for the working class. (The C.P. advocates gaining workers' power by passing a constitutional amendment abolishing capitalist ownership of the means of production!) In the end the "lesser of two evils" theory brings fascism ever closer to actuality and makes us less prepared to fight it.

Opportunism in its various forms grows from a lack of confidence in the ability of the working class to relate immediate demands to long-range political goals. Sectarianism does the same but from the "other side of the coin."

A revolutionary program must advance immediate goals as well as long-range goals. When revolutionary and militant workers isolate themselves from the immediate struggles of the workers out of fear that reforms only create illusions, they commit a serious sectarian error. Such self-isolation prevents revolutionaries from showing the relation between the fundamental nature of the state and other political principles, and the day-to-day class struggle. They cannot help build the organizations of workers nor learn the necessary tactics, through actual battles, to defeat the capitalist class enemy.

They fail to raise the political, class and socialist consciousness of workers by learning correct lessons from the workers themselves. Thus, they become armchair generals who fear to lead troops in actual battles against the enemy; as a result there are no troops who follow their leadership.

A "revolutionary" strategy that dismisses immediate demands is not revolutionary at all. It offers no opportunity to change the relationship of forces within a union, between the union and the boss, or between the working class and ruling class plus its state. It is just the kind of "revolutionary" the bosses love–all on paper with no workers to follow.

To try to build a base for long-range goals without immersing oneself in the immediate day-to-day struggles (because "fighting for reforms spreads illusions that things can be patched up under this system") will produce no base at all. Fear that the bosses will take over the workers' victory and therefore "there is no point in fighting for short-range demands" indicates that those building the base are unable to point out why the victory was won –based on the workers' strength–how it can be taken away and what has to be done next time to get to a higher level. Workers– and communists among them–learn lessons from struggle that can be learned in no other way. Those looking for a quick and easy road to the destruction of the U.S. ruling class will only end up cutting themselves off from the mass of workers, and more than likely leave themselves open to bribery and corruption by the enemy.

A correct political line does not automatically influence masses of workers solely by it being presented to them. In the Progressive Labor Movement–forerunner of the Progressive Labor Party–this error was made as an over-reaction to the opportunism of the Communist Party. In attempting to overcome the sellout of communist principles in the C.P., and to reassert the necessity for a communist organization, the PLM concentrated most of its activities in public street-meeting forums. It did not patiently attempt to build a base among particular groups of workers and thereby involve itself in struggles over less advanced demands, struggles from which important lessons could be learned. Had this sectarian practice continued, the PLM would have generated into a sect "preaching revolution" without any ties to the people. Though this error was recognized and its lessons brought to the PLP, it still is a constant danger and must always be guarded against.

Sectarianism is not restricted to communist movements. It can infect anyone desiring social change when others do not see it "his way" immediately. Unless one adopts a patient, long-range outlook, and is ready to become involved in even minor struggles, then the best ideas and most honest intentions will be wasted. The person presenting them will become cynical or worse, while his potential for leadership to a movement will be undermined. Without a base in which to test ideas they will eventually become sterile and wrong.

In summary: The decline of militant trade unionism in the 1950's was not due solely, or even mainly, to the attack by the ruling class but rather to the Left's lack of political base-building around a correct line prior to the bosses' post-war offensive. If we are to overcome the present objective problem of the misleadership of the trade union movement; if we are to take full advantage of the emerging strengths in the working class; if we are to forge it into an antifascist, antiracist Left-Center coalition–and ultimately into a revolutionary force that will overthrow capitalism–we must overcome the main subjective drawbacks–primarily opportunism and secondarily sectarianism, both of which grow out of fear of the working class.

Workers Must Unite in Class Struggle

The bosses use the method of "divide and conquer" to prevent the working class and other sections of the population from challenging their power. The more these groups clash, the less they are able to fight the ruling class. The principle that must guide the U.S. working class among its various sections as well as in its relations with other groups with whom it has common interests must be the principle that is fundamental to the very term "union"—unity around a fighting class program.

Racism Divides Working Class

U.S. bosses extract billions in superprofits from the special oppression of Black workers. The overwhelming majority of Black people are workers; approximately 1,500,000 are in trade unions. At least 75 per cent of the Black people live in urban areas. Through the propagation of racism by the ruling class—the lie that Black people are inferior to whites (and therefore don't deserve as much as whites)—a deep division has been created between Black and white workers.

The superexploitation of Black workers is a class question, not one of race. It benefits the class that owns the means of production; when Black workers fight against it they must fight, as workers, the same ruling class that exploits the entire working class, nationally and internationally. If white workers do not support the fight of Black workers for liberation from special oppression, they strengthen the same ruling class that is exploiting them and weaken their own class position in relation to the bosses' much the same as if they scabbed during a strike.

Though at certain high points of class struggle white workers will drop their passive or active support of the ruling class' racist ideology and unite with Black workers around common demands, they generally allow themselves to be used on behalf of the ruling class' goal of superexploitation of the Black workers.

The misleadership of the trade union movement, while sometimes paying lip service to the fight against racism, actually fosters it. This is especially true in the old AFL lily-white craft unions, which join forces with the bosses to freeze Black workers out of skilled jobs, apprenticeships, etc. In the old CIO unions, among the unskilled workers in the mass production industries, Black workers get most of the dirtiest and hardest jobs, such as in the foundries in the steel industry. White workers tend to hold the higher-paying jobs, the more skilled jobs, where they exist.

Nearly all the union officials, especially at the middle and top layers of leadership, are white, although there may be as many as 20 to as high as 60 per cent Black membership in some of these unions.

One of the sharpest effects of this special oppression is seen in the South. Since the trade union movement has never made a serious attempt at mass organization in the South, wages and working conditions are far worse, for Black and white workers, than anywhere else. This annual differential amounts to $30-billion extra profits for the bosses. To organize unions throughout the South would mean tackling racism head on; but the trade union misleaders shun such a struggle like the plague. The South continues to be a low-wage haven for Northern bosses, a condition that drives down wages and conditions of all workers.

However, Black workers are not waiting for some benefactor to hand them their freedom; they are fighting for it. Since 1964 the Black urban ghettos have risen in massive rebellions, related to the working class in two ways:

1. Those active in them are workers for the most part–employed and unemployed–and they are generally making class demands: against discrimination in jobs, housing, education, etc. Their fight is directed towards obtaining some of the superprofits stolen from them by the ruling class. Their struggle weakens the ruling class; it has been forced to deploy army troops normally used to protect profits in colonial countries to suppress these domestic rebellions.

2. Since the Black people who participate in these rebellions are mostly workers, they inevitably bring their militant class demands into the working class' general fight against the bosses. This has become increasingly evident in recent years in many strike movements, especially in basic industries, where Black workers are becoming a larger and more decisive part of the work force. In the Newport News shipbuilding strike of 15,000 (mostly white) workers, it was 200 Black workers in the transportation department, victims of discrimination by the company's refusal to upgrade classifications, who struck over an issue affecting all workers–compulsory overtime–and whose action led di-

rectly to the first walkout in the company's 81-year history. (Significantly, this strike occurred at the same time as the Newark rebellion; it saw Black and white workers demolishing the loan sharks, installment plan businessmen-robbers and finance companies located across the street from the plant in a white area.)

"Black and white fought us like (they were) brothers," said the sheriff. Class contradictions were so sharp that the bosses' tool of racism was useless at that peak of struggle, proving to all the workers that this kind of unity is not only possible but necessary if their demands are to be won.

Two wildcat strikes in 1967 and 1968 occurred in Ford's Mahwah, N.J., plant, sparked by Black workers' reaction to a white foreman's racist remarks, and supported by large numbers of white workers who also feel class pressures on the assembly lines. There was also the historic strike of 1,300 sanitation workers in Memphis, Tenn., 98 per cent of whom were Black, which panicked the ruling class because it encouraged trade unionism throughout the South among both Black and white workers. Here again the initial spark was racism against the Black workers; their reaction became an inspiration to all workers fighting for decent union conditions.

Thus while the rebellions of the Black workers are national in form—that is, based on the heightened consciousness of the Black people as a group—they are also working class in content: They are directed against a ruling class and its henchmen, not against white people as a group, and they consistently evolve into some form of struggle that also represents the class interests of white workers.

If white workers do not grasp the class content of this Black rebellion they will inevitably react in a racist way. They will either support the bosses' suppression of the Black workers' rebellions and strike actions, support racism against Black workers or remain passive while the oppressors do their dirty work. Either way they will be acting against their own class interests.

One specific form that the militancy of Black workers takes within the trade union movement is the organization of all-Black caucuses to fight for some of the special demands of Black workers, especially in those industries where discrimination is very sharp.

Some of the most militant strikes and actions in recent years have found Black workers either leading or deeply involved—always over working-class demands. They follow a classic pattern.

Because of a lack of union representation or because of special discrimination or oppression at the hands of the bosses, or both, Black workers organize as a group (national form) and begin to struggle against the boss to alleviate those conditions (class content). Usually these Black caucuses put forth many class demands that reflect the aspirations of all workers in the shop (against speedup, company harassment, etc.). Included in those demands are ones that fight against the special oppression of Black workers. This national form indicates Black workers cannot wait for white workers to reach their level of understanding of the necessity to fight the bosses, a fight which is invariably working class in content.

The special oppression of Black workers often places them in the vanguard of the struggle against the bosses and corrupt union leadership. The recognition of this fact often results in white workers electing Black workers to represent them as shop stewards.

The Black workers' militancy is also directed against the sell-out policies of much of the trade union misleadership, advancing the struggle of all rank-and-file workers. Just as the Black workers' fight for unionization encourages organization of all workers, so too do the actions of all-Black caucuses tend to spark white workers' rank-and-file activity against the boss and union misleaders. Historically, all-Black caucuses fighting for working class demands have generally joined with the more progressive, class conscious white workers to become rank-and-file caucuses representing all workers.

Of course the bosses and their labor lieutenants will do all in their power to destroy the movement of Black workers or direct it against white workers and for nationalist demands–which are reactionary. On the one hand they tell Black workers that white workers are the source of their oppression. On the other, they tell white workers that Black workers want to "take away what is yours."

This attempt to divide white from Black workers is growing because Black workers have become an increasingly higher percentage of the total work force in the basic industries. They compose 30-35 per cent of all auto and steel workers, two industries in which there is blatant discrimination against Black workers by the bosses as well as by the Reuther and Abel misleadership. In a number of locals they are a majority. Successful movements of

Black workers in these two industries will affect Black workers in the entire trade union movement, as well as give leadership to unorganized Black workers. It will set an example for all workers in these two key industries, and therefore in these two key unions, and will be an important and possibly a decisive step in changing the character of class struggle and union leadership in these two areas. This will in turn affect the entire trade union movement.

No wonder the bosses try every scheme imaginable to prevent and crush the development of Black caucuses in such key areas. Already they, with the aid of the union misleaders, are intensifying their efforts to divide Black and white workers and smear Black worker efforts in fighting racism. This was evident in the way they incited white workers to "honor" Robert Kennedy and Lurleen Wallace as their "right" to react the way Black workers reacted to the assassination of Martin Luther King. Racism is the bosses' key weapon–along with anticommunism–in these basic industries to keep workers divided and unable to challenge union misleadership and the exploitation of all workers–Black and white.

Since the old method of just misdirecting white workers with racism is sometimes insufficient, the bosses now try to misdirect Black workers through nationalism. They try to buy off Black militants with such schemes as building "ghetto plants" for and by Black owners who will make a "reasonable profit." This is just another form of exploitation and will split the working class. Such "Black capitalism" will continue to oppress Black workers.

Black communists struggling among Black people understand that the only way they can truly liberate themselves will be through workers' rule–the dictatorship of the proletariat and the establishment of socialism. They cannot settle for a change from white bosses to Black bosses. The class content of the Black Liberation Movement must become the fight for workers to seize state power. The bosses will always try to use demagogic Black misleaders to obscure any class demands of Black workers. They encourage nationalist demands for Black foremen, Blacks on boards of directors, profit-sharing for Black workers, etc. Therefore all workers, Black and white, must judge the direction of a particular Black caucus by whether or not it has class demands.

But there will be other ways to fight racism besides the emergence of all-Black caucuses. In those areas where there are larger numbers of Black workers, and where the conditions of both Black and white are relatively at the same wage level, it is possible to begin rank-and-file movements composed of both Black and white workers. Even here the Black workers will put forth certain special demands to make up for the special oppression they have suffered for years. But again, these must be seen as weakening the class enemy, and therefore as class demands, not a blow to the white workers. As happened in some of the auto wildcat strikes, in the New York City transit and sanitation strikes and in the Newport News shipbuilders' strike, Black and white workers can aim their joint fire at the same class enemy, despite the fact that white workers in those industries are not notably free of racism. In fact, to form a Black caucus when it is possible to form a rank-and-file caucus of Black and white workers would be a step backward. When the class contradictions are the sharpest, it is then that the greatest potential for unity exists between Black and white workers. And if rank-and-file caucuses of both Black and white exist at those times and are doing their job, still greater unity will be forged against the boss and the union misleaders.

The potential for success in the fight against racism is greatest at the point of production where the class contradictions are the sharpest, where the boss is more easily seen, despite differences in degree, as a common exploiter of both white and Black. White workers do not have to worry about Black workers laying down special demands. More often than not Black workers are happy to see white workers joining a rank-and-file fight against the boss. What Black workers ask at this point is not necessarily the end of racism among white workers before they will join a united struggle, but just that a fight be made against this racism and that it not become an obstacle to fighting the boss at that particular time.

However, the struggle of the Black people is not limited to the trade union movement. In fact in recent years much of this struggle has centered in the Black communities. The issues have usually been slum housing, police brutality, bad schools, extortionate prices and interest rates and generally an intolerable lack of "city services." One drawback has been the absence of strong, organized working-class leadership in these struggles. Unfortunately, many of them have been led—or mis-led—by government agents in the guise of so-called antipoverty agencies, or with bosses, recognizing the great militancy of the Black people, attempt to subvert every movement that threatens their hold on the Black people and the superprofits produced from it.

For this reason it is imperative that the experience in organized class struggle being gained by Black workers in the shops, in caucuses and in unions be brought into the community–an experience that is steeled in class understanding against the very same bosses that exploit the Black people in the ghetto. As this process begins, the Black workers will become the key force that unites the struggles of the entire working class–Black and white–at the point of production with the fight of the Black people–led by Black workers–for their liberation. This could become an unbeatable force in the long-range fight for workers' state power and the defeat of U.S. imperialism.

Naturally, such movements of workers don't happen automatically, especially with such a deep-rooted division as this one. No doubt one of the main factors tending to heal this division will be the actions of Black workers themselves. But it is also the special responsibility of the more advanced and left-revolutionary white workers to consciously destroy the racism among their fellow white workers. In their actions these white communists and advanced workers must know who the enemy is, must sharply rebuke white workers who make racist remarks, must show that such attitudes serve the boss, are anti-union and stem from lies spread by the bosses and their propaganda media. Racism is anti-working class and must be labeled as such. White communists and Left forces must set the example for all white workers in fighting racist practices.

Fighting racism is a class responsibility. If white communists accept the racism of their fellow white workers they are abdicating that responsibility. If white communists "fear isolation" because of a fight against racism they will fall into the same old opportunistic bag: Not having fought for this aspect of class and political consciousness among white workers, their political base (and the level of the workers' understanding) will have been considerably weakened so that when the boss launches a red-baiting attack these communists may really be isolated. Thus, fighting racism is an integral part of any political base the Left intends to build.

None of this is easy in a country filled with racism 24 hours a day. It will start slowly, perhaps with just the reduction or elimination of open racist remarks by white workers. It will especially grow as the class struggle sharpens and the bosses' role in fostering racism is seen more clearly as a weapon directed against all workers. But unless white militants and revolutionaries do the necessary groundwork, day in and day out, when the peaks of class struggle occur the boss will be able to use racism to split and defeat the workers.

The importance of the fight against racism among white workers is one that cannot be underestimated. Its elimination will be a long and difficult task, but it cannot wait. As long as it exists the ruling class will have a primary weapon for use against the entire working class. Because of its all-embracing character in the U.S., racism also acts as a pattern-setter to similarly divide many different groups of workers along national and racial lines.

State power may very well be the trump card that the ruling class has in all battles with the workers, but racism is one that it will always play first in the hope that it will prevent the workers' challenge from getting to that higher level.

The fight of white workers for their own demands cannot include demands that accept racism, as did the actions of the Shanker leadership in the 1968 New York City school shutdown. The fight for a trade union movement that battles in the class interests of the working class is inseparable from the fight against racism, the key antiworker weapon of the bosses. No broad rank-and-file movement in U.S. trade unions can succeed without fighting racism sharply. Such boss-inspired division directly contradicts the basis of the union—unity.

Government vs. Non-Government Workers

Twelve million local, state and Federal government workers are increasingly fighting their boss—the state—for the same things as non-government workers. The ruling class has attempted in two ways to break this new front of class struggle by using the rest of the working class against the government workers.

1. It tells the rest of the workers that any increases in wages and conditions for government workers will force tax increases for the whole working class, impelling the rest of the workers to blame the bigger tax bites on government workers.

2. When government workers are provoked into striking for just demands—similar to demands of all other workers—the bosses blame the ensuing hardships of a transit or sanitation strike, for instance, on the government workers.

Both tactics get the real culprit off the hook, the bosses who exploit all workers—government and nongovernment alike—and skimp on needed services while paying huge sums of interest to the big banks. (See Section I.) These maneuvers help the bosses get support from nongovernment workers for antistrike and anti-union legislation that eventually is used against all workers. This is done in the name of the "public interest"—in reality the corporate and banking interests.

The only way this new kind of ruling-class offensive can be beaten is for ALL workers to unite around a fighting program that would include such things as smashing all antistrike and union-busting legislation, taxing the profits of the banks and big corporations to get the money for working-class needs in the cities, industrial unions among government workers, and government worker support for demands of working-class communities in the areas of education and welfare. The workers must pin the responsibility for low wages and lousy conditions on the ruling class.

Women Are Specially Oppressed

The ruling class' propaganda machine spreads the ideological poison of male supremacy among men workers: Women are inferior; they are a threat to men's jobs; their place is in the home. The second-class status of women drags down the pay rates, working conditions and union strength of the entire working class and adds billions to the bosses' profits. And by spreading the idea that a woman's role is to "look pretty and take care of the children," they have established a million-dollar market that caters to this ruling-class image. Thus the bosses direct women's energies towards "serving men" rather than fighting as part of the working class against their special oppression. When men fall for this propaganda they are hurting their own ability to fight those same bosses.

Women historically have been the leaders of struggles in the community against the hardships created by the system. They have fought for a decent education for their children, against exorbitant rents, for decent housing, against the high cost of living, for more traffic controls, parks, playgrounds, etc. Therefore, the fight of the working class against the special oppression of women can yield good results in the communities as well as in the shops and offices (and in the unions organizing there).

To unite men and women workers against their common enemy requires a real fight by the working class—and especially the Left—against the bosses' ideology of male supremacy and for special demands such as equal pay for equal work, women in leadership of unions of which they are members, special provisions for maintenance of seniority while women workers are on maternity leave, two years maternity pay from the boss, special recognition of the demands of Black and other minority group women.

Women must become part of the leadership of rank-and-file caucuses. Where women are segregated into the worst and lowest-paying jobs, consideration should be given to the organization of caucuses among women. They can grow to include all workers in a particular situation when class leadership is shown by the women's caucus.

Minority-Group Oppression

The ruling class gains great advantages from the special exploitation of many minority groups–Mexican-Americans, Puerto Rican workers, other Latin Americans, various Asian nationalities, Indians, etc. Many of the principles put forward in relation to Black workers hold for these groups. Black workers plus these other specially exploited workers make up more than one-fifth of the U.S. work force. Unity with them, and support for their special demands, puts 15 million workers with special reason to fight class battles, into the field against the bosses. Every time one worker utters a racial or national or religious slur against another group of workers, the bosses smile. This kind of disunity must be fought by all workers, who have nothing to gain and everything to lose by it.

The working class must unify itself in many other ways, to overcome divisions created by the boss: skilled and unskilled, employed and unemployed, senior and junior workers, white collar and blue collar.

Locals must not allow selfish interests to split them from sister locals. There must be unity among all locals in a given struggle until the demands of each one are won.

Workers should not develop a strategy of organizing dual unions by taking all the militants out of present unions and further splitting the working class. However, depending on circumstances, if independent unions will actually unite the vast majority in a situation, they must be considered as a tactic.

Many more extended analyses must be made about each of these aspects of working class unity.

Worker-Student Alliance

Since the effects of U.S. ruling class wars of aggression fall more heavily on the workers here at home, any rebellion against that policy is directly in the workers' class interests. Students are one of the leading forces against these imperialist wars. They are militantly resisting the bosses' use of the working class as cannon fodder to kill other workers abroad.

The bosses try to smear the students in workers' eyes. They recognize the potential strength of a rebellion by the students united with the workers' fight against the "national interest," which is put forward to support the war. Therefore, the alliance of workers and students is important to the success of workers' demands, whether it be directed against the effects of the war on workers, against a draft which dumps workers into graves in Vietnam and ruins the future of students, or manifests itself on picket lines in strikes and against university trustees, who are both the oppressors of students and the directors of corporations that exploit workers.

Through the form of a worker-student alliance, the identity of interests between both groups can be established and a fight made against the same ruling class that oppresses both.

Independent Political Action

It is useful for workers to participate in electoral politics, not as a strategy for taking power (as stressed by the revisionists) nor as support for a "lesser evil," but as a tactic for organizing workers around common demands and raising political and class consciousness. The ruling-class politicians, both directly and through their labor lieutenants, make constant appeals for the workers' vote. This can be turned around and thrown back at them by militants and the Left by organizing independent candidates right out of the shop and local union to expose the class bias of the two major-party candidates. It could also include joining with community political groups who oppose the ruling-class parties over community issues, and to which trade union issues could be brought and made part of the campaign. And it could express itself in an organized boycott of the bosses' candidates. But electoral activity is just one tactic in organizing workers against the class enemy. It is not the main one and most definitely not one that will fundamentally change things. It is an organizing and educating tactic over issues to place workers—many times allied with other sections of the population—in motion against the ruling class.

The working class must be united with every part of the population oppressed by the U.S. ruling class. If the bosses are able to prevent such alliances, it will be that much more difficult, and probably impossible, for the working class to overthrow the capitalist class. Sections of the people not allied with the working class will be used against it, such as student scabs, parents against teachers, or a whole community against a strike affecting that community.

Unity in class struggle as a guiding principle for the trade union movement is a strategy that must be applied in any area of class battle against the bosses.

Program for Victory

For a New Type of Unionism

For U.S. workers to launch an all-out struggle in their class interests against the bosses, they must throw out the Meany-Reuther axis. They must not be fooled by Reuther's "split" with Meany over the AFL-CIO's "lack of social vision." These misleaders are worried about a working-class rebellion, which they must divert into a harmless direction or it will be all over for them. Reuther's "social visions" don't blur his eyesight when it comes to crushing wild-catting auto workers fighting GM or Ford.

Reuther's "rival" labor federation with the Teamsters and other unions is designed to contain the growing rank-and-file militancy and allow workers to "blow off steam" against the reactionary Meany by setting up a "lesser evil" similar to the Democrats being a "lesser evil" to the Republicans. Reuther will not change his sellout policies one bit but will try to use the Alliance for Labor Action as a power base to fight for supremacy in the labor movement (after having lost out to Meany in the AFL-CIO). A second labor federation controlled by the likes of Reuther is just another gimmick to check the workers and prevent them from organizing a long-range fight to throw out the Meanys and the Reuthers.

At this stage the organized caucus within a local union can become the key form of struggle, along the lines of a Left-Center coalition as already outlined. It can be organized around some or all of the following points (and others that workers will add; it is not our intention, nor are we able, to detail every future struggle that will take place).

• Against the Boss—a fight for higher wages with protection against the skyrocketing cost of living; for job security, especially through shorter hours without a cut in pay; rigid contract enforcement, with the right to strike over grievances if the boss violates the rules; against no-strike clauses in the contract; two-year maximum contract length; ironclad protection against discrimination for Black, Latin and women workers; labor unity in all directions —"vertically" throughout one international union and one industry or national company, "horizonally" across all local lines, especially between rank-and-file movements.

• For a Better Union—democratic rank-and-file control over all decisions of the union, from local to international; absolute membership power over ratification of contracts; intensive establishment of, and backing for, an all-embracing shop steward system, always elected by the steward's crew; no union official to be paid a higher salary than the average of the unit that elects him; specific campaigns to organize the unorganized and the unemployed within the realistic possibilities of each level of the union; no split in strikes by one-at-a-time local back-to-work movements within national companies; locals to be run by committees and officers from the shop; all negotiating and policy committees to have a majority of rank-and-filers on them.

• Against Racism—smash the bosses' tool that divides workers and prevents them from fighting in their class interests; upgrading and preferential hiring of Black and Latin-American workers into jobs denied them because of boss-inspired and union-supported racism, thereby reducing the bosses' ability to break the workers' strength; support for the inclusion of militant, class-conscious Black and Latin workers in all levels of union leadership; support for and unity with Black caucuses fighting for class demands against the boss; defense of Black and Latin people in the ghetto.

Against the Bosses' Government—repudiation of the "national interest" and all state-invoked wage freezes and "guidelines" as a bosses' tool; smash all strikebreaking, union-busting laws; fight the shoving of the burdens of city growth onto the workers through the profiteering of banks (unity between Government and non-Government workers against the common enemy); no support of ruling-class parties or candidates; no submission of contract disputes to arbitration or other "neutral" Government boards.

Contained within previous sections of this program are suggestions that lead to many other programmatic demands, depending on the groups of workers involved and the stage of struggle. Suffice it to say now that unity of all sections of the working class around a militant, class struggle line should be the guiding principle that governs every short- and long-range action of any group of workers. The eventual goal must be a national rank-and-file movement that will unify the workers as a class and sweep the labor fakers out. That can only be accomplished by forging a broad Left-Center coalition which in turn will be created only through the building of a long-range political base for revolution by communists.

For a Party of a New Type

For our part, in the Progressive Labor Party, as the earliest communists said 120 years ago, we "disdain to conceal our aims." We openly proclaim the necessity for the working class to smash the bosses' state, establish workers' power, take over the means of production and create a socialist society in which the workers will reap all the fruits of their labors.

We dedicate ourselves to tirelessly fighting the bosses and their servants in the trade union bureaucracy, exposing the state as the bosses' weapon by which the working class is held in check, and exposing the two-party system as the political circus it is.

We will never fail to continuously point out at every level of struggle the necessity of replacing the dictatorship of the bosses with the dictatorship of the proletariat.

We will circulate our ideas on these vital questions at all times, under all conditions, and will never be bound by the ruling class' ground rules. We offer our words and actions for the most penetrating scrutiny, criticism and self-criticism to the masses of workers. Without this type of testing and retesting, no vanguard workers' party can hope to correct its errors and maintain itself.

It is only in this way that we can really serve the people: by becoming part of their struggles and making their fight our fight; by joining these common experiences to a mastery of communist ideology which will enable a real revolutionary vanguard to emerge with a long-range program that will involve millions in sharp struggle leading to total victory for the working class and its allies; and by combatting every aspect of subjectivity and individualism that separates ourselves and our party from the people.

We attempt to develop a strategy and tactics of the class struggle, not as a chess game to be played with the ruling class, but as a life-and-death matter. We believe that Marxism-Leninism has proved itself as the best servant of the workers and the people and therefore is an indispensible weapon to lead us to our goals, shaped by our particular experiences.

Those goals are not only "bread on the table," a chance for our children to grow up strong and healthy, without having to die killing other workers' children to protect some boss' profits; not only an opportunity for a real working class art and culture to flower. Our goal is also a system of society in which no small, minority class can take away any of this once it has been won. Any less of a commitment than this is insufficient.

We believe that such a society can only be achieved with a vanguard party to lead the way. Therefore, the struggle within the trade unions essentially must build a strong communist party, under any and all conditions, to guarantee that such a working class vanguard will exist. We aspire to that role and welcome–and will join with–all others who have that goal.

We have a rich heritage to draw on in trying to carry out this struggle: those who dared to fight at Pittsburgh in 1877, at Homestead in 1882, at Haymarket in 1886, with Debs at Pullman in 1894, with Haywood and the miners of the West, with the IWW, with Foster and the steel workers in 1919, with the unemployed marching in 1932, with the Flint sit-downers in 1937, with the unionization of Ford in 1941, history's longest steel strike in 1959, the armed struggle of the Kentucky miners in 1963, the uprisings in the Black ghettos of the mid-1960's, the militant longshore walkouts of 1964-65, the rebellion of 15,000 shipbuilding workers at Newport News in 1967, and the current wave of militant government workers' strikes.

We must build on this inherent strength of the working class—its unfailing capacity to wage the class struggle–and take up the eternal challenge to the exploited down through history: Dare to fight! Dare to win!

The Future Is Bright

JUNE 1970

> *The proletariat will become an invincible force only when its ideological unity around the principles of Marxism is consolidated by the material unity of an organization, which unites millions of toilers in the army of the working class.*
>
> –V. I. LENIN

The sixties are best described as the years in which a communist movement emerged in the United States. This may sound presumptuous, because we are referring to the Progressive Labor Party. However, the facts speak for themselves. The Communist Party of the U.S. was corrupt and dormant because of revisionism. The Trotskyist movement, which is simply another trend of revisionism, was a domestic and international farce.

The central problem of our party has been the struggle to make it a working class party in ideology and composition. And that problem arose from the fact that our party grew primarily from the student movement. Would workers respond to such a party, even assuming its tactics were correct?

In the years since PLP's birth, we have waged a serious ideological fight for the pre-eminence of the working class in the revolutionary movement. Most radicals were, to varying degrees, opposed to this concept. Some said workers were too corrupt. Others believed it correct for other countries—but not ours. The general view was that the United States ruling class had the workers in its hip pocket. We recognized, of course, severe problems in the working class: Its leaders were corrupt. Anticommunism and racism were rampant. And it appeared that the bourgeoisie had won the workers first to the cold war and then to the wars in Korea and Vietnam.

But as the anticommunist crusade groaned along at home and abroad it was becoming painfully clear to workers that they were paying the lion's share of it. Real wages dropped. Conditions worsened. The cost of living soared. Racism was intensified to maintain maximum profits and splits in the working class. Wars in Korea and then Vietnam were rejected by the working class as it saw that workers' sons were simply cannon fodder for the rich. In sum, the working class was becoming more politically conscious.

Over the years it became apparent that no movement in our country would win anything significant unless workers took part in it. And it became clear, at least to the ruling class, that Marxism-Leninism was a threat. Workers would respond to Leninism, and old-line anticommunism alone wouldn't keep them from it. So the bosses had to add a few other guns to their arsenal. The CPUSA was kept alive. An assortment of "left radicals" were foisted on the antiwar movement and on workers.

By the end of the sixties everyone and his brother "saw the need" for workers. This new view was stimulated by student-worker rebellions in France. It became fashionable for various so-called socialists and radicals to pay lip service to the need to unite with workers. Most of the traditional left organs, which had previously written them off, began to prattle about workers and their struggles. We in PL sarcastically called 1968 The Year of the Worker.

In our party the ideological campaign for students to win workers was something less than sensational. While most members were in agreement with this idea, agreement was skin deep. One of the big mistakes we made was to perpetuate the old C.P. notion of sending students to work in industry. We thought it was only their revisionist politics that made a shambles of the "colonization" plan, and that since PL's line was correct our students in industry were guaranteed success. But we had made only a superficial analysis of the problem.

In the first place the transformation of students to factory workers under capitalism is an enormous job. And we underestimated changing objective conditions in the country. Workers in large numbers were responding to a communist line. Thus we were left, in this increasingly favorable situation, with only the efforts of students newly entered in the working class. In addition, typical student arrogance showed itself in the belief that workers wouldn't move unless students joined them at the "point of production." These obstacles limited integration with workers and limited winning workers to the party.

But another phenomenon occurred: The circulation of *Challenge-Desafio,* PLs national newspaper, rose in two years from

5,000 to 50,000 and is still rising.* The increase in circulation is primarily at factories, usually trustified sections of big industry. So we believe an historic trend is taking place. The advanced, class-conscious workers, of whom Lenin spoke, are becoming evident. All the conditions of life for U.S. workers are worsening and they are fighting back—and looking around for new ideas. The sixties could be called years in which Marxism-Leninism reappeared in the U.S. The seventies will see workers seizing Marxism-Leninism. The main thing in life is the class struggle. Its main manifestations are a communist party and workers joining it. Intellectuals and sophisticates may scoff, but American bosses are losing much sleep over it. All aspects of class struggle are developing.

Class Struggle at a New Stage

Perhaps this editorial should have been titled "U.S. Workers in Search of a Communist Party," or "Workers Are at Least as Smart as Students." In any event, while talking to a friend of the party in California (a young white student type) he told of his experiences selling *Challenge-Desafio* at a big plant. One story went like this: "I met a young black worker while I was selling the paper at the plant. We talked a while, because it was too early for the shift to start. He bought the paper. After talking more he asked for my phone number. As we talked still more I asked for his. The conversation went on about conditions on the job, etc., and he asked was I going to be home this Sunday so he could come over and talk some more. I said I was busy that day and that I would call him soon. Well after a week or so he called me and invited himself over to my house on the following Sunday."

The point of this story is that the worker took the initiative in almost every step of the relationship. (Our friend did make the party a reality for the young worker.) Workers are going to seize Marxism-Leninism because their struggle with the bosses is taking on more of a life-and-death character. Marxism-Leninism offers them the only way to avoid destruction. Not only does it offer a way out, but a way forward.

Suppose you made $125 a week and had a family of four. Suppose it bought a good deal less than it used to. Perhaps you

*100,000 in August, 1970.

live in a building that is falling around your ears. Maybe you send kids off to school never knowing whether they'll come home pummeled by some cop or hooked on drugs. Suppose your kids were taught that you and your wife were really unsuccessful dullards. What do you think happens if you or your kid gets sick—even if you have a medical plan? Suppose you looked out the window and saw the street littered with debris and garbage.

We could go on and on about the deteriorating conditions of life for most workers. The end of this deterioration is not in view. It is becoming obvious that millions never made even the $125. And millions who did are now out of work. Millions more are on short work weeks. And even if a full-blown depression doesn't materialize, economic prospects for workers are still bleak. The Nixon budget for the coming year is full of guns but very little butter. Every aspect of the budget concerning schools, hospitals and welfare has been cut. These cuts have been made in the name of halting inflation. But facts are persistent. Prices are still soaring and so is unemployment.

U.S. imperialism is becoming more and more unworkable. That is why millions of workers and students challenge it in some way. The difference is that once workers seize Marxism-Leninism they will not let go. Workers will go faster and farther than others because their very lives are at stake. For that reason they will eventually emerge in the forefront of the revolutionary battle.

Workers understand the class battle better than nonworkers because they have to try and live under the capitalist system based on their labor. And in the overwhelming majority of cases selling their labor power buys them less than what it takes to survive. Latest Government statistics claim that it requires over $11,000 per year for a family of four to live modestly in New York City. How many workers in New York end up with $11,000? Even relatively high-paid construction workers don't reach this on an average. How do you think garment workers stack up to this figure? And they compose 40 per cent of the industrial work force in New York City.

When American workers buy communist literature they are talking a big step forward in fighting class oppression. And when they seek out communists they are taking a giant step—a qualitative leap forward. Moves towards Marxism-Leninism by workers are not simply acts of curiosity, as they may be for others. They are attempts to find a way to fight the boss in order to survive. Unquestionably, this attitude of workers is a new development. Workers tend to be practical. Idle curiosity that could get them into trouble with union leaders and their bosses is usually avoided. When workers bring PL literature and organization to work the class struggle is at a new stage.

Workers Need the Party

The sixties were marked by the war in Vietnam and the fight of black people against racial oppression in the United States. Both of these developments were important stimuli to our movement and to the antiwar movement. As we pointed out previously, worker participation was low, particularly in the antiwar movement and in our party. However, the seventies may give rise to different types of struggles by the people. It appears that the nitty-gritty struggles for survival will emerge. This means that such things as wages, hours, speed-up, runaway shops, rents, schools, garbage and hospitals will take their place alongside of war and racism, and every other form of oppression will become clearer.

Though workers hung back in the sixties, they will soon take over the leadership of much of the emerging mass movement. The facts are pretty apparent. In the black liberation movement, the integrationist leadership of Martin Luther King gave way, at least in large part, to various forms of virulent nationalism. Integrationist or nationalist, the results have been the same, not much.

In the antiwar movement, anti-imperialism teeters on the brink of winning. It never quite makes it, because workers have not entered into it. The bosses have been able to keep workers out of the movement by using a host of devices. By building the image of the "crazies" they have been able to portray much of the youth as freaks and kooks. They have also dredged up the CP-SWP-pacifist cabal to ensnare many in liberal-type pap. These pseudoradicals have had little luck in winning and holding workers. So though the antiwar movement has made some good efforts its effect has been severely limited.

Many people wonder how if workers can't even challenge seriously the betrayal of their own union leaders they can be expected to take the leadership of a mass movement. It is becoming clearer that workers are starting to assert themselves in their struggles. After 14 weeks of strike against G.E., many of the larger G.E.

shops turned down the sellout agreement. Some stayed out beyond the settlement. Workers in the telephone, teaching, packing-house and maritime industries, to mention a few, have shown more vigor than ever. However, the crucial aspect in all of this is whether our party will grow. If it doesn't, the chances are the economic struggles won't grow into broader political struggles. And what is more, even the economic struggles will lag. A worker we knew in Buffalo used to say that "when there was a party in the plant at least we could fight the boss." The point is that without the party the workers are at the mercy of union goons, bosses and cops.

The Nixon bunch has no intention of marking time while the class struggle heats up. Recently, the Administration's response to the possibility of a national rail strike went far beyond usual antistrike legislation. Nixion imposed a compulsory settlement on the workers. This new noose is being designed for all workers. The Nixon crew are frightened out of their minds by working class action. After the legislation there were militant wildcat strikes by rail workers around the country.

Shortly after Nixon's blast at the rail workers, New York's Gov. Rockefeller demanded that striking gravediggers return to work. When they told Rocky to dig his own, he imposed sanctions on the gravediggers similar to those Nixon sprung on rail workers. Nevertheless, the gravediggers held out for a time and won a slightly better contract.

The best answer to Federal and state strikebreaking has come from postal workers. They were well aware of the lengths to which Federal bosses will go to break their strike. Despite the attempts of most of their union leaders to sell out, the strike spread way beyond New York. Nixon demanded they return to work. This demand was buttressed by fake union leaders. But the men stuck to their guns. Apparently, the threat of Army intervention held little fear for the postmen.

If the postmen can strike militantly—the first in their history—there is no end in sight. Already, there have been significant actions by thousands of city workers in San Francisco. Their short strike brought immediate support from thousands of workers. If the strike had lasted another day or two a general strike might have gotten under way. At this writing the sanitation workers in Atlanta are out. And though the Mayor has fired them all, and is desperately looking for scabs, workers' militancy grows.

These actions and others show the emergence of new militant leaders in the working class, and it creates ever broader possibilities for our party's growth.

Over the last 25 years there has been an endless stream of militants who emerge, make a bit of a splash and then sell out. They become either foremen or union hacks–or worse. A militant emerges and does battle with the company and union for a while. But the objective nature of the struggle is such that he and his mates will eventually lose. The militant begins to see this and eventually comes to terms with the union and the boss. It isn't because he was always basically crooked or corrupt, but because a serious person sooner or later must estimate the situation; and when he does, the fundamental question is usually asked: Can the struggle my shopmates and I are engaged in come to a successful conclusion? Except for winning some minor reforms (and even this is very hard and often unsuccessful) it is unlikely that basic conditions in the shop or in life will change. When this is seen, and no alternative is in view, a militant will either come to terms or drop away from struggle.

But if a communist party exists, militants can see an alternative to rotten conditions. What is more important, they can learn about an alternative to capitalism. Even if the struggle for socialism were to go on for centuries, workers would have an alternative to see and to work for. So the party eliminates the frequently almost automatic shifting of sides or passivity. *Because the party is the general staff of the working class, and its only interest is to serve that class, it develops the winning tactics for the working class.* Thinking in terms of being able to win is vital to the class struggle. After all, why should people persist in their efforts if they know they are bound to lose?

Through the party's perspective of internationalism, working class unity at home, and other important outlooks, workers can see how their local fights are linked to the over-all fight and why political issues of all sorts are crucial to winning anything. Actually, the emergence of the party is the main factor in the class struggle. Without it the workers are powerless. Without Marxism-Leninism workers have no set of ideas for how to reverse political power. Workers are beginning to see this problem–in a small way. The fact that our party is slowly beginning to gain in numbers and in influence in the working class is the most important development in our country. Those who call themselves communists and fail to understand this development had better take another close look at themselves. *Growth of the Progressive Labor Party among workers is vital for workers to defeat the imperialists. Defeating United States imperialism is vital for the victory of the international working class.*

Ruling Class Will Counterattack

The bosses always seem more capable than radicals of evaluating trends. And bosses are more adept at smashing resistance than we realize. This doesn't mean they are omnipotent. It does mean they are strong, ruthless and often clever. If we want to beat them we must have some understanding of what they are doing to stop the development of Marxism-Leninism in the country. To sit back and call them rotten and stupid won't be much help to the class struggle. The main weapon in the arsenal of the bosses isn't only repression or terror, though naturally they are used vigorously if the situation calls for it. Another way the bosses hold sway is using political ideas. Probably the chief aspect of the ruling class' ideological attack against workers is to push harder to divide them. Everyone knows that a divided group–at one another's throat–is usually no match for a more cohesive enemy.

In the coming years there is going to be an intensification of racism whipped up by the bosses and their stooges. In the last six months this was seen more clearly than ever. The organization of some building trades workers to oppose more hiring of blacks is a significant event. Attempts by Southern politicos to push for national busing is an attempt to whip up racist feelings. Nixon's appointment of Haynsworth and then Carswell for the Supreme Court is another important sign. After all, why should the ruling class undermine all the illusions in the Supreme Court by appointing an open racist and a judicial imbecile? The Supreme Court has been a vital cog in maintaining illusions in bourgeois democracy. Why should Nixon give up on a good thing? Is Nixon stupid? Is Carswell's appointment just political pique shown by Nixon because Haynsworth was rejected? We think not! Is his appointment just a political ploy to win the South? Only partially. It is a calculated risk for the ruling class to appoint Carswell. They feel they must openly encourage racism (being an open racist is good and will be rewarded) instead of maintaining illusions in the

Court. Of course there is much opposition to this thinking in ruling circles. But one can see that stupidity or pique is not the reason for these political acts.

The ruling class hopes the attack against the Black Panthers will serve to whip up racist sentiment. By picturing the Panthers as wild-eyed bomb throwers, bosses hope to inculcate white workers with the idea that it is black workers and not the bosses who threaten their survival.

In addition to this racist drive launched and led by the bosses, the ruling class hopes the black masses will move, totally, in a nationalist direction. The workers will then be fighting among themselves while the bosses pretend to be neutral umpires.

Another device the ruling class dredged up to intensify racism is school busing. The Nixon and Agnew gang is playing both sides of the street on this one. On one hand the bosses' Supreme Court has called for busing to integrate schools. Nixon and the Court want to look good to the black people and assorted white liberals. On the other hand, Nixon and Agnew make statements about how integration should go slow, and that they favor the concept of neighborhood education. In effect they are maneuvering black and white workers into a confrontation. Relying on racist sentiments of white workers to oppose busing–and knowing that the black community has little interest in this issue–the Nixon bunch hopes for just enough racist action by some whites to divert the whites from working class action on vital questions. And they hope they can generate a little more nationalist heat in the black community in response.

If bosses can turn working class militancy away from our party to racism and nationalism, they will have bought themselves some more time. But not unlimited time in any case, because eventually workers will catch on to this game and beat it.

To sum up: The emergence of our party and its ideas among the more militant class-conscious workers is the most significant political development of the past 25 years. The party must emerge as an important factor in the industrial working class. This is necessary for the workers to have a tool to defeat imperialism in the short run and long run. Party members and radicals should rely on the workers and not use ersatz political methods of organizing. Old C.P. methods are doomed to failure even if a better line is in effect. Workers have more than enough going for them to grasp Marxist-Leninist ideas.

The coming period will be marked by increased economic oppression and more suffering by workers. *The fight against racism is more vital than ever.* Nationalist efforts will give way to class action in the shops and communities. Bosses will try to crush the move to our party by introducing more racism and nationalism. They will also use more fake radicals and the revisionists to isolate students from workers. And they will use all these devices to separate our party from workers. However, workers will fight back and will continue to respond to our party as long as we dare to win the working class.

Win Fight Against Racist Firing

200 Boston students get cafeteria worker rehired (see campus pages) ▶

Vol. VII #1. April 1970 Progressive Labor monthly 10¢ (non-NY stands 25¢)

Postal Strikers Inspire All Workers

Neither Laws nor 'Leaders' can push Rank & File Around

Angry letter carriers shout down union mis-leaders at W. 142 St. Armory mass meeting

Busing Children: Rulers take People for a Ride